Doing Women's History in Public

ABOUT THE SERIES

The American Association for State and Local History Book Series addresses issues critical to the field of state and local history through interpretive, intellectual, scholarly, and educational texts. To submit a proposal or manuscript to the series, please request proposal guidelines from AASLH headquarters: AASLH Editorial Board, 2021 21st Ave. South, Suite 320, Nashville, Tennessee 37212. Telephone: (615) 320-3203. Website: www.aaslh.org.

ABOUT THE ORGANIZATION

The American Association for State and Local History (AASLH) is a national history membership association headquartered in Nashville, Tennessee, that provides leadership and support for its members who preserve and interpret state and local history in order to make the past more meaningful to all people. AASLH members are leaders in preserving, researching, and interpreting traces of the American past to connect the people, thoughts, and events of yesterday with the creative memories and abiding concerns of people, communities, and our nation today. In addition to sponsorship of this book series, AASLH publishes *History News* magazine, a newsletter, technical leaflets and reports, and other materials; confers prizes and awards in recognition of outstanding achievement in the field; supports a broad education program and other activities designed to help members work more effectively; and advocates on behalf of the discipline of history. To join AASLH, go to www.aaslh.org or contact Membership Services, AASLH, 2021 21st Ave. South, Suite 320, Nashville, TN 37212.

Doing Women's History in Public

A Handbook for Interpretation at Museums and Historic Sites

Heather A. Huyck

ROWMAN & LITTLEFIELD
Lanham • Boulder • New York • London

Published by Rowman & Littlefield
An imprint of The Rowman & Littlefield Publishing Group, Inc.
4501 Forbes Boulevard, Suite 200, Lanham, Maryland 20706
www.rowman.com

6 Tinworth Street, London SE11 5AL, United Kingdom

British Library Cataloguing in Publication Information Available

Library of Congress Cataloging-in-Publication Data Available

ISBN 978-1-4422-6416-8 (cloth: alk. paper)
ISBN 978-1-4422-6417-5 (pbk. : alk. paper)
ISBN 978-1-4422-6418-2 (electronic)

∞™ The paper used in this publication meets the minimum requirements of American National Standard for Information Sciences—Permanence of Paper for Printed Library Materials, ANSI/NISO Z39.48-1992.

For all those who tell the whole story

Contents

Part IV—*Interpretation*

List of Figures and Tables

List of Figures and Tables

Acknowledgments

As with any such book, many people made this one possible, from Dr. David Wallace, who told me decades ago that he had a good career as a PhD public historian "and so can you," and all those who encouraged me, especially Dr. Sara Evans, my advisor and friend, as well as my co-workers, colleagues, and friends. Thank you all so very much.

For over a decade, I've been deeply involved with two women's history groups, the National Collaborative for Women's History Sites (NCWHS, www.ncwhs.org) and the Maggie Walker Community, a wonderful multiracial group that processed over 15,000 documents found in the St. Luke Hall in Richmond, Virginia, and built a 23,000-entry database of that African American community and the indomitable Maggie L. Walker. The NCWHS has undertaken many projects to support and strengthen women's history at historic sites and museums with academic and public historians working together.

Many friends and colleagues have been crucial in writing this book. Thank you! Staffs from key museums and sites who have been particularly helpful include Dinah Gewalt, Mike Tramel, Matthew Cahill, Judy Kesler, and Phoebe Gilbert (Alaska National Park Service, including Klondike NHP, Kennecott at Wrangell-St. Elias NP, and Sitka NHP); Carolyn Brucken (Autry Museum of the American West); Michael Rose, Kelly Whitfield Bradley, and Jessica Rast Van Landuyt (Atlanta History Center); John Carson (Bent's Old Fort NM); Steve Black (Big Hole NB); Lesley Barker (Bolduc House Museum, New France: The Other Colonial America); Robert Munson (Cabrillo NM); Lisa Heuvel, Mary Carter, and Carl Childs (Colonial Williamsburg Foundation); Ed Roach (Dayton Aviation Heritage NHP); Leonard DeGraaf (Edison NHS); Franceska Marcal-Urban (Eleanor Roosevelt NHS); Elizabeth Bertheaud and Michael Showalter (Historic Ephrata Cloister, Pennsylvania Historical and Museum Commission); Bill Manhart (Fort Davis NHS); Tracy Fortmann, Theresa Langford, and Meagan Huff (Fort Vancouver NHP); Lori Osborne (Frances Willard House Museum and Archives); Sherrie Smith-Ferri (Grace Hudson Museum & Sun House); Lisa H. Beede, Elizabeth Burgess, and Chelsea Farrell (Harriet Beecher Stowe Center); Adam Prato (Herbert Hoover NHS); Marsha Mullin (The Hermitage, Andrew Jackson's home); Nancy Cass and Missy McDonald (Historic Fort Snelling, Minnesota Historical Society); Kirsten Stalling (Harry S Truman); Jean Ellis (Keweenaw Heritage Center at St. Anne's); Jeremiah Mason, Jonathan Fairchild, and Wyndeth Davis (Keweenaw NHP); Beth Wear (Longfellow House, Washington Headquarters NHS); Emily Levine (Lowell NHP); Eola Dance, Cindy McLeod, Ben Anderson, Ajena Rogers, Ethan Bullard, and Andrea DeKoter (Maggie L. Walker NHS); Jascin Finger (Maria Mitchell House & Archives); Phil Wallis, Bonnie Stacey, Ann DuCharme (Martha's Vineyard Museum); Tara Morrison (Mary McLeod Bethune NHS); Anna Altschwager (Old World Wisconsin); Ellen Mast Carlson and Callie Hawkins (President Lincoln's Cottage); Dr. Karen Nickless (in memorandum) and Priya Chhaya (National Trust for Historic Preservation); Barbara Lau (Pauli Murray Family House NHL); Dan Schwartz, Susan Barron, and Amanda Phillips (Pope-Leighey House, National Trust for Historic Preservation); Elizabeth Tucker and Ann Roos (Rosie the Riveter/World War II Homefront NHP); Emily Murphy (Salem Maritime NHS); Anita Badertscher (Tumacácori NHP); Julie Northrip and David Newmann (U.S. Grant NHS); Noemi Ghazala, Dinah Gewalt, and Kim Szewczyk (Women's Rights NHP).

My public historian colleague-friends, especially Stephanie Toothman, Diana Pardue, John Dichtl, Peg Strobel, Vivien Rose, Susan Ferentinos, Callie Hawkins, Arnita Jones, Marie Rust, Shaun Eyring, Bob Beatty, Beth Boland, LuAnn Jones, Turkiya Lowe, Dwight Pitcaithley, Judy Hart and Mary Melcher. My academic historian-colleague-friends, especially Sara Evans, Nancy Hewitt, Vicki Ruiz, Mary Beth Norton, Kitty Sklar and Tom Dublin, Gail Dubrow, Antonia Castañeda, Nupur Chaudhuri, Anna Agbe-Davies, Barb Howe, Lynn Weiner, and Erin Krutko Devlin. Thanks also to Jill Cowley, Megan Spainhour, Isabel Ziegler, Toni Cottrell, and Chris and Shelia Morse for their generosity in providing images. Thanks to the Stallings family for access to the Maggie Walker documents.

My dear ones, especially Kevan Huyck O'Connell, Holly Huyck and Daniel O'Connell; and all the Berryhill family; Doris Crump Rainey, Jean and Jerry Jackson, Valena Dixon, Connie Cook-Hudson, Jean Parrott, Liz Smith, Shelby Hawthorne, Andrea Li, Vivian Short, Joanne Poehlman SSND, Alla Bozarth, Marie Rust, Bruce Vento, and Ames Sheldon. Thanks to Rachel Wallace, Kathryn Abbott, and Rebecca Harrison for their work, and to the Collington Community for their encouragement. Thanks to Peggy Latimer, Nathan Ryalls and especially to Jessica Milstead for their much-appreciated editing.

Most of all, for all who he is and all he has given, in his support for Women's Rights National Historical Park and the restoration of the Statue of Liberty, in his willing immersion in women's history, and for his extensive and varied support, my dear husband, Charlie Clapper.

Note: Throughout this book, NPS is National Park Service, NHL is National Historic Landmark, NRHP is National Register of Historic Places; NHP is National Historical Park; NHS is National Historic Site; NB is National Battlefield; and NCWHS is National Collaborative for Women's History Sites.

Introduction

When I was a child, my mother mercilessly dragged my sister and me to historic sites—to Ephrata Cloister, with its wooden pillows, and to Mesa Verde, where we climbed a ladder up into rock-walled rooms whose ancient denizens seemed so close. I loved museums and went to the Smithsonian so often I memorized its colonial American exhibits. I wanted to share these amazing places with others. Sadly, I found that my enthusiasm for public history was not shared by many faculty members when I began graduate school. Fortunately, Dr. Sara Evans, a protégé of the pathbreaking women's historian Dr. Gerda Lerner and even as deeply committed to women's history, joined the faculty and became my advisor. Since then, my career has been to build bridges between academic and public history, specifically to encourage and strengthen women's history as integral to American history. In addition to working for the National Park Service (NPS) and the House of Representatives Subcommittee on National Parks and Public Lands, I have taught at the College of William and Mary and been a board member/president of the National Collaborative for Women's History Sites.

While working for the NPS, I visited Gettysburg National Military Park. At the Slyder farm near Devil's Den (where especially heavy fighting had taken place), the interpreters were using Living History techniques to convey the history by wearing nineteenth-century clothing and having pigs and kittens again living there. A senior NPS historian had gruffly asked me, "What is a Living History farm doing in the middle of a battlefield?" I told him I didn't know. Interpreters portrayed how the battle affected the Slyder farm and its family, presenting a compelling perspective on a battlefield I'd visited often. I returned with a question for him—"What was a battle doing in the middle of a family's farm?" I then understood that battles were often fought on family farms, profoundly affecting the farm women and men whose lives and livelihoods then changed drastically. The Civil War affected the 4 million enslaved African Americans (and nearly half a million free Blacks) who fought for their freedom. Wars are more than battlefields; they include women manufacturing munitions and fighting on the other home front.

History has both acute and chronic aspects, the dramatic unique events as well as the subtle but crucial slogs, trajectories easily missed. Women's history includes the *traditional* category of domestic/biological reproduction of family and culture; the *underappreciated* but constant category of livelihood production to gathering, farming, industry, and technology; and, as *essential* a category, the production of the social glue of numerous and diverse organizations and communities that support and supplement the first two categories. Women have built the third category powerfully with Puritan prayer circles, abolition petitioners, suburban women's clubs, Girl Scouts, and dinners of U.S. women Senators, from Black neighborhood improvement groups to the American Red Cross. Our accomplishments in all three sectors are awesome, if unseen. Our history needs to document and share these categories. We would not have our country without them. Without us!

Several National Park Service historians once kept a list of parks we believed lacked any women's history, which we whittled down until only Alcatraz Island in California remained. Actually, women and girls lived there as the wardens' families, and the male prisoners had women in their lives. Women's stories and objects have been found in *every* museum and historic site. Happily, the appreciation for women's history has grown exponentially in the past forty years.

Just as the larger discipline of history has accepted new forms of evidence that extend our ability to study more fully many different groups. Women's history has also become a lively field with a strong knowledge base. Seen through the lens of race, ethnicity and class, region, religion, gender roles, and/or LGBTQ communities, women's history is exciting, diverse, and transformative for American History. Three important women's history lines of inquiry focus on the social construction of gender that sees gender as culturally defined; the benefits of tangible resources for research and interpretation; and intersectionality, the recognition that we all experience varied aspects of identity simultaneously. For example, Black women are not African Americans one moment and women another, as both attributes are profoundly intertwined.

Those of us who work in museums and historic sites have amazing opportunities to welcome literally millions of people long past their school days with stories of women (and men) using the objects, buildings, and landscapes we interpret. The Statue of Liberty embodies a proud female proclaiming our promise to the world. Women's quilts and baskets reveal great artistry. House museums from extravagant to humble demonstrate female agency. We can convey women's lives and accomplishments in seemingly small but critical artifacts used daily—wood-handled pastry blenders, beaded moccasins, hand-cranked sewing machines, and typewriters, to name a few. We should welcome everyone to come discover the women who shaped this country in often-unappreciated ways. We also need to present the diversity of women's lives and honor women whose lives were stunted by circumstances far beyond their control. Their stories deserve to be shared just as those of famous women are. Examples from many museums and sites have been included here to show their wondrous variety and to encourage the identification of similar ones in your museum or historic site.

Interpretation engages us with the past and helps us interpret the women and girls who made us who we are. It helps us discover women we did not expect and so enlarges our worlds. Interpretation provides quality connections with visitors using professional programming and products, so they encounter historic women, their lives, and their accomplishments in their historic context. This book provides a strategic approach, specific tools, and numerous sources to interpret women's history based on three elements:

- *Significance*—why women's history matters and the importance and purpose of fully interpreting women at museums and historic sites—the emotional element;
- *Knowledge base*—the foundation for women's history preservation and interpretation through mastery of existing research and completion of new research and investigations—the intellectual element;
- *Tangible resources*—the preservation of physical evidence—the objects, buildings, structures, and landscapes—that shaped American lives and help to make the women's history interesting, vibrant, and accessible—the physical element.

Interpretation melds the other three elements together. With *interpretation* we can share these stories, bring together these crucial elements, together appreciate the women (and men) who came before us—even the scoundrels. We all construct own understanding; good interpretation nudges us to new ones based on *significance* so that we appreciate women more, *knowledge base* so we comprehend them intellectually, and *tangible resources* so we encounter their physical historical elements. Here, interpretive programming includes all the programs and products from traditional house tours to staged suffrage debates to exhibits, books, and reproduction dolls—as well as all things digital. It's every way that museums and historic sites share past women with present people.

Chapter 1 of this book discusses the question of significance. Why does women's history matter? Why is it important to recognize and incorporate women into museums and historic sites? Chapter 2 discusses basic research that every organization needs for a solid foundation in women's history. Chapters 3 through 5 present primary sources that historians use for research—the written, visual, and oral sources. Chapters 6 through 8 discuss women's interactions with the tangible resources—landscapes, architecture, and objects—that comprise museums and historic sites. Chapter 9 provides the basics of preservation that cares for tangible resources. Finally, Chapter 10 combines these elements with current interpretive approaches for visitors to provide hospitable and inclusive interpretation at your historic locale for stronger visitor experiences of women's history. Note the emphasis of working *with* visitors. Finally, the Tools in each chapter cumulatively build locale-specific women's history interpretation that is useful everywhere. The Bibliography lists sources by different categories.

This book is deliberately full of many examples and designed to encourage *everyone* engaged in interpreting the women's history found in museums and historic sites with the public and everyone interested in women's history. May it help you to find, research, preserve, and interpret the many women whose history is associated with your locale and to respond to skeptics of the benefits of doing so. Telling the whole story responds to concerns of public relevance and attraction. I have spent decades searching for—and finding—women's history that is *not* just a sliver of the American history pie. It appropriately includes everyone, for women intersect with every other human group. Let's tell the whole story together.

Cheers, Heather A. Huyck

Part I

Significance

1

Why Women's History Matters

Watch a young girl wearing a long dress with a straw hat on her head, carrying a basket as she walks past houses, shops, and stocks, lost in her thoughts as she considers life in a colonial village. As a visitor to Colonial Williamsburg, she smells wood fires, hears church bells, and sees women hawking their gingerbread. Stepping carefully, she may imagine she has successfully time-traveled back into history. She hasn't. She is encountering another girl's life centuries earlier and appreciating all the women who preceded her.

Determining Significance

We save what we believe is important and what we want to share with future generations. In other words, we preserve those things we consider significant. Often events or values are embodied in tangible resources—landscapes, architecture, and objects—from the Great Plains to the Statue of Liberty to grandmother's teapot. Things we find unimportant are frequently left to disintegrate while we invest huge sums to protect those we value. Inherent in our decision of the significance of places is our identification with them—how we remember them or learned about them. Each generation has key moments and stories that lose their potency when their last witnesses die, whether the 1941 Pearl Harbor bombing, or hospital wards filled with women dying from septic pregnancies before 1973, or the 1969 Woodstock festival. Some events and forces become woven into our nation's self-understanding while others vanish. When subsequent generations lose connections, maintenance of significance can be quite difficult. Ritualized memories such as commemorations of centennials can revive our sense of significance as the 1976 Bicentennial did, but much still gets lost. Historic homes succumb to termites and neighborhoods to "urban renewal."

To decrease such physical losses, in 1966 the National Historic Preservation Act that established our nation's preservation program used "significance" as a core concept, as elaborated by the regulations that implemented this crucial law.[1] Furthermore, preservation decisions often hinge on the "period of significance," the most important era within the longer history of a building. Often coinciding with the time when the most important person(s) associated with it were present, the "period of significance" has practical effects because it guides which building elements will be restored, thrown away or replicated. Significance reflects powerholders and national debates. The February 2006 designation of the Sixteenth Street Baptist Church in Birmingham where four young Black women were murdered as a National Historic Landmark came only with greater respect for and political potency of African Americans in this country. Finally, significance changes as decisionmakers do. Greater numbers of women historians in politics and in higher positions in academia, museums, and historic sites, as well as men sympathetic to women's history, have been crucial for greater recognition of the significance of women's history.

American history needs greater appreciation of the significance of women in it. We are all part of that process.

While progress has been made in preserving and interpreting places that document women's lives, much remains to be identified at existing places and more places need to be preserved, both of which require changed attitudes and more research. For example, a few years ago, the Johnson State Historic Site in New York completely omitted Mohawk leader Margaret (Molly) Brant on their website. Brant lived complex roles as a tribal leader and Loyalist diplomat, as well as the common-law wife of British Indian Agent William Johnson; they had six children together. She managed their complex estate, Johnson Hall, for eleven years until his death.[2] With her brother Joseph Brant, she was crucial in keeping the powerful Iroquois nations pro-British, first fighting the French and later the American patriots. Today, her impressive accomplishments are recognized. Interpreting the agency of Molly Brant improves our comprehension of Iroquois decisions and both U.S. and Canadian history. Omissions of women such as Molly Brant need to be seen as problematic and rectified everywhere.

Museums and Historic Sites: Commonalities and Distinctions

Museums and historic sites show us how women in the past lived, worked, worshiped, and coped with crises and change. The insights gained from visiting these cultural institutions simultaneously encourage and challenge us. They help us understand similar forces at work in our own lives to understand how the present developed. With their objects—whether Girl Scout founder Juliette Gordon Low's well-worn traveling bag or a wedding dress made from a parachute—museums and historic sites illuminate cultural values, attitudes, and behavior from the past and provide evidence of how people decided where to live, where to work, when to marry, and when to migrate. Understanding these forces at work in our ancestors' lives can help us better respond to them in our own, because we perceive past issues more clearly, both wonderful and tragic. Museums and historic sites play important roles in our culture as bridges between newer scholarship and the public who are years past their formal education. We save what we believe important and what we want future generations to know. While named women's sites and museums are few, every such institution contains women's history whether recognized as significant or not.

This book seeks to provide insights and methods for the research, preservation, and interpretation of women's history at institutions of all sizes, from single rooms with cases of woven hair jewelry to those with huge acreage and generous resources for multiple exhibits and programs. As *places* of the past, both museums and historic sites allow us to enter and intensively feel with our senses. As informal learning places, these institutions allow us to experience history in ways appropriate to our different backgrounds and learning styles. They provide social experiences with family and friends of all ages—or highly personal ones—and help us know who we are and where we've come from.

While museums and historic sites share a common mission to preserve our material culture, their approaches to that mission may differ somewhat. Museums range from single rooms filled with lovingly collected items arranged in cases and on the walls, to enormous, well-funded institutions with large staffs and impressive collections. Historic sites include single-room cabins, repurposed churches, and schools—as well as mansions with sprawling, ornate gardens. Some, such as Colonial Williamsburg or the Atlanta History Center, combine museums with historic sites with in situ historic buildings, transplanted ones, and massive museum collections. Many state and federal parks and historic sites have associated visitor centers with interpretive exhibits and museum collections that preserve objects not on display. Known for its parks, the National Park Service curates a 43-million-object museum collection nationwide. Historic sites' landscapes, buildings, and objects each have their own character, and while rooms may be restored, or objects added, they generally retain their same appearance for decades, although the interpretation of their rooms and objects can change more frequently. Museums generally store most of their collections, displaying only a portion in their permanent or temporary exhibits. Because historic sites show roomfuls of objects together, individual objects receive less attention than rooms overall do. Museum exhibits often display assemblages of objects together, making it easier to compare and contrast their characteristics and to focus on particular objects. The vocabulary varies. Museums generally focus on objects and have curators, conservators, and docents. Historic sites preserve and interpret objects, buildings, and landscapes with the help of architects, archaeologists, landscape architects, curators, resource managers, maintenance crews, historic housekeepers, interpreters, and historians. Large institutions such as the Atlanta History Center with its Swan Mansion, transported buildings, and museum collection frequently combine museums with historic sites.

Doing Women's History

Historic sites and museums vary, but all can interpret women's history by incorporating recent scholarship, by reconsidering older interpretation, by collecting female-related objects, and by recognizing everyone who shaped the history of that museum or site. *Every* historic site and museum has women's history, although some ignore it or render it nearly invisible. For example, maritime museums usually focus on the men who sailed on whaling ships, a la *Moby Dick*. Women are included primarily as recipients of gifts such as pie crimpers that sailors made from whale teeth. The important role that whale hunting played in the lives of American women and girls gets little attention. Whale baleen stiffened women's corsets, creating fashionable twenty-three-inch waists. Whale oil shone brighter in household lamps and made perfume. An industrial lubricant, it greased looms tended by young women who had left New England family farms for wage work at places like Lowell mills.[3] Showing visitors that their great-grandmothers once read by whale oil, spun on whale-lubricated looms, and wore whale parts in their undergarments (!) makes maritime exhibits more relevant to visitors and thus more accessible to a larger public. Museums and historic sites demonstrate the impressive variety of American women's lives, the challenges they faced, and resilience they showed. Contemporary Americans, both women and men, can then better appreciate that women can now vote, own property, obtain credit, and have jobs and rights to their children. We know that any of these hard-won rights can disappear, as has happened in the past, making us more protective of them. History comforts and confronts us.

"History" here contains *both* the past that happened and our understanding of that past. While the past itself is immutable, interpretations change dramatically with different questions, sources, and attitudes. The "history of women" refers to the experiences, perceptions, and accomplishments of all women, explicitly recognizing them as significant. In contrast, gender history is an analytical approach that uses the lens of gender to study all humans. Both utilize categories of race, sexual orientation, and class to explore varied gendered experiences. Unlike gender history, women's history explicitly makes *women* its subject matter because they are half of humanity. A major challenge here is recognizing the many variations of women's lives while focusing on how best to research, preserve, and interpret them for the public at your museum or historic site with its own mission and story. We need to balance distinct aspects with shared ones. Often, women's history has been portrayed as a small slice of the pie of distinct human groups rather than being understood as encompassing *half* of that pie, including all races, classes, and sexualities. Some cross-cutting groups—such as age cohorts, LGBTQ, and disabled people— are parts of other groups. Barring major disruptions of war, violence, or disease, Kongolese Americans, Latinx, Swedish Americans, and Cherokee Americans with time and reproduction become half-female populations, which their histories reflect. While this may seem minor, it recognizes the generative aspect of human survival and reproduction. As the celibate Shakers show, human reproduction requires both sexes. People have lived their entire lives within one race or creed but not with only one sex. Women do not experience their gender one day and their race another. Clearly intertwined, race and gender cannot be fully separated, as the activist the Rev. Dr. Pauli Murray articulated in her concept of "Jane Crow" in her foundational 1965 article.[4] More recently, African American scholars have developed "intersectionality" to recognize such complexity.[5]

Finding Women's History Resources

Decades of research show how integral women and girls have been throughout human history, even if they remain sorely missing from much history publications and teaching. Expanding beyond "events" and written sources shows much female activity; we can shift to *assuming female presence*—and go find them. Examples of finding women in previously unexpected places abound. For example, maritime resources such as large vessels, lighthouses and light stations, life-saving stations, shipwrecks, and so forth may not immediately conjure women's history.[6] As with many other traditionally male-identified pursuits, we now recognize how many women were directly involved in maritime activities on board vessels or indirectly sending and using objects shipped from elsewhere. When poor or nonexistent roads made land travel difficult, people commonly traveled by water along the coasts, on inland rivers, or on the Great Lakes simply because it was faster, easier, and more comfortable. Women sailed on vessels large and small; women and girls lived at lighthouses with their husband/father–lighthouse keepers with some women officially designated assistant lighthouse keepers or lighthouse keepers.[7] Women salvaged shipwrecks while others were rescued by men from lifesaving stations. In World War II, women welded and riveted ships and mailed letters to family sailors, some preserved at the USS *Becuna*.[8] Nearly every woman and girl who immigrated here before 1940, by choice or by force, arrived by ship. Some women lived on canal boats, steering or walking beside the mules pulling them, and performing all the usual domestic duties with their children tied onto the boat to prevent them falling off and drowning.[9] Fiery steamboats lurched up the Mississippi and Missouri Rivers, transporting women and their army husbands from St. Louis upstream to Fort Snelling in Minnesota and saving weeks of difficult overland travel.[10] Some museums and historic sites interpret maritime history, but most focus on landscapes. Waterscapes including shorelines and favorite lesbian beaches need recognition too. A few historic ships still float in Baltimore, Salem, Philadelphia, and San Francisco, while historic lighthouses guard our coasts and can remind us of women active in maritime history.

Women's History Changes American History

When we fully recognize women's roles in all aspects of life, it changes American history. American women played more substantial economic and political roles than has been historically recognized. Indigenous women who gathered berries, nuts, fruits, and tubers distinguished nutritious plants from poisonous ones and knew their locations, seasonality, and proper preparation. Colonial women protested British actions before the American Revolution by refusing to drink imported tea. By combining environmental, political, and indigenous history, Susan Sleeper-Smith has rewritten our narrative when she rightly credits the women agriculturalists who farmed prosperous villages from the Ohio River Valley to Wisconsin, a world deliberately disrupted by George Washington to pay Revolutionary War soldiers with western lands.[11] Later, farm wives provided large if little-appreciated family income by selling butter and eggs to urban dwellers. They also ran family businesses when menfolk were away, as Abigail Adams supported her husband, John Adams, while he worked in Philadelphia to form a new nation.[12] Our image that western fur trappers were European men braving the wilderness alone to collect beaver pelts for men's hats distorts reality. Those men could not have survived without their Native American women partners who had crucial environmental knowledge and diplomatic relationships. Here, indigenous women found that the more beaver trapped, the more wealth and work they had. They processed the beaver skins into tanned hides, a skilled but nasty process. Here, the inclusion of women provides a fuller and more accurate understanding of fur-trading *men*—women's history changes everyone's history.

Frequently overlooked, women have fought invisibly in every American war, and more visibly as Civil War telegraphers, military uniform sewers, and ammunition manufacturers; during World War I they volunteered as Red Cross workers who ran hospitals and canteens, drove trucks, and even did medical research on gangrene. Their experiences in a larger world shaped their determination to gain greater rights when they returned.[13] During World War II, wives who accompanied their husbands to top-secret Los Alamos, New Mexico, where we developed the atomic bomb, played diverse roles there.[14] Women served as cryptographers who broke enemy codes, grew Victory Gardens, and kept watch at Cold War missile silos. These are just a few of the important roles to be documented in museum and historic sites, with the added challenge of interpreting women who served overseas. The Women in Military Service to America, which honors "all women who have defended America," makes women's integral service visible.[15] Recognition of women who were officially civilians during conflicts remains inadequate, a real problem given how many historic sites are battlefields or forts.

We now recognize women's centrality in ways not once understood. Women persisted, contributed, bore children, and fulfilled many other roles and accomplishments, some recognized and others not. Millions of enslaved women involuntarily worked for and enriched their owners or captors; some enslaved women sought their freedom from horrendous mistreatment while others endured. Historically thousands and thousands of women's lives have been misrepresented, even obliterated, especially women of color—at early Spanish missions, on antebellum plantations, and growing cotton in the Texas-Mexico desert and pineapples in Hawai'i in the early twentieth century. Many historic sites mislead when they are named solely for a man, as if he alone lived there. Interpretive signs read "Farmers provided laborers with room and board," as if one man were doing all the work himself, rendering women and their labor invisible.[16]

As we acknowledge the enormous range of women's accomplishments, we also need to recognize them in museums and historic sites, exhibits, and signs. For two generations, historians of women have searched for more of our story and found a bounty hardly imagined. Scholars have documented the lives and community at Jane Addams Hull-House and other settlement houses. They have uncovered the roles played by lesbians who conceptualized a changed society with maternal housekeeping. Historians have described early astronauts' wives who functioned as single parents operating under intrusive publicity with constant fear for their husbands' safety. Women's work and women who buttressed their husband's public accomplishments need much greater recognition. We know about the gold rushers, but little about wives who financed their husbands while coping with their legal limitations as females or who fed their husbands thrice daily in near-impossible conditions.[17] By interrogating these women's differences—and commonalities—we better understand all people's lives, including our own.

We frequently equate history with dramatic events—wars, elections, economic crashes—where males have been most evident, or catastrophic natural disasters were blamed on "mother nature." Historians study the reasons and processes of change to understand the past and shape a better future, teasing out the significant changes from the exciting flash-in-the-pan events but actually ephemeral ones. Yet some of the most potent change agents are subtler, more chronic forces, whether demographic, technological, environmental, or cultural. For example, museums need to interpret the complexity that White women in the seventeenth-century Chesapeake

Bay area lived in a much richer ecosystem but as the female sex had more constrained lives.[18] Profound population shifts occurred when millions of indigenous Americans died from European-imported diseases and warfare; when women had fewer children in the 1780s; as 500,000 White Americans migrated west in the 1840s–1860s, or when 6 million Blacks in the Great Migration traveled out of the south from the 1910s on.[19] For centuries, death was a dreaded risk of pregnancy, killing women and leaving their families bereft. (Please see Appendix, p. 15.) Research using the 1910 *Annual Report of the Secretary of State on the Registration of Births and Deaths, Marriages and Divorces in Michigan* found more Michigan women died from childbirth than men from mining accidents, reversing our assumptions from interpretive tours full of descriptions of death and injuries.[20] Around 1927, high maternal mortality rates plummeted with sulfa drug use and improved obstetrical practices; infant death rates decreased more slowly. Although these changes made enormous differences to women and their families, they are little publicly recognized and need more interpretation.

Important shifts came as generations of women worked to challenge cultural values and changed many. For example, in the early twentieth century, suffragists used San Francisco sidewalks, storefront displays, and Washington, D.C., streets to claim space and gain visibility to demonstrate that women belonged in public—and in voting booths too.[21] Women were arrested and beaten when they paraded in Washington streets on the eve of President Wilson's 1913 inauguration. Generations of women have sought greater rights and recognition, which have come with reverses and high personal costs. Since then, women have repeatedly used public spaces for their causes of lesbian rights, pro- and anti-abortion rights, and voting rights. American women using their bodies to proclaim their beliefs in public has long been an especially powerful display of democracy.

Surprising resistance still remains to the full recognition and integration of women's history into many museums and historic sites. Some historians attribute this to unconscious bias and prescribe greater sensitivity; others see political power plays and argue for resisting them. Visitor

Figure 1.1.   Women protesting for suffrage outside of the White House, here "college day" in 1917. Suffrage was finally achieved for most women in 1920. Some women were arrested and jailed at Occoquan workhouse in Virginia, beaten, and force-fed when they went on a hunger strike. When two of the women's husbands came to visit, they did not recognize their own wives. Leader Alice Paul was kept in solitary confinement.
RETRIEVED FROM THE LIBRARY OF CONGRESS, HTTPS://WWW.LOC.GOV/ITEM/97500299/. ACCESSED FEBRUARY 10, 2017.

comments, advisory group recommendations, and scholarly writings often nudge managers, although the National Register of Historic Places continues to omit *gender* or *women* as categories. Some historians and historic resource professionals have truly not believed that women's actions were significant. Others are not interested, claiming that interpreting women is simply an effort to assuage their feelings or that women's roles were incidental rather than essential to the past. The invisibility of any group of humans, especially one that constitutes *half* the population, distorts history and denies us all a genuine understanding of our shared past. Women's history is too often treated as *just another category.*

The history of women includes women of all races, ethnicities, regions, social classes, and sexual orientations. Scholars have introduced the concept of intersectionality—the idea that women experience several of these categories simultaneously. Thus, the experiences of White women differ from those of Asian American women or Latinx women, and the experiences of heterosexual women are not interchangeable with those of lesbian or transgender women.[22] Initially, historians of women wrote primarily about wealthy White women, women married to notable men, and women involved in the suffrage movement because historical evidence for these women was the most accessible. Gradually as research built upon research, historians found more sources and used old ones in new ways. As thousands of women's history projects have accumulated, researchers from all disciplines have become more sophisticated and creative in their questions, use of diverse sources, and determination to *tell the whole story.* As scholars have refuted binary conceptions that humans are either male or female and have recognized the diverse factors that affect individual women's lives, such as birth order, physical ability, or educational access, generalizations about women's experiences have become more difficult.

Even as gender is a social construction, most female humans share key biologically based experiences in having menstrual periods, as well as potentially being pregnant, having miscarriages, and nursing babies, and later menopause—each of which can have major life implications. However, because most women live in close proximity with the other half of humanity—men and boys—gaining insights into a distinctive women's perspective can be difficult. As Supreme Court Justice William Douglas declared, "the two sexes are not fungible; a community made up exclusively of one is different from a community composed of both; the subtle interplay of influence of one on the other is among the imponderables.[23] Concurrently, single-gender women's groups (nuns, lesbians, women at single-sex colleges) often develop more incisive analyses of gender relationships.

From History into a History Museum

When the Tenement Museum first located an appropriate building, at 97 Orchard Street, on the Lower Eastside of New York, there were four open commercial storefronts in its lower floor and twenty sealed apartments in its upper floors, vacant since 1935 rather than having been upgraded to meet new residential requirements. The Tenement Museum bought the building and restored it using census, court, and voter records, and photographs, as well as oral history, to give historical "comfort, inspiration and perspective."[24] Its primary resource was the tenement building itself, supplemented by artifacts and its minimal landscape, a yard with laundry and outdoor toilets. Here tangible resources provide superb ways to share different women's history.

Relying on the memories and family artifacts of Josephine Baldizzi [Esposito], Henry Rosenthal, and other former tenants, the museum restored the Rogarshevsky apartment to 1918 and the Baldizzi apartment to 1935.[25] In 1994, the museum unveiled the latter apartment as part of its first guided tour: Morning glories bloomed in window boxes that once held Home Relief provisions, Josephine Baldizzi Esposito's mother's pink shawl draped an armchair, and rosary beads hung from a bureau. When Esposito saw her resurrected apartment, she said, "I felt like I'd gone back in time and was a little kid again."[26] The museum "had planned to use fictional composites of immigrant families to bring the tenement experience to life. Inspired by Esposito's connection to 97 Orchard Street where she lived as a child, the Museum changed its approach."[27] Since then, additional apartments have been added, the most recent one dating to the 1980s. The front room of the Gumpertz' 1878 apartment appears as if the struggling seamstress (whose husband had deserted his family) had just stepped outside, with fabric near her Singer sewing machine and clothes draped over a dressing area screen. This museum preserves and interprets a streetscape, a building, its collections of furniture and artifacts, and its yard. Its significance comes as an intact example of housing for many thousands of immigrants. Many immigrants—women—produced industrial work in their tenement rooms; others worked in factories. Only a portion of its urban landscape with few related buildings—public baths, Jewish synagogues, factories—survives now, often with different uses, making provision of historic context for these women's lives even more important.

Diversity and Commonalities of Women's Experiences

We need to recognize and respect the sheer diversity of women's experiences and accomplishments. As museums and historic sites associated with women show, women lived very different lives, with every woman's story deserving to be told. At the same time that we recognize variety and change, we need to remain aware of women's common experiences beyond potentially becoming mothers. In most societies, women were historically less powerful than men, legally, politically, economically, and socially—and were alleged to be intellectually and morally inferior as well. Such generalizations ignored the continuums most embodied traits have, with considerable overlap between the genders. Women as generally closely connected to men as daughters, sisters, wives, and widows were affected by men's lives and livelihoods as farmers, tavernkeepers, or scientists. Women's life cycles and sexual orientations, and their roles as daughters, mothers, and grandmothers, have socially constructed meanings shared by diverse groups of women. Such gender expectations of roles for women have been much more flexible and variable over time than most people realize. Seventeenth-century European beliefs that women were the morally weaker gender flipflopped by the nineteenth century to proclaim women morally stronger, with Victorian women held responsible for protecting familial and societal morality. As social constructions, gender roles changed over time.

Women's History Everywhere

Whether or not museums or historic sites are named for women, they all have women's history—even if not fully recognized. The surprisingly frequent assertion that "no women were there" especially overlooks women of color. Focus only on Lewis and Clark and their intrepid guide Sacajawea disappears, as do all the indigenous women the Corps of Discovery encountered.[28] If you assume that women were present, you will find them. Evidence from women's lives may not be found in as many written documents as men's, but sites and museums preserve their history in tangible resources of landscapes, buildings, and objects. Using those sources as well as other sources and scientific research, we can identify and interpret women-shaped history and weave the past back together, using every available source to present as "complete, accurate and reliable" an American history possible, one that includes all women and girls.[29] At the Dorothy Molter Museum, her cookstove and canoes survive as testaments to her determination to live year-round in the Minnesota wilderness. At the Emily Dickinson Museum, her desk shows where she wrote her poetry. Even though some historic site interpreters still proclaim "there's no women's history here," there most certainly is. Some history sites focus on famous women—Jane

Addams Hull-House, Alice Paul Institute, National Cowgirl Museum and Hall of Fame, Marian Anderson House, Harriet Beecher Stowe Center, Women's Rights National Historical Park, and women's institutions such as the Women's Christian Temperance Union, National Association of Colored Women's Clubs, and the Daughters of the American Revolution headquarters. Yet other sites—family homes such as Hacienda La Peralta, Andrew Jackson's The Hermitage, George Washington Birthplace NM, Cahokia Mounds State Historic Site, and military and industrial sites such as Springfield Armory NHS, Klondike Gold Rush NHP, the Alamo, Edison [Laboratory] NHS, Alcatraz prison, and the Autry Museum are also *places* of women's history.

Doing Women-Centered History

Women-centered history goes beyond finding and documenting their lives. Like a kaleidoscope, by turning our perspective to focus on women, different events become significant and patterns change. Women's work was critical in sustaining industrializing America. For example, women's work running homes and boardinghouses was essential to men working in mines, factories, and farms. There, women did such unglamorous tasks as milking the cows, feeding chickens, churning butter, darning socks, washing dirty clothes, and preparing twenty meals weekly from scratch—all without refrigeration or electricity. Industrial work assumed that someone, usually the wife, did all the home-based work so that the man/husband could work in the mine, factory, or farm. Many families depended on the work of every member, sending husband and children out to work while the wife/mother took care of their material needs at home. Women's history helps us understand patterns and appreciate how much hard work was necessary to build our world. Putting women in the center asks how Chicanas coped with annual migrations between Texas and Washington state, packing their families and essentials including *comino* (cumin) for six months away, transporting their values, cooking, music, religion, and community with them.[35]

When women are central, different patterns emerge—as happened at the Ludlow massacre during the 1914 Colorado coal strike.[36] A men's labor union story becomes more comprehensible when we discover women running boardinghouses connecting miners, and joining protests, not only being observers. To comprehend the awful rituals of lynching African American men, we need to recognize the terror being inflicted on all the Black community, and ask how mothers, wives, and daughters felt and reacted. We need to recognize that Black women were also lynched and include them in our interpretation.[37] Imagine how our understanding of American history can change if every museum and historic site fully included women.

Significance: Saving What's Important

Our museums reflect what *we* think important in our history, as people save objects and buildings believed important—and trash the rest. As preservation involves considerable effort, historic buildings and artifacts preserved in museums and historic sites reflect our values. The Wesleyan Chapel, site of the first women's rights convention in 1848, provides an excellent example of the impact significance has on tangible resources. Over the years that church became Johnson's opera house, a telephone exchange, car dealership, and when Women's Rights National Historical Park opened, it was the self-service Seneca Falls Laundromat with washers spinning away. Much of the historic building had been "obliterated" although the church window openings remained.[31] Today it has been reconstructed, again providing a meeting place we can envision as filled with an estimated 300 activists.[32] Many other tangible resources are "found" again and restored when their historical significance is appreciated, as also happened with the Elizabeth Cady Stanton house also in Seneca Falls, New York.

Figure 1.2.   Elizabeth Cady [and Henry] Stanton House, Seneca Falls, New York. Now painted classic Greek revival white, the house was a vivid turquoise when Women's Rights NHP acquired it, helped by a donation by actor Alan Alda.
COURTESY WOMEN'S RIGHTS NATIONAL HISTORICAL PARK, NEW YORK.

Museums and historic sites provide space, experiences, insights, and tangible objects that encourage people to learn about their own past and our nation's history. Who is included in museums and historic sites' stories—and who is ignored—matters to all of us. We have long struggled to decide who and what should be remembered in our museums. When sites don't fully interpret women, they lose their explanatory power, distort the past, and deny fundamental respect to half. Not understanding *why* a site is significant, and why its history matters, can damage it as much damage as a flood or earthquake because people will not support its long-term preservation and interpretation.

The significance of women's history comes from our recognition that understanding and appreciating the roles of women in our past helps us live better and make better decisions. Once we understand the significance of women's history, we can utilize the knowledge base and tangible resources that provide the methodology and evidence for women's past to develop excellent interpretation of women's history and understand the larger human experience. Significance then simply means that these objects, places, stories, and interpretations are important to us and our understanding of American history. At the same time, significance has drastically different meanings for people. Consider this 1846 account of Lucy Henderson Deady from her Oregon Trail journey:

> At a meeting of the men of the wagon train it was decided to throw away every bit of surplus weight so that better speed could be made. A man named Smith had a wooden rolling

pin that it was decided was useless and must be abandoned. I shall never forget how that big man stood there with tears streaming down his face as he said, "Do I have to throw this away? It was my mother's. I remember she always used it to roll out her biscuits and they were awful good biscuits."[33]

His rolling pin—far more than an object used to roll out dough—was adding too much weight to a wagon train. Its significance was inextricably tied to the nurturing work that his mother did when he was a child.

Significance is often fluid, changing from generation to generation. One generation's beloved silver tea set is a later one's polishing chore; one childishly wrought sampler is a great-granddaughter's attic fodder or donated to a museum. Today, people think of the Lincoln Memorial as a protest site as much as a presidential one.[34] We remember it for the 1939 Marian Anderson concert and the 1963 March on Washington, where Dr. Martin Luther King Jr. gave his famous "I Have a Dream" speech and only one woman, Daisy Bates, was allowed to speak. She had been a mentor to the Little Rock Nine, six of whom were girls. Different generations and people value different pasts. The result of women history's being recognized as significant will be full acceptance and integration into existing museums and historic sites, the creation of additional ones, and a deeper and livelier understanding of women as a crucial part of our past and present. Without significance, tangible resources, knowledge base, and interpretation, we cannot be proper stewards of women's history.

Telling the Whole Story

Honest history tells the story of *everyone* who once lived here, including women who left only fleeting hints or whose history is found hidden under many layers of other people's views and biases. This book deliberately includes a variety of women because women's lives are more diverse than usually recognized. Consider Latinas replastering Texan missions, Chippewa women harvesting Minnesota wild rice, Italian women saying Novenas in Massachusetts, and Filipina nurses providing elder care in California. The history of these women requires us to interpret it in our locales and makes them the wonderful places they are. Integrating women into the history at museums/sites provides a richer, more genuine story—and a more interesting one, partly because it so often surprises us. Our goal is interpretation that appreciates all our foremothers, and understands how they experienced their lives, and what they accomplished in them. Significance, knowledge base, and tangible resources reinforce each other to develop vivid interpretation—and interest in women's history. In other words, for genuine understanding, we need to knit together the affective, intellectual, and physical aspects of our past.

Interpreting women's history begins with understanding its significance—why women and their history are important—then developing its knowledge base and preserving its tangible resources. Significance recognizes the important visitor experience for a girl and all of us immersing ourselves in Colonial Williamsburg, gaining new insights about ourselves and our shared past. That can only be properly done with a good knowledge base and tangible resources. Building a comprehensive quality knowledge base takes time and effort and is never finished as new scholarship, interpretive theories, and issues arise, all of which require ongoing work. The benefits of that work are credibility and connections with academic historians and the public. Likewise, tangible resources as physical entities require never-ceasing efforts to preserve them whether dusting objects or repointing masonry walls. It's a process of continual insights and attention that revives and enriches our history.

Those of us associated with museums and historic sites have a superb opportunity to share American women's history with the larger public. We have the significant stories, the tangible resources, the interpretation, and the potential audiences to reveal American women's history in ways that respect our predecessors and can excite our successors. We can do this by researching, preserving, and interpreting this crucial part of our past, and in so doing understand our history in ways more comprehensive and comprehensible. The following chapters provide the rationales and methods for the preservation and interpretation of women's history. The tools following each chapter are designed to build on each other to develop strong women's history interpretive programs, products, and presentations. With a stronger understanding and appreciation for the significance of women's history at your historic museum/site, let's begin.

Tools for Chapter 1: Significance

Each chapter ends with a set of Tools that together are designed to provide experience and resources useful for your specific museum or historic site. The more you invest in these tools, the greater benefit you will have. Best done together in a work team.

Tool 1.1 Write a bumper sticker that summarizes your museum's significance.

Study your mission statement, legislation, or similar documents and brainstorm a bumper sticker. This can force clear thinking by shortening a concept to a few words. An imaginary museum could use *Where History Comes Alive* or *Where Maria Gonzalez Changed History*.

Tool 1.2 Identify Focal Women and Associated People

Begin to build a list of *everyone* crucial to your history, both focal women and everyone closely associated with your museum or site. Include everyone you can find to make a strong and comprehensive list but concentrate on the women and girls there. If yours is a "Great Man" museum, list him and the other males. Be inclusive—especially search for minority women. Go as far back as you can, until noon yesterday, and include their birth/death dates as possible. You may be surprised at the length of your list; there may be some duplicates because some women had several names, such as those who followed patriarchal practice and changed their names upon marriage. An enslaved girl initially identified in a slave census only by gender and age may match a named woman with the same birth year in a later U.S. census. Genealogical pedigree charts are useful to track family members.

Try to find the woman behind "Mrs. George Smith" by collecting as much information as you can about her and other women there—Anne Jones may have become Mrs. George Smith. Cross-reference dates, locations, and incidents to identify Anne Jones Smith (Mrs. George). Do the same for immigrants, enslaved women, and girls. Finding children is often more difficult than finding adults, yet we know they were present and so we need to include them. Cradles, baptismal gowns, and an occasional toy remain, but often little else. Childhood clothing, such as diapers, once called "clouts," became rags or were recycled, making original ones rare.[38] As most women breastfed their children until the twentieth century (except for wet nurses), finding baby bottles is hard—although here archaeology helps. Except for prescriptive literature, childrearing practices have surprisingly few written descriptions about specific girls, making it harder to research them. Memoirs can help. Girls help us connect with our audiences, especially those girls fascinated with girls in history, who bring their families to sites and museums. Biographies of historic girls and dolls from different eras intrigue some girls. Watch girls during programs to see what reaches them best.

Next, identify the universe of people *associated* with your museum/site. The Associated People list should add the following:

1. People who stayed for lengthy time periods, such as aunts, grandchildren, friends, and tutors;
2. People who visited for shorter time periods, such as a doctor who paid house calls, a seamstress who came twice annually, a slave buyer, or elderly parents;
3. Neighbors and other key local people such as the minister or midwife;
4. People important in preserving the resources and establishing the museum.

These steps will enable your site to begin building the knowledge base necessary for telling your whole story. Once this information is compiled, it will provide the basis for research and interpretation. May you find some fascinating women.

Appendix

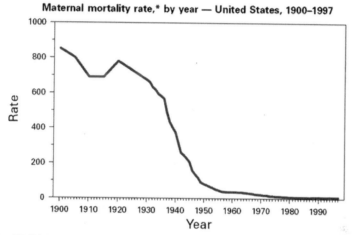

Maternal mortality rate,* by year — United States, 1900–1997

*Per 100,000 live births.

Figure 1.3. U.S. Maternal Mortality, 1900–1999. Deaths per thousand. Centers for Disease Control and Prevention. Note the dramatic mortality drop around 1927 as sulfa drugs and better obstetrical method became available. The high death rate for children left grieving families and dramatically skewed "life expectancy" ages. Child mortality rates decreased less drastically.

NATIONAL PARK SERVICE, CENTERS FOR DISEASE CONTROL AND PREVENTION (CDC). ACHIEVEMENTS IN PUBLIC HEALTH, 1900-1999: HEALTHIER MOTHERS AND BABIES, 1999. MMWR MORB MORTAL WKLY REP. 48(38): 849-58.

Notes

1. "National Historic Preservation Act," Pub. L. No. 89–665, § I, 16 U.S.C. 470(b), 1 (1966), https://www.nps.gov/history/local-law/FHPL_HistPrsrvt.pdf. Canadians with their Anglophone and Francophone worlds have wrestled with significance a great deal, identifying five key characteristics: *Importance* to those who experienced an event; *Profundity*, how deeply they felt its effects; *Quantity* of people affected; *Durability*, whether it left lasting or ephemeral effects; and *Relevance*, the impact on historical understanding. The United States focuses on whether an event took place fifty years ago, assuming that several generations will be the Test of Time. Both countries struggle to assess chronic forces that so often reflect women's lives. See Stéphane Lévesque, "Special Issue: New Approaches to Teaching History Teaching Second Order Concepts in Canadian History: The Importance of 'Historical Significance,'" *Canadian Social Studies* 39, no. 2 (WINTER 2005), www.quasar.ualberta.ca/css.

2. Cataraqui Archaeological Research Foundation, "Molly Brant: Who Was Molly Brant?" *Http://Www.Carf.Info/Kingston-Past/Molly-Brant*.

3. National Park Service, *Lowell: The Story of an Industrial City: A Guide to Lowell National Historical Park and Lowell Heritage State Park* (Washington, DC: Government Printing Office, 1992).

4. See Pauli Murray and Mary O. Eastwood, "Jane Crow and the Law: Sex Discrimination and Title VII," *George Washington Law Review* 34, no. 2 (December 1965): 232–56; Pauli Murray, *Proud Shoes: The Story of an American Family* (New York: Harper & Row, 1956), and Rosalind Rosenberg, *Jane Crow: The Life of Pauli Murray* (New York: Oxford University Press, 2017).

5. Kimberlé Williams Crenshaw, "Mapping the Margins: Intersectionality, Identity Politics, and Violence against Women of Color," *Stanford Law Review* 43, no. 6 (1991): 1241–99.

6. https://www.nps.gov/maritime/ref/landmarks.htm.

7. Mary Louise Clifford and J. Candace Clifford, *Women Who Kept the Lights, An Illustrated History of Female Lighthouse Keepers*, 2nd ed. (Alexandria: Cypress Communications, 2000). Seamond Ponsart Roberts and Jeremy D'Entremont, *Everyday Heroes: The True Story of a Lighthouse Family* (Portsmouth: Coastlore Media, 2013); Meg Jones, "Newly Found Photos Document Lighthouse Life at Wisconsin's Apostle Islands—[Female] Lighthouse Keeper's Negatives Surface on eBay," *Wisconsin Journal*, June 24, 2014, http://archive.jsonline.com/news/wisconsin/.

8. Mary Louise and J. Candace Clifford, *Women Who Kept the Lights, An Illustrated History of Female Lighthouse Keepers*, 2nd ed. (Alexandria: Cypress Communications, 2000).

9. Chesapeake and Ohio Canal NHP exhibit, 2012; Great Falls Tavern Visitor Center, Potomac, Maryland.

10. Lea VanderVelde, *Mrs. Dred Scott: A Life on Slavery's Frontier* (New York: Oxford University Press, 2009).

11. Susan Sleeper-Smith, *Indigenous Prosperity and American Conquest: Indian Women of the Ohio River Valley, 1690–1792* (Chapel Hill: University of North Carolina Press, 2018).

12. David McCullough, *John Adams* (New York: Simon & Schuster, 2002). Marla Miller in Betsy Ross provides another perspective on the difficulties patriot women faced during the American Revolution. See Marla Miller, Betsy Ross and the *Making of America.* (New York: Henry Holt, 2010).

13. Nancy O'Brien Wagner, "Awfully Busy These Days: Red Cross Women in France During World War I," *Minnesota History* 63, no. 1 (Spring 2012); my thanks to Ames Sheldon.

14. Peggy Pond Church, *The House at the Bridge of Otowi, The Story of Edith Warner and Los Alamos* (Albuquerque: University of New Mexico Press, 1959), Jennet Conant, *109 East Palace Ave. Robert Oppenheimer and the Secret City of Los Alamos* (New York: Simon & Schuster, 2005),

and Liza Mundy, *Code Girls: The Untold Story of the American Women Code Breakers of World War II* (New York: Hachette Books, 2017).

15. Women in Military Service to America Memorial, https://www.womensmemorial.org/memorial.

16. Rebecca J. Siders and Anna V. Andrzejewski, "The House and Garden: Housing Agricultural Laborers in Central Delaware, 1780-1930," in *Exploring Everyday Landscapes*, vol. VII (Knoxville: University of Tennessee Press, 1997).

17. Linda Peavy and Linda Smith, *Gold Rush Widows of Little Falls: A Story Drawn from the Letters of Pamelia and James Fergus* (St. Paul: Minnesota Historical Society, 1990).

18. Philip D. Curtin, Grace S. Brush, and George W. Fisher, eds., *Discovering the Chesapeake: The History of an Ecosystem* (Baltimore: Johns Hopkins University Press, 2001).

19. Isabel Wilkerson, *The Warmth of Other Suns: The Epic Story of America's Great Migration* (New York: Vintage Books, 2010), 556.

20. My thanks to Jean Ellis and Greta Erm, who researched the *Annual Report of the Secretary of State on the Registration of Births and Deaths, Marriages and Divorces in Michigan: For the Year*, vol. 44, Part 1910 (Lansing: Wynkoop Hallenbeck Crawford Co., State Printers, 1912). Google Books.

21. Jessica Ellen Sewell, *Women and the Everyday City: Public Space in San Francisco 1890-1915* (Minneapolis: University of Minnesota Press, 2011).

22. Pauli Murray and Mary O. Eastwood, "Jane Crow and the Law: Sex Discrimination and Title VII," *George Washington Law Review* 34, no. 2 (December 1965): 232-56. See Murray's *Proud Shoes: The Story of an American Family* (New York: Harper & Row, 1956).

23. Pauli Murray, November 14, 1963, quoting William O. Douglass to the National Council of Negro Women Leadership Conference, Washington, DC.

24. Andrew Dolkart, *Biography of a Tenement House in New York City: An Architectural History of 97 Orchard Street* (Santa Fe: The Center for American Places, Inc., 2002), 17.

25. Dolkart, *Biography*, 117.

26. Mort Sheinman, *A Tenement Story* (New York: Lower East Side Tenement Museum, 2004), 9.

27. Dolkart, *Biography*, 9.

28. W.S. Pillow, "Sex and Race in the Corps Expedition," in *Connexions: Histories of Race and Sex in North America* (Urbana: University of Illinois Press, 2016).

29. Robert R. Page, "National Park Service Cultural Landscapes Inventory Professional Procedures Guide" (Washington, DC: National Park Service, January 2009).

30. Antonia Castañeda, "Engendering the History of Alta California, 1769-1848," *California History* 76, no. 2/3 (1997): 235.

31. Sharon Brown, *Historic Structure Report: Historical Data Section: Wesleyan Chapel, Women's Rights National Historical Park* (Denver: National Park Service, 1987), https://irma.nps.gov/DataStore/DownloadFile/474799.

32. https://www.nps.gov/wori/learn/historyculture/the-first-womens-rights-convention.htm.

33. As quoted from Lucy Henderson Deady, 1846, in Joyce Badgley Hunsaker, *National Historic Oregon Trail Center: The Story Behind the Scenery* (Las Vegas: KC Publications, 1995).

34. At the 1922 racially segregated dedication of the Lincoln Memorial only R.R. Moton, then-president of Tuskegee Institute, was invited to speak as a keynoter. http://americanhistory.si.edu/changing-america-emancipation-proclamation-1863-and-march-washington-1963/1963/lincoln-memorial.

35. Antonia Castañeda, "Comino Chronicles: A Tale of Tejana Migration," *Chicana/Latina Studies* 9, no. 1 (Fall 2009).

36. Ludlow site visit August 2011; "Working American: The Human Experience of the Colorado Coalfield Strike of 1913-1914," *Teach Ludlow*, 2004, www.teachludlow.com.

37. Crystal N. Feimster, "Ida B. Wells and The Lynching of Black Women," *New York Times*, April 30, 2018. Wells identified at least 130 Black women lynched between 1880–1930.

38. Karin Calvert, *Children in the House: The Material Culture of Early Childhood, 1600–1900* (Boston: Northeastern University Press, 1992).

Part II
Knowledge Base

2

Researching Women's History

A knowledge base is simply an organized collection of everything you can learn about your museum's resources and story. Having a strong knowledge base differentiates professional museums/historic sites from tourist traps. Solid research supports quality interpretation that offers insights into both women and their larger historical context and connects tangible resources and visitors. Without research support, interpreters may tell stories passed from one to another that lack any relationship with historical evidence, such as the myths that colonial people were short because their beds were, or that window pane scratches came from antebellum women testing their engagement rings to see if they had real diamonds. Actually, four poster beds are optical illusions and diamonds were uncommon antebellum stones. Research that builds knowledge bases helps avoid such fallacies. Knowledge bases are not stacks of books, but knowledge in every form, everything we know about a site/museum, its people—especially its women—and its tangible resources. Along with significance and tangible resources, knowledge bases help us interpret our female heritage. It builds our credibility.

Knowledge bases consist of *primary* sources, *secondary* sources, and *tertiary* sources. Primary sources refer to the documents, objects, art, music, and buildings produced by the women and men who lived during the historic time period being preserved and interpreted. Chapters 3, 4, and 5 will focus on written, oral, and visual primary sources. Secondary sources, from textbooks to children's books, synthesize the past into coherent narratives. Here, "tertiary" is used to distinguish management-related documents that are seldom formally published but profoundly shape present and future decisions. Tertiary sources—often called gray literature—help manage sites/museums with myriad studies, reports, site-specific analyses, conference papers, archaeological surveys, and plans created from research or during decision-making processes. This chapter focuses how to access and use secondary sources of women's history—reference works, textbooks, online resources, scholarly monographs, and academic journal articles. In our electronic age, many sources of all kinds are available on paper and digitally. Although museum/historic site knowledge bases cover different kinds of sources—written, oral, visual, and scientific—they work best together when they reinforce, expand, and even apparently contradict each other. Together, these varied sources provide stronger evidence and enable better interpretive presentations, just as an image "shows" a written description visually. Later, consider how you want to share your women's history knowledge base with the public, in person and virtually. Most of it should be available, but some entries such as copyrighted images or the location of sensitive archaeological sites may need protection.

A knowledge base answers key questions about the women's history and resources available at your museum or site. Having a strong one makes research accessible about the women and their histories, and it identifies what is already known and what is missing and needs to be known. This guides future research priorities and methods. Because research is cumulative, sources

Figure 2.1.   With millions of men in the U.S. armed forces during World War II, many young mothers, such as Josephine Stober, shown here holding her daughter, Diane, went to work in wartime factories such as Union Oil in Long Beach, California. The federal government provided quality childcare while the mothers worked in shipyards and factories.

and historical research ideally form a conversation that enables criticism and strengthening of our historical knowledge. Articles and books written today build on earlier findings. Although a museum/site knowledge base should document everyone, the focus here is on women. Consider these questions:

- Who were all the women here? What experiences did they have? What differences did they make by their lives? How did they affect history? How did they interact with men? With each other?
- What women's history *context* is interpreted at your museum/site? What should be?
- How do your site's tangible resources shape a deeper understanding of women's pasts? Are there "missing" resources that need interpretation, such as outbuildings or ponds?
- What must be known to tell the whole story well and preserve its tangible resources?
- What is inadequately known or not known at all?
- What do you need to do to tell the whole story?

Research and Knowledge Bases

Answering these questions requires a robust knowledge base, one created and maintained by research. This iterative process becomes more sophisticated with time as intellectual discovery continues because articles and books written today build on earlier findings. This chapter focuses on how to begin building your knowledge base through research on the women's history of your museum/site, rather than from its tangible resources, which follow in Chapters 6–8. Invest the time and effort to build your knowledge base on the relevant women, tangible resources, and historic era of your museum/site. Begin with a survey of your existing knowledge resources—a list of the key books, articles, papers, reports, etc. that you already have. In addition to on-hand sources, look at electronic databases, including Project Muse, which lists over a thousand recent and relevant books, and JSTOR, which electronically curates peer-reviewed journals; and investigate content descriptions of online booksellers. Access to electronic databases is generally available only through subscribing universities, although partial access is available, supplemented by interlibrary loans or alumnae access from some colleges.

If you can't locate a source in your knowledge base, you don't really have that source! Finding aids help locate specific items in the more comprehensive knowledge bases that include all kinds of sources. Some museums/sites have impressive libraries with thousands of books and sophisticated databases, while others have a corner shelf of materials. Finding aids come in many forms—commercial museum management software, library catalogs, property cards, or simple lists—reflecting the complexity of their sites/museums. The effort involved in developing these aids pays off in time and aggravation saved. Finding aids identify pertinent knowledge, whether a scholarly article, a master's thesis, a catalog card recording a needlework sampler, a DVD describing an archaeological dig, a YouTube webinar, or a database.[1] Aids complexity depends on the scope and size of a specific museum/site. Actually, museums and historic sites often have different finding aids for objects, books, or master plans. Every kind of aid must be kept current to work well. Increasingly, museum management systems or collection management systems increase efficiency. Whether electronic or paper, it's important to invest in finding aids that cover all your holdings, especially when your knowledge base includes your tangible resources. Internet searches complement site-specific knowledge bases but cannot substitute for them.

Existing site-related knowledge bases vary in comprehensiveness and content, making it crucial to snoop around in their entries to determine if and how they cover women and girls and related topics. See what's there—don't assume that Planned Parenthood will be found under "Women and Medicine." Don't expect that *everything* you seek in a collection will be in its finding aid. Your search will net all kinds of tidbits, many irrelevant but still potentially useful. You may need to modify your collection management system to ensure that visitors can find women's history and associated resources. Can "women" and related terms such as "gender" be easily located in your existing system, or must query terms be added?[2] As you explore, it is crucial to keep track of your sources by constantly copying the URLs, adding "date accessed," and bookmarking online sources for later use. This approach will save untold amounts of time. Free, historian-developed Zotero, Notes, and similar software have replaced 3-by-5-inch cards for notetaking—and bibliographic references that only need to be entered once. Develop a system that everyone can easily grasp for their research and to avoid a formidable and unfriendly backlog of sources not in your knowledge base. People can help. Public historians handling land disputes have expertise in land records and court cases, while curators know marks on fine china as well as changes in fashion and different manufacturing methods. Historic architects research buildings in telling detail. Historic sites and museums need these disciplines to research the people, the lands, the events, and the processes that comprise their history.

Getting Started

This chapter focuses on how to begin research on the women's history of your museum/site, rather than on their tangible resources; this follows in Chapters 6–8. Strengthening your knowledge base begins with reviewing the basics. Survey the existing knowledge base at your historic site/museum to identify major knowledge gaps and fill them. Depending on the sophistication of the staff at your site/museum, it's best to begin by reading a current textbook in U.S. and women's history for the general context and then sections of relevant reference works and key articles. Seminar-style reading can engage all staff members as well as anyone else who may be interested. Weekly discussions of key chapters will encourage everyone to do the readings and apply their insights to the women at your site/museum. Readings should be of reasonable length, not 2,000 pages that have been inflicted weekly in graduate school seminars.[3] Asking everyone to write down three questions on how the chapters/articles relate to your site/museum—and then answer them—works well, as does rotating the discussion leader. Such discussions increase understanding of the women who were at your museum and how best to apply that knowledge.

Reference Works and Textbooks

Durable and authoritative, these tomes or their online equivalents are intended to be consulted as needed; they are foundational and protect us from egregious errors. Everyone serious about researching women's history needs to access them. Keep your readings current. Although some topics are extensively researched for a few years and then not studied for years, some older sources become classics. Secondary sources will only cite works published *before* their copyright date. Look closely at all these books and mine their bibliographies and footnotes for books and articles relevant to your site by topic or by geographic proximity.

- *Notable American Women*, a thirty-year, five-volume project, is still *the* reference work for women's history. The first three volumes, *Notable American Women, 1607–1950: A Biographical Dictionary*, cover women who died before January 1951. The fourth volume, *Notable American Women: The Modern Period*, includes women who died 1951–1975. *Notable American Women: A Biographical Dictionary, Completing the Twentieth Century* covers women who died 1976–1999.[4]

- *A Companion to American Women's History*, Nancy Hewitt and Anne Valk (eds.), is an excellent foundation with extensive scholarly bibliographic essays on our myriad facets.[5]
- Depending on your location and focus, consider the two-volume Darlene Clark Hine, *Black Women in America: An Historical Encyclopedia* and Jessie Carney Smith, *Notable American Black Women Book II*; Vicki Ruiz and Virginia Sanchez Korrol, eds., *Latinas in the United States: A Historical Encyclopedia, and volumes of El Mundo Zurdo, conference papers from* SSGA/EMZ, Society for the Study of Gloria Anzaldúa; also Elinor and Robert Slater, *Great Jewish Women*.[6] For Asian American Pacific Islander women, see Gary Y. Okihiro, *Women and Gender: The Columbia Guide to Asian American History*, and Shirley Hune and Gail M. Nomura, eds., *Asian/ Pacific Islander American Women: A Historical Anthology*. Books on Native American women include Patrick Deval, *American Indian Women*; Erin H. Turner, *Wise Women: From Pocahontas to Sarah Winnemucca*; and Carolyn Niethammer, *Daughters of the Earth*.[7]
- Susan Ferentinos thoughtfully synthesizes LGBTQ women in *Interpreting LGBT History at Museums and Historic Sites*; Megan Springate edited *LGBTQ America: A Theme Study of Lesbian, Gay, Bisexual, Transgender, and Queer History* with excellent essays; Lillian Faderman, *Odd Girls and Twilight Lovers: A History of Lesbian Life in the 20th Century* and Paula Martinac, *The Queerest Places: A Guide to Gay and Lesbian Historic Sites* (New York: Henry Holt and Company, 1997) are insightful.[8]
- Choose a women's history textbook. Sara Evan's *Born for Liberty* provides a brief, succinct narrative of American women's history while other, more comprehensive texts combine primary documents with essays on relevant topics. Ellen Carol DuBois and Lynn Dumenil, *Through Women's Eyes: A History with Documents*; Sharon Block and Ruth Alexander, *Major Problems in American Women's History*; Linda Kerber and Jane Sherron De Hart, *Women's America: Refocusing the Past*, or S. Jay Kleinberg, Vicki Ruiz, and Eileen Boris, *Women's History and Narratives, Intersections, and Dialogues*.[9]
- For textbooks on African American history, consider Darlene Clark Hine, *A Shining Thread of Hope: The History of Black Women in America*; Darlene Clark Hine, Wilma King, and Linda Reed, eds., *We Specialize in the Wholly Impossible: A Reader in Black Women's History*; and Hine's haunting, "Some Preliminary Thoughts on Rape, the Threat of Rape and the Culture of Dissemblance," which everyone should read.[10]
- A number of excellent works include readings on diverse groups of women. Especially helpful is *Unequal Sisters: A Multicultural Reader in U.S. Women's History*, which documents an amazing variety of women.[11] Other titles to consider include Vicki L. Ruiz and Virginia Sanchez Korrol, eds., *Gender on the Borderlands: The Frontiers Reader*; Yolanda Flores Nieman and Susan Armitage, *Chicana Leadership: The Frontiers Reader*; and Linda Trinh Vo and Marian Sciachitano, eds., "The Derivative Status of Asian American Women," in *The Force of Domesticity: Filipina Migrants and Globalization*.[12]
- Allan G. Johnson, *The Gender Knot: Unraveling our Patriarchal Legacy*, provides crucial insights on our culture, as well as Patricia Collins and Sirma Bilge, *Intersectionality*, and Paula Rothenberg, *Race, Class, and Gender in the United States: An Integrated Study*. Understanding the concept of intersectionality provides insights into the complexity of women's lives. Reading the lively literature helps explain the range of women's experiences when race and gender (and myriad other factors) combine and intertwine.[13]

Online Resources and Research

After you have surveyed the knowledge base for your museum/historic site, prepare a summary outline of its sources and then go further using online sources. Just as good ingredients make delicious meals, use only solid websites whose information is well-sourced, accurate, relevant, and appropriate. *Every* statement should be traceable back to a genuine, high quality, original source—online fakes happen! Websites and blogs are flexible and easily accessible, and they can be very helpful in strengthening a site's knowledge base with their vast amounts of information. Use excellent websites (see Appendix) such as the Library of Congress, National Archives and Records Administration; National Park Service; the Smithsonian Institution; the American Association for State and Local History; the National Council on Public History; the Organization of American Historians; the American Historical Association; the National Trust for Historic Preservation; the Vernacular Architecture Forum; the National Association for Interpretation; and the Association for Living History, Farm, and Agricultural Museums.[14]

Review the holdings at the three major women's history archives: the Sophia Smith Collection at Smith College; the Schlesinger Library at Radcliffe/Harvard University; and the Sallie Bingham Center for Women's History and Culture at Duke University.[15] Nearby archives and libraries will most likely have research about local women and events. Search out your state's resources—many have developed excellent websites from their state historical society, state library, and state archives. In addition, organizations' websites often have resource sections with presentations, lesson plans, and insights from distinguished historians but may require some hunting. Blogs provide current discussions and perspectives that reflect current understanding, but can be ephemeral. Major universities—as well as those with exemplary public history, museum study, or curatorial programs—can be particularly helpful. Public history organizations and interpretive ones also have useful websites, as do regional/racially based organizations. Identify possible sources and then go search for them. Alexander Street Press publishes the broadly defined "Women and Social Movements in the United States, 1600 to 2000" website begun by Kathryn Kish Sklar and Tom Dublin, accessible by subscription.[16] Ellis Island's American Family Immigration History Center has over 50 million searchable online records; the University of North Carolina has "Documenting the American South."[17] Websites change content frequently but usually have up-to-date approaches, program ideas, and colleague names. Less scholarly websites can be valuable but often mislead or omit information—Wikipedia, for example, has a decided dearth of women's history entries. Websites ending in .org, .edu, and .gov for organizations, educational institutions, and governmental websites are generally more trustworthy than the highly variable commercial ".com."

Genealogical Research

Traditionally, there has been a huge gap between historical research and genealogical work, probably because they have had two different audiences—one professional and published and the other more personal and private. Genealogists have been very successful in developing tools and techniques to trace back generations, using written, oral, and visual sources to explore women's history. Genealogists work to fill out their family trees, whether to document everyone in their lineage for their personal satisfaction, for bragging rights (as descendants of saints or scoundrels), or to qualify for membership in hereditary organizations. These last include the Daughters of the American Revolution, who trace back to male ancestors who fought for the Patriots; the United Daughters of the Confederacy, descended from those who fought against the Union during the Civil War; or Children of Colonial Clergy. There are many such organizations whose members claim virtue by their ancestors' actions. Historians generally cringe at this approach, believing that we can take neither credit nor blame for our ancestors' actions, as we had nothing to do with their deeds. Still, many people find deep satisfaction in genealogical research and pursue it passionately. Because members of The Church of Jesus Christ of Latter Day Saints (LDS, or Mormons) trace lineages as part of their theology, many genealogical tools are located at LDS FamilySearch Centers. There are also extensive resources in Cincinnati at the National Underground Railroad Freedom Center, and in Washington, D.C., at the DAR Museum. Excellent genealogical books and websites, along with other organizations and commercial sources, also assist research. If the women you are researching had husbands or sons who fought in a war, there should be military records—especially if she became his widow—although some records have been lost. Women's petitions for pensions created pension records, which are good evidence of their lives. In addition, soldiers in early wars, including the American Revolution, received payment in bounty lands, again creating pertinent records.

The sheer quantity and variety of available records is awesome. The NARA published a *Guide to Genealogical Research in the National Archives*, which details information available in its census records, passenger arrival lists, U.S. naturalization records, military records, records of pensions for widows, civilians during wartime, records of Indians and African Americans, civilian government employees, land records, claims, court records, miscellaneous records, and District of Columbia records. This guide provides good assistance for anyone researching historic women.[18] The NARA website has a section for genealogists but organizes *all* its records by giving each originating department or commission its own Record Group number. For example, the indispensable Census Bureau records, including the ten-year censuses, are RG 29. Because professional document repositories arrange their collections according to the people or organizations where they came from, thinking like an archivist will ease your search.

Court records, trials and proceedings, useful in women's history generally, are especially pertinent for genealogy. For example, *Courthouse Research for Family Historians: Your Guide to Genealogical Treasures* focuses on local records—often county, city, or state.[19] This resource provides considerable information on how to research courts' legal findings and the numerous kinds of records generated, including land records and criminal cases. While few records are specific to women, women were involved in most of them. *Genealogy Online for Dummies* has an integrated approach especially useful for beginning research.[20] Genealogical research systems can help discover a great deal about families and individuals.

Genealogical websites are useful for researching women's lives. Two popular sites are Ancestry.com (free and by subscription) and FamilySearch.org, a free website by a nonprofit arm of the LDS.[21] Ancestry.com has webinars, databases, specialized forms, and resources for everyone from the raw beginner to the professional genealogist, with extensive lists of other pertinent databases. These databases include Castle Garden for immigrants who came to New York before Ellis Island opened; college/high school yearbooks; and 3.5 million patents.[22] Ancestry.com describes how to find photographs and "Searching for Maiden Names of Female Ancestors," while FamilySearch.org has a large, growing collection of records, books, photos, and family trees—including more than 1,500 historical record collections from around the world, and more than 177,000 digitized books. Two excellent books are the *Unofficial Guide to Ancestry.com* and the *Unofficial Guide to FamilySearch.org*.[23]

Expanding Your Knowledge Base

Once you are comfortable with the background literature and available web-based materials, including genealogy, you will want to go more in depth and read books and articles relevant to your historic site or museum that were written for an academic audience. This may seem daunting at first, particularly if you do not have a history background, but the more you learn about your museum/site, the more expert you will become. Soon you will be comfortable reading academic writing, especially as it relates to "your" topic. Nobody has ever perished from footnotes, which sometimes have wonderful gems tucked in them. Local librarians and college faculty can be very supportive in helping to enhance your knowledge base. WorldCat, a free online resource, identifies books, articles, reviews, and primary documents valuable for research. To avoid future misery, track *all* your findings in Zotero or another bibliographic site.[24]

Scholarly Books

The past fifty years have produced an astonishing outpouring of scholarship on women's history, with thousands of scholarly monographs, articles, theses and dissertations, exhibits, letters, and diaries being researched, analyzed, synthesized, mounted, and published. The challenge is matching the best sources with your museum/historic site. Secondary sources are especially useful to understand the all-important *historical context* of the women at your museum/site. Being able to fill in specific gaps in your knowledge base is crucial for current and future projects. New research, newly discovered primary sources, dissertations, translations, and secondary sources especially useful to understand the historical context of the women at your museum/site will continue to be published. These publications help you become truly knowledgeable about women's history at your locale. One of the most difficult issues is ferreting out—or working around—information that's missing, hard to find, or unknowable.

Every museum/site should have (and read!) the basic secondary sources relevant to the key women and tangible resources. Secondary sources provide a framework and context for primary resources by providing comparisons and showing contemporaneous events. Begin by doing a catalog search. If you have access to a top research university in your area, a field trip to snoop in its library will help immensely. Visit the reference librarian first and let him or her know what you are looking for. Examples of excellent and useful books include *Betsy Ross and the Making of America*, which centers on an iconic tradeswoman and shows how her life intertwined with the American Revolution—helping us understand both. Especially pertinent, *Keeping House: Women's Lives in Western Pennsylvania, 1790–1850,* answers many historic site–related questions. *Kit Carson's Three Wives: A Family History* shows complex frontier relationships among indigenous Mexican and "American" women and men. *Mrs. Dred Scott: A Life on Slavery's Frontier* on Harriet Robinson [Scott] at Fort Snelling in Minnesota, provides the biography of a woman whose freedom suit had dire consequences. *On the Edge of Purgatory: An Archaeology of Place in Hispanic Colorado* analyzes a now-displaced nineteenth-century Hispanic settlement, while *Mine Towns* analyzes families in northern copper mines. The bibliography has additional secondary sources.[25] The fascinating *Three Decades of Engendering History: Selected Works of Antonia Castañeda* centers on Latina women's lives as explanatory and provides a powerful alternative American history.[26]

Other books cover particular aspects of women's history in greater detail. Finding such books entails tracking journals, professional association magazines, and websites. Regionally oriented books contribute context—*Women in Pacific Northwest History; Beyond Schoolmarms and Madams: Montana Women's Stories; Homes in the Heartland: Balloon Frame Farmhouses of the Upper Midwest;* and *Women Building Chicago, 1790–1990: A Biographical Dictionary.*[27] Chapter-length biographies of women are being published for southern states by the University of Georgia, while several states have published books on women there such as Genevieve McBride, *Women's Wisconsin: From Native Matriarchies to the New Millennium.*[28] Finally, the Depression-era state-by-state WPA Guides—though now dated—remain fascinating summaries.[29] Handbooks published by museums and sites similar to yours in period and locale can be especially helpful.

Academic Journals and Other Sources

Beyond historical monographs, consider that the most current research in any field, after papers at conferences, usually first appears in academic journals. Key journals for women's history include *SIGNS: Journal of Women in Culture and Society, Frontiers: A Journal of Women's Studies* (western and multicultural emphasis), *Gender and History*, and the *Journal of Women's History, Chicana/Latina Studies.* The Asian American Feminist Collective has published its first zine.[30] Other important journals not focused on women or gender, but often publishing relevant articles, include *The Journal of American History,* the *American Historical Review,* and smaller journals such as the *William & Mary Quarterly* (colonial), *Ethnohistory,* the *Western Historical Quarterly,* the *Journal of Southern History,* the *Journal of the Gilded and Progressive Era,* the *Public Historian,* and *History News.* The excellent *Winterthur Portfolio: A Journal of American Material Culture* and *Buildings & Landscapes* (Vernacular Architecture Forum, VAF) consistently publish relevant high-quality articles. There are myriad others. Contact your local reference librarian.

H-Net (http://www.h-net.org) has reviews and bibliographies analyzing the most recently published books. Women's history organizations post bibliographies and professional meetings, have advertisements from publishers in their programs, and publish prize-winning books from the Organization of American Historians, the Association of Black Women Historians, National Council on Public History, Mujeres Activas en Letras y Cambio Social, and Society for the Study of Gloria Anzaldua. Other organizations include the Southern Association of Women Historians and the Western Association of Women Historians. For LGBTQ, see Lesbian Herstory Archives and Committee on Lesbian, Gay, Bisexual and Transgender History; National Collaborative for Women's History Sites; and the grandmother of Women's History Conferences, the Berkshire Conference on the History of Women and Gender.[31]

After completing your initial survey and identification of those sources most useful to your knowledge base, there are several ways to enhance it.

- Search for books published by academic presses specializing in women's history. Search for relevant journals, magazines, and websites; find newsletters and annual meeting programs that list scholars and their research; look for work by those scholars.
- Access JSTOR, which publishes many journals electronically but requires a subscription (worth it!); it's part of the "gated web" that also includes PhD dissertations with thousands produced annually (available online for a fee).
- Search in fields of anthropology, archaeology, women's studies, fashion, geography, etc. Read professional publications such as *Historic Preservation, Legacy,* and academic journals such as *Signs, Frontiers: A Journal of Women Studies,* and *Journal of Women's History.*
- Seek relevant MA theses and PhD dissertations (JSTOR and local universities).
- Attend relevant professional meetings and conferences to hear some of the hundreds of papers given with their prodigious research and analysis and to meet the authors. In addition to national and regional women's history conferences, national history, American Studies, and Women's Studies conferences often include women's history sessions. Join appropriate groups to access their networks and expertise.

Tertiary Sources

Professionally managed museums and historic sites conduct intensive studies and develop many types of plans—strategic plans, general management plans, historic structure reports, Environmental Impact Studies, etc. While academic research begins with intellectual questions, museum and historic site research begins with our collections, tangible resources, upcoming events, and management concerns. Many institutions and organizations use or undertake tertiary sources that provide in-depth analyses of the associated tangible resources and the people who once lived there, or analyze alternatives for future development. Little known to the public and profession, tertiary sources with their tangible, resource-based research are useful to other museums and historic sites. Some are reports from major multiyear archaeological excavations, while others employ the latest technology to determine curatorial object conditions. While public meetings or in-depth market analyses can be involved, often these studies have few authors and small readership, but huge effects in preserving resources, determining public programs and

Figure 2.2.   Charlotte Hopper driving a Ford automobile, Dorrance, Kansas, by Leslie Winfield Halbe, June 7, 1913.
COURTESY KANSAS STATE HISTORICAL SOCIETY.

access, or documenting eligibility for National Register of Historic Places protection. Their obscure titles hide research and analysis very useful for many other museums/sites.

Major museums and historic parks have impressive sets of tertiary literature. Identify the tertiary sources of pertinent studies, plans, reports, and specialized publications your museum already has and their dates. These works explain earlier decisions and document past conditions. Unlike secondary literature that synthesizes a large scale, tertiary sources are locale-specific but still useful. For instance, at Herbert Hoover National Historic Site in West Branch, Iowa, the National Park Service prepared a *Historical Base Map and Grounds Study, Herbert Hoover, 1874–1886*, available online. This study remains very helpful for understanding that village and other post–Civil War Midwest towns, including the women who lived there and ran boardinghouses, and the Hoover family. The West Branch one-room schoolhouse furnishings plan is available online.[32] The *Historic Furnishings Report*, Clara Barton National Historic Site, analyzes Barton's frugality and determination, her minimal interest in housekeeping, and her difficulties managing a combination national headquarters and boardinghouse—with drunken workmen, unhappy housekeepers, and international gifts—full of insights into her personality and organization.[33] An archeological assessment, *The Buttrill Ranch Complex: Evidence of Early Ranching in the Big Bend* (TX) discusses ranching families, women, and governesses, as well as former slave Susie Payne and her husband, Monroe—research applicable to other ranching women in the Greater Southwest.[34] Such site-specific studies contrast with the more generalized research of the Colonial Williamsburg Foundation or Old Sturbridge Village. These tertiary sources contain a surprising wealth of women's history.

NPS Tertiary Sources: Plans, Reports, and Studies

Used here, tertiary sources are simply management documents—studies, reports, and plans—that guide museums and historic sites and help implement directions. They differentiate museums and sites from the academic world. As "gray literature" (published in small print runs or online), tertiary sources can be elusive but extremely helpful. If your site is near another one or one that is comparable in age and subject, seek these often-relevant tertiary sources. For example, the Herbert Hoover NHS, the *Historic Base Map* includes a typescript of the 1880 manuscript census for West Branch Iowa property and church records, and photographs building a vivid understanding of village's time and place. Museums and sites that interpret that era in the Midwest will find it quite pertinent. Few tertiary documents are mesmerizing, but their research can fascinate, and their recommendations have profoundly shaped historic resource management. *The Skagway, District of Alaska, 1884–1912, the Historical and Preservation Data on the Skagway Historic District* has extensive photographs and architectural drawings designed for decision making; its many women counter stereotypes of Alaskan sourdoughs.[35] Plans for sites such as Mary McLeod Bethune Council House, the First Ladies Library/Ida Saxton McKinley home, and the Susan B. Anthony House have research and interpretive alternatives.[36]

This list below provides key tertiary sources useful for your knowledge base:

- *The National Register of Historic Places* identifies places of local, regional, or national significance. National Register (NR) properties need to be fifty years old and still maintain their historic physical integrity. NR nomination quality varies, but often has excellent research on the 90,000 NR properties that contain more than 1.4 million individual resources, including buildings, sites, districts, structures, and objects that weave together our local, state, and national heritage. Nearby Register property nominations can be helpful. *National Register of Historic Places Travel Itineraries*, with over sixty itineraries, features key historic buildings and structures with short descriptions, including "Places Where Women Made History" in New York and Massachusetts, and *Teaching with Historic Places Lesson Plans* combines pedagogy with locations to demonstrate how places teach; eighteen lesson plans portray women-associated places.[37]
- *National Historic Landmarks* (NHL) are nationally significant properties designated by the Secretary of the Interior after considerable research and evidence of public support. Since 1935, some 2,700 NHLs based on scholarship and outstanding national significance have been designated.[38]
- *Environmental Impact Statements* (EIS), Environmental Assessments, Furnishing Studies, Furnishing Plans, Grounds Studies, Special Resource Studies, etc. (Warning! Names change). These studies are rich in analysis and research.
- Organizations do many different kinds of studies and inventories—they make research management decisions, identify key resources and interpretive themes, and develop comprehensive plans, strategic plans, and annual plans. By whatever name, these plans are often very useful, even if sometimes difficult to locate.
- National Park Service (NPS) sites and parks—look for one near you, including the "natural" parks, which have a surprising amount of women's history. Women ran hotels in Yosemite, were Army wives in Yellowstone, and fought for the preservation of the Everglades. The NPS has prepared many helpful tertiary sources. Their museum collections, scientific studies, furnishing studies, and plans are all potentially useful.[39]

Evaluating Sources

Evaluating the quality of any source you find is *crucial*. Historians constantly research and with surprising frequency find new sources, by asking different questions of existing primary sources, using new techniques, or sometimes by finding "new" ones in basements, attics, and in unlikely places. If you know of resources in such locations, remove them from any place too wet/dry, cold/hot, or fluctuating to prevent their damage or destruction. Good scholarship has footnotes that mix older and newer sources, primary and secondary ones, with well-known names and publishers. View sources whose authors have obvious axes to grind with skepticism. What did they omit? Overstate? Skew? There are earnest but amateur articles, websites rife with misstatements, and simply inaccurate sources—all of which must be identified. Go for the strongest sites first—homemade ones can be wildly misleading. Magazines, journals, newspapers, and websites publish writings that range from awesome to awful. Their content must be analyzed more carefully than peer-reviewed publications where experienced professionals carefully critique each other's work. Unless deemed classics, avoid works that only cite books and articles from the 1950s or before, or those that only reference one or two sources, or those without any source notes and bibliography. Evaluate every source by asking how well it documents the women/girls in your museum/site. Does it fit with what you already know? Does it raise new questions or provide new insights? Does it make sense? Seem prejudiced? Do you know the authors? What are their credentials, whose website or blog? Suddenly, your climbing gets steeper. Some sources are obvious, others are possibly useful, and still others are weird, with unsubstantiated assertions. Experience will hone your judgment of quality sources.

Our social and political system reflects cultural attitudes that long declared women as *auxiliary* members of society rather than primary ones. For example, women tried for decades to serve on juries so that women could judge each other. Only in 1975 did the U.S. Supreme Court in *Taylor v. Louisiana* support jury equality, calling women a "distinctive group," and overturning centuries-old common law that generally kept women from serving on juries because of their "defect of sex."[40] Enjoy your search and discoveries!

Research Notes

- Words and terms change meaning. Consult the *Oxford English Dictionary* for history and to prevent embarrassing misusage.
- Life expectancy means the likelihood that a person will live to a certain age. Because historically so many children died before age five, that average is skewed. A more accurate calculation is the average life expectancy *at age five*, after a person has survived childhood's high death rates, although that obscures young children's death rates. See the 1910 Michigan state report, which shows how many children died before age five. One can only imagine the grief their families experienced.[41]
- Correlation and causality are often confused; correlation shows that two events have occurred together, which may be significant or may simply be coincidence. Causation shows that event A causes event B.
- We underestimate how much inflation lessens the value of money so that $100 in 1930 is $1,504.14 in 2019! The inflation calculator from the Bureau of Labor statistics calculates comparable dollar amounts (https://data.bls.gov/cgi-bin/cpicalc.pl). Please refer to historic *and* current amounts.[42]

Tools for Chapter 2: Knowledge Base Research

In Chapter 1, you began a list of Focal Women and Associated People affiliated with your museum/site. The present chapter has identified useful secondary and tertiary sources to enhance that list. To strengthen your knowledge base, continue to refine that list, build a Women's History Chronology, and map your Women's History Knowledge Base. With these elements you can build a strong site-related knowledge base, a longtime investment that will yield much. As you fill in the Focal Women and Associated People Lists, the Women's History Chronology, and the Women's History Knowledge Base Sources, additional questions, people, dates and sources that require more research will become obvious. For example, to research a particular school teacher, look for alumnae records from the State Normal School (now probably a college) she attended and her yearbook there, for schools where she taught, or for a court case she had. Museums with excellent research libraries will benefit from these tools as a summary of your women's history, convenient for interpreters and everyone else. Museums and historic sites that lack strong libraries will find that the knowledge base increases your ability to plan and provide excellent interpretive programs and products.

Tool 2.1 Build a Chronology of Women and Resources

This chronology, which captures important dates, women, and sources in one place, should emphasize the women involved with relevant dates, major events, long-term trends, and national context. Entries should reference museum/site evidence. Depending on the museum/site's complexity, the chronology can be a Word table, an Excel file, or whatever format works, as long as it is regularly updated. Because this chart will grow-as-you-go, don't worry about having only few dates initially. Using this chronology regularly will build it faster and stronger. Sharing it in the Cloud, on Google.Drive, or in a similar location will allow more people to add entries so it will become an electronic master list. It's unnecessary to include *every* event in American history—focus on those that most affected the women at your museum/site and that are especially important to interpret. Rows by decade can be refined later with specific years, months, days, or even hours as events require; additional columns can track different women. Include events that women affected or were affected by at your museum/site, such as when land was purchased/homesteaded, when buildings were constructed, when people migrated there, when people died, and when major events in American history happened. Abbreviations are fine if they are understood by users.

Your own chart of names, dates, and sources summarizes research in one place. An example, designed as a template for your use from the fictitious María González de la Cruz and José Rojas de la Cruz State Museum, Table 2.1, follows on page 34.

Tips for Completing Knowledge Base Chronology

1. The dating format of 1920.05.23 allows electronic sorting. Start with the year and refine it.
2. The Comments column is a place for questions, to note patterns, and to add information.
3. To prevent later problems, fully cite critical information or link it with your Women's History Knowledge Base Sources (see Tool 2.2). As soon as you begin a note or quote a source, *capture that citation*. Zotero, developed for historians, is an excellent program for tracking notes and sources and will prevent major hassles later.
4. Track complete names as accurately as possible, noting alternative ones.
5. Many questions and blank spaces will be resolved later. Early information is usually incomplete, which is why it's called "research"! This also helps identify research priorities.

Tool 2.2 Map Women's History Knowledge Base Sources

Prepare your Women's History knowledge base of key primary, secondary, and tertiary *sources* at your site/museum, with a prioritized list of those additional sources most needed to acquire.

Table 2.1.   Chronology for María González de la Cruz and José Rojas de la Cruz [Fictitious!] Museum.

Person	Date	Event	Tangible Resource	Source	Comment
María de la Cruz	1920.05.23	Born in San Antonio, Texas	House no longer exists; seek artifacts	Biography, p. 24.	Born to Josefina Pilar and Juan de la Cruz. [Check names!]
María de la Cruz	1928–1938	Great Depression	Rental house extant	Natl Reg. Nomination, p. 77.	Family loses land; moves to town. Dates approximate.
María de la Cruz	1940.00.00		Dress she made	Museum Collection	[Accession # here]
José Rojas	1942	Listed as a mechanic	Garage gone; replaced by office building	City directory	Only under his name—need to link together!
María Gonzalez	1942.02.12	Gave first major speech	[Seek copy of speech]	Biography p. 34	[Check location; title??? When did she marry?]
María Gonzalez	1951.03.06	Jailed for civil disobedience	[Seek jail]	Local newspaper	See article, March 6, 1951; look for other records.
Samuel Jones	?????	Political activism	Letter to María Gonzalez	Museum collection	[Accession # here]
María Gonzalez	1967.00.00	Inherited home	Home to House Museum	Museum collection	Listed on National Register in 2019
María Gonzalez	1988.02.14	Interviewed as an activist	Oral history tape	Newsletter Centro Cultural refers to this	Need to get copy from woman who interviewed her!

Include full citations! Use it as a community reading list to build shared knowledge and teamwork. Review/develop a staff handbook with charts showing essential information about written sources (primary, secondary, tertiary), oral sources, visual sources, key readings, relevant articles, and FAQs (especially on sensitive topics). A chart form helps sort the knowledge base so that everything available about a particular year, or all books by a particular author can be shown. For example, your Women's History Knowledge Base Sources could have the following sections: Written Sources, Primary, Secondary (reference only), Tertiary; and FAQs. Your Written Sources chart should include: author, date, type (diary, letter), original location, current location, and the ever-useful "Comments" column.

Notes

1. Julia G. Costello and Adrian Praetzellis, *Excavating L.A.'s Brothels*, VHS (Venice: Furman Films, 1999).
2. Past Perfect and Re:Discovery are among several dozen museum management programs.
3. Personal experience, University of Minnesota.
4. Edward T. James, Janet Wilson James, and Paul. S. Boyer, eds., *Notable American Women, 1607–1950: A Biographical Dictionary*, 3 vols. (Cambridge: The Belknap Press of the Harvard University Press, 1971). See the two subsequent volumes, Barbara Sicherman et al., eds., *Notable American Women: The Modern Period* (Cambridge: The Belknap Press of the Harvard University Press, 1980) and Susan Ware and Stacy Braukman, eds., *Notable American Women: A Biographical Dictionary, Completing the Twentieth Century* (Cambridge: The Belknap Press of the Harvard University Press, 2004).
5. Nancy Hewitt and Anne Valk, eds., *A Companion to American Women's History,* 2nd ed. (Malden: Wiley-Blackwell, 2020).
6. Darlene Clark Hine, *Black Women in America: An Historical Encyclopedia,* 2nd ed. (New York: Oxford University Press, 2005); Jessie Carney Smith, ed., *Notable Black American Women: Books I–III* (Gale Publishing, 1991; Vicki L. Ruiz and Virginia Sanchez Korrol, eds., *Latinas in the United States: A Historical Encyclopedia* (Indianapolis: Indiana University Press, 2006); T. Jackie Cuevas, Larissa M. Mercado-Lopez, and Sonia Saldivar-Hull, eds., *El Mundo Zurdo 4* (San Francisco: Aunt Lute Books, 2015); Elinor and Robert Slater, *Great Jewish Women* (Middle Village: Jonathan David Publishers, 2015).
7. Patrick Deval, *American Indian Women* (New York: Abbeville Press, 2015); Erin H. Turner, *Wise Women: From Pocahontas to Sarah Winnemucca* (Guilford: GlobePequot, 2009); Carolyn Niethammer, *Daughters of the Earth* (New York: Touchstone Books, 1996); Laura F. Klein and Lillian A. Ackerman, eds., *Women and Power in Native North America* (Norman: University of Oklahoma Press, 1995).
8. Susan Ferentinos, *Interpreting LGBT History at Museums and Historic Sites* (Lanham: Rowman & Littlefield Publishers, Inc., 2014); Megan Springate, ed., *LGBTQ America: A Theme Study of Lesbian, Gay, Bisexual, Transgender, and Queer History* (online: National Park Service and National Park Foundation, 2016), www.nps.gov/subjects/tellingallamericansstories/lgbtqthemestudy.htm; Lillian Faderman, *Odd Girls and Twilight Lovers: A History of Lesbian Life in the 20th Century* (New York: Columbia University Press, 2012); Paula Martinac, *The Queerest Places: A Guide to Gay and Lesbian Historic Sites* (New York: Henry Holt and Company, 1997).
9. Sara Evans, *Born for Liberty* (New York: Touchstone Books, 1994); Ellen Carol DuBois and Lynn Dumenil, *Through Women's Eyes An American History with Documents*, 5th ed. (New York: Macmillan Higher Education, 2018); Sharon Block, Ruth M. Alexander, and Mary Beth Norton, *Major Problems in American Women's History*, 5th ed. (New York: Wadsworth Publishing, 2013); Linda Kerber and Jane Sherron De Hart, *Women's America: Refocusing the Past,*

8th ed. (New York: Oxford University Press, 2015); S. Jay Kleinberg, Vicki Ruiz, and Eileen Boris, *Women's History and Narratives, Intersections, and Dialogues* (New Brunswick: Rutgers University, 2007).

10. Darlene Clark Hine and Kathleen Thompson, *A Shining Thread of Hope: The History of Black Women in America* (New York: Broadway Books, 1998); Darlene Clark Hine, Wilma King, and Linda Reed, eds., *We Specialize in the Wholly Impossible: A Reader in Black Women's History* (New York: Carlson Publishing, 1995); Darlene Clark Hine, "Some Preliminary Thoughts on Rape, the Threat of Rape, and the Culture of Dissemblance," *SIGNS: Journal of Women in Culture and Society* 14, no. 4 (Summer 1989): 912–20.

11. Vicki Ruiz and Ellen Carol DuBois, eds., *Unequal Sisters: A Multicultural Reader in U.S. Women's History*, 4th ed. (New York: Routledge, 2007). Excellent!

12. Yolanda Flores Niemann and Susan Armitage, eds., *Chicana Leadership: The Frontiers Reader* (Lincoln: University of Nebraska Press, 2002); Shirley Hune and Gail M. Nomura, eds., *Asian/Pacific Islander American Women: A Historical Anthology* (New York: New York University Press, 2003); Gary Y. Okhiro, *The Columbia Guide to Asian American History* (New York: Columbia University Press, 2001); Linda Trinh Vo and Marian Sciachitano, eds., "The Derivative Status of Asian American Women," in *The Force of Domesticity: Filipina Migrants and Globalization* (New York: New York University Press, 2008).

13. Allan G. Johnson, *The Gender Knot: Unraveling our Patriarchal Legacy*, 3rd ed. (Philadelphia: Temple University Press, 2013); Patricia Collins and Sirma Bilge, *Intersectionality* (New York: John Wiley & Sons, Inc., 2016); Paula Rothenberg, ed., *Race, Class, and Gender in the United States: An Integrated Study.*, 6th ed. (New York: Worth Publishers, 2004). See Kimberlé Williams Crenshaw, "Mapping the Margins: Intersectionality, Identity Politics, and Violence against Women of Color," *Stanford Law Review* 43, no. 6 (1991): 1241–99; Anna Carastathis, "The Concept of Intersectionality in Feminist Theory," *Philosophy Compass* 9, no. 5 (2014): 304–314; and Lynne M Woehrle, ed., *Intersectionality and Social Change."* (Bingley, UK: Emerald Group Publishing, 2016); John D'Emilio and Estelle B. Freedman, *Intimate Matters: A History of Sexuality in America*, 3rd ed. (Chicago: University of Chicago Press, 2012).

14. Library of Congress (www.loc.gov); National Archives and Records Administration (https://www.archives.gov); National Park Service (https://www.nps.gov); Smithsonian Institution (https://www.si.edu); the American Association for State and Local History (https://aaslh.org); the National Council on Public History (https://ncph.org); the Organization of American Historians (https://www.oah.org/); American Historical Association (https://www.historians.org); The National Trust for Historic Preservation (https://savingplaces.org); the Vernacular Architecture Forum (www.vernaculararchitectureforum.org), the National Association for Interpretation (www.interpnet.com), and the Association for Living History, Farm and Agricultural Museums (ALHFAM, https: www.alhfam.org).

15. See the Sophia Smith Collection at Smith College (https://www.smith.edu/libraries/special-collections/about/sophia-smith-collection); the Schlesinger Library at Radcliffe/Harvard University (www.radcliffe.harvard.edu/schlesinger-library); and the Sallie Bingham Center for Women's History & Culture at Duke University (library.duke.edu/rubenstein/bingham).

16. Kitty Sklar and Tom Dublin, "Women and Social Movements in the United States, 1600–2000," womhist.alexanderstreet.com.

17. American Family Immigration History Center, https://libertyellisfoundation.org/family-history-center and "Documenting the American South," https://docsouth.unc.edu.

18. *Guide to Genealogical Research in the National Archives*, 3rd edition. (Washington, DC: National Archives Trust Fund Board, U.S. General Services Administration, 2000).

19. Christine Rose, *Courthouse Research for Family Historians: Your Guide to Genealogical Treasures* (San Jose: CR Publications, 2004).
20. Matthew L. Helm and April Leigh Helm, *Genealogy Online for Dummies*, 6th ed. (Hoboken: Wiley Publishing, 2011).
21. https://www.ancestry.com/; https://www.familysearch.org/en/.
22. Nancy Hendrickson, *Unofficial Guide to Ancestry.com: How to Find Your Family History on the #1 Genealogy Website* (Cincinnati: Family Tree Books, 2014).
23. Nancy Hendrickson, *Unofficial Guide*, 2014; Dana McCullough, *Unofficial Guide to FamilySearch.Org: How to Find Your Family History on the Largest Free Genealogy Website* (Cincinnati: Family Tree Books, 2015).
24. See https://www.worldcat.org/.
25. Marla Miller, *Betsy Ross and the Making of America* (New York: Henry Holt, 2010); Virginia K. Bartlett, *Keeping House: Women's Lives in Western Pennsylvania, 1790–1850* (Pittsburgh: University of Pittsburgh Press, 1994); Marc Simmons, *Kit Carson & His Three Wives: A Family History* (Albuquerque: University of New Mexico Press, 2003); Lea VanderVelde, *Mrs. Dred Scott: A Life on Slavery's Frontier* (New York: Oxford University Press, 2009); Bonnie J. Clark, *On the Edge of Purgatory: An Archaeology of Place in Hispanic Colorado* (Lincoln: University of Nebraska Press, 2011); Alison K. Hoagland, *Mine Towns: Buildings for Workers in Michigan's Copper Country* (Minneapolis: University of Minnesota Press, 2010).
26. Linda Heidenrich, ed., *Three Decades of Engendering History: Selected Works of Antonia Castaneda* (Denton: University of North Texas Press, 2014).
27. Karen J. Blair, *Women in Pacific Northwest History*, Revised (Seattle: University of Washington Press, 1988); Martha Kohl, ed., *Beyond Schoolmarms and Madams: Montana Women's Stories* (Helena: Montana Historical Society, 2016); Fred W. Peterson, *Homes in the Heartland: Balloon Frame Farmhouses of the Upper Midwest* (Minneapolis: University of Minnesota Press, 2008); Rima Lunin Schultz and Adele Hast, eds., *Women Building Chicago, 1790–1990: A Biographical Dictionary* (Bloomington: Indiana University Press, 2001).
28. Genevieve McBride, *Women's Wisconsin: From Native Matriarchies to the New Millennium* (Madison: Wisconsin Historical Society, 2005). Joan M. Jensen, *Calling This Place Home: Women on the Wisconsin Frontier*, 1850–1925 (Minneapolis: University of Minnesota Press, 2006).
29. John A. Stahlberg, ed., *Montana: A State Guide Book*, Compiled and Written by the Federal Writers' Project of the Works Project Administration for the State of Montana, American Guide Series (New York: The Viking Press, 1939), 307.
30. See https://www.asianamfeminism.org/events/2019/5/30/asian-american-feminist-history-in-action; they also held Asian American Feminist History in Action, an interactive workshop in New York City.
31. H-Net (http://www.h-net.org); Organization of American Historians (https://www.oah.org); the Association of Black Women Historians (truth.abwh.org); National Council on Public History (https://ncph.org) (Mujeres Activas en Letras y Cambio Social (MALCS, http://malcs.org); and Society for the Study of Gloria Anzaldua (SSGA, http://www.gloriaanzaldua.com). Other organizations are Southern Association of Women Historians (thesawh.org); Western Association of Women Historians (https://wawh.org); Lesbian Herstory Archives (www.lesbianherstoryarchives.org); and The Committee on Lesbian, Gay, Bisexual, and Transgender History (clgbthistory.org); National Collaborative for Women's History Sites (www.ncwhs.org); and the Berkshire Conference on the History of Women and Gender (https://berksconference.org).
32. See https://irma.nps.gov/DataStore/Reference/Profile/2246130; Edwin C. Bearss, *Historical Base Map and Grounds Study, Herbert Hoover, 1874–1886* (Washington, DC: National Park Service, 1968), https://www.nps.gov/parkhistory/online_books/heho/base_map.pdf.

33. Sandra Weber, Katherine Menz, and Diana Pardue, "Historic Furnishings Report, Clara Barton National Historic Site" (Washington, DC: National Park Service U.S. Department of the Interior, 1983), https://www.nps.gov/parkhistory/online_books/clba/hfr.pdf.

34. Virginia A. Wulfkuble, *The Buttrill Ranch Complex: Evidence of Early Ranching in the Big Bend*, Office of the State Archeologist Report 34 (Austin: Texas Historical Commission, 1986), 26.

35. Robert L. S. Spude, *Skagway, District of Alaska, 1884–1912: Building the Gateway to the Klondike* (Fairbanks: Anthropology and Historic Preservation, Cooperative Park Studies Unit, University of Alaska, Fairbanks, 1983).

36. National Park Service, "Final General Management Plan Environmental Impact Statement Mary McLeod Bethune Council House N.H.S." (Washington, DC, 2001); National Park Service, "Saxton House and National First Ladies Library Special Resource Study" (Canton: National Park Service, 2001); National Park Service, Boston Support Office, "Susan B. Anthony Special Resource Reconnaissance Study" (Boston: September 2001).

37. National Register of Historic Places, https://www.nps.gov/subjects/nationalregister/index.htmr, Travel Itineraries, https://www.nps.gov/subjects/heritagetravel/discover-our-shared-heritage.htm; Teaching with Historic Places, https://www.nps.gov/subjects/teachingwithhistoricplaces/index.htm.

38 National Historic Landmarks, https://www.nps.gov/nhl/.

39 National Park Service, https://www.nps.gov/parkhistory/online_books.

40. Holly McCammon and Soma Chaudhuri, "Becoming Full Citizens: The U.S. Women's Jury Rights Campaigns, the Pace of Reform, and Strategic Adaptation," *American Journal of Sociology* 113, no. 4 (January 2008): 1105–47. See Tracy Thomas and Tracey Boisseau, *Feminist Legal History: Essays on Women and Law* (New York: NYU Press, 2011).

41. Michigan Dept. of State, *Annual Report of the Secretary of State on the Registration of Births and Deaths, Marriages and Divorces in Michigan: For the Year*, vol. 44, Part 1910 (Lansing: Wynkoop Hallenbeck Crawford Co., State Printers, 1912).

42. https://data.bls.gov/cgi-bin/cpicalc.pl. The calculator covers 1913 to the present.

3

Written Sources

Read All About Her

"Her death was very sudden she died Tuesday mourning [sic]." Feb. 25, 1918 at 8.30 a.m.[1]

Written sources can have powerful immediacy that startles us a century later, such as this letter reporting a mother's death only twelve hours after she gave birth. To interpret history effectively, we must be able to trace to evidence found in primary sources created by or about historical women. Written primary documents—on paper and now increasingly digitized—have long been crucial for women's history. They have impressive variety, as shown in this partial list: letters, diaries, certificates, official memoranda (including those written by historic site staffs), laws, court decrees, congressional testimony, recipes, speeches, sermons, sewing patterns, obituaries (mini-biographies), grocery lists, magazine articles, building permits and deeds, drivers' licenses, musical scores, and tree ring data. This journey of discovery connects us to the women who authored them, because documents witness directly to their lives. For us, such close connections with those who came before us are part of the joy of being human. They challenge us to understand women on their terms, to unravel mysteries and to discover missing parts of their lives. This chapter focuses on written primary sources. It helps you identify which sources to research first and the value of working with reference librarians and other professionals to track down the documents that you need to enrich your museum or historic site—as well as the utter importance of tracking every source and every note taken. This chapter discusses specific research issues in doing women's history.

Finding Documents

You never know where or when you may find a treasure trove of original documents. For example, Clara Barton's diary was found hidden in the walls of her Maryland home and, simultaneously, the national American Red Cross headquarters. Search for such treasures in historic buildings—in attics, basements, outbuildings, and in second-hand bookstores with books covered in ancient dust. Students found thirty boxes of documents, 1898-1940, of Maggie L. Walker, an intrepid entrepreneur, organizer, banker, and "Race Woman" during American Apartheid, in the attic of her former national headquarters. Ask neighbors, descendants, leaders, or school libraries if they have any old books or paper records. Look any place where the women you are researching may have left traces. In this day and age, this means old computers too. Don't give up—such primary sources are worth it. Some primary documents have been collected into easily accessible anthologies.

Looking for primary sources begins with the women (and men) historically present at *your* museum, at your historic site, or in a nearby repository. Finding appropriate documents and reading antique handwriting and idiosyncratic spelling can be daunting. Few collections contain both incoming letters and their responses—although carbon paper and copying machines have made complete sets more likely. Your reward comes in the retrieval of women previously little sought, unknown, or barely visible—but who are now found and who so enrich our understanding of the past. While working on the Maggie Walker Collection, the women processing it learned not only about this amazing woman's deeds, but heard her moods, insights, and even her frustrations.[2] Broadening your sources and analyzing them is crucial to building the knowledge base of your historic site or museum. For example, the Mujeres Latinas Project of the Iowa Women's Archives at the University of Iowa states, "Despite their significant presence in Iowa, Latinas remain largely invisible in our state's history due to the lack of historical documents available to researchers. The Mujeres Latinas Project . . . collects and preserves materials which document the lives and contributions of Latinas and their families to Iowa history."[3] By looking for documents about Latinas, the Mujeres Project has made a significant contribution to Iowa's history. The LGBT Historical Society provides collecting advice for LGBTQ materials.[4]

American historians have primarily used English-language sources and heard men's voices, often by reading their handwriting and deciphering obscure vocabulary. They seldom read more than one or two foreign languages, usually Spanish, French, or German. Yet when Susanah Shaw Romney examined seventeenth-century documents in old Dutch, she uncovered the multiple roles that women played in Dutch colonial enterprises. From their homes, Dutch women financed, supported, and benefited from the men associated with the Dutch East India Company's enterprises, even as they also carried out crucial domestic work.[5] Romney's research counters assumptions that only women who physically accompanied men were integral to colonial enterprises. To be successful, you must include women and girls in every research question that involves document acquisition and access. Seek people fluent in other languages to enrich your knowledge base. Happily, repositories often prepare excellent finding aids. For example, the Library of Virginia's "Using Women's History Sources" identifies pertinent holdings, including 1888 "pensions for all [Confederate] veterans and family and an 1890 special census of Union veterans—documents from the postwar South."[6] These collections, along with curated digitized collections, contain potentially relevant documents.

Challenges of Women's Written History

We cannot research what has not been saved. Historians—being prisoners of our sources—need quality ones to do good history and need female-created sources to hear women's voices directly. More men wrote letters, diaries, and official papers—and their organizations saved their documents more than women's were saved. Most of the women who kept diaries were better educated and wealthier. Before their emancipation, reading and writing were illegal for enslaved Black women, making our hearing their voices more difficult. To help future generations, the adage "Don't throw it away," encourages that more women's history documents be kept *now* to ensure many more documents from more diverse women are placed in archives to have more women's history resources in the future.[7] It can be surprisingly difficult to get people to keep their personal papers, and even harder to get people to deposit them in an archive. Many women believed—and still believe—that their lives weren't sufficiently interesting or valuable, or they were simply shy, resulting in many female writings being burned, trashed, or lost to natural causes. References to women often are omitted from finding aids or hidden under their husbands' names; databases and book indexes sometimes lack key words that identify women. We need to do much more to collect, preserve, and make accessible women-related sources. As a cautionary tale, Zora Neale Hurston's biographer wrote about the author and anthropologist:

> She [Hurston]not only vanished from Eatonville but also from the public record. Exhaustive searches of archives from this period have unearthed no census listing, no city directory entry, no school file, no marriage license and no hospital report. . . . In 1911, it was relatively easy for someone, particularly a black woman, to evade history's recording gaze.[8]

Written communication never captures everything said or gestured among people. Full communication includes tone of voice, posture, gestures, and nonverbal cues. When reading written documents, query their context and consider how creative, even cunning, people can be in writing letters or memorandums, even when taking minutes. When reading documents, ask if they make sense given what you know about a particular woman. Did she always sound so negative? So shy? Why was she being so formal in that letter? Only by collating many bits of evidence can you get a clear picture of what was really happening. Test each document against what is already known and check the document itself—some documents are outright frauds.

In addition, many women's traditional activities were unlikely to be discussed in writing. How much can one write about doing laundry? Or canning spaghetti sauce? Or cleaning the baby? Discussions about marital problems, losing children, becoming and being a widow, having menstrual cramps, spousal abuse, being a stepmother or stepdaughter, or getting pregnant were seldom discussed in writing. Yet we all live within our own bodies and lives, and these bodily aspects affect us deeply. One can sometimes find a surprisingly intimate reference and extrapolate a fuller meaning from it. For example, in the early nineteenth century, a happily married Pennsylvania woman wrote her bishop complaining that he had decreed that married people should only have sex twice a year, "Sex is sometimes the only way it is possible to hold love together. *For a great many people, it is the only way.*"[9] Did this woman represent that popular opinion among her peers? Was she an exception among married women at the time? Or was she exceptional because she was willing to state her views so forcefully and clearly to a bishop in an age when women were expected to accept religious direction?

To find sources by/about women and surmount barriers—such as documents being listed under their husband's/father's names or as "Mrs. Smith"—different sources must be knitted together to compile as much information about your key women as possible. The Focal Women and Associated People and Chronology lists you began in Chapter 1 can help refine knowledge about such key individuals. As your knowledge base accumulates information about different individuals, it will help identify connections among them.

Documents By, For, and About Women

While many documents are relevant to women's history, analyzing their purpose and audience shifts our understanding. One approach is to sort these documents into three categories—those written *by* women, those written *for* (or addressed *to*) women, and those written *about* women—in order to clarify each author's purpose. Descriptive documents written by women, such as letters and diaries, usually provide women's actual perspectives and behavior on a particular event or topic. Prescriptive documents written for women—speeches, sermons, or medical advice—generally direct females to believe and act in particular ways. Some writings *about* women necessitate reading *between the lines* to find women's perspectives; others are analytical, such as medical reports—although they contain their own biases. Mistaking prescriptive literature for women's actual lives can confuse visitors into thinking that women once did as they were told, even though prescriptive sources seldom describe actual circumstances. Determining the "targets" of documents clarifies their authors' purpose and audiences. In addition, some documents were generated during or just after an event while others were retrospective; some documents describe intentionally remembered past events, while others were haphazard leavings of life. Before official vital records were kept, only family Bibles recorded births or baptisms, marriages and deaths.

Historians have traditionally divided written materials into those published (books, articles, memoirs), and those not-published (letters, diaries, etc.), because libraries kept published materials and archives/special collections had unpublished ones. With more books and documents digitized online, this division has become less germane.

Prescriptive Literature

Speeches, sermons, and lectures provide the presenter's idealized future and the actions necessary to achieve it. In contrast, descriptions purport to present current reality. While descriptive sources discuss what women were actually doing, prescriptive ones direct what women should do. Mistaking prescriptive literature for women's actual lives confuses the author's ideals with women's realities, whether in a cookbook or in a sermon. Prescriptive sources seldom reflect actual circumstances. For example, Catherine Beecher and Harriet Beecher Stowe wrote *The American Woman's Home or, Principles of Domestic Science: Being a Guide to the Formation and Maintenance of Economical, Healthful, Beautiful, and Christian Homes.* One of many such household guides, its title exemplifies prescriptive literature.[10]

Women's Private Writings

Of course, the best sources are those written by the historical women themselves. Although women were not as literate or prolific in their writings as men (their lives being circumscribed by hard work, less education, and expectations that they "know their place"), their private documents broaden our understanding of women's reality and personalities. Written by the actors themselves, women's private thoughts provide research insights and powerful quotes for interpretive programming.

Letters

The largest category of women's descriptive primary documents—letters—ranges from small love notes to official reports from organizations. These letters and diaries tell us as much about their authors as about their lives and times. Letters are written by, about, to, and for women, and have different purposes, from the deeply personal to the coldly official. Most collections only have the incoming correspondence, requiring searches elsewhere for the other half. Unless writers saved copies of their outgoing letters, responses have often been lost—as happened to Benjamin Franklin's letters to his sister Jane Franklin.[11] Business letters, while formal, often have subtle differences in tone that reveal relationships between the writer and her recipients—or that she's dictating her letters. The development of typewriters, carbon paper, mimeographs, and later, photocopiers makes finding and using primary sources easier, especially when carbon copies of responses exist or documents are available electronically.

Letters women wrote to their family and friends provide excellent evidence because they reveal motives, attitudes, and experiences. Letters written by men about women are often excellent sources, but are mediated through their male-imprinted perceptions. For example, the 1850s Dumville family correspondence of mother Ann Dumville, and her daughters Jemima,

Hephzibah, and Elizabeth, provide "a rarely seen look at antebellum working women confronting privation, scarce opportunities, and the horrors of civil war with unwavering courage and faith."[12] In 1873, Victorian writer Isabella Bird described her Rocky Mountain travels with a "desperado" (outlaw), later published as *A Lady's Life in the Rocky Mountains*, where Bird vividly described both terrain and people there.[13] Isabella Bird's letters provide images useful for any nineteenth-century museum interpreting the people and terrain of the Rocky Mountain West—as well as Victorian attitudes toward adventurous women. Written documents that first appear to have limited applicability are often quite useful. Historians knit together primary documents with extensive supplementary research to write books such as *Gold Rush Widows of Little Falls [Minnesota]*, detailing women's lives whose husbands had departed to make their fortunes in the Rocky Mountains—but who later needed to borrow money from their wives.[14] Showing wives supporting their gold rusher husbands brings nuance to our common perceptions of Victorian marriages. Today, telephone calls and emails that have replaced correspondence leave less evidence, complicating future research.

Diaries

Women kept diaries for many reasons and under many circumstances. These intimate records often served as their confidants. Some entries may seem trivial, but in the aggregate brim with significant evidence and provide perspectives missing from men's accounts. Even in sparse entries, because ink and paper were dear, careful reading says much. Martha Ballard, a Maine midwife, kept her diary for twenty-seven years, writing by candlelight while her family slept, recording her experiences of caring for women during pregnancy and childbirth and ministering to the health needs of everyone. Her diary become the basis of Laurel Thatcher Ulrich's *A Midwife's Tale: The Life of Martha Ballard Based on Her Diary, 1785–1812*. Supplementing her diary with other written records, Ulrich showed Martha Ballard's busy and skilled life, enmeshed in a frontier community and building a "web" of relationships.[15] Ballard's diary provides insights for our interpretation of childbirth and women's health. Six-year-old Laura Jernegan kept a diary as she sailed from 1868–1871 on the "whale ship" *Roman* with her captain-father, mother, and brother from Massachusetts to Hawaii and back. She shared her perspective on girlhood, kittens, lessons, and whaling. One entry reads: "Would you like to hear some news well I don't no [sic] of any. Good by for to day" [sic].[16] In the 1700s, Abigail Bailey of New Hampshire wrote of her "wicked" husband's "vile intentions" toward their daughter; Mary Holyoke of Massachusetts recorded giving birth to twelve children, and burying nine of them; Elizabeth Fuller simply wrote of household work. "I spun three skeins," was all she wrote one day. At first glance, some entries may seem trivial, but read together they brim with relevant information missing from the accounts men penned then.[17]

Such diaries remain crucial sources for understanding women's lives. In the mid-nineteenth century, as an estimated 250,000–500,000 men, women, and children (of the U.S. population of 23 million) migrated westward, some women kept diaries on their covered wagon journeys as they rode (others walked) hour after hour. Historian Lillian Schlissel analyzed 103 diaries from women traveling the six-month journeys along the Oregon and California trails during the 1840s–1860s, published as *Women's Diaries of the Westward Journeys*.[18] Schlissel explains that some women kept a diary so that families subsequently moving west had guidance. Like most women then, these diarists were profoundly reticent about discussing their female health issues. While women's diaries recorded births, they rarely discussed pregnancy. Being written "in real time," diaries directly capture their authors' feelings, as in 1962 when a twelve-year-old girl wrote, "Pres[ident] Kennedy real angry today at Cuba," referring to the Cuban Missile Crisis as her neighbors built bomb shelters or prepared to evacuate Washington, D.C.[19] She wrote that entry to record her feelings, not to show us her deep concern. Her diary has an immediacy that

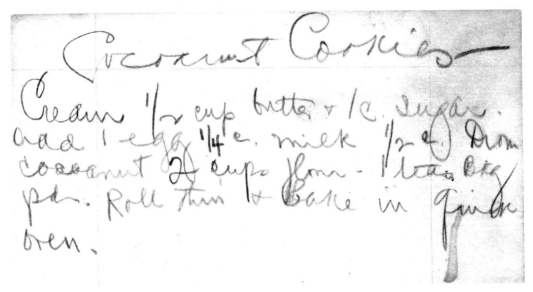

Figure 3.1.   Cocoanut [sic] cookie recipe, Bess Truman, wife of President Harry S Truman.
COURTESY HARRY S TRUMAN NATIONAL HISTORIC SITE, INDEPENDENCE, MISSOURI.

exposes a girl's concern, even though it tells us nothing about her subsequent responses as the crisis developed. Unlike diary writers, we know the "time between" that they could not foresee. We see the intervening years, which side won or lost, when beloved people died—what happened between then and now.

Ephemera: Receipts, Calling Cards, and Scrapbooks

While easily ignored or dismissed, bits of paper can be valuable in showing purchases and consumer behavior, bills, tickets for events, even poll tax receipts. Each receipt reflects a particular historic situation that helps us understand these women. Lori Osborne, processing papers of Frances Willard, head of the Women's Christian Temperance Union, found "the kinds of things that would be in anyone's piles from the nineteenth century—train tickets, notes on scrap paper, concert programs, calling cards, newspaper clippings (too many!), letters (to and from), [and] telegrams."[20] A set of 1920s dance cards that culminated in fifty-two years of marriage illustrates a woman's evolving relationship with a man, as many listed names became only one.

Scrapbooking, very popular in the late nineteenth and early twentieth centuries, is discussed in *Writing with Scissors: American Scrapbooks from the Civil War to the Harlem Renaissance*, where women pasted cherished items into their scrapbooks, now common in museum holdings. Their scrapbooks expressed their experiences and values, places they visited and sights they saw, and how they created their own histories by saving mementos from their most valued experiences.[21] Scrapbooks provide insights beyond memorabilia.

Memoirs

Classic memoirs provide depth to interpretation, as they share first-person accounts of women encountering and besting difficult experiences. They also represent rare documents by women that were usually meant for a larger reading audience. Harriet Backus's *Tomboy Bride* recounts her experiences when she accompanied her husband to the mining camps high in the Rocky Mountains. Her excellent early twentieth-century account details the difficulties and dangers of running a household at 11,500 feet above sea level and partnering with her husband by "checking his reports."[22] Because memoirs entail the act of remembrance that often intensifies emotions, they need cross references, as detailed in *Swept Under the Rug: A Hidden History of Navajo Weaving*. Its author mined the Hubbell Trading Post financial records and her interviews with Navajo women to refute many myths, demonstrate the women's agency, and show how the grossly low amounts that traders paid expert Navajo weavers contributed to their impoverishment.[23]

At the same time, authors sometimes omit key aspects of their lives because they are ashamed or simply reticent about them. For example, Elizabeth Lord, who traveled to Oregon at the age of eight, wrote about her experiences in *Reminiscences of Eastern Oregon*. Her account frustrates, as we want her to disclose more about her significant life-changing events:

> Of the many things connected with our family I do not care to speak in these pages, such as my marriage, the loss of my first child and the birth of my second, which meant much to all of us and was a great event in our lives, and is something that especially belongs to ourselves.[24]

Public and Published Sources: Literature and Cookbooks

Some of women's most important expressions come in public writings, such as Elizabeth Cady Stanton's "Declaration of Sentiments," based on the American Declaration of Independence, that argued for comprehensive women's rights throughout American life. Although a written document, Stanton had it read and signed at the 1848 Woman's Rights Convention in Seneca Falls, New York.[25] While less likely to reveal emotions, these documents show the determined efforts women made to reshape their world.

Libraries are full of literature written by women—poetry, short stories, plays, and articles on many topics. In addition to providing evidence, they can provide lively presentations of women's voices at contemporary sites.[26] Novels provide insights into the author's life and perceptions and reveal a place, its people, and their values. Artistic writings require the same analysis all historic research does—ensuring authenticity, considering its context, understanding its audience and purpose, and describing how the author shaped the final product. Analyzing their public reception and staying power are also important. During the nineteenth and twentieth centuries, American women wrote novels eagerly read by the public. While *Little Women* and *Their Eyes Were Watching God* provided literary insights into women's lives, *Uncle Tom's Cabin* inflamed political anger.[27] In 1862, President Lincoln allegedly greeted Harriet Beecher Stowe with, "So you're the little woman who wrote the book that started this Great War."[28] While Lincoln might not have said this, it suggests the enduring power of Stowe's novel.

Within close relationships, women have often shared recipes with their dear friends and family, evidence that they probably ate together in their affective networks. Mothers gave daughters favorite family recipes; daughters-in-law begged for childhood dishes their husbands remembered. Some—but certainly not all—recipes were written down, even published. Women's organizations and churchwomen published cookbook collections as fund-raisers; these now provide us evidence of food accessibility and changing tastes and diets. Gelatin salads gave way to mushroom soup–based casseroles to internationally influenced recipes and prepared foods. Lacking a family cookbook or recipe cards, many excellent period cookbooks have been reprinted, showing us more about lifestyles, as well as health and housekeeping instructions. The Swan Mansion at the Atlanta History Center uses the 1928 *The Southern Cookbook* interpretively for its authentic regional recipes.[29] Other notable cookbooks include Lydia Maria Child's *The Frugal Housewife* (1829)[30]; Catherine Beecher's textbook, *A Treatise on Domestic Economy* (1841); and, coauthored

NAME	RELATION.	PERSONAL DESCRIPTION.								
of each person whose place of abode on June 1, 1900, was in this family. Enter surname first, then the given name and middle initial, if any. Include every person living on June 1, 1900. Omit children born since June 1, 1900.	Relationship of each person to the head of the family.	Color or race.	Sex.	DATE OF BIRTH.		Age at last birthday.	Whether single, married, widowed, or divorced.	Number of years married.	Mother of how many children.	Number of these children living.
				Month.	Year.					
3		5	6	7		8	9	10	11	12
Johnson, Charles L.	Head	W	M	Ab	1868	32	m	5		
Olivia J.	Wife	W	F	Sep.	1866	33	m	5	2	1
Gladies M.	Daughter	W	F	Jan.	1898	2	S			

Figure 3.2.   Manuscript Census 1900, Ottawa County, Kansas. Note questions on how many children a woman had borne and how many of her children were alive. This reflects the high death rate for infants and children to age five.

OTTAWA COUNTY, KANSAS. 1900 U.S. CENSUS, POPULATION SCHEDULE T623, ROLL 6. WASHINGTON, DC: NATIONAL ARCHIVES AND RECORDS ADMINISTRATION 1900.

with her sister, Harriet Beecher Stowe, *The American Woman's Home* (1869).[31] Many have been republished. Even though they were published, these reprinted published sources should be considered as primary sources. *The Fannie Farmer Cookbook* (1896), *Settlement Cookbook* (1901), *The Joy of Cooking* (1931), and *The Betty Crocker Cookbook* (1955) were popular.[32] Ethnic groups had their own food traditions and cookbooks. Cookbooks provide authentic recipes and insights into aspirational worlds. Cookbooks with "Sunday Night Suggestions" indicate wealthier homes with paid cooks who had that night off. Presumably the homemaker herself prepared simpler dishes such as "Cheese Pudding."[33]

Organizational and Group Records

Consider all the organizations that women have created, joined, and supported—the famous national ones, the quiet local ones, the temporary ones responding to crises such as the American Revolution. Unlike personal documents, these records cover many women's activities, usually over lengthy time periods. Here are a few women's organizations: The Woman's Christian Temperance Union (WCTU), the National Organization for Women (NOW), nonprofit clubs, camps, political organizations, fraternal organizations' auxiliaries, sororities, Girl Scouts, Girls' Friendly Societies, the Daughters of Bilitis, American Red Cross, National Council of Negro Women, and Daughters of the American Revolution have their own collections. Many women's religious organizations and orders also have impressive collections.

To access records often entails extensive travel to visit appropriate collections, which can be invigorating— and expensive. Reading online descriptions of repositories helps. Because every repository has its own rules for collection use, it is best to contact repositories before leaving home.[34] Religious records are organized locally and nationally, requiring searches for their repositories. The Southern Baptist Church has an extensive website including guidance on setting up church archives and protecting documents. Specialized archives amass organizational and personal documents topically, such as the Social Welfare History Archives at the University of Minnesota and the National Cowgirl Museum and Hall of Fame.[35] Individuals sometimes keep group records because they lack a repository to donate them to or they don't want to give them away. You may also find report cards, diplomas, and student identification cards as well as certificates attesting that women had graduated from academies for young ladies or passed their examinations and received teacher certificates. School papers and projects expressed girls' interests and personalities. Many college special collections have records donated from their alumnae and faculty (rather than systematically collected) that preserve any activity that generated paper trails. Student organizations generated protest posters, flyers, minutes, and programs for concerts and theater. Alumnae offices keep records of former students. When my grandmother's college yearbook was missing from the library shelves, the helpful alumni office found it. To our surprise, she had edited the 1920 yearbook.

Newspapers and Periodicals

Clementina Rind, the publisher of the *Virginia Gazette* after her husband died in 1773, was the official printer for Virginia; Deborah Franklin published the *Pennsylvania Gazette*.[36] With greater literacy, more American newspapers were published. Famous newspapers include *The Lily*, a temperance and suffrage newspaper edited by Amelia Bloomer (1849–1853); *Frank Leslie's Illustrated Weekly* (185–1922); and *The Revolution*, published by the National Woman Suffrage Association (1868–1872). National papers included the *New York Times* (1851–), *Washington Post* (1877–), and the *Chicago Defender* (1905–), are available online. Journalists Ida Barnett Wells, Nellie Bly, and Eliza Nicholson (owner of the *New Orleans Times-Picayune*) all wrote professionally. Newspaper publishing was often a family business. Sallie Lindsay White, wife of famous editor William Allen White (aka "the Sage of Emporia" in Kansas), wrote for the *Emporia Gazette*, which she published when he was frequently away.[37] Environmentalist Marjory Stoneman Douglas wrote society pages in Florida.[38] Many local newspapers ran columns by women detailing readers' visits, travels, and illnesses.[39]

As mass media grew after the Civil War, more newspapers were published in places large and small, such as the *West Branch* (IA) *Times*, the *Skagway News* (AK), the *Boston Gazette*, and the *Richmond Planet*. Many of these have been microfilmed and/or digitized and can be obtained online. Major current newspapers such as the *New York Times*, the *Washington Post*, *Seattle Times*, the *Los Angeles Times*, and *USA Today* have back issues online. Newspapers published before 1923 have been digitized at the Library of Congress. For more recent issues, a digital subscription or access through Lexis/Nexis is required. Newspapers were published weekly or daily (morning or afternoon), with smaller newspapers reprinting "boilerplates" from national press services. Newspapers often found women's activities less newsworthy, and omitted stories about many women's lives and activities unless the women were famous, criminal, or married to prestigious men. Many people believed that women should only appear in newspapers twice—upon marriage and upon death. Newspapers published obituaries of women based on family member interviews, resulting in uneven accuracy. These very short biographies hint of considerable skills and accomplishments. Consider Marie-Louise Creighton (1934–2006), wife of the Episcopal bishop of Washington, D.C. Her obituary hints at her capacity and the work she did that helped make him successful:

> During her husband's tenure (1958–1977), Creighton was responsible for many social functions held at the cathedral and at the bishop's home in Washington. She entertained Queen Elizabeth II of Great Britain at a reception and supervised many of the cathedral's arrangements surrounding the funeral of President John F. Kennedy in 1963.[40]

Until the 1960s, many newspapers had women's pages—separate sections dedicated to high society events, gossip, and women's clubs. Before they were ruled discriminatory in 1973, classified advertisements listed separate job openings for men and women.[41] Some women's organizations published their own newspapers, or newsletters full of women's news as alternative worlds to "mainstream" journalism, and also published members' obituaries. The much-researched *Richmond Planet* covered African American men's news extensively, but wrote much less about African American women.

Local papers and their advertisements show women's cultural context. Today most advertising sells things or experiences. Ads have included detailed nineteenth-century notices of runaway slave women with descriptions of their appearance and abilities, and early twentieth-century plaintive requests to adopt a child. Advertising, initially in print and then on radio, television, and online, was another source of societal prescriptions—what women should wear, "problems" of body odors or rough skin, or guidance such as the 1948 advertisement that promoted "the first frozen foods to melt a man's heart." Some ads solved real problems, while others published recipes featuring the advertised product—dishes full of Kraft Velveeta cheese—to entice consumers to try something new, or to feel they had to use certain products. Some ads provided useful content, while others were merely sales pitches.

With a larger reading public and improved transportation systems, mass publications emerged in the nineteenth century. By mid-century, two key periodicals—*Godey's Lady's Book* (a woman's fashion magazine) and *Frank Leslie's Illustrated Newspaper* (a general interest periodical)—were widely available and are now online at http://www.accessible-archives.com. In 1837, Sarah Josepha Hale became editor of *Godey's Lady's Book* (1830–1877) and she remained in that position for forty years. This 150,000-circulation publication, which featured articles and current fashions, also encouraged the preservation of Mount Vernon and increased education for women. Other publications targeted farm women. Since 1885, *Good Housekeeping* and similar magazines have documented women's lives. *American Girl* (for Girl Scouts) and *Seventeen* magazine have long publication histories; *Ms.* magazine has documented second-wave feminism since 1972.[42] These publications described women's lives and prescribed their fashions and attitudes. The *History of Underclothes* researched such women's magazines and clothing to document how the contortions and restrictions of women's undergarments evolved.[43]

Mail-order catalogs document once-common agricultural, household, and personal goods. In the absence of a large retail store, Sears catalogs sold a huge variety of goods, including clothing that showed rural women the latest fashions. Sears catalogs, 500 pages long, were mailed nationwide and increased the range of goods available to consumers beyond country stores. Now reprinted, they document available middle-class goods and changing tastes, helpful in identifying appropriate objects in exhibits. They underscored women's emerging roles as consumers and gave African Americans access to better goods and privacy because mail order bypassed White-controlled country stores.[44] From 1908 to 1940, Sears sold over 100,000 mail-order houses in models that reflected classic American domestic architecture.[45]

Business Records

Every business generates records, and every transaction creates a document—unless a sole proprietor kept it all in her head. Business documents can be hard to access as they may still be proprietary or may no longer exist. But they are crucial, however, to understanding our history. Most corporations have their own archives or have arrangements with companies such as the History Factory or Iron Mountain to keep their documents. Businesses distinguish between current records management and the older archives. Archived documents can help determine a number of things related to women's history, including female-owned businesses—more common than ever imagined—women as bosses, employees, consumers, and protestors. Women documented everything necessary to form and manage their businesses for themselves and regulators, from accounting records to advertising. Government regulations provide historians with additional records. For example, the A. L. Avery General Store in Charlemont, Massachusetts, recorded the huge quantities of butter women sold between 1861 and 1892.[46] Women's earnings from the sale of butter and eggs was income informally recognized as their own. Milliners, needlewomen, and other businesswomen tracked their sales in their journals. Many women's economic activities were informal—taking in one or two lodgers (often relatives) or swapping childcare. Illegal activities such as numbers runners, prostitutes, or bootleggers were accordingly hidden.[47] Farm wife Elizabeth Porter Phelps of Hadley, Massachusetts, kept her memorandum book for fifty years, detailing not only women's quilting but also the number of hired men she fed and pounds of candles dipped, demonstrating the complexity of the New England economy just before the industrial revolution.[48] Midwestern businesswomen kept journals that detailed their enormous sales of butter, eggs, and poultry.[49] Other women kept financial records for their husbands, who were shopkeepers, tanners, doctors, and insurance agents.[50] As the Great Depression bore down, African American banker and activist Maggie Walker struggled as a landlord to keep her paying tenants.[51] When pieced together with other business evidence, these records clearly show women as much more active and entrepreneurial than previously appreciated, encouraging more research and different interpretation.

Insurance records detail how buildings were designed and constructed, their contents, and when fires broke out and thefts occurred. Clara Barton's 1892 insurance policy with the Montgomery Mutual Fire Insurance Company, for example, reveals that her 10,000-square-foot building in Glen Echo, Maryland, was originally a "cottage dwelling" she occupied in the summer. She moved into it year-round when it became the American Red Cross headquarters. Credit reports provide additional information about women not found elsewhere. R.G. Dun & Company has done credit reporting for nearly 170 years, with 2,580 volumes analyzing the financial well-being of companies, while Dun & Bradstreet Corporation Records document the company from the 1840s to the late twentieth century.[52] Shipping manifests, train schedules, stock reports, inventories, even work contracts that included overseers' wives on some South Carolina plantations, can provide insights into women's lives and business. For a discussion of Sanborn Fire Insurance Maps, which provide detailed spatial and construction information useful for understanding cities and neighborhoods and for preservation documentation, see Chapter 6.

Professional trade journals illustrate changing technologies and attitudes with their advertisements of products and services, which always claimed improvements. For example, one trade journal advertisement promoted "Jack Frost" toilets, which promised they would not freeze. Early twentieth-century space and plumbing constraints resulted in toilets being installed on cold porches or in basements as improvements over outdoor privies, which risked contaminating wells and causing typhoid.[53] The Winterthur Museum online has a 900-item trade journal collection that includes many journals focused on women's clothing.

City and town directories that preceded telephone books listed residents at their addresses, noting "wid." for "widow" and "c." for "colored." Women show in the commercial listings as boardinghouse keepers, milliners, and dressmakers. In 1921, the Business and Professional Women of Richmond, Virginia, published a *Directory of Business and Professional Women of Richmond*, a list that mixes common occupations—secretaries, clerks, and registered nurses—with defunct ones— corsetry, comptomer [calculator] operators, and tea room managers.[54] County histories and atlases reveal women landowners. Once available only by subscription, some are now available online, and they sometimes provide information unavailable elsewhere—albeit with uneven accuracy.[55] *Who's Who in American Women* has published entries of "leaders and achievers" since 1899, with specialized versions such as *Who's Who in Science* and *Who's Who in the West*. Another company published *Who's Who in Colored America*. These volumes included basic information about "worthy" individuals, who approved their entries and were then encouraged to purchase a copy.[56]

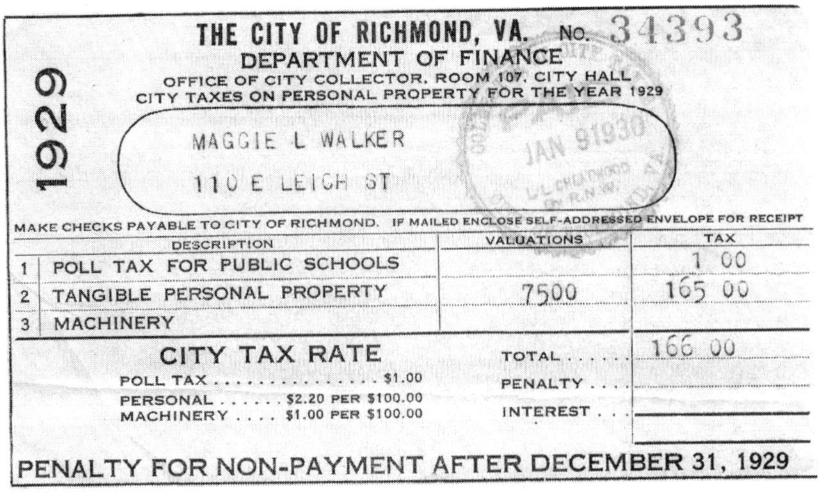

THE CITY OF RICHMOND, VA. No. 34393
DEPARTMENT OF FINANCE
OFFICE OF CITY COLLECTOR. ROOM 107. CITY HALL
CITY TAXES ON PERSONAL PROPERTY FOR THE YEAR 1929

1929

MAGGIE L WALKER
110 E LEIGH ST

JAN 9 1930

MAKE CHECKS PAYABLE TO CITY OF RICHMOND. IF MAILED ENCLOSE SELF-ADDRESSED ENVELOPE FOR RECEIPT

	DESCRIPTION	VALUATIONS	TAX
1	POLL TAX FOR PUBLIC SCHOOLS		1 00
2	TANGIBLE PERSONAL PROPERTY	7500	165 00
3	MACHINERY		

CITY TAX RATE
POLL TAX $1.00
PERSONAL . . . . . . $2.20 PER $100.00
MACHINERY . . . . $1.00 PER $100.00

TOTAL 166 00
PENALTY . . . .
INTEREST . . .

PENALTY FOR NON-PAYMENT AFTER DECEMBER 31, 1929

Figure 3.3. Poll Tax receipt for Mrs. Maggie L. Walker, 1929. She paid $1.00 [$14.95 in 2019 dollars] poll tax for (segregated) schools and $165 .00 [$2,496.87 in 2019 dollars] for owning her Pierce Arrow automobile.
COURTESY MAGGIE L. WALKER NATIONAL HISTORIC SITE, RICHMOND, VIRGINIA, NATIONAL PARK SERVICE.

Government Records

Both the National Archives and Records Administration (NARA) and the Library of Congress have enormous collections with more women's history than most people imagine. The challenge is matching our information needs with their particular systems, which their websites explain how to do. NARA collects federal records from all three branches of government, whether congressional (laws, oversight, and appropriations), executive (all federal departments and agencies, civilian and military, domestic and foreign, from Children's Bureau to Department of the Treasury, FBI, and presidential libraries) or judiciary (courts). Public historians access NARA records to research historic events, better understand laws, and conduct genealogical research. The U.S. Constitution requires a census to be taken every decade, an irreplaceable source in that it provides women's data unavailable elsewhere. Since 1790, the census has provided snapshots of the U.S. population, invaluable as household-by-household surveys providing information about relationships within households and in neighborhoods. Although the information collected has changed, every museum or site since 1790 will benefit from having all its relevant censuses in its knowledge base. States also take censuses, often on the alternate five years. Each census asks slightly different questions, such as level of education, occupation, and ethnicity—providing various insights. Because census takers ("enumerators") walked up and down neighborhood streets to collect the census data, neighborhoods can be reconstructed. To provide privacy, censuses are opened only after seventy-two years, with the 1950 census the next available, in 2022. NARA also documents military and civilian employees, with a surprising number of women postmistresses, lighthouse keepers, or military washerwomen drawing rations.[57] States have impressive research sources as well although they use different names and configurations—state libraries, state historical societies, state archives. While they focus on documents from and about their respective states, don't assume that those documents are restricted to that state. WorldCat helps (see www.worldcat.org). The Library of Congress (LC) collects books and accepts donations of personal (e.g., Clara Barton's papers and jewelry) and organizational (e.g., National Association for the Advancement of Colored People) records.

The LC has key tangible, resource-related documents from HABS (the Historic American Building Survey), HAER (the Historic American Engineering Record), and HALS (the Historic American Landscape Survey), as well as millions of photographs, personal collections, books, and historic newspapers and periodicals; because of copyright laws, only newspapers before 1922 are available online.[58]

Interpreting Written Sources

Many visitors find the act of touching original paper enthralling. Because fragile paper cannot take much handling, facsimiles of original documents work well—although they lack the "real" association. Living History interpreters have long used reprinted cookbooks, the *1897 Sears Catalog*, and the *McGuffey Eclectic Readers* in facsimile versions, which are authentic and intriguing for visitors. One site gave a Girl Scout troop copies of the original 1848 "Declaration of Sentiments" and asked the girls to develop new amendments, an exercise that deeply engaged them. They eagerly shared their amendments with each other—and earned a badge.[59]

Having visitors struggle reading handwritten diaries and letters and then "update" them connects past and present. Well-delivered historic speeches mesmerize audiences, whether as speeches given again or as staged arguments for and against women's suffrage. Powerful quotes are frequently used in exhibits, brochures, and websites—it's important to always seek such passages. Provide translations of obsolete words and phrases to help visitors understand historic writings, whether "salaterus" for early baking powder or "alligator pears" for avocados. Some women have found transcribing women's historic documents—working as a group to discern context, build a database, and discuss current issues together—very powerful.

For generations, historians primarily used written documents as their sources, eschewing other kinds as less professional. Today, written sources are often successfully combined with oral history and other sources to strengthen historical interpretation. Business and commercial records are ripe for additional research, as is deeper research into nonelite women's groups and ways that women internalized, resisted, or affected strongly patriarchal cultures. Written documents in languages other than English offer considerable opportunities for research. Inviting visitors and staff to articulate the different kinds of knowledge they themselves bring to better understand the women and girls interpreted in public historical locales of museums and historic sites has strong potential. Having written documents requires active preservation efforts, which entail constant security and climate control to protect them. As the National Archives states, "The records you are using are irreplaceable original documents."[60]

Tools for Chapter 3: Written Sources

Tool 3.1: Finding Documents about Women

Beginning research in written women's primary sources can be daunting. The organizations and resources listed below can help. Visit several websites to ascertain the most applicable ones:

- Schlesinger Library on the History of Women in America, Harvard University, http://guides. library.harvard.edu/schlesinger_rg_home.
- Sophia Smith Collection, Smith College, http://www.smith.edu/libraries/libs/ssc/index.html.
- Sallie Bingham Center for Women's History & Culture, Duke University, http://library.duke. edu/rubenstein/bingham/.
- The Latina History Project, Southwestern University, http://latinahistoryproject.omeka.net/ and Mujeres Latinas Project of the Iowa Women's Archives at the University of Iowa, https:// www.lib.uiowa.edu/iwa/mujeres.
- Native American: National Museum of the American Indian, https://nmai.si.edu.
- Center for Asian Pacific Island Women, www.apawomen.org.
- Association of Black Women Historians, www.abwh.org.

- LGLBT Historical Society Archives & Museum, www.glbthistory.org/archives.
- The Jean-Nickolaus Tretter Collection in Gay, Lesbian, Bisexual and Transgender Studies, University of Minnesota, https://www.lib.umn.edu/tretter.
- Schmidt, Laura, "Using Archives: A Guide to Effective Research" (Society of American Archivists), www2.archivists.org/usingarchives.
- Women's History Consortium Collections, Washington State, http://www.washingtonhistory.org/research/whc/WHCcollections.[61]
- Your state/local museums, libraries, archives, historical societies and state historic preservation offices as well as nearby states and locales.

Tool 3.2: Evaluating Sources

Develop a list of ten to twenty primary documents and their repositories relevant to the women at your museum/historic site. To determine your priorities, look at your list of documents and analyze each one, either informally or in a group. Score one to five for each factor: Authoritative? Accurate? Appropriate? Timely? Applicable/useful? Consider the purpose for each source, its perspective and biases, and its best interpretive uses. Add the sources to your knowledge base.

Notes

1 Maggie Walker Collection, Box 33 Folder 86, Melvinia Coleman to Walker, 1918.11.02.
2. Maggie Walker Community, Williamsburg VA, 2009–2017.
3. Mujeres Latinas Project of the Iowa Women's Archives at the University of Iowa.
4. Barry Loveland and Malinda Triller Doran, "Out of the Closet and into the Archives: A Partnership Model for Community-Based Collection and Preservation of LGBTQ History," *Pennsylvania History: A Journal of Mid-Atlantic Studies*, vol. 83, no. 3 (Summer 2016): 418–424.
5. Susanah Shaw Romney, *New Netherland Connections: Intimate Networks and Atlantic Ties in Seventeenth-Century America* (Chapel Hill: University of North Carolina Press, 2014). Romney found the Dutch enterprise part of a merchant empire "that actively sought to control space via the bodies of women," 191. Also, Romney, "'With & Alongside his Housewife': Claiming Ground in New Netherland and the Early Modern Dutch Empire," *William & Mary Quarterly*, 3rd, 73, no. 2 (April 2016): 187–224.
6. Jennifer Davis McDaid, "Using Women's History Sources in the Archives at the Library of Virginia, Research Notes Number 10," 2002. The Virginia General Assembly passed laws to support Confederate veterans and their families.
7. Sandra Florand Young, *Don't Throw It Away! Documenting and Preserving Organizational History* (Chicago: Special Collections Department, The University Library, University of Illinois at Chicago and Jane Addams Hull-House Museum, 2006), http://www.uic.edu/depts/lib/specialcoll/pdf/DTIA.pdf.
8. Anne Trubek, "Zora's Place," *HUMANITIES*, December 2011; review of Valerie Boyd, *Wrapped in Rainbows: The Life of Zora Neale Hurston* (New York: Scribner, 2004).
9. Virginia K. Bartlett, *Keeping House: Women's Lives in Western Pennsylvania, 1790–1850* (Pittsburgh: University of Pittsburgh Press, 1994). Very useful.
10. Catherine E. Beecher and Harriet Beecher Stowe, *The American Woman's Home or, Principles of Domestic Science: Being a Guide to the Formation and Maintenance of Economical, Healthful, Beautiful, and Christian Homes* (Hartford: Stowe-Day Foundation, 1975).
11. Jill Lepore, *Book of Ages: Life and Opinions of Jane Franklin* (New York: Knopf Doubleday Publishing, 2014), xiii.
12. Anne Heinz and John Heinz, eds., *Women, Work, and Worship in Lincoln's Country: The Dumville Family Letters* (Urbana: University of Illinois Press, 2016).

13. Isabella Bird, *A Lady's Life in the Rocky Mountains* [1879] (New York: Ballantine, 1960).
14. Linda Peavy and Linda Smith, *Gold Rush Widows of Little Falls: A Story Drawn from the Letters of Pamelia and James Fergus* (St. Paul: Minnesota Historical Society, 1990).
15. Laurel Thatcher Ulrich, *A Midwife's Tale: The Life of Martha Ballard Based on Her Diary, 1785–1812* (New York: Vintage Books, 1990).
16. "Girl on a Whaleship," exhibit, Laura Jernegan Diary. Martha's Vineyard Historical Society, Edgartown, MA. See http://www.girlonawhaleship.org.
17. See http://www.pbs.org/wgbh/amex/mwt/sfeature/sf_diaries.html.
18. Lillian Schlissel, *Women's Diaries of the Westward Journey* (New York: Schocken Books, 1982). See http://www.census.gov/history/1850 for the U.S. census.
19. Diary, Heather Huyck, 1962. In author's possession.
20. Lori Osborne, "A Critical Eye," New Post on Reflections on Archives and Public History (blog), February 16, 2016, https://loriosborne.wordpress.com/2016/02/15/a-critical-eye/.
21. Ellen Gruber Garvey, *Writing with Scissors: American Scrapbooks from the Civil War to the Harlem Renaissance* (New York: Oxford University Press, 2012).
22. Harriet Fish Backus, *Tomboy Bride: A Woman's Personal Account of Life in Mining Camps of the West* (Portland: Westwinds Press, 1980), 25–26.
23. Kathy M'Closkey, *Swept Under the Rug: A Hidden History of Navajo Weaving* (Albuquerque: University of New Mexico Press, 2002).
24. Elizabeth Lord, *Reminiscences of Eastern Oregon* (Portland: Irwin-Hodson Co., 1903), in Julie Roy Jeffrey, *Frontier Women, Revised Edition* (New York: Hill and Wang, 1998), 63.
25. See https://www.nps.gov/wori/learn/historyculture/declaration-of-sentiments.htm.
26. For example, see Marietta Holley, *Samantha Rastles the Woman Question*, ed. Jane Curry (Urbana: University of Illinois Press, 1983). Humorist Holley shares her insights.
27. Harriet Beecher Stowe, *Uncle Tom's Cabin, 1852*; Louisa May Alcott, *Little Women*, 1869; *Their Eyes Were Watching God*, Zora Neal Hurston, 1937.
28. See https://www.harrietbeecherstowecenter.org/utc/impact.shtml.
29. Mrs. S.R. [Henrietta] Dull, *Southern Cooking*, Reprint 1928 (Athens: University of Georgia Press, 2006).
30. See http://uudb.org/articles/lydiamariachild.html.
31. See https://www.harrietbeecherstowecenter.org/hbs/beecher_family.shtml.
32. Fannie Merritt Farmer, *Fannie Farmer 1896 Cookbook* (New York: Skyhorse Publishing, 2011); *Settlement Cookbook* (1901), http://www.wisconsinhistory.org; *Better Homes and Gardens Cookbook* (1930), https://archive.bhg.com/issue/1930/12/; Irma Rombauer, Marion Rombauer Beck, and Ethan Beck, *The Joy of Cooking*, 8th ed. (self 1931; Hoboken: Scribner 2006); and *Betty Crocker Cookbook* (New York: John Wiley & Sons, 1950).
33. *The Bronxville Women's Club Cook Book* (Bronxville: Bronx Valley Press, Inc., 1934).
34. National Archives and Records Administration Research Rules, http://www.archives.gov/research.
35. See https://www.lib.umn.edu/swha, and http://www.cowgirl.net/museum.
36. Martha J. King, "Clementina Rind: Widowed Printer of Williamsburg," in *Virginia Women: Their Lives and Times*, Vol. 1 (Athens: The University of Georgia Press, 2015). Personal communication Kara K. Clapper from visit to Franklin Court, Independence NHP, October 2015.
37. See http://www.kshs.org/places/white/pdfs/brochure_genealogy.pdf.
38. Marjory Stoneman Douglas, Everglades National Park, https://www.nps.gov/ever/learn/historyculture/msdouglas.htm.
39. The *West Branch Times* (Iowa) is available on microfilm; the *Richmond* Planet is a historic Black newspaper digitized by the Library of Congress.
40. "Marie-Louise Creighton, Bishop's Wife," *Washington Post*, February 11, 2006.
41. *Pittsburgh Press v. Pittsburgh Commission on Human Relations* (413 US 376), 1973 under Title VII of the Civil Rights Act of 1964.

Written Sources

42. *Godey's Lady's Book,* Sarah Josepha Hale, editor; and *Frank Leslie's Illustrated Newspaper, Good Housekeeping, and American Girl.*
43. Cecil Willett and Phillis Cunnington, *The History of Underclothes* (New York: Dover Publications Inc., 1992).
44. *1897 Sears Roebuck & Company Catalogue* [reprint] (New York: Skyhorse Publishing, 2007). See "Mail Order Catalogs as Resources in Material Culture Studies," in Thomas J. Schlereth, *Artifacts and the American Past* (Nashville: American Association for State and Local History, 1980). Also, Louis Hyman, "How the Sears Catalog Was Revolutionary in the Jim Crow Era," *All Things Considered*, October 16, 2018. Also, Louis Hyman, "How the Sears Catalog Was Revolutionary in the Jim Crow Era," *All Things Considered*, National Public Radio, October 16, 2018.
45. See http://www.searsarchives.com/homes/index.htm.
46. "A.L. Avery General Store Records, 1859–1905," Historic Deerfield Collection, https://static1.squarespace.com/static/595e3b72099c01fedbac5c15/t/59c553bebce17630ed5a3839/1506104254210/Avery_General_Store_Records.pdf; Joan Jensen, *Loosening the Bonds: Mid-Atlantic Farm Women, 1750–1850* (New Haven: Yale University Press, 1988).
47. Lashawn Harris, *Sex Workers, Psychics and Numbers Runners: Black Women in New York City's Underground Economy* (Urbana: University of Illinois Press, 2016); Doris Crump Rainey account, October 2017.
48. Marla R. Miller, *The Needle's Eye: Women and Work in the Age of Revolution* (Amherst: University of Massachusetts Press, 2006).
49. Lucy Eldersveld Murphy, "Her Own Boss: Businesswomen and Separate Spheres in the Midwest, 1850–1880," Illinois Historical Journal 80, no. 3 (Autumn 1987): 155–76.
50. Susan Branson, "Women and the Family Economy in the Early Republic: The Case of Elizabeth Meredith," *Journal of the Early Republic* 16, no. 1 (Spring 1996).
51. Maggie Walker Collection.
52. Harvard Business School, "The R. G. Dun & Company Credit Report Volumes."
53. Maggie Walker Collection.
54. Available at www.donslist.net, which digitizes many local directories and yearbooks.
55. Some 150 county histories (of 5,000) at http://www.accessible-archives.com. Harold E. Way argues they can be the "best available resource for local information." Way, "A White Paper: American County Histories: Their Uses, Usability, Sources and Problems with Access," November 2010, http://www.accessible-archives.com/collections/.
56. *Who's Who in American Women* (New Providence: Marquis, 1958–1985). Joseph Boris, ed., *Who's Who in Colored America: A Biographical Dictionary of Notable Living Persons of Negro Descent in America* (New York: Who's Who in Colored America Corp., 1927–1950).
57. U.S. Census, https://www.census.gov/history/www/genealogy/decennial_census_records/; Mary Louise Clifford and J. Candace Clifford, *Women Who Kept the Lights, An Illustrated History of Female Lighthouse Keepers*, 2nd ed. (Alexandria: Cypress Communications, 2000).
58. See https://www.loc.gov/newspapers.
59. Kim Szewczyk, Women's Rights National Historical Park, 2016.
60. National Archives and Records Administration, http://www.archives.gov/research/start/researcher-orientation.pdf.
61. In addition to the National Archives which has branches across the country as well as the Library of Congress, the many state entities are helpful. For example, see a state library such as the Library of Virginia, www.lva.virginia.gov, a state historical society, such as Utah State Historical Society, https://history.utah.gov/utah-state-historical-society, a state museum such as the Alaska State Museums in Juneau and Sitka, https://museums.alaska.gov/asm/asmhome.html, state archives such as the Alabama Department of Archives and History archives.alabama.gov and historical trusts such as the Maryland Historical Trust, https://mht.maryland.gov. They all have riches.

4

Oral Sources

Listening and Recording

In a 2017 oral history interview, Doris Crump Rainey, an African American, recounted an incident that happened when she was an eight-year-old living in Virginia in the 1930s. The story features a parrot owned by a White woman whose house she and her friends passed on their way to school:

> One of the older boys got tired of a parrot yelling the "N" word at us children every time we walked by her house. He took that parrot and swung it—and that was the end of that parrot yelling at us. The woman who taught the parrot that awful word never knew who did it, but we couldn't take that shortcut anymore.[1]

This revealing incident illustrates that young Black children in the early 1930s Virginia clearly understood—and resisted against—the racism hurled their way from a White woman who had taught her bird the epithet. The children risked much by killing the bird. This small, insightful story illuminates a Black woman's lifelong dedication to breaking racial barriers—beginning in second grade. Such insights highlight the value of oral sources in history.

Oral sources bring sensory reality and help interpret the historic soundscape. History is a world full of many sounds that women made and heard, sounds important to recover and interpret. Many sounds—thunder, baby cries, grief at funerals in unknown languages—are shared at museums and historic sites. Other sounds are now less familiar to most of us—African languages of enslaved women, chants, whippoorwill calling, or winds straining wagon covers. Sounds had different meanings as well. Oral sources—both soundscapes and oral history—have great potential in strengthening women's history interpretation, literally giving women their "voices" often too little heard. Including the historic soundscape in exhibits and historic rooms and house museums enhances emotional connections visitors make with resources. Powerful speeches women gave as they claimed their citizenship, chants sung by sisters at Ephrata Cloister, songs mothers used to calm babies, and hymns sung in churches are all useful oral sources. A farm exhibit made noisy by animal sounds or hearing crying children while also hearing cooking sounds increases accuracy and reflects women's historic conditions more than quiet does. As important, sounds provide realism and context—a train whistle or ferry horn hints of the larger world. Websites with sounds attract more attention.

Soundscapes

Sounds enhance historic accuracy and interpretive potency by adding sensory experiences and creating distinct visitor experiences. Soundscapes have changed—earlier generations heard bells, wolf howls, and iron pots rather than radio music or sonic booms. Such once-familiar sounds as a pump drawing up water are now rare, while thunderclaps have a different meaning. Noises from animals, domesticated and wild, can animate exhibits. Like most early industrial machinery, the mills of Lowell, Massachusetts, were extremely noisy; their floors vibrated from the looms and the air was full of dust. Lowell mill girl Lucy Larcom complained that "buzzing and hissing and whizzing of pulleys and rollers and spindles and flyers around me often grew tiresome."[2]

Women proximate to U.S. western forts "lived by the bugles" that blared daily schedules.[3] Adding historic sounds to exhibits brings them alive so we can better experience noisy kitchens or cities. Instead of misleading battlefield quiet now disturbed only by a passing car or barking dogs, replicate historic sounds before, during, and after battles make them more realistic and horrifying with cries of wounded men and dying horses. Once-ordinary sounds now foreign to us can be especially helpful to understand women's lives—the crank of a butter churn, the crackle of a fire, or bodies shifting on a straw mattress. We live in layers of sounds that require careful research and reconstruction. Consider the many overlapping sounds women heard and made themselves—personal (moans, laughs), family (cries, slurps), and community sounds (threshing, milking cows, typing). Research the sounds once heard at your museum or historic site and add them as appropriate, layering the varied sounds once heard there, such as children at their particular ages, work activities, and women's voices. Add her cat's meows to Rachel Carson's home. Using the many sounds available online will enhance the historic scene and help visitors recognize the genuine complexity of the past. In her account of working in the Lowell, Massachusetts, textile mills in the 1830s, Lucy Larcom spoke of the long hours and challenge of working in the rigid environment "enforced by the clangor of the bell."[4]

Types of Oral Sources

Some people limit oral sources to formal recorded interviews, but many existed long before audio recording became more easily available in the late 1940s. Generations of people carefully memorized stories, speeches, lectures, and sermons initially given orally. Some cultural groups and families preserved their own history and remembered people and events separate from written records. These accounts are their important markers. Often, individuals who made mistakes in their group's stories were corrected, protecting the narratives.

Once viewed by scholars with skepticism, oral history has repeatedly proven its value, especially when supplementing written sources or in their absence, providing new or different insights. Oral history provides female perspectives often unavailable in newspapers, which seldom covered women's lives until the late twentieth century, or only as news of the wealthiest or deviant women who broke laws or social norms. Today, decades of formal oral history interviews give us access to women we would never otherwise know. Beginning with folklorists, and then historians, researchers have asked thoughtful questions and listened carefully. Folklorists used to lug around heavy tape recorders to capture folk songs now preserved in the Library of Congress' Folklife Center (loc.gov/folklife). Today's digital recordings on miniature equipment allows more spontaneous interviews.[5]

Oral history has particular value because it can provide insights into women's emotions and reasons, literally giving them a voice that can be heard by visitors in exhibits, rooms, and programs at museums and historic sites. Hearing an individual woman's voice has authenticity and power for visitors. Hearing Eleanor Roosevelt's *own* voice describe their home connects us to him, her, and Hyde Park. Play women's voices and their favorite music, and sing popular songs from contemporary song sheets. Consider the prime relationship in George Root's 1864 popular song, "Just Before the Battle," which continued, "Mother, I am thinking most of you." That reflected the demographics of younger Union soldiers.[6] Imagine "hearing" women's gatherings, working in factories, or cooking dinners.

Oral sources—whether formal speeches or sermons, verbal accounts, community traditions preserved orally, or formal interviews—can form the basis of interpretive presentations that transport our visitors into the past. Although we know speeches from reading their transcripts, they were first performed before audiences who heard them. Written speeches express intentions and aspirations even when we cannot hear every pause, change in tempo or pitch, or audience response. Maggie L. Walker gave powerful speeches with phrases still potent in her analysis and calls for action. We can only imagine how her full performance sounded with her audience's claps, cries, and affirmations. Roughly a century ago, in a 1925 speech, Walker decried centuries of mistreatment of women, proclaimed marriage as a "partnership," and argued for the elimination of the sexual double standard. She finished with, "Let us unite and stand by one another; let us deal kindly with our sisters—Let us join hands and hearts and sympathies, and God will bless us, and save us from the snares of the world and receive us in the world above."[7] Audio recordings of speeches and sermons help evoke their historic cadences and meanings. Consider the different ways past women heard sermons quoting St. Paul that directed their "proper" behavior. Or how Americans in the early twentieth century heard speeches for—and against—women's suffrage.

For decades, women who addressed males and females together broke social codes with so-called promiscuous speeches. During the nineteenth century, this began to change. In 1832, African American abolitionist Maria Stewart gave the first-known public speech that included a mixed audience. By 1836, the Grimké sisters from South Carolina, whose father was a slave owner, spoke to mixed audiences on the same topic. The women's rights movement, which began with the 1848 Seneca Falls Convention, explicitly challenged social norms for women speaking in public. As the nineteenth century ended, many women proclaimed their right to speak in public—as lecturers, labor organizers, social workers, even political candidates. After the United States deposed her in 1893, Hawaiian Queen Liliuokalani spent her imprisonment adding to women's public voices by composing hymns and prayers and stitching a colorful protest quilt; over her lifetime, she wrote more than 160 hymns and songs.[8] Many women's presentations are available in print or online collections. Retrieving oral sources remains a major challenge, but they enhance our understanding of the women who wrote them, gave them, heard them, or tried to live by them.

Many cultural groups have preserved their history orally across generations, recounting their past and their understanding of it. African American accounts of enslavement and its horrors have told stories long inaccessible to the White community, which are corroborated by written records and archaeology.[9] Hawaiians memorized lengthy poems detailing their history, risking punishment for incorrect recitations. Maintained over a century, Inuit oral accounts "keeping the old stories alive" were crucial in finding the long-lost ships of the 1845 Sir John Franklin Arctic expedition after British written records proved inadequate.[10] His widow, Lady Jane Franklin (and Charles Dickens) had attacked Inuit versions of the disaster. But Inuits were "vital links in the chain of knowledge. Among them, two figures loom particularly large, William Ouligbuck and Tookoolito ['Hannah']."[11] Two distinct communities across several generations employed oral history to solve a mystery, with women playing key roles.

Some oral accounts were later written down. General Washington's wife, Martha Washington, visited Valley Forge, where she improved troop morale by feeding, clothing, and nursing the soldiers who were so important for the Patriot army's survival when winning the American Revolution seemed unlikely.[12] Diarists have recorded firsthand oral accounts of women otherwise little

Figure 4.1.   Oral history interview with Mrs. Doris Crump Rainey, Williamsburg, Virginia, May 2017.
PHOTOGRAPH BY LEAH BROWN.

known. Doña Angustias de la Guerra, a California woman who "had just given birth to a daughter a few days before," effectively used her recent childbirth, wits, position, and determination to hide and protect a Californio (an ethnically Mexican Californian) man being hunted by the U.S. Army. She hid him in her bed and successfully employed male squeamishness and Victorian propriety to prevent the U.S. soldiers from conducting a thorough search there. Women seeking to preserve their own history have used a journal-writing technique explained in *Asian Pacific Islander American Women* to capture Filipina history. After dinner, and guided by experts, the Filipinas began with the familiar concept of *kitchen* and gradually processed into deeper thoughts and emotions they shared with each other, becoming increasingly confident. They shared their memories, including difficult ones never divulged before. Museums and historic sites can use this technique to retrieve history believed inaccessible.[13]

Oral History Research Projects

Oral history projects at museums and historic sites differ from scholarly research. Rather than emerging from scholarly curiosity or debates, museum and historic site oral history usually focuses on developing its knowledge base and/or interpretive programs and products. In other cases, oral history seeks answers to specific questions, such as memories of an earlier building configuration. When combined with written sources, photographs, and tangible resources, oral history research is especially useful in creating interpretive programs, movies, and lively historic rooms with music, human voices, and weather noises—the entire soundscape.

Oral history differs from other kinds of research for two primary reasons. If recorded, it can bring out women's (and men's) emotions in the very sounds of their voices, providing information about their accent, emotions, even their health. Second, it's interactive. The relationship between the research participants, interviewee, and the interviewer profoundly affects the history being created/researched, especially when the interviewer is perceived as having authority.[14] Historians have struggled with being *too* sympathetic to those they interview, even fearing they may inadvertently support despicable beliefs and actions. Without interviewing oppositional women and men, we diminish our understanding of the awful conditions, social structures, and individuals resisted by women we find sympathetic and honor.[15]

Given the two often-overlapping categories of oral history interviews for building the knowledge base and for answering particular questions, your approach will vary depending on whether you have a well-established set of oral history interviews or none at all. The National Cowgirl Museum & Hall of Fame has now collected 200 interviews of its honorees, "information from the source."[16] Identification of gaps between complementary written and tangible resources should guide the oral history research. Good oral history research projects first conceptualize the completed project, then choose the best women (and men) to interview, develop thoughtful questions, identify women and men to be interviewed, conduct the interviews, transcribe them, and preserve the digital formats and ensure access to insights gained that are often unavailable elsewhere.

Identifying core questions that your museum/site most needs answered and who can best answer them begins the process. These core questions should then be used for many interviews. Don't waste people's time on questions better suited to written sources such as dates and spelling of names by researching those sources in advance yourself or with a basic questionnaire. Having sets of questions to guide interviews helps avoid rabbit trails of potentially interesting but probably unimportant information. The first, introductory, factual questions simply ask the interviewee's name and role, such as who they are, what they do, and how long they've done it. The second set focuses on the key research concerns; these questions allow you to compare answers and better understand the groups' shared understanding with each individual's one. The third set are individual questions that focus on more specific issues fewer people know, or on *this* woman's expertise. Other people will be asked different questions to build a strong understanding of the events, processes, and personalities involved. The fourth set are those questions that emerge as you proceed. During the interview(s), listen with compassion and a bit of skepticism. We all have our own propaganda! Break up the interview into smaller portions so that the interviewee doesn't become exhausted. Oral history is more demanding than most people realize. Be kind! You want to be invited to come back.

As public historians, we have a responsibility to the future to do the best oral history possible so that our interviews will be truly useful decades from now. You are embarking on an important project. Treat it as such; lay out your research strategy and your priorities and address your challenges thoughtfully and carefully. Map out the issues you need to research and the background information you need to gather to develop good questions. Then match those individuals most crucial and best suited to provide information on these questions, the people willing and able to sit down and share their perspectives. Look at the people you have identified as crucial, and prioritize interviewees for the quality of their knowledge, their age, and their health. Don't interview the most important person first, but gain understanding and confidence with others so that the key people can be asked the complex questions or those questions only they can answer. Oral history requires interviewees of sound mind and good memory. People with muddled memories cannot give good interviews.

Equipment and Advance Permissions

Use the best equipment quality you can acquire; sound quality requirements change, and getting the highest quality possible will give you the most longtime flexibility because it can be used in different situations. Knowing your equipment well avoids having to fuss with it during interviews, especially as people can be surprisingly skittish about being recorded. Set up in a quiet place where you won't be disturbed and your equipment won't be bothered. Test it to ensure it's working before the interview starts. Check your sound level to make sure you are picking up her voice (a microphone is helpful). Begin by identifying yourself, the location, and date, and having the interviewee identify herself. Although it can be impossible *not* to interview people in a group, avoid it. Untangling their different voices (and attitudes) later is a real hassle. Also avoid having other people in the room listening to your interview.

Happily, the equipment for doing oral history has greatly improved, from huge suitcases of tape recorders with plastic tape that easily snarled, to smaller ones that used tape cassettes, to digital recorders. Given the constant changes in the technology, it's best to seek expertise to pick out a good digital recorder. You want clear sound so you can hear it easily and have a permanent record available for exhibits years from now. Extensive technical information on the best equipment is available at the Vermont Folklife Center.[17] Consult with an oral history program or expert to find the best equipment when you're ready to do the interviews. There are several key oral history organizations that have a great deal of expertise, such as the Oral History Association, the Library of Congress, or the Baylor Institute for Oral History.[18] Whatever equipment you are using, be sure you can make it work and record well. Try it. Then try it again. Make sure you have more than enough power—extra batteries, cords—for the entire interview. Getting home to find that you did not actually record a wonderful interview is heartbreaking and problematic if you have to go back and ask to conduct it again—it strains your credibility.

Interviews

Good oral history interviews are a dance between two partners, with the interviewee leading and the person doing the interview following her lead. Develop your questions in a thoughtful order so that the person being interviewed can follow their logic and focus on their answers rather than puzzling over them. This is neither a cable news interview nor a tabloid story, so there should be not be any "gotcha" questions. Write out your interview questions and consider how interviewees may hear them for order, tone, and vocabulary. You can ask key follow-up questions, something impossible to do with most written sources. As you become more experienced doing oral history, your instincts will be honed, and you will be able to wait more patiently (counting to yourself helps) as your interviewee rummages through her memory. You'll more easily recognize when someone being interviewed is pausing too long, which may indicate that she is thinking too hard about what she's telling you. As you do additional interviews, one person may share a great deal of information, another may give key details, while a third person may demand excessive confidentiality. You'll need to test each person's perspective and statements. At times during interviews, I've asked questions that indicated that I already knew more than she thought I knew—or apparently wanted me to know.

Oral history interviews should be done partway into the research process, after the foundation of the museum's knowledge base has been built. Interviews you do now that may seem quite basic will probably become more valuable with time. This approach increases your credibility and avoids asking superfluous questions, such as "When did that happen?" Get that kind of information beforehand if possible. Now it's time to practice doing interviews. Some people are so genuinely busy that you may only be able to ask them a few questions. I had to do that once while driving an interviewee in heavy traffic. Although I could not give the interview my full attention, I asked my key questions and got his invaluable insights and extraordinary guidance. It wasn't ideal, but it was preferable to not getting that interview.

Establishing rapport and credibility with the person being interviewed is crucial. Oral historians are aware of the challenges of researching complex people, doing them at different intervals, and that different researchers obtain quite distinct versions. Without a good relationship, interviewees withhold the most important information or state it so cautiously it is hard to use. If an open, but honest tone is not immediately established by the historian (you), the interview can be a dud. To hear what the other person *really* thinks, be as silent as you can be. Handling yourself and your equipment with quiet confidence goes far, as that shows respect to the person being interviewed (as does being on time, being fully prepared, etc.). You are collaborating with her on this project as cocreators of this oral source. I knew I had succeeded in researching rapport with an elderly Friends (Quakers) couple when they began using their preferred "Thee" term with me. Sometimes women will be sharing difficult or painful parts of their lives—they need assurance they can entrust such confidences to you. Consider that some women may be ashamed they didn't graduate from high school or college. Others assume responsibility for having opportunities closed to them, or they apologize for being "just housewives." Some older women are intimidated by a PhD or graduate student interviewing them—be gentle and appreciate their gift. Respect them, their knowledge, and their time, and honor all three. Historian Judy Yung interviewed Lee Puey You, a woman who interned at Angel Island for twenty months, then was deported back to China after she had tried to enter the United States. Yung later concluded, "I believe she would have told us more if we had only persisted."[19] At the same time, pain-filled oral histories must balance what the woman being interviewed can stand with what you as interviewer needs to learn. I once interviewed a man who headed an opposing group from my own. Afterward he said, "And now that you understand our position, I'm sure you'll join us." I demurred. There was no way I would join his group. I was very glad we'd established a positive atmosphere in our tone, questions, and my responses to him—verbally, in body language, and in command of the tape recorder. He felt he had been truly heard and his approach understood because I had listened to his beliefs and had respected the strength of his opposition.

Various challenges await researchers using oral history because the researcher can so affect the resulting interview. An interviewee may mislead or omit key information, either intentionally or inadvertently. That's why it's important to interview as many people as practicable on a particular topic so that different interviews and viewpoints can be compared to provide a more accurate account. Some of your questions may involve actions people prefer not to discuss as too painful to remember.[20] Or they wish they had acted differently or because they have come to tell a story that exaggerates the truth. Some people regret their actions and prefer that they not be discovered. Ego, shame, anger—all kinds of emotions—may be involved, complicating developing interpretation that explains what actually happened. Remember that human sources will talk, text, tweet, and email each other, sharing your questions and their evaluations of you—for your knowledge of the issues, your mastery of oral history techniques, your fairness, your hair, and anything else. Consider the politics of the sequence of the people you are interviewing, the way of phrasing questions, what you are going to wear, even where you stay. If there are factions involved, it may cost less in the long run to stay a few miles away. In other words, avoid annoying or angering people. Consider their cultural values and how you come across to them. I have found that dressing conservatively and being very careful how I phrased questions works best.

After you ask a difficult or complex question, give your interviewee time to formulate her answer. Avoid interviewing over a meal as it's difficult to focus on both, and the likelihood of confusing fancy salad dressings with gazpacho soup is too high—I did that, and it made me look and feel like an idiot! Be aware of the physical comfort of the person being interviewed, especially if they are elderly or frail—don't exhaust them. It's better to come back (soon!) and do more than to try to get it all in one sitting. Every interview needs to be carefully considered for attitudes, accuracy, and perspective. For example, one Michigan family remembered that a mining company had forced their newly widowed relative out of her house, but mining company records show that she received $5,300 in insurance and funeral money.[21] Written and oral records used together work best.

Do not record interviews without obtaining written permission in advance. As intellectual property, oral history interviews require clarity of ownership, which is obtained by a release form—get one! Samples are easily available online. The Oral History Association publishes and updates its excellent "Principles and Best Practices."[22] Oral historians must have permission before they can use interviews in publications, exhibits, films. Once you have completed the oral history interview, then the work begins. Indexing interviews provides a quick way to find their key elements. Make a copy of all your interviews as soon as you can and keep them in a separate and secure place. Transcription takes much more time and effort than anyone expects, approximately a 10:1 ratio of transcription time to recording time. You can pay someone to do it, get software to help you, or index interviews for their topics, matching them to the counter on the recorder, and then transcribe only the key phrases. This has the advantage of much greater speed, but it risks that future researchers will probably want to see the entire interview. Transcribing takes time and work, but the good news is that you will get to know your material well. Because technology keeps changing quickly, the medium you use may not be able to be played back in ten years' time, while the transcription should still be fine. The problem of long-term preservation of audio materials—and ongoing access to them—remains a huge issue among the preservation community, not only for audio and video recording but for all the different formats. Digital recording should diminish issues of transcription and preservation.

Interpreting Oral Histories

Many oral history interviews of women and girls provide unique insights, better explanations, and better interpretive quotes than the written record alone. While there are many homesteading accounts, Dora Rosenzweig's account includes her parents' disagreements over her education and her determination that she (and later, her daughters) get educated. This example provides an important perspective on cultural prescriptions versus women's actual experiences.[23] Lue-Rayne Culbertson, a shipyard welder during World War II, recounted hiding her pregnancy from her employer and later washing diapers during her time off—without her husband's assistance. These examples highlight the differences between cultural norms and women's actual experiences—discovered only by interviewing them.[24] Women's voices are often omitted from written accounts, as they are less likely to speak *for* organizations or to be interviewed by the media. Except for Rosa Parks, too few female activists in the modern Civil Rights movement have had their stories fully told, which profoundly misleads us. Social change required many people, not only a few famous men. For instance, in Black Montgomery, Alabama, women were already organized before their bus boycott began.[25]

The power of using oral sources for interpreting women's history becomes clear at Big Hole National Battlefield, where the interpreters consider the experiences of Nez Perce women "a very important part of our story." Their names are lost but not the significance of their lives.

> Anytime you have the U.S. Army shooting women and children during a war, there is a chord that is struck in our visitor. It brings it home to almost everyone we [Nez Perce] tell the story too. When the staff uses a photo of their great-great-great-grandmother who was here in 1877 and saw horrible things done to women and children, and that staff member tells the

stories passed down to them, it becomes very real for our visitors. It is no longer an event that happened many years ago, it is something that is very real and raw and the Nez Perce staff member telling those stories that are full of emotion, the visitor becomes involved, and I feel, takes away a better understanding. Our park is not about soldiers fighting Nez Perce warriors, it is about people and the stories that we tell make it so much more meaningful.[26]

One of the great values of oral history is how it can provide many perspectives on the same issue. For example, the Peralta Hacienda in Fruitvale, California, works hard to be a multicultural museum, with Hispanic, Ohlone, Italian, African American, and Cambodian peoples all coming together to learn about and enjoy each other's heritages. One of the park's exhibits includes shared stories about each culture's foods that included the voices of women and men associated with the various cultural groups. Being able to hear women's voices implicitly welcomes other women and confirms the value of their shared history. This strongly recommended approach also provides an opportunity for local and online interpretation. As women from different groups discover their shared experiences, they find it easier to talk about those they don't share—and hear each other more clearly.

Often battlefield interpreters assure visitors that no women could possibly have been present there, that the arguments that precipitated war had nothing to do with women, which was essentially, even exclusively, the world of men. Oral history can disprove this. Thomas Powers used Dakota oral history to recount the Battle of the Little Bighorn, famous for the death of George Armstrong Custer and his men.[27] The *Smithsonian Magazine* account "How the Battle of Little Bighorn Was Won" discusses how integral Dakota women were in the battle, from being an early warning system that U.S. troops were coming (because they were dispersed in large area as they gathered wild turnips) to being early victims when two women and their three children were killed at the outset. One Hunkpapa woman known as Good White Buffalo Woman recounted her story years later. "The Sioux that morning had no thought of fighting," she said. "We expected no attack." The Dakota women taunted their men to fight, singing "Brothers-in-law, now your friends have come. Take courage. Would you see me taken captive?" After the battle, remembering the mutilations done to their niece who had been beheaded twelve years before at Washita Battlefield NHS, two elderly southern Cheyenne women mutilated Custer's body. Anyone who imagines battles as places without women should read this account. First-person accounts from the American Revolution and Civil War exist from women who experienced battles on their family farms or as refugees.

Oral histories from women can provide first-person perspectives on a variety of subjects, not only the obvious topics related to childbirth and health and the construction of gender in different cultures, but also accounts of lesbians, women in heterosexual marriages, immigrants, young mothers, girls, and relationships between women such as employer/employee or teacher/student.[28] Oral interviews can also illuminate women's experiences in places where men are generally excluded, for example, lesbian clubs, sorority initiations, women's colleges, bridal showers, women's locker rooms, quilting parties, church missionary societies, and other female-only organizations. Oral histories document people's attitudes and feelings, can recover the "contradictions" in their values, and can hear women's "silences" in their interviews. Be sure to interview those women who have been *least* seen or heard historically.

One very useful source of information on major events is the spouses of important and famous men—politician's wives, for example. In researching the history of the ordination of women in the Episcopal Church, I found that many (male) bishops had been "over-interviewed" and had well-rehearsed answers. Their wives who had been beside them throughout the years involved provided more thoughtful and spontaneous answers. Their insights and anecdotes were crucial to understanding key events. One bishop who had not been particularly active in women's ordination suddenly became much more so. Known as a liberal and generous man, his absence had puzzled me. What had happened? His wife explained that one morning as he was in their glass-doored shower, she essentially trapped him there, asking, "Dear, what are you going to do about women's ordination?" The effort suddenly became quite personal to him and he responded accordingly.[29]

Initially many researchers doing oral history clung to the model of scholar/informant, with the scholar being the expert and the informant providing gist for their intellectual mill. That very hierarchical model denied their mutual dependence. Today, most people who are part of oral history projects expect to read their own interviews, believing that the research is a cooperative effort. This approach results in richer relationships and stronger research. You absolutely must get their full permissions with release forms in order to share interviews with the public.[30]

Building for the Future

The interviews have gone well, have been carefully cataloged to prevent future confusions, and have been transcribed. Thank-you notes have gone out to the participants (yes, thank-you notes). You know what's in the interviews, when they confirm written sources, when they contradict each other, and you are analyzing that. You're finding ways to incorporate them into your museum's exhibits. This project began because you wanted real people's voices and now you have them. You want to integrate their voices into your museum's research and its public interpretation. You're circling back to those who have generously shared their lives and let them know where "they" will now be heard. Because you never know where their networks extend, this step is more important than it may sound. Be extravagant in thanking them, just as you are diligent in preserving their interviews.

Other Oral Sources

Words and phrases can explicate earlier practices, such as "sanitary napkins," which were folded cloths that caught menstrual blood and then were scrubbed clean for use the next month, or "prime the pump" referred to pouring water into a pump to get it started. In Russian Alaskan colonies, Russian loan words in Yup'ik language that referred specifically to female garments supplemented archaeological findings.[31] Families often pass on their own stories. My mother shaped my world understanding when she shared pranks my great-grandmother Katie played on her nine children. Her kitten Mehitable caused havoc in my grandmother's meticulous house when, still soapy, she escaped her bath. Her mother's friend stitched an oilcloth (plastic) pocket into her husband's coat so he could feed his family during the Great Depression. These snippets can reveal and help us understand women's lives and reactions.

Oral sources have particular advantages and joys, allowing us to *hear the past*, whether in old sermons, speeches, traditional now-written history, anecdotes, or formal oral history projects and sounds. Think of all the songs composed as part of the nearly-century-long effort for American women to gain federal suffrage. You planned your oral history program, found and interviewed amazing women, got all the proper paperwork done, transcribed them so you could use the interviews later, and preserved them in secure, temperature- and humidity-controlled storage. The oral history interviews you collect now, shared with its interviewees, will soon become irreplaceable; the questions you ask now may well be the only time such insights are gained. Such interviews are challenging—and fun. Songs and hymns add atmosphere to historic homes, especially when former residents once performed them there. Now you know you have added to our understanding, shared that understanding through many different media, and have

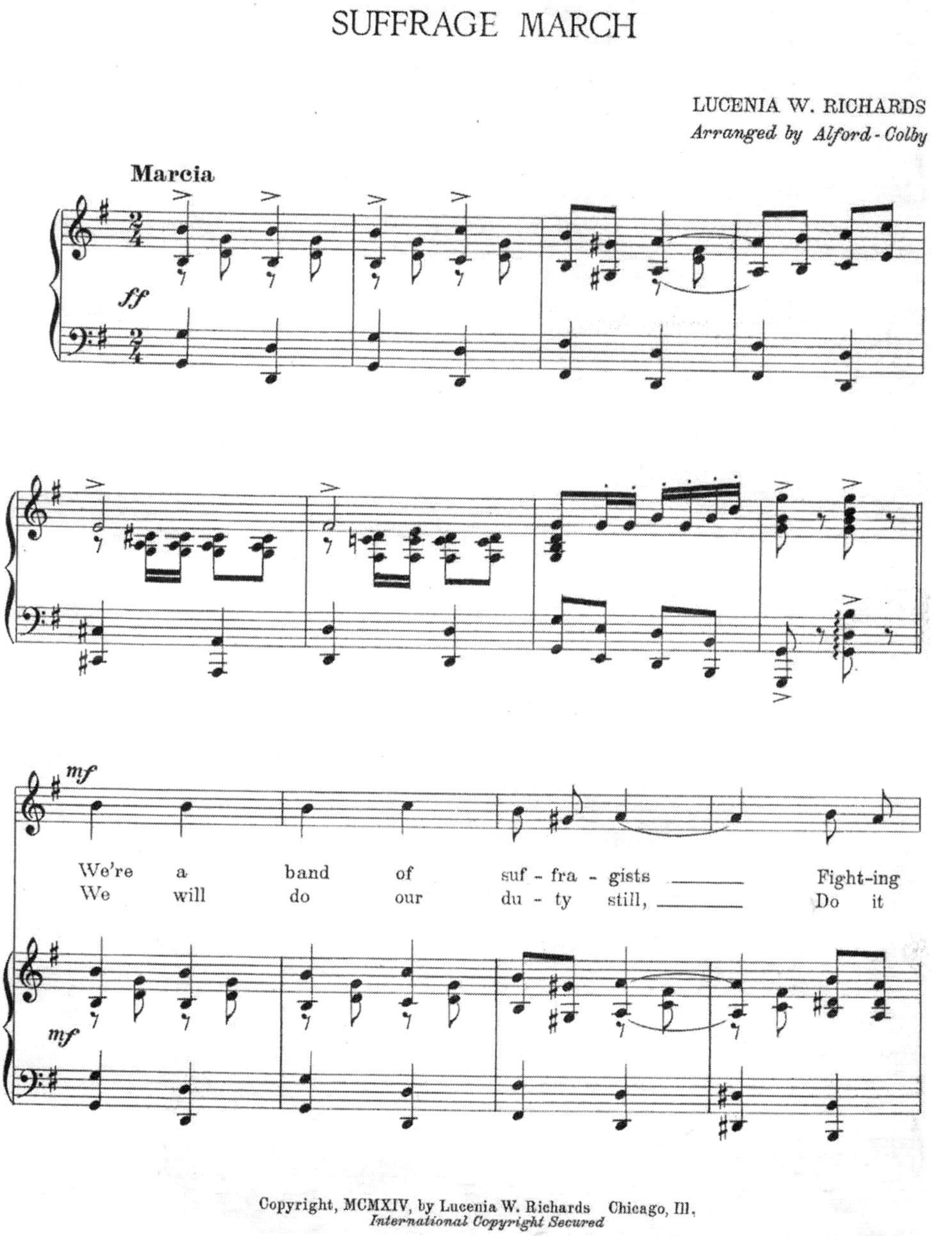
SUFFRAGE MARCH
LUCENIA W. RICHARDS
Arranged by Alford-Colby
Marcia
ff
mf
We're a band of suf - fra - gists Fight-ing
We will do our du - ty still, Do it
mf
Copyright, MCMXIV, by Lucenia W. Richards Chicago, Ill.
International Copyright Secured

Figure 4.2. Suffrage March, 1914, by Lucinia W. Richards, one of many musical protest songs.
COURTESY JOHNS HOPKINS UNIVERSITY. LESTER S. LEVY COLLECTION OF SHEET MUSIC, SHERIDAN LIBRARIES.

added to the knowledge base. You will be rewarded in marvelous ways, by having people want to help you truly understand their worlds and why they did what they did. You've made a difference.

Hearing interviews recorded to high technical standards provide visitors with recordings, videos, and exhibits so they can encounter people and have the powerful experience of hearing their actual voices. At the Rosie the Riveter World War II Homefront National Historical Park, visitors hear oral history interviews in "Blossoms and Thorns" with Japanese American flower growers and nursery owners about their internments during World War II.[32] The Dorothy Molter Museum in Ely, Minnesota, interviewed her relatives, friends, visitors, and other canoe outfitters about her life. A humorous sign by her cabin reads, "KWITCHURBELIAKIN."[33] Oral sources help us appreciate dissimilar women's lives.

Resources

- Oral History Association, https://www.oralhistory.org.
- Oral History Center—UC Berkeley Library, www.lib.berkeley.edu/libraries/bancroft-library/oral-history-center.
- Institute for Oral History—Baylor University, https://www.baylor.edu/oralhistory; see the excellent "Introduction to Oral History Manual" online there.
- Oral History Archives at Columbia—Columbia University Libraries, https://library.columbia.edu/locations/ccoh.html.
- Digital Collections, Oral Histories, Audio Recording—Library of Congress, https://www.loc.gov/collections/.
- Oral History—Oklahoma State University Library, https://library.okstate.edu/oralhistory/.

Tools

Tool 4.1 Practice an Oral History Interview

These guided conversations are much more complex than many researchers realize, making practice crucial in order to learn how to listen in the particular way that prizes hearing another person's actual words, their unspoken ones, and their deeper meaning. Try a realistic practice interview. Find someone you want to interview who is unrelated to your historic site and, based on your purpose, develop ten key questions that logically create "flow." Interview her in a realistic situation using your equipment. Afterward ask for her feedback on your technique and analyze the insights gathered. Practice interviews improve technique and confidence.

Tool 4.2 Listening for History

Choose a dozen natural and human-made sounds heard during your key era and decide how best to use them interpretively in exhibits, rooms, and shows. Be creative—dogs barking are too obvious! Which female-associated sounds epitomize women's lives? What sounds are now missing at your museum? What "new" sounds were not heard historically? How can you improve the soundscape of your exhibits and rooms? Does it have as many layers as real soundscapes have?

Notes

1. Doris Crump Rainey, interview by Heather Huyck, Williamsburg, Virginia, January 11, 2016.01.17. Used with permission.
2. Lucy Larcom, *A New England Girlhood* (1889).
3. Anne Brunner Eales, *Army Wives on the American Frontier: Living by the Bugles* (Boulder: Johnson Books, 1996). Memoirs often describe local soundscapes.
4. Lucy Larcom, *A New England Girlhood*. See Mark M. Smith, *The Smell of Battle, the Taste of Siege: A Sensory History of the Civil War* (New York: Oxford University Press, 2015).
5. Sue Armitage and Laurie Mercier, *Speaking History: Oral Histories of the American Past 1865–Present* (New York: Palgrave Macmillan, 2009).

6. George Root, *"Just Before the Battle, Mother"* (Chicago: Root and Cady Publishers, 1864), or John L. Zieber, "The Girl I Left Behind Me" (J.H. Johnson, Philadelphia, 1862), https://www.loc.gov/item/amss.cw101980/.

7. "Traps for Women" speech delivered by Maggie L. Walker, March 5, 1925, p. 24. Maggie L. Walker NHS Collection.

8. Her hymns include: Aloha Oe ("Farewell to Thee"); "Go and Tell"; "He Lives on High"; and "He's Coming Soon." She wrote "'O kou aloha nö" in 1893 while she was imprisoned; see http://www.hymntime.com/tch/non/haw/okoualoh.htm.

9. Edward Baptist, *The Half Has Never Been Told: Slavery and the Making of American Capitalism* (New York: Basic Books, 2014). Excellent use of oral accounts.

10. President Stanley Anablak, *Nunatsiaq News*, "Feds announce money for Nunavut-based centre to house Franklin relics, Parks Canada also working with Kitikmeot Inuit to develop National Historic Site." http://www.nunatsiaqonline.ca/stories/article/65674feds_announce_money_for_nunavut-based_centre_to_house_franklin_relics.

11. Russell Potter, "Inuit historians that helped search for Sir John Franklin," http://www.canadiangeographic.ca/magazine/jf16/inuit-historians-franklin-ships-search.asp.

12. Helen Bryan, *Martha Washington: First Lady of Liberty* (New York: John Wiley & Sons, Inc., 2002). Thanks to the Colonial Williamsburg Foundation.

13. Gail M. Nomura, "Filipina American Journal Writing: Recovering Women's History," in *Asian/Pacific Islander American Women: A Historical Anthology* (New York: New York University, 2003), 141.

14. Katherine Borland, "'That's Not What I Said': Interpretive Conflict in Oral Narrative Re-search," in *The Oral History Reader*, 2nd ed. (New York: Routledge Taylor & Francis Group, 2006).

15. Kathleen Blee, "Evidence, Empathy and Ethics: Lessons from Oral Histories of the Klan," *The Oral History Reader*, 2nd ed.; Susan Armitage and Sherna Berger Gluck, "Reflections on Women's Oral History: An Exchange," in *The Oral History Reader*, 2nd ed.

16. "National Cowgirl Museum and Hall of Fame," http://www.cowgirl.net/.

17. See http://www.vermontfolklifecenter.org/archive/res_audioequip.htm.

18. See www.loc.gov, www.oralhistory.org, or Baylor Institute for Oral History, *Introduction to Oral History* (Waco: Baylor University, 2016), http://www.baylor.edu.

19. Judy Yung, "'A Bowlful of Tears': Lee Puey You's Immigration Experience at Angel Island," in *Asian/Pacific Islander American Women: A Historical Anthology* (New York: New York University, 2003). Lee later returned to the United States and remained here.

20. Amy Shuman, "Reticence and Recuperation: Addressing Discursive Responsibility in Feminist Ethnicity Research," *Journal of American Ethnic History* 26, no. 4 (Summer 2007).

21. Alison K. Hoagland, *Mine Towns: Buildings for Workers in Michigan's Copper Country* (Minneapolis: University of Minnesota Press, 2010), 114.

22. Oral History Association, "Principles and Best Practices," 2009, http://www.oralhistory.org/about/principles-and-practices-revised-2009/.

23. Doris Crump Rainey, personal communication, January 11, 2016.

24. Dorothy Molter Oral History Project 2015, Ely, Minnesota, http://www.rootbeerlady.com/wp-content/uploads/2016/02/Dorothy-Molter-OH-Transcript-Collection-1.pdf.

25. Such women include Maude Ballou SCLC Secretary; Myrlie Evers; Diane Nash; and many others. See Lynne Olson, *Freedom's Daughters: The Unsung Heroines of the Civil Rights Movement, 1830–1970* (New York: Touchstone Books, 2001).

26. Steve Black, Big Hole National Battlefield, Wisdom, Montana, June 2015.

27. Thomas Powers, "How the Battle of Little Bighorn Was Won," *Smithsonian Magazine* (November 2010). http://www.smithsonianmag.com/history/how-the-battle-of-little-bighorn-was-won-63880188/#eFWvtxMPRDiGYio.

28. Elizabeth Lapovsky Kennedy, "Telling Tales: Oral History and the Construction of Pre-Stonewall Lesbian History," in *Oral History Reader*, 2nd ed.

29. Heather Huyck, "To Celebrate a Whole Priesthood: The History of Women's Ordination in the Episcopal Church" (PhD, Minnesota, 1981).

30. See The American Folklife Center, Library of Congress Release Form, 2005, http://www.loc.gov/folklife/fieldwork/releaseform.html.

31. Louise M. Jackson, "Cloth, Clothing, and Related Paraphernalia: A Key to Gender Visibility in the Archaeological Record of Russian America," in *Those of Little Note: Gender, Race and Class in Historical Archaeology* (Tucson: University of Arizona Press, 1994), 38.

32. Sherna Berger Gluck, *Rosie the Riveter Revisited: Women, the War, and Social Change* (New York: Plume, 1988); Ken Kokka, *Blossoms & Thorns: A Community Uprooted*, 2012. Video.

33. Dorothy Molter Oral History Project 2015 Ely, Minnesota, http://www.rootbeerlady.com/wp-content/ uploads/2016/02/Dorothy-Molter-OH-Transcript-Collection-1.pdf. Susan Armitage and Sherna Berger Gluck, "Reflections on Women's Oral History: An Exchange," in *The Oral History Reader*, 2nd ed.

5

Visual Sources

Pictures, Maps, and Photos

Visual sources add a vivid dimension to our museums and historic sites. Paintings and drawings record past experiences, while portraits show how people appeared and how they presented themselves. Maps depict landforms and land claims both locally and globally with historic photographs especially valuable for their research value and interpretive possibilities. When combined with written, oral, and tangible resources, visual sources provide important opportunities for research, interpretation, and preservation. We are so surrounded by visual sources that we sometimes miss seeing them. They play a key role in so many visitors' first question, "Where's the restroom?" The answer? "Over there, by that sign." We have more visual sources than previous generations did with all those directional signs, millions of photographs, television shows, movies, and YouTube. Visual sources reflect the dramatic technological changes over the past 150 years. Would all of the Donner Party have made it to California in 1857 instead of dying in the high Sierras had there been an overhead sign warning, "Avoid Hastings Cutoff"?

Museums and historic sites need huge quantities of visual sources for interpretation in exhibits, publications, and programs. Visual sources provide visitors access to historic landscapes that no longer exist or buildings now too dangerous to enter. Creative use of images can form a semblance of movement from still photographs by zooming in or panning. In preservation, visual sources guide curators how best to restore tangible resources to their near-original state and how to replicate long-rotted carved woodwork.

In some cases, visual sources are the only way to communicate. Constructing buildings today would be nearly impossible with only verbal instructions and without blueprints. Maps and graphs condense huge amounts of data into useful products. Art forms in all their imagination and creativity convey emotion in ways census schedules cannot. In our visual culture, it's hard to remember how rare photographs were 150 years ago, or when parents photographed their dead children because that would be the only image they would have.[1] Visual sources show a world frozen in time. As such, it's crucial to examine them slowly and carefully to see everything one can in each of them. Some were posed photographs; others composed paintings. Still others are especially valuable for their unintentional information—the reflection in the window of men watching women or a wind-whipped girl pumping water from her family's well. In women's history, visual sources can be especially powerful in showing women doing unexpected things—working on lathes during world wars, conducting research at the Edison laboratory in New Jersey, or driving cars in 1913 Kansas (see Figure 2.2, p. 30). We have long been surprised by women's long woolen swimming suits; seeing pictures of men in similar long swimming suits shows that everybody once wore such bulky garments. Haunting photographs of women grieving, refugees of every color and background, or protesting suffragists on horses shape our feelings about the past. This chapter considers the best ways to use visual sources for women's history at museums and historic sites, focusing on historic photographs as especially useful, while recognizing the many earlier visual sources of drawings, maps, and paintings.

Varieties of Visual Sources

The many kinds of visual sources—drawings, prints, paintings, photographs, maps—convey the world to our eyes rather than our ears. While some visual forms—pictographs (painted rocks) and petroglyphs (incised rocks) are ancient, even maps and drawings that required paper and ink can be centuries old. The printing revolution of the fifteenth century first made mass production of maps, books, and images possible. That distribution of knowledge was essential to creating the modern world in politics, society, and religion—the 1455 printing of the Gutenberg Bible contributed to the Protestant Reformation.

Signs

In societies with low literacy rates, visual sources were crucial, whether signs identifying a shop for women or religious stories told in stained glass. Shop signs displayed their products—Mary Dickenson's millinery shop in Williamsburg, Virginia, had a sign with crossed feathers and a fan to signal that she sold hats, fans, and gloves. Millinery shops—once a major industry run by and for women—were unusual female spaces, part of the female economy active from the mid-eighteenth century to the mid-twentieth century.[2] In the 1960s, as many women stopped wearing hats to church, Black women still prized their elaborate hats as crowns.[3] Signs served as trademarks when merchandise brands became nationwide and chain stores such as A&P grocery stores wanted easy identification.[4] Signs also excluded, such as segregationist "Colored Women" and "White Women" or "No Spanish or Mexicans" ones.

Maps

Maps convey the three-dimensional world in two-dimensional images that are portable and reproducible, allowing people to share their particular spatial version of the world. Historically, maps provided information about maritime and land routes worldwide, identified where people lived, showed ownership claims, and indicated so-called empty and unknown places to some people. Analytically useful maps show complex information sets as understandable images, such as urban population density or pre–Civil War slave populations along major southern rivers. Recently, Lisa Brooks found key insights by mapping Mary Rowlandson's famous seventeenth-century captivity narrative onto Wabanaki territories.[5] She used Native American Indigenous Studies (NAIS) expertise, linguistic study, and GPS/GIS (Geographic Information Systems) recording; she personally hiked trails and canoed rivers. She identified the indigenous world and demonstrated that places foreign to Rowlandson were well-known Wabenaki locations. While published maps and guidebooks have sometimes claimed authority beyond their expertise, matching current and historic maps with present landforms provides invaluable insights into earlier women's perceptions. Maps that illustrate colonial claims and U.S. territorial acquisitions help trace legal and property rights for women in "common property" states.

Maps show land divisions in increasingly smaller parcels, from continents to backyards. Public lands claimed by the United States and opened to homesteaders, including single women, with the 1862 Homestead Act were divided into 160-acre homesteads for farming, and might be subdivided into smaller village lots that were platted—mapped and legally recorded. Some states have digitized these land maps and put them online; many such maps feature village streets, public institutions, and some residences. These maps help identify neighborhoods surrounding historic sites. For example, on the *Kansas Memory* website, online maps show once-thriving villages on the Union Pacific rail line that boasted a dairy, school, train depot, and two churches, but are now ghost towns.[6] Local maps, especially old ones, can be invaluable in tracing a historic place's earlier environment or a museum's original layout when country surrounded it instead of cities and suburbs.

Maps use different scales, features, and color schemes. Their respective levels of formality and efforts to show different elements have implications for research and interpretation. Several kinds of maps are particularly useful: bird's-eye maps that show towns as though from the air; Sanborn insurance maps; and the United States Geological Survey Quadrants, the 7.5-minute topographic maps at a 1:24,000 scale where one inch equals 2,000 feet.[7] Sanborn fire insurance maps (1867–1967) documented 12,000 locales. They are invaluable because they show building construction materials, whether brick, stone, wood, or adobe, and land use patterns—the commercial, industrial, and residential jumble of different functions before zoning homogenized neighborhoods. For example, close by the Richmond home of Maggie Walker on "Quality Row" in segregated African American Jackson Ward were a grocery, funeral parlor with a casket storage building, and a vulcanizing tire garage.[8]

Maps and place names served political purposes, as competing European nations and later the United States documented discoveries, claimed territories, and named battlefields. Using maps entails awareness of these political aspects to avoid confusion. Adversaries have given battlefields different names, usually referencing geographic locations, so that the Union called it First Manassas, and the Confederates, Bull Run. Even though the Lakota were victorious in the 1876 battle, for decades the United States named the locale the Custer Battlefield for the man they had defeated. Amid contention, the Congress finally renamed it Little Bighorn, referring to the nearby river where the Lakota had camped. Archaeology combines aerial maps, which combine high-altitude photography with GIS to identify unseen land features, permitting recognition of unusual patterns such as straight or nearly straight lines of fences and fields, as well as evenly circular corrals and mounds that are seldom found in nature and invisible from the ground. The few female place names on maps reflect a lack of female power and recognition. Notable exceptions include the Commonwealth of Virginia, named for Elizabeth I of England, "the Virgin Queen," and Spider Rock on the Navajo Reservation, named for Spider Woman, a Navajo holy being who dwells on the high monolith (see Figure 6.1).

Atlases that combine maps with other data to portray geographic patterns provide useful context, although *they seldom* adequately portray gender. *The Routledge Historical Atlas of Women in America* is an exception. It's useful, if generalized.[9] A national or regional atlas places a specific location into larger spatial and temporal world comparisons, while a local atlas shows more detailed spatial development.[10]

Paintings and Drawings

This painting, which swirls together joy and sadness, shows the emotive witness to women's lives that these forms of art provide. African American Loïs Maillou Jones painted the "Flying Horses" carousel on Martha's Vineyard, featuring bright colors and a powerful sense of motion. Women have painted much less than they have been favorite subjects of paintings. Especially known for her art depicting her life in New Mexico, Georgia O'Keeffe painted scenes in self-consciously feminine ways. In Northeast Louisiana, Clementine Hunter, a self-taught twentieth-century African American artist, painted scenes of Melrose Plantation, where she had long worked. Lenore "Lee" Krasner, an American abstract expressionist, and Mary Cassatt, an American impressionist

Figure 5.1.   *Flying Horses*, Oak Bluffs, Massachusetts, by a key Harlem Renaissance artist, Loïs Maillou Jones, who had a sixty-year career as a painter, textile designer, and educator (Howard University) (1905–1998).
COURTESY OF THE GRANARY GALLERY, WEST TISBURY, MASSACHUSETTS.

famous for paintings of mothers with children, each show powerful if differing styles.[11] Much less frequently, women have had sufficient means to help other artists. Philanthropist Isabella Stewart Gardner assembled an impressive collection. Although Rose O'Neill was best known for her Kewpie dolls, she was a serious sculptor who helped other women artists as well.[12]

If your museum or historic site is fortunate enough to have such art or access to it, consider how it reflects the artist's life, how it portrays the women of her era, and how it can help us understand them. Hunter gives us a sense of African American life on a cotton plantation in the fields where she worked for decades. Maillou Jones, best known for her use of color, taught at Howard University for many years and designed high-end fabrics. In the twentieth century, Jacob Lawrence's famous paintings, *The Migration Series*, shows Blacks migrating from the Jim Crow south, a powerful interpretive source when he showed African American women working and suffering. Before photography and photocopying, few exact copies of a painting existed. Portraits documented family lineages and sometimes included female family members. Popular magazines often published images of the latest women's fashions.

Paintings and drawings can convey other insights than photographs. For example, today visitors hear airplanes landing at the nearby Minneapolis–St. Paul airport as they drive the interstate highway to Historic Fort Snelling. As this painting depicts (see Figure 6.4), that access to the dramatically altered landscape masks the fact that Fort Snelling's location was chosen at the confluence of the Mississippi and Minnesota rivers. Historically, most people arrived by canoe, then later by steamboat in the 1820s. During the fort's period of significance, the European Americans and African Americans who lived in and near the fort had close neighbors, the Ojibwas, who lived on its riverbanks. Nineteenth-century images of Fort Snelling such as this one shows the fort's strategic and impressive location on the high river bluffs. This painting of the 1850s fort hints at its future as farmlands for the European American settlers who soon arrived. Looking closely at this painting reveals a variety of land and water uses, different types of peoples, and how the topography influenced their lives. Knowing that women lived in the fort, on top of the river bluff, at the Indian Agency, and in tipis surrounding it encourages comparisons and questions, insights difficult to discern elsewhere.[13] Here, the U.S. Indian Agent to the Sioux Nation, Lawrence Taliaferro—owner of enslaved Harriet Robinson [Scott], wife of Dred Scott—lived close to the fort, surrounded by several hundred Dakotas in tipis.[14]

Analysis of advertising images aimed at women, whether paintings, drawings, or photographs, provides us with numerous prescriptive sources encouraging the purchase of new appliances, clothing, and personal products. Each of them implies an ideal American woman or shows a serious problem for women that purchases could solve, such as a 1920 Odorno deodorant advertisement that showed a woman alone in "the most humiliating moment of my life."[15]

Figure 5.2. Daguerreotype, unknown woman with book, American mid-nineteenth century. A matching photograph of a man exists. Note the elegant frame.
PHOTOGRAPH BY RACHEL WALLACE.

These portrayals had emotional pitches, as the "Chessie the Kitten" mascot that promised the Chesapeake and Ohio Railroad was the best train for women to ride, or the many versions of the Betty Crocker trope that real women showed their love by baking.[16]

Photographs

Photographs provide some of the very best documentation for women's lives because they are so useful for research and interpretation. In historical documentation, there is almost "BP" and "AP"—before photographs and after photographs—given how profoundly they increase our ability to "see" the past. If the photographer were documenting a scene rather than showing technical prowess, their work would provide better evidence than a painter, who might miss details that mar accuracy. Photographs give us a realistic sense of being present at the very moment of action. At the same time, fewer images of women and girls exist than of men, and many images have lost their identification, seriously limiting their historical value.[17] A set of photographs forms a powerful exhibit illustrating women at different life stages and their changing lives. A photograph of an elderly woman, known only as "Cousin Mildred" and who always offered children candy from her store, paired with one taken decades before when she was a ruffled, pert young girl holding a bright-eyed kitten, shows both her individual life and women's changings ones. Photographs are excellent in showing changes, aging, and generations, along with how much has happened in the century between her girlhood and today. When you explore photography as a key source, invest in a book on the history of American photography and contemplate its pictures. A published book encourages careful looking time and again, training your eye to appreciate what these images can convey and to discern details not otherwise found.

Not seeing a woman in a historic photograph does *not* prove she wasn't there—she just wasn't in the printed picture. The famous photograph of *The Last Spike* at Promontory Summit, Utah, commemorates the moment in 1869 when the transcontinental railroad connected the rail lines between the Atlantic and the Pacific oceans. That photograph features two men triumphantly shaking hands. Another photograph exists that shows women there as well, presumably the wives of the men in the first photograph. Historian Martha Sandweiss points out that just "beyond the frame" of that photograph were Chinese laborers, who provided 90 percent of the western railroad construction labor and suffered many of the casualties involved in building the transcontinental railroad.[18] Often our historical accounts privilege the investors and architects of a building, rail line, or ship over their *users,* impacts, and the wider story, obscuring women from our history. Within a few years after this photograph was taken, entire families, their furniture, and their livestock traveled west by railroad to their new homesteads. Photographs challenge us to appreciate why and how they were taken, that their meanings change, and that they contain information unavailable elsewhere, even if unintentionally.

Photographs truly change our ability to see the past. Delving into women's history that happened after the advent of photography has more and richer sources to offer us. Once photographs became relatively available, questions could be asked and answered about what people actually did or had. Ironically, the same historic photographs are published over and over, partly because the most poignant ones are so rare—the same nineteenth-century desolate family of three women, four children, and a man resting in front of their two horseless wagons appears repeatedly. We know that enslaved women were whipped, but we only see the same picture of a formerly enslaved man with welts on his back.[19]

Most early photographs, known as daguerreotypes, were portraits that made a single copy without any negative—such as Figure 5.2, which shows some damage. Next came easily broken glass-plate negatives, which allowed sharp images and multiple copies of Matthew Brady's Civil War images, or of the great nineteenth-century land surveys that mapped North America as the

Figure 5.3. Florence Thompson, a destitute agricultural worker, with one of her seven children, as photographed by Farm Security Administration Dorothea Lange in 1936 near Nipomo, California.

LIBRARY OF CONGRESS. CALIFORNIA NIPOMO, SAN LUIS OBISPO COUNTY, UNITED STATES. FEBRUARY OR MARCH 1936. HTTP://WWW.LOC.GOV/ITEM/2017_762907/.

United States acquired additional acreage. Initially, flash photography literally "flashed" magnesium and nitrate powders, which explains the startled looks on some women's faces in Jacob Riis's tenement pictures in *How the Other Half Lives*.[20] His investigative photographs spurred recognition of New York City's deplorable conditions—dank basements filled with discouraged-looking women, some holding barely alive babies, suddenly became visible. During the Great Depression, Farm Security Administration photographs painfully documented hardships Americans faced. Seeing the faces of women enduring disasters brings home their calamitous situations when we come face-to-face with them—and their emotions become ours.[21]

Relatively few women became professional photographers during the early decades of the technology from lack of exposure to the equipment and techniques as well as from outright discouragement—as Marion Post Wolcott found in her 1930s career.[22] Yet women photographers have created impressive work, much of it now available online. Four especially memorable women photographers—Frances Benjamin Johnston, Marion Post Wolcott, Alice Austen, and Dorothea Lange—took photographs familiar to us, especially when they turned their cameras on women's experiences. The Library of Congress has extensive collections of digitized photographs and a good overview section on women photographers.[23] The iconic *Migrant Mother* [Florence Thompson, widow, 1936 (Figure 5.3)] by Dorothea Lange epitomized the tragedy of the Great Depression. Working for the Farm Security Administration (FSA), Lange labeled her photograph,

"Destitute peapickers in California; a 32-year-old mother of seven children. February 1936."[24] While working for the FSA from 1938–1942, Marion Post Wolcott traveled thousands of miles, often alone, and collected an "insightful photographic portrait of American life."[25] Wolcott and the other women worked extremely hard for little pay or recognition in their time. Earlier, Frances Benjamin Johnston photographed people and travel scenes. Her most famous photograph was her rebellious 1896 self-portrait *New Woman*—of a woman smoking a cigarette and holding a beer stein with her petticoats showing. Professional women photographers successfully gained access to different kinds of people and places and had varying interests in their craft, bequeathing us powerful images. Most photographs were taken informally by amateurs documenting family gatherings, school graduations, and travel. As the technology developed, cameras captured informal scenes far more spontaneous than the early daguerreotypes, whose sitters had to be still for a minute. Although photographs can be manipulated, they have high information value as they often show details large and small that no longer exist, such as rooms in now-demolished buildings. Photographs of female teachers and students beside their schools, disappeared landscapes, and specific people associated with your locale provide vivid interpretive details.

Postcards

Historically, people mailed postcards much more frequently than now, when smartphones allow instant transmission of photographs. Usually high-quality photographs, postcards provide a huge range of topics useful as documentation, from lovely gardens to a lynching as young White girls watched.[26] From 1898 to 1978, the Curt Teich Company published some 300,000 postcards covering most of the United States, with many now digitized.[27] Check whether this enormous collection has ones relevant to your locale, remembering that postcards were often made with commercial or artistic purposes rather than documentary ones. Postcards of restaurants, hotels, etc. were designed to encourage customer patronage rather than document existing conditions. Postcards have a code that dates them, helping us avoid anachronisms.

Film and Video Sources

Visitors, staff, and students accustomed to living our heavily visual lives find videos and similar media compelling evidence. Quality media are produced independently for public television, by major cultural institutions (Library of Congress, the Smithsonian, C-SPAN), and by some commercial producers. C-Span videos on the First Ladies or political topics and the PBS series *American Experience* link scholarship with women's history.[28] In *Midwife's Tale*, Laurel Thatcher Ulrich's book became more vivid as we see Martha Ballard paddling a small boat to go care for her patients. Commercial productions such as *Hidden Figures* show the extraordinary roles Black women played as "human computers" in launching U.S. astronauts to the moon.[29] The Library of Congress has numerous free-access videos and presentations, including a webcast concert of the "Lili'u Project," which features the music and poetry of U.S.-deposed Hawai'ian Queen Lili'uokalani.[30] The History Channel offers programs broadcast during Women's History Month in March, such as a tour of Louisa May Alcott's Orchard House in Concord, Massachusetts. In that video, executive director Jan Turnquist explained the Alcott's family dynamics and politics and used the house as evidence, showing the archway between the parlor and dining room where the "March" daughters had staged plays and the desk (built by her father) where Louisa May Alcott wrote *Little Women*. Watch for special March programming on PBS and CNN as well. The History Channel also broadcasts films that trained men how to supervise women in World War II industrial jobs, and the National Women's History Project has various videos. In addition, YouTube has a powerful lecture, "Disappeared . . . Enslaved Women and the Armies of the Civil

War" by historian Thavolia Glymph.[31] Alice Kessler-Harris of Columbia University has taught MOOC (Massive Open Online Course) classes including "Women Have Always Worked," which provides worldwide electronic access to quality women's history.[32]

Analyzing Visual Sources

Consider the specific relevance of each image to your museum and interpretation. Visual analysis, like textual analysis, requires thoughtful review, as outlined below. Preparing the descriptive metadata *first* helps deeper analysis and ensures completion of the basics. Is the image genuine and congruent with the prime historical period of your museum? Has it been altered? If so, how? How can we tell? Why spend time researching fake or profoundly distorted images? A unique identifier, which can be as simple as date-place-initials-item number for that day, as in 2020.05.23-cc-017, creates a useful nonrepeating code; quick analysis of condition (good, fair, poor); basic description of item (photograph, black & white, 2" x 2" mounted on stiff cardboard with "Cousin Mildred" written on back); date as exact as possible (c. 1900 from clothing, age six from teeth); place (Frankfort, New York, on photo); photographer (W.H. Pearce); description (Cousin Mildred as a girl, missing front teeth, holding a kitten); comments (smiling, wearing ruffled dress); and finally editor and date (HH and April 24, 2020). If the particular photographic form is known, such as daguerreotype or Kodachrome, include that information for its conservation implications. Write *nothing* on the photograph itself and handle it only by its edges.

Figure 5.4.   The Chrisman sisters on a claim in Custer County Nebraska, 1887. Photograph by Solomon Butcher. Women could legally file for homestead claims under the 1862 Homestead Act and "proved up" acquiring land.
RG2608.PH-1053. NEBRASKA STATE HISTORICAL SOCIETY.

Knowing the photographer provides information on their purposes, style, equipment, etc. If the document is a map, include the publisher; if a drawing, the artist.

The quietly confident sisters in Figure 5.4 counter Hollywood-conjured images of the West, giving us evidence of female presence, agency—and success. When examining photographs, consider these key perspectives:

- *Purpose.* Why was the image taken/made? Purpose informs subject matter, including how complimentary or hostile a picture appears. Published photographs of women can be quite unflattering. Was it taken as a special memento, for a news story, or to illustrate the social status of a homesteading family by including its prized possessions, such as carriages and horses, sewing machines, organs, dog, cows, cats, and everything else? From 1886 to 1912, Solomon Butcher traveled Nebraska and made his living by selling/bartering almost 3,500 glass-plate photographs he took of families living in primitive conditions in sod houses. He believed this era would end once they could afford to build using lumber. Today, the Nebraska State Historical Society has his wonderful collection.[33]

- *Overall Sense of Picture.* What is its subject? Who/how many/what kinds of people are in it? What are their postures, and where are they looking? What actions and things are portrayed? Is the image indoors or outdoors? Was the weather sunny or inclement? For photography, was it taken with a flash or with available light? What technology was used? In earlier photography, the technology, such as the aperture and exposure time, greatly affected the kind of picture taken. Look at the image in general and then very carefully. If safe to do so, use a card or piece of paper to mask portions of it and draw it slowly across the image, writing down what you see, noting anything unrecognized or unusual. Crucial to using visual sources for research is to look, and then look again.

- *Context—Its Time and Place.* Clothes (hemlines, sleeves), hairstyles, jewelry, toys, and car models help date images. Also use seasons (snow, bare trees, leaves), and holiday decorations. Place includes topography (hills, mountains), physical features (rivers and other bodies of water), plant species, and architectural styles. Plants are especially useful in determining locations—palm trees grow in a different climate than Colorado blue spruce do. Look at age, gender, class, race, occupation, etc. Look for any religious or ethnic evidence—a Virgin of Guadalupe, the patron saint of Mexico, suggests that origin. All these elements are in photographs and paintings. Looking again and again helps find them.

- *Focus.* Is there a clear foreground, middle, and background to the composition? Are there partial elements at the edges that indicate cropping? Look at people's clothing—what were they wearing? What did they do? What were they carrying? What did this woman most value—is her teapot shining? Is there paper edging on her shelves? Is she holding children? Are the pictures of women sexual or suggestive? Is this a formal, posed picture with people in front of a television set, leaning on a post, or sitting in a chair? Or is it a candid picture taken during other events? What was the event? Look for anything adjacent to your image—other buildings, cows, etc. Look carefully at the photograph of urban laundry in Figure 5.5 for plants on wooden porches, women, a boy, and a man, as well as the morning's work. Here, women's work was displayed for all to see.

- *Quadrants.* Now divide the picture into quarters and carefully study each quarter and its contents, covering the rest of the picture. What do you see now? What questions arise? Can you identify anything special to this image—anything now unusual? Were people arranged to make a "better" picture? Look for anomalies—anything unexpected. This can be subtle—an extra arm, or shadow of another person. Could the image be propaganda? Why?

- *Enlargements.* If you have a digital version of the picture, enlarge it until it becomes blurry and pixelates. What becomes visible when each of the four quadrants is enlarged? What more

Figure 5.5.   Drying laundry, "old rear tenement in Roosevelt St." Washing laundry required carrying and heating approximately 200 pounds of water per load and dumping dirty water, as well as removing stains, scrubbing, rinsing, and wringing out each load. Photograph by reformer Jacob Riis, who exposed slum living conditions in New York City.
JACOB AUGUST RIIS (1849–1914)/MUSEUM OF THE CITY OF NEW YORK. 90.13.1.100.

can be seen with the strongest magnification? For example, store signs become legible, and a baby and baby carriage become visible. In another, by manipulating the digital image one can "see" inside a window. With digital photography, one can play with images, blowing up corners until they fuzz into pixels to see a ruffled dress or dog's collar. Facial expressions, directions of gazes, and arm/hand placements are especially telling.

- *Features.* What are its landscape features? The architectural (buildings and structures) features? Objects? Who is shown in the picture? Numbers, demographic data, activities, and posed/informal/action? Is this a special occasion or daily living? Look for "ghosts" that show changes in the building when things were removed or unusual connections between parts of a building that may show additions. Knowing basic building styles helps identify such changes.
- *Surprises.* Does anything seem amiss—something broken, or a part missing, or interrupted action? Any explanations why? Follow arm and hand positions. Many people are surprised to discover how many different things women did. For example, *One Woman's Gold Rush: Snapshots from Mollie Brackett's Lost Photo Album 1898–1899* published from her photograph collection dispels the myth of male-only Alaska gold rushers more powerfully than any paragraph.[34] We know that photographs can be altered, but we realize that most are not and we appreciate having such interpretive evidence to refute common stereotypes.

Digital Collections

The Minnesota Historical Society has digitized historic photographs appropriate for other Midwest museums and sites, as does Kansas Memory. Begin with your own state institutions and then nearby states and archives known for relevant topics to find the most useful places. Most historical societies have local maps, some digitized. State historical societies and archives—such as those in Kansas, Minnesota, and Virginia—have excellent collections, as do the Autry Museum of the American West and Harvard University. An impressive collection of historic U.S. and earlier maps is available at the Perry-Castañeda Library Map Collection in Texas and with wide-ranging resources in the David Rumsey Collection at Stanford University, including digitized copies of the famous 1895 Hull-House neighborhood ethnicity maps.[35] Commercial websites include aerial maps, environmental information, title information, and public records.

The Library of Congress has an amazing collection of digitized photographs in its American Memory collection, as well as maps from many eras and sources, including Historic American Building Survey (HABS), Historic American Landscape Survey (HALS), Historic American Engineering Record (HAER), and Sanborn maps. The National Archives and Records Administration (NARA) has its own sets of images and maps generated from the work of various federal agencies. The Library of Congress publishes reasonably priced books of photographs; National Archives photographs are available on its website. The National Oceanographic and Atmospheric Administration (NOAA) has large collections of charts and maps, and the U.S. Census Bureau combines geography with statistics.[36] The National Park Service has a historic photograph collection including images of specific parks.

Visual Sources Conservation

Discussions of how best to protect and ensure future access to visual sources continue. Debates over photograph care are especially vigorous—whether to put them in cold storage, to digitize them all, or to accept some losses—because photographs were made with so many different chemical processes. Conservation processes are highly technical for paintings in all media as well. Note that curators use "conservation" while historic preservationists use "preservation" for the similar processes of extending the "lives" of tangible resources. Photographs are *extremely fragile*, and some—with nitrate film, for example—are *very dangerous*. Inspect all of those in your collection to see if there are any nitrate films or other flammability issues, as well as to get a general understanding of their condition. Never touch anything except by the edges—it's safest to assume photographs will fall apart if you do *anything* thoughtless with them. While dated, Robert A. Weinstein and Larry Booth's *Collection, Use, and Care of Historical Photographs* has excellent advice on all kinds of photographs. When supplemented with good Web materials and good sense, their book works well. The key advice? When in doubt, call a conservator.[37] NARA has a great deal of relevant information, and the National Archives of Britain website has an introductory brochure.[38] The Getty Conservation Institute has intensive website courses in photographic conservation and materials, and the.Northeast Document Conservation Center has online materials including publications and webinars on conservation of materials.[39] Remember: If you *ever* open old film and smell an acrid odor, act immediately and contact a conservator—it's probably highly flammable nitrate film.

Using Visual Sources Effectively

It's one thing to hear that women took up bicycling in the late nineteenth century, but another to see a picture of four women in long white dresses and large hats bicycling along. How did they do it? No wonder bicycling spurred women to wear different clothing—it's hard enough to pedal in a skirt, much less a very long one. The photograph of Frances Willard, head of the Women's Christian Temperance Union, riding a bicycle in a long skirt on the cover of her book, *How I Learned to Ride the Bicycle: Reflections of an Influential 19th Century Woman*, shows her success and recognizes her determination.[40] The famous photograph *Four Sisters on their Claims* in Nebraska shows four women who homesteaded land for themselves and their families (see Figure 5.4).[41] The Chrisman sisters stand in front of a small sod house (soddy) constructed by laying tiles of sod upon each other in masonry fashion to build walls, leaving space for a door and sometimes a window, and adding a roof of more sod. While the number of women who homesteaded was not huge, a surprising number did, and many "proved up" their claims successfully, becoming landowners when few women could. These four women exemplify grit in the high grass with their two horses and soddy. In contrast, "A young evacuee of Japanese ancestry waits with the family baggage before leaving by bus for an assembly center in the spring of 1942," by Clem Albers, California, April 1942.[42] Her face mixes confusion and fear. Each of these photographs, whether posed or documentary, has different elements of women's experiences: challenging the old order with the freedom of bicycling; literally claiming their own land and homes; and persevering through difficult racist times. Here emotions become clearer, as do their associated tangible resources—landscape, buildings, and objects. The women's clothing hampers their actions in the two older photographs, the soddy seems to use a single board for the roof and a couple of boards for the door, and the pile of suitcases shows everything a Japanese family was allowed to take to the World War II internment camps. Beyond words, they enrich our understanding of the joys and struggles our foremothers experienced. Visual sources have practical aspects as well; for interpretive programs they show us how earlier generations appeared in period clothing, and they document earlier configurations of buildings, assisting in their preservation. Consider Lewis Hine's famous photograph of a young girl tending a spinning machine as propaganda to fight child labor and the difference it helped make (see Figure 5.6). We are fortunate to have a plethora of visual sources, from family photographs to comics to high-style designs, all of which help us better perceive past women's lives to document and interpret them today.

Tools for Chapter 5: Visual Sources

A warning!

The wonderful images and published materials available on the internet are available for research as part of "fair use," but they may be copyrighted, making public use illegal, as in *theft* of intellectual property. Look but don't steal—find out every image's status, always credit their maker, and pay as appropriate. The U.S. Copyright Office website explains Fair Use.[43]

Figure 5.6.   Sadie Pfeifer, a 48-inch-tall girl working a spinning machine in 1908. Lancaster Cotton Mill, Lancaster, South Carolina. Photograph by Lewis Hine, who documented the travesties of child labor.
LEWIS WICKES HINE, PHOTOGRAPHER. NOVEMBER 30, 1908. LANCASTER, SOUTH CAROLINA. RETRIEVED FROM THE LIBRARY OF CONGRESS, HTTPS://WWW.LOC.GOV/ITEM/NCL2004001284/PP/. ACCESSED FEBRUARY 12, 2017.

Tool 5.1 Finding Visual Sources

Interpretation, websites, and label-and-exhibit copy/products are all visually voracious. Go to your state historical society or library/archives website. Look for digitized images that show women and girls, places, and eras relevant to your museum/historic site. Search at least twenty-five images, and identify ten potential images for use. What useful information do you see in each image? How do these images enhance the interpretation of women? Keep notes!

Tool 5.2: Conserving Visual Sources

Review your collections and identify their major kinds of visual sources—paintings, photographs, postcards, etc. Sample ten key items, research how best to meet their conservation needs, and develop a priority list. Document your work well!

Notes

1. Michael Lesy, *Wisconsin Death Trip* (Albuquerque: University of New Mexico Press, 2000).
2. Marla R. Miller, *The Needle's Eye: Women and Work in the Age of Revolution* (Amherst: University of Massachusetts Press, 2006).
3. Wendy Gamber, *The Female Economy: The Millinery and Dressmaking Trades, 1860–1930* (Champaign: University of Illinois Press, 1997).
4. Marc Levinson, *The Great A&P and the Struggle for Small Business in America* (New York: Hill and Wang, 2011).

5. Lisa Brooks, "Awikhigawôgan Ta Pildowi Ôjmowôgan: Mapping a New History," *William & Mary Quarterly*, 3rd, 75, no. 2 (April 2018).

6. Kansas Historical Society, Bennington, Kansas, 1902. http://www.kansasmemory.org/item/209393/page/29.

7. Special thanks to Aaron Berryhill for his cogent explanation and assistance on these maps.

8. Library of Virginia, Sanborn map, Jackson Ward, Richmond, Virginia, vol. 3, 1925, Map section 307.

9. Sandra Opdycke, *The Routledge Historical Atlas of Women in America* (New York: Routledge, 2000).

10. Derek Hayes, *Historical Atlas of the United States* (Berkeley: University of California Press, 2007); Derek Hayes, *Historical Atlas of the Pacific Northwest: Maps of Exploration and Discovery: British Columbia, Washington, Oregon, Alaska, Yukon* (Seattle: Sasquatch Books, 1999). Eric Homberger, *The Historical Atlas of New York City: A Visual Celebration of 400 Years of New York City's History*, Rev. (New York: Owl Books, Henry Holt and Company, 2004) ignores Emily Roebling and Margaret Sanger.

11. Exhibit of Loïs Maillou Jones, Martha's Vineyard Historical Society Exhibit, 2015; Mary Cassatt, https://www.marycassatt.org; and Gail Levin, *Lee Krasner: A Biography* (New York: Harper & Row, 2011).

12. See the Isabella Stewart Gardner Museum in Boston, www.gardnermuseum.org and Rose O'Neill, Bonniebrook Gallery, Museum and Homestead, Missouri, www.roseoneill.org.

13. Edward K. Thomas, *View of Fort Snelling*, Oil, c. 1850, Minneapolis Institute of Arts, The Julia B. Bigelow Fund, www.bridgemanimages.com.

14. Lea VanderVelde, *Mrs. Dred Scott: A Life on Slavery's Frontier* (New York: Oxford University Press, 2009), 13–19. Superb!

15. Sarah Everts, "They Smelled Bad," *Smithsonian*, August 2, 2012, https://www.smithsonianmag.com/history/how-advertisers-convinced-americans-they-smelled-bad-12552404. Specific ad is August 1920, no publication, Courtesy JWT Archives, Duke University.

16. C & O Railroad Advertisement, "If Ever There Was a Train Designed for Women It's the George Washington," COHS *archives*, n.d., www.cohs.org.

17. There are many websites with historic photographs of American women, but it's still worth buying a large-format book of quality published images to immerse yourself in them. See also "Discovering American Women's History Online" at http://digital.mtsu.edu/cdm/landing-page/collection/women and https://www.nps.gov/articles/taas-womenshistory-intro.htm.

18. Martha A. Sandweiss, *Print the Legend: Photography and the American West* (New Haven: Yale University Press, 2002).

19. Erin Blakemore, "The Shocking Photo of 'Whipped Peter' That Made Slavery's Brutality Impossible to Deny; The Widely Circulated Image of Peter's Wounds Helped Turn White Northerners against Slavery," History Channel, *History Stories* (blog), February 7, 2019, https://www.history.com/news/whipped-peter-slavery-photo-scourged-back-real-story-civil-war. Image is in Library of Congress; no known image of a woman with such scars has been found yet.

20. Jacob Riis, *Italian Ragpicker with Her Baby in Home near Jersey St.*, 1890, photograph, https://allthatsinteresting.com/jacob-riis-photographs-how-the-other-half-lives#13; see Riis, *How the Other Half Lives*, 1890, http://www.gutenberg.org/4/5/5/0/45502/.

21. See Farm Security Agency, http://www.loc.gov/pictures/collection/fsa.

22. See http://www.loc.gov/pictures/search/?q=Marion%20Post%20Wolcott&co=fsac.

23. See http://www.loc.gov/rr/print/coll/596_womphotoj.html.

24. See http://www.loc.gov/rr/print/list/128_migm.html.

25. See http://www.loc.gov/pictures/search/?q=Marion%20Post%20Wolcott&co=fsac.

26. *Lynching of Rubin Stacy. Onlookers, including four young girls. Fort Lauderdale, Florida*, Gelatin silver print, 8" x 10", July 19, 1935, www.withoutsanctuary.org/pics_51.html; James Allen, *Without Sanctuary: Postcards and Photographs of Lynching in America*, 13th ed. (Santa Fe: Twin Palms, 1999).

27. Curt Teich Company, postcard collection, 300,000 items, 1898–1978, https://www.new-berry.org/curt-teich-postcard-archives-collection.

28. "Orchard House and Louisa May Alcott" (C-SPAN, June 19, 2017), https://www.c-span.org/video/?430723-1/orchard-house-louisa-may-alcott.

29. Theodore Melfi, *Hidden Figures* (Twentieth Century Fox, 2017).

30. "First cook book written by an American and published in the United States," Library of Congress, https://www.loc.gov/item/96126967.

31. Thavolia Glymph lecture, Vanderbilt University, "Disappeared: Enslaved Women and the Armies of the Civil War," February 25, 2011, https://news.vanderbilt.edu/.

32. Alice Kessler-Harris, *Women Have Always Worked: 1700–1920*, n.d., https://www.bing.com/videos.

33. See http://memory.loc.gov/ammem/award98/nbhihtml/aboutbutcher.html.

34. Cynthia Brackett Driscoll, *One Woman's Gold Rush: Snapshots from Mollie Brackett's Lost Photo Album 1898-1899* (Kalamazoo: Oak Woods Media, 1996).

35. See https://www.davidrumsey.com/view.

36. Perry-Castañeda Library Map Collection: www.lib.utexas.edu/maps; Office of Coast Survey, NOAA, www.nauticalcharts.noaa.gov.

37. Robert A. Weinstein and Larry Booth, *Collection, Use, and Care of Historical Photographs* (Nashville: American Association for State and Local History, 1977).

38. The United States is http://www.archives.gov/preservation/formats/index.html#photos, and for Britain, see http://www.nationalarchives.gov.uk/documents/archivesconservation_photo.pdf.

39. See the Getty Conservation Institute website, http://www.getty.edu/conservation/about/overview.html, for extensive resources, including its Archives and Resources for Feminist Research. See also Northeast Conservation Center, https://www.nedcc.org.

40. Frances Willard, *How I Learned to Ride the Bicycle: Reflections of an Influential 19th Century Woman* (San Francisco: Fair Oaks Publishing Company, 1991).

41. Solomon Butcher, *The Chrisman Sisters*, photograph, 1886, Nebraska State Historical Society. "The Chrisman Sisters Hattie, Lizzie, Lutie and Ruth, Four Sisters On A Claim," NARA.

42. NARA Photograph No. 210-G-2A-6. Japanese American evacuee.

43. See https://www.copyright.gov/fair-use/more-info.html.

Part III
Tangible Resources

6

Landscapes

Fields and Gardens

"I knew every farm, every tree, every field in the region around my home and they all called out to me. My deepest feelings were rooted in this country. . . ." —Willa Cather, 1921[1]

Landscapes surround us, shape us, and inspire us, and have for generations. Navajos believe that Spider Rock is home to their holy person, Spider Woman, who taught their women how to weave.[2] (See Figure 6.1.) Willa Cather wrote about the Nebraskan prairie landscapes she knew, that sheltered "pioneer" women living in its villages and dugouts.[3] Although we seldom adequately appreciate landscapes in their "rich, glorious, messy, confusing, ugly, and beautiful complexity," they have major interpretive force because they have so shaped women's lives and women have so shaped them.[4] Every museum and historic site has landscapes that bring together land, sky, and sometimes water, and provide locales for their tangible resources. Landscapes include South Pass on the Oregon Trail, the route across the Rocky Mountains that women traveled in wagon trains; the East Coast fall line, the natural location for port cities, as the farthest place boats could go upstream and later for Interstate I-95; and the Mississippi River, simultaneously a barrier and a major travel route cutting through the North American continent from Minnesota to Louisiana. They also include small kitchen gardens useful for growing herbs and flowers, and formally designed gardens; as well as industrial landscapes of manufacturing complexes, shipyards, or space launch facilities; and even wilderness. As tangible resources, they combine natural- and human-made or cultural resources; referring to them as "tangible" resources removes the artificial boundary between natural and cultural resources here. In all of these landscapes, *assume* women's presence. Women traveled through and lived in these locales; their reactions to particular landscapes ranged from delight to horror.[5] When Elizabeth Cady Stanton and Susan B. Anthony visited Yosemite in 1871, Anthony enjoyed the trip, but Stanton complained, "I have been in no mood for scenery. I have been constantly watching my hands and feet lest I should come to grief."[6]

This chapter introduces landscapes as *tangible resources* in contrast to written, oral, or visual sources, and discusses the diverse ways women interacted with them. Look for women's presence in all kinds of landscapes—they were there. The gendered world masked female visibility, even as women provided much of human subsistence in paid and unpaid workplaces. Interpreters have amazing opportunities to experience landscape resources intimately and to share them with the public so they can tap all their senses. We appreciate spatial relationships among buildings and their settings, and the ways women moved around their landscapes from house to garden to barn. At our museums and sites, we see and smell seasonal changes, crunch oyster shells un-

Figure 6.1. Spider Rock, Canyon de Chelly, Navajo Nation, Arizona, home of Spider Woman, who is credited with teaching Navajo women how to weave.

derfoot, and hear Alaskan river ice breakups that made travel treacherous. With their daily and seasonal changes, landscapes provide opportunities to interpret different aspects of women's lives such as planting and harvesting gardens. Please, go outside now and look around. If you are fortunate, an intriguing landscape welcomes you there.

Defining Landscapes

With amazing variety in North America alone, landscapes are best understood as human-shaped environments that ground our regional identities. As the largest kind of tangible resources, landscapes include mountains and valleys, high plains, cotton fields, lovers' lanes, and eastern crazy-quilt land ownership patterns that contrast with ordered square western sections. Landscapes range from tiny urban gardens to western ranches of many thousands of acres and include vast fields of agrarian history, waterways for travel, and mountain ranges that shape climates and cultures. In Hawai'i, sweet potatoes grow on 800-year-old terraces while in the arid North American West, scraggly lines of cottonwood trees mark streambeds, and a square of planted trees indicates a former home site. In Virginia, the Colonial Williamsburg Foundation preserves the capital landscape with streets and buildings designed to impress colonists with royal power and instill hierarchical values—the Governor's Palace, the Capitol, and Bruton Parish Church.[7]

Focusing on biogeographical areas provides a solid foundation for understanding landscapes and their historic impacts. The ecosystem of your museum provides its natural context; this expands interpretive options because landscape analysis can stress biogeographical, cultural, and/or design aspects. Applying them together ensures greater understanding of landscapes' complexity. One of three ways to conceptualize U.S. landscapes comes from the Cooperative Ecosystems Studies Units (CESU), a federal program that divides the United States into seventeen biogeographical areas (ecosystems). These help us see how landscapes and waterways affected

Figure 6.2. Map showing U.S. biogeographical regions.
COOPERATIVE ECOSYSTEMS STUDIES UNIT MAP, CESU NETWORK.

historical processes and events.[8] The CESU map correlates well with American settlement and political patterns and helps us identify historically present plants and animals.

Two other approaches come from the National Park Service and the American Society of Landscape Architects (ASLA). The NPS divides cultural landscapes into four overlapping categories: designed, vernacular, historic, and ethnographic. Designed landscapes are planned by professional landscape architects; historic landscapes identify locales where specific events or historic processes occurred; vernacular landscapes reflect common usage; and ethnographic landscapes are places or sacred sites used by specific ethnic, racial, or tribal groups. Specific landscapes don't always neatly fit these categories, but they are frequently referenced in diverse laws, regulations, and official studies. A third approach from the ASLA that especially applies to formally designed landscapes uses *character-defining features* that shape a cultural landscape—topography, vegetation, circulation, water features (aesthetic and functional), structures (non-habitable), site furnishings (e.g., benches), and objects. Used together, these three different approaches provide tools to analyze and interpret cultural landscapes.

Varieties of Landscapes

Landscapes around museums and historic sites seldom appear as they once did, due to missing elements and new intrusions. Once-lively historic sites are now tranquil; for example, Fort Laramie in Wyoming, which once bustled with wagon trains; or New Bedford in Massachusetts with its fleet of tall-masted whaling ships. Some landscapes have lost key species, including bison, salmon, and bees, or have been inundated with invasive species such as grasshoppers, kudzu, or wild pigs, profoundly changing those ecosystems. Large properties have been subdivided, leaving disconnected patches of land instead of habitats covering many thousands of acres. Modern highways and development intrude on historic scenes with highway noise; office and apartment buildings tower over Margaret Mitchell's Atlanta residence.[9]

Recognizing the many layers of landscapes helps us understand them. Their geology—the earth and its surface, its coastlines, mountains, rocks, coasts, and soils—provided distinct environmental and economic situations. Water sources and features distinguished hospitable locations, while climate and seasons as well as pollution levels affected what lived and grew in them. These factors affect native and imported life forms, along with pests and invasive plants. Other forces, natural and human, eliminated bison, passenger pigeons, chestnuts, and elm trees. Cultural landscapes are "composed of a collection of features which are organized in space. They include small-scale features such as individual fountains or statuary, as well as patterns of fields and forest that define the spatial character of the landscape."[10] Few people would confuse Atlanta with Alaska, simply because their ecosystems are as distinct as their history was. In 1916, Alaskan schoolteacher May Wynne Lamb remembered "the scene that left the most lasting impression on me was the awe-inspiring golden sunset across the tundra as the sun seemed to go in a blaze of fire."[11]

Landscape analysis emphasizes connections among plants, animals, climate, weather, and humans. Use the categories below to identify the landscapes at your historic site/museum.

Designed Landscapes

Colonial Philadelphia, Pennsylvania, and Savannah, Georgia, were designed landscapes with planned streets and parks. In Washington, D.C., Pierre L'Enfant designed its infamous circles that confound tourists and provide parks for locals. Frederick Law Olmsted, father of landscape architecture, designed Central Park in New York City with each curve, rock, and tree placed for optimal effect.[12] Minneapolis designed parks around its lakes, creating places where women have

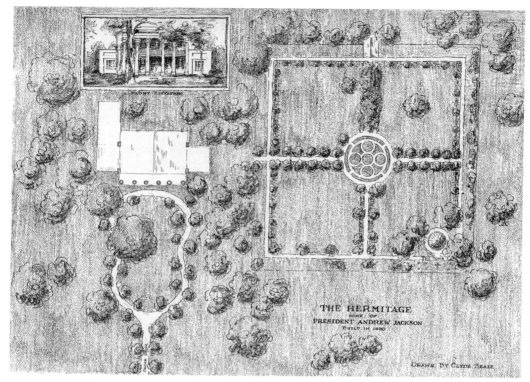

Figure 6.3.   Design for Rachel Jackson's garden at The Hermitage, Tennessee.
COURTESY TENNESSEE STATE LIBRARY AND ARCHIVES.

long walked or canoed. Hospital and asylum landscapes, such as the Athens Lunatic Asylum in Ohio, were designed to heal patients. During the 1920s, the Ball Nurses' Sunken Garden and Convalescent Park was "a beloved space for Indiana University student nurses."[13]

Although women have farmed and gardened extensively through the centuries, most landscape architecture scholarship focuses on large, formally designed landscapes. Few women had access to the formal education and personal connections required for professional careers in landscape architecture. Those few women who became professional landscape architects often designed private estates and gardens because they seldom won attention-getting major contracts for the large public projects that garner professional recognition. Recently, the American Society of Landscape Architects held a contest, "Documenting the Cultural Landscapes of Women," which identified diverse landscapes designed for and by women, including Wiawaka on Lake George, New York, an affordable vacation spot for working women; as well as gardens; camps; mansions; estates; and university campuses, including those of Princeton and Yale Universities.[14] Suzanne Spencer-Wood explained the situation:

> First, when women's organizations were creating parks, playgrounds and children's gardens, they were willing to give men the credit for these socially transforming programs in order to convince men to permanently adopt and institutionalize them. Second, historians have traditionally constructed history from men's public institutional records and books that have focused on men's leadership and important contributions.[15]

With her New York social connections, Beatrix Farrand gained "major estate commissions and quickly developed a reputation for her elegant, restrained style and rich architectural detail," still thriving in her famous Dumbarton Oaks gardens in Washington, D.C., a twenty-six-year-long project.[16] For fifty years, Vilma Pérez Blanco designed many Puerto Rican projects, including train stations, shopping centers, schools, and homes; and the restoration of the Old San Juan gardens.[17] A historic preservationist, Alice Longfellow, hired landscape architects Martha Hutcheson and Ellen Biddle Shipman to rehabilitate the nineteenth-century colonial revival garden that her father Henry Wadsworth Longfellow had designed.[18] Marian Cruger Coffin designed naturalistic gardens, Martha Brooks Hutcheson fashioned landscapes with native habitats, and Marjorie Sewell Cautley created urban "self-sustaining landscapes."[19] In Lynchburg, Virginia, the garden of Anne Spencer, African American poet and civil rights activist, has been restored. The house and garden of author Eudora Welty have been restored to the original 1925–1945 design of her mother, Chestina Welty.[20] The vibrant Eloise Butler Wildflower Garden and Bird Sanctuary in Minnesota is the oldest public American wildflower garden. Botany teacher Eloise Butler acquired fifteen acres of parkland, designed the garden, collected and cared for its plants, and retired from teaching to become its curator. Aided by the Minneapolis Woman's Club, its Wildflower Garden with prairie, bog, and woodland flowers opened in 1907. With a donation from Butler's former student, Minne-

Figure 6.4.   Fort Snelling, founded in 1819 on the bluffs above the confluence of the Minnesota River and Mississippi River marked U.S. claims against Great Britain and efforts to have peaceful relationships among resident tribes the Dakota and Ojibway. Here, the fort, the fur trading post, and the tipis are all shown, as well as Anglo American fields being planted—with women of several nationalities living there.
VIEW OF FORT SNELLING, C. 1850; EDWARD K. THOMAS (1817-1906). MINNEAPOLIS INSTITUTE OF ARTS, MINNESOTA, UNITED STATES. THE JULIA B. BIGELOW FUND/BRIDGEMAN IMAGES.

apolis businessman Clinton O'Dell, creator of the Burma Shave roadside signs, they enlarged the garden.[21] Today, the garden continues to evolve but remains a mesmerizing place. As a designed garden, it requires intensive labor lest it become a jumble of weeds and brambles.

Cemeteries as designed landscapes provide insights into women's lives. Some were elaborately designed nineteenth-century landscapes, such as Mount Auburn Cemetery in Cambridge, Massachusetts, or Forest Hills Cemetery in Boston, which became favorite picnic grounds with their "meandering paths, scenic vistas, and lovely Lake Hibiscus."[22] In some cemeteries graves were placed wherever space allowed, while in others burials were by religion. In Tin Cup, Colorado, a late nineteenth-century mining camp, the cemetery has separate sections for Protestants, Catholics, Jews, and outcasts. Kate Fisher, an African American woman known for her friendliness to local children, ran a restaurant and rooming house in Tin Cup. Her burial in the Protestant cemetery demonstrates her acceptance there. Epitaphs on grave markers hint at women's lives and accomplishments.

Vernacular Landscapes

In contrast to designed landscapes, most museums and historic sites are surrounded by vernacular gardens that have grown with minimal planning. Vernacular landscapes are the largest category, which include historic and ethnographic landscapes. In his popular 1842 book, *Cottage Residences*, Andrew Jackson Downing greatly influenced American landscapes as he encouraged moves away from cities and gave detailed instructions for suburban cottages and their gardens for beauty, convenience, and propriety.[23] As the American Industrial Revolution gathered steam and the "Cult of True Womanhood" encouraged middle-class White women to retreat into domestic lives of purity, piety, and submission, Downing proclaimed the female-created home the best retreat from the competitive male commercial world. He promoted the home as exemplified in cottage architecture, "as an unfailing barrier against vice, immorality and bad habits," added flower borders and foundation plantings to gardens, and replaced work yards with flowers and lawns. His extensive plant lists include more than three dozen once-available pear varieties.[24]

Magazines such as nationally distributed *Godey's Lady's Book*, while focused on women's fashion, also included gardening advice. In 1852, its recommendations for women's ornamental gardens directed that, "In a geometrical flower garden, the colors must be contrived so as to produce a striking effect contrasted with each other, and the plants must be so chosen as to be nearly of the same size, so that the garden, when seen at a distance, may have the effect of a Turkey carpet."[25] American gardeners brought and adapted techniques, styles, and plants from other countries. In the desert southwest, courtyard gardens provided refreshment, as well as medicinal and culinary herbs and fruits that included rosemary, olive, and apricots.[26]

Other vernacular landscapes have included trailer parks, inner city slums, and glitzy skyscraper cities with plazas and concrete sidewalks. Finnish community landscapes had houses, barns, fields, and distinctive saunas where families bathed and where women gave birth. In World War II internment camps, Japanese American women who had previously been commercial flower growers planted garden plots outside their barracks where "potatoes, onions, Chinese cabbage, and watermelon vie[d] with chrysanthemums, nasturtiums, roses, and carnations."[27] Industrial landscapes surrounded factories of many-storied mills for cloth or copper processing, or mines and slag piles with intense pollution—quite dissimilar to Downing's idealized landscape. Industrial landscapes had worker and management housing, schools, railroads, and heavy equipment. At the Kennecott copper mine in Alaska, infamous for its brutal climate, single women nurses and teachers, and wives and children of male managers, lived in nearby company housing.

Landscapes

Historic Landscapes

These landscapes reflect specific events or longer historic processes, with battlefields being the most commonly preserved examples. Some historic landscapes shaped events by constraining movement in built-up urban spaces or narrow canyons. While battles have dramatically re-arranged landscapes with earthworks that still remain a century later in women's front yards, demonstrations in city streets usually leave little evidence. In 1913, just before President Woodrow Wilson's inauguration, Alice Paul, leader of the National Woman's Party, held the largest suffrage march in history in Washington, D.C. Here the protest landscape was a constricted streetscape with Pennsylvania Avenue squeezed between commercial buildings, sidewalks, and trees. Women on floats, foot, and even horseback—8,000 of them—demonstrated for women's suffrage, an act then considered so outrageous that male bystanders attacked the women as policemen stood by. Photographs easily available on the internet provide the only permanent evidence of that impressive display of female determination.[28] In contrast, battle scars remain over 150 years later from Civil War earthworks that still mark landscapes. Many battles were fought on family farms, where kitchen gardens, peach orchards, and wheat fields flourished before battles, and where dead and dying soldiers and horses lay after them.[29] It's crucial to remember that while fathers/husbands held legal title, *families* cultivated these farms whose houses and barns were shot full of holes, and fences became breastworks on these now-historic landscapes. Declarations that "there's no women's history here" on battlefield landscapes distort the past by removing women and girls from them.

Many women witnessed and participated in Civil War battles—and left their accounts. Mrs. Judith Carter Henry and enslaved girl Lucy Griffith were the first civilian casualties during the 1861 First Battle of Manassas when shelling injured the elderly Mrs. Henry, who had refused to leave her house.[30] Lucinda Hardage, "the last living link to the battle," described the battle at Kennesaw Mountain Battlefield at ninety-one years of age when she "pointed out key locations that would never have been found without her help."[31] Confederate Mary Ann Webster Loughborough survived the siege of Vicksburg in a cave dug into the bluffs there. She lived and wrote, "How rapidly and thickly the shells and Minié balls fell . . . until I was almost deafened by the noise and explosions. . . . Our little home stood the test nobly."[32] During the Battle of Wilson's Creek, Roxanna Ray with her nine children, enslaved Aunt Rhoda with her three children, and Julius Short, a farmhand, "all took shelter in the cellar." When they emerged hours later, they found their house full of "wounded and dying Southerners."[33] Officers' wives accompanied their husbands, including General Ulysses S. Grant's wife, Julia, and John Wesley Powell's wife, Emma, who nursed her wounded husband.[34]

The public asks, "Why were so many battles fought in parks?" Think of these landscapes in time slices—before, during, after battles—and finally, now. Making Civil War battlefields into historic sites often inadvertently reduces wars solely to men fighting battles, ignoring everyone else involved. People who also affected the war's outcome included 4 million enslaved people, refugees who clogged roads and women everywhere compensating for their men's departures in an agricultural economy. Further, changing attitudes among Southern White women reveal a very different version of the war.[35] Accounts of Gettysburg include grisly details of the post-battle landscape. Women worked to clean up the carnage left behind—dead and dying men and horses, cast-off equipment, buildings with bullet holes, animals wandering about.[36] After the battle, eyewitness Matilda Pierce recounted, "The whole landscape had been changed and I felt as though we were in a strange and blighted land."[37] Cleanup after battles was difficult and lengthy. Historian Margaret Creighton explains that, "Before they became the honored dead . . . they were the awful dead—decayed, bloated, and partially buried."[38] After the battle of Gettysburg, pregnant Elizabeth Thorn and her elderly father dug "close to a hundred graves."[39] Widow Lydia

Figure 6.5. Slyder Farm, a vernacular landscape, saw major fighting during the battle of Gettysburg. The family moved away shortly after the battle had left dead men and horses there and destroyed their crops and orchard.

PHOTOGRAPH BY JASON MARTZ, COURTESY OF THE NATIONAL PARK SERVICE, GETTYSBURG NATIONAL MILITARY PARK.

Leister returned to find "her home severely damaged by artillery fire, and seventeen dead horses . . . around her best peach tree . . . her wheat had been trampled, her spring spoiled, and all her fences burned."[40] Many whose homes and farms were damaged never received any compensation. During the Indian Wars, some battles fought in the West killed more women than men. At the Sand Creek Massacre in southeastern Colorado Territory, the U.S. Army killed more Southern Cheyenne and Arapahoe women than men, and at Wounded Knee killed more Lakota Sioux women. These and many more examples provide ways for interpretation at every battlefield to reconsider female presence and agency.

Ethnographic Landscapes

Ethnographic landscapes preserve a particular definable people's place—meaning any group that over time has come to identify itself as a group with common beliefs, perspectives, and often biological connections. Such groups can connect through racial, ethnic, religious, or other designations, with common language, clothing/physical adornment, food, celebrations, and other rituals. The challenge for women's history is that women are—and have been—part of almost every such group. The relationships in these societies were varied and complex, but how each group defines itself inevitably includes gender norms. In some Native American cultures, women made, owned, and controlled their group's homes and determined who lived in them. During the eighteenth century, Plains Indians developed a mobile, horse-based culture and moved from earthen lodges to tipis produced and owned by women. Tipis dotted the plains landscape with tribal families and communities but sat lightly on the land, challenging archaeologists to search for their subtle marks. In Montana, archaeologists identified three tipi rings marking such housing in Bighorn Canyon National Recreation Area (NRA), where rocks weighed down buffalo hide edges. Using high-tech methods, archaeologists have identified many sites of ephemeral but once crucial buildings. At Big Hole National Battlefield, also in Montana, some 800 Nez Perce (nimí·pu) families and 200 warriors fleeing the U.S. Army camped near the Big Hole River. Archaeological investigations there have identified a maternity tipi, where a mother, her newborn baby, and her midwife were killed during that dawn 1877 battle there.[41] Another woman, pıná.?wınonmay (Helping Another) recounted a child's death: "The little girl was killed. Killed under my arm."[42] Nez Perce women are now central to park interpretation.

Other vernacular landscapes are regional. Southern yards extended the work areas of the houses. In these warmer climates, women worked on their porches or under shade trees, or in yards cleared to bare soil to deprive snakes of any cover. The Atlanta History Center portrays a classic swept yard at the Smith Family Farm, with dirt and small stones in its center while a bed of flowers several feet wide bed blooms along its fence line. Photographs show African American women, brooms in hand, daily sweeping their yards. If your museum is in the South, it may once have had this distinctive kind of landscape.[43] Vernacular urban yards show webs of clotheslines publicly drying family washing, the product of women's labor (see Figure 5.5, p. 79). Yard usage reflected economic and aesthetic priorities.

Landscape Perceptions

Interpreting how women perceived, experienced, and altered their landscapes is crucial to public understanding at museums and historic sites. Three sites show their variety. In the New Mexican desert, an enormous 7,296-foot-high promontory, El Morro, as tall as a 700-story building, marks a 200,000-thousand-gallon pool at its base.[44] Travelers who gratefully found its water—Anasazi, Spanish, U.S. Army, and nineteenth-century American wagon trains—carved their names into its soft sandstone. Women settlers accompanied Juan de Oñate in 1605 as he wrote "Pasó por aquí" on his way to establishing Santa Fe in far northern Spanish Mexico. Centuries later, wagon train traveler Miss A.E. Baley added her name beside the other ones.[45] In the early nineteenth century, Sacajawea successfully guided the Lewis and Clark expedition through "wilderness" (to them) carrying her baby on her back, crucially showing by her presence that they traveled in peace. Today automobiles make historic distances seem much shorter. But in 1848, Elizabeth Cady Stanton lived a snowy half-hour walk from downtown Seneca Falls, a strenuous effort with her three-, four-, and six-year-old sons, with her abolitionist husband often away.[46]

Landscapes powerfully shape our self-perceptions. Many peoples believe their native landscape to be the "best," not always recognizing that other people felt the same way about their own landscapes. Santa Clara Tewa Pueblo people perceived landscapes as holistic rather than the separate natural and human worlds so prominent in Western thought. For many indigenous peoples, landscapes remain "living, sacred texts" with homes of deities off-limits to humans. Other locales such as Spider Rock in Canyon de Chelly are places where humans can communicate with deities.[47] Gender differentiated reactions to landscapes. Annette Kolodny found that the European American "frontiersman imagined the wilderness as virgin land, an unspoiled Eve to be taken, [but] the pioneer woman at his side dreamed more modestly of a garden to be cultivated."[48] European American men perceived the American landscapes as feminine places to be conquered. Women saw landscapes to be enjoyed and to feed their families; they carried favorite seeds and seedlings to frontier homes and planted trees as windbreaks in practical symbolism.

Landscape Interactions

Women have found all kinds of sustenance in landscapes by collecting wild foods and by extensive formal farming and gardening. They have harvested, gathered, cooked, and served from their "natural supermarkets," consuming berries, grapes, plums, chestnuts, roots, dandelion leaves and other greens, camas, and other edible bulbs. They built fish weirs across creeks and walked salt flats to harvest clams for crucial nourishment and sometimes cash. Their harvesting required expert knowledge of where particular plants and animals lived, when they ripened, and if they were edible. They knew which plants and mushrooms were poisonous, even fatal.

Women have shaped and been shaped by agricultural landscapes, as agrarian Haudenosee (Iroquois), Pequot, and ancient Puebloan women farmers grew the "Three Sisters" of corn, beans and squash for millennia. Before the nineteenth century, indigenous women were highly successful farmers who grew impressive crop surpluses when "the Ohio River Valley was one of the most fertile landscapes in North America."[49] In country and city, yards served as workplaces where women cooked, laundered, raised (and killed) chickens, and where they grew flowers, fruits, and vegetables as well as medicinal herbs to feed and heal their families. Women sold *quantities* of eggs, butter, and produce at markets and to country stores. Frontier U.S. Army wives fed their families from their gardens when they lived in remote and poorly supplied forts. On once-barren Alcatraz Island in San Francisco Bay, military wives planted trees and vegetables and cultivated roses in formal gardens. Harriet Backus, wife of a Tomboy Mine engineer in Telluride, Colorado, recalled the challenges of living at 11,500-feet altitude, often buried under many feet of snow, writing, "Such lack of wood increased the work entailed in getting it; and encouraged burning coal instead." [50] On the treeless Great Plains, children twisted straw for burning and gathered dried dung, politely called "buffalo chips."

Some landscapes became deeply personal—battlefields where a son or husband died, rivers where a woman was baptized, gardens where a lover proposed marriage, or woods where a woman was raped.[51] After discovering the infidelities of her husband Franklin D. Roosevelt, Eleanor Roosevelt often retreated to Augustus Saint-Gaudens's heavily hooded statue of a woman *Grief*, surrounded by high shrubs. In this contemplative garden, she found "the resolve to remake her life as 'an independent life.'"[52] When they faced discrimination and exclusion, lesbians created their own community spaces in parks, playgrounds, and beaches.[53] For example, Cherry Grove on Fire Island. New York, provided safety and freedom for lesbians when they were so ostracized.[54]

Women Travelers' Landscapes

When women traveled, they encountered disparate landscapes, often crossing them for new homes during migrations westward (from the eastern seaboard and Midwest) and northward (from the deep south and Mexico). Women reacted to similar landscapes quite differently. For some women, travel was a grand adventure; for others it was a daily struggle. Susan Magoffin found both while traveling on the Santa Fe Trail, beginning in luxury before an accident that caused her miscarriage.[55] Harriett Bidwell Shaw described that same trail in 1851, writing, "Here the eye stretches hundreds of miles & not a tree to be seen."[56] In 1909, when automobiles were novelties and roads barely existed, four women drove across the country in two Model A Fords; one woman later admitted it was harder than she expected.[57] A few years later, in 1926, Marguerite Lindsley Arnold rode her motorcycle to Yellowstone Park from Philadelphia, where she was working on her master's degree in microbiology.[58] While most women traveled with others, one woman who drove west and camped by herself in the 1920s always placed a pair of men's boots outside her tent and never encountered any problems, while another woman camping alone fifty years later met incredulity at campgrounds but found picnic tables good places to write up her research.[59] Some women discovered American landscapes under duress. *Homeless on the Range: Life on the Road in a Model A Ford* gives a poignant picture of a couple and their four-year-old daughter driving through the U.S. West during the Great Depression, looking for work and discovering scenic wonders between coping with punctured tires and mud holes. Early women botanists and naturalists in Rocky Mountain National Park became the first park interpreters who explained wildflowers to visitors. Women botanists who researched far above timberline worked under brutal conditions to unlock the survival mechanisms of the minuscule plants living there.[60]

Women Homesteaders' Landscapes

Many single and widowed women filed claims under the 1862 Homestead Act that allowed them to do so as "head of households" (see Figure 5.4). In the 1880s, independent Adeline Hornbeck homesteaded with her four children at a 10,000-feet elevation in the Rocky Mountains, where she cut twenty tons of hay yearly.[61] North Dakota women "proved up" (acquired) their land at a rate nearly the same as men's rates, often staking their claims near other family members. In Nebraska, Solomon Butcher photographed *Four Sisters on A Claim*.[62] These women valued "land in her own name," even if initially discouraged by treeless plains and hard times when crops failed.[63] In the early twentieth century, Carrine Gafkjen Berg was among this surprising number of women; she successfully homesteaded on the northern plains thirty miles from Williston, North Dakota, getting her patent in 1905. She farmed her own land, worked as a housekeeper during winters, fed threshing crews in summers, and walked five miles to do her weekly laundry. To successfully homestead, many women took jobs as teachers, housekeepers, and sewers/milliners to earn the cash necessary to "prove up" their claims. One woman bicycled seventy-five miles each way to take her state teacher's exam, returning to teach the next day—a still-impressive feat! These women provide examples for interpretive programs and publications showing their varied actions and sheer guts.

Women and Public Landscapes

Increasingly, women claimed access to public spaces as their right, and not only to get their work done. Slowly, women of all backgrounds became more accepted in public arenas. Victorian culture had decreed that women should be domestic, and some wealthy women were home-focused, but gradually *attitudes* shifted toward greater acceptance of women's activities outside their homes. In the City Beautiful movement, Progressive Era women's groups successfully pushed for more female presence in public landscapes, arguing that parks and playgrounds developed "character" through recreation.[64] Tea rooms, public libraries, clubs, and other female-focused buildings increasingly provided separate places for women's groups and activities. Women defied social conventions by demanding their rights, and they blurred their roles as consumers "window shopping" and as protesters parading for the vote. Suffragists demonstrated on sidewalks to assert their rights as citizens. Later, women risked arrest and even death, as at Kent State in 1970, when they demonstrated alongside men in civil rights marches, in the Stonewall riots for gay rights, and in anti-Vietnam war marches that all showed their participation in national crises. During the Prohibition era, previously male-only saloons became tea rooms. Restaurants frequented by both genders became more common as men and women socialized more together in places such as movie theaters and amusement parks.

As Americans became more consumer-oriented and families had fewer backyard farms, women shopped daily for perishables and ran frequent errands to the dressmaker, milliner, and pharmacist, which exposed them to unwanted attention on public streets.[65] Carriages and cars protected wealthy women, but most women walked or used public transportation. The San Francisco streetcar system tried special shopping cars so women could avoid contact with unknown men. Streetcars, trains, ferries, and other public transportation were especially fraught locales for Black women under American apartheid.

Many women—especially working-class women—had always traveled through public spaces for work, play, worship, or simply to return home.[66] Women had entered male spaces by accident when lost, in desperation to locate a missing husband, or for business as prostitutes. Female "incursions" into public spaces slowly changed attitudes as men became more accustomed to seeing middle- and upper-class women there.[67] Still, gender boundaries prevailed. For example, in early twentieth-century Denver, Colorado, male-oriented businesses such as banks and insurance companies lined Seventh Avenue, while parallel Sixth Avenue featured female-oriented department stores—in a still visible landscape.[68] Consider the continuum where females were welcome, accepted, tolerated, and prohibited; and that different kinds of women were "allowed" in different places at different times. Decades of greater female presence in American landscapes slowly increased acceptance for women's public life.[69]

During the severe economic distress of the 1930s Great Depression, New Deal policies forced many married women to return to their homes, reinforcing "traditional" gender divisions. The Civilian Conservation Corps (CCC), which provided jobs primarily for White males who remitted 80 percent of their salaries to their families, still has an enormous impact on the U.S. landscape. The CCC planted three billion trees and constructed hundreds of public landscapes— playgrounds, roads, campgrounds, and facilities such as the Red Rock Amphitheater near Denver. These facilities still provide greater public recreation access for women and girls. The New Deal REA (Rural Electrification Administration) brought electricity and paved roads to rural areas, easing farm women's work and lives with electricity to turn on lighting and radios; to pump water from wells; and to run appliances such as stoves, refrigerators, and irons.

With World War II, women's roles changed again, as the war effort needed them to replace men who had become soldiers. While many remained in known localities, major migrations to industrial sites and the nation's capital rearranged those landscapes, some permanently. The 6 million women that were memorialized as Rosie the Riveter and Wendy the Welder worked industrial jobs building thousands of ships and airplanes. Many suffered industrial accidents.[70] Some 10,000 female clerks and cryptographers moved to Washington, D.C., to fight the war with typewriters and early computers; "code girls" cryptographers broke secret German and Japanese codes while living in extremely crowded conditions.[71] Women protected the home front as air raid wardens wearing steel Office of Civil Defense helmets and as scrap metal collectors. During World War II, women cooked with rationed fats, meat, and sugar and planted 20 million home Victory Gardens, growing an impressive 40 percent of domestic produce.[72]

After the Second World War, as 8 million veterans returned home to housing shortages, new suburban subdivisions sprang up and shopping centers replaced cornfields as inner cities deteriorated. Highway construction, redline bank policies that denied mortgages to minorities, and federal loans and housing policies transferred desirable housing to suburbia, profoundly altering the American landscape. Suburban landscapes substituted earlier use-oriented backyards with blocks of front yards with well-fertilized lawns, clipped shrubs, and flower beds melded together that displayed their owners' class and race privilege. The Garden Magazine and Better Homes & Gardens published designs and plant selections as women gardened and men mowed competitively. Homes now showed off their ornamental shrubs and flowers. Families entertained with barbeque grills and swimming pools, but suburban women without cars were isolated in such affluent places. The interstate highway system has replaced waterways as our basic national framework, yet few travelers realize how relatively recent the extensive interstate highway networks in the United States and Canada landscapes are or appreciate their impacts on women's commuting or recreational travel.

Women and Contested Landscapes

Historically, women's lives were often restricted by time and location. A landscape safe by day was frequently not safe at night, whether urban or rural, whether a risk to her reputation or to her body. Women traveling the Santa Fe Trail erroneously feared nighttime attacks from native peoples.[73] The public long assumed that no "proper" woman ventured alone after dark, although many women had no choice to commute to and from their work. Women risked being seen—and treated as—prostitutes, even if out getting milk for a baby or coming home from night work shifts. They had to discern where they were welcome and where they were not, such as walking by construction sites.[74] Women's movements were carefully monitored for propriety; women themselves had to consider where, when, and with whom they were seen. These subtle, personal forms of regulation are difficult to discern from the historical record.[75] Self-policing from fear of being labeled deviant or from physical risk—as well as official policing—kept women out of areas deemed inappropriate or "unsafe" for them. Socially acceptable places for middle- and upper-class women increased during several generations as women became more active in clubs, social activities, and political campaigns, especially for temperance, suffrage, and consumers' rights. In their unpaid benevolent work—justified as "municipal housekeeping"—women became physically more visible on the streets. They turned inside-out old arguments against women exiting their homes, by redefining "home" as the entire world. Today, American women's presence extends into most of the physical and social landscape.

Enslaved African American women encountered especially harsh restrictions. They found travel dangerous when they required passes to prove they had permission to leave home. They risked severe punishment when they visited their husbands on other plantations or attended secret religious meetings or parties.[76] Margaret Garner, while running away, killed her young daughter to prevent her child from being captured into slavery; her story is the basis of Toni Morrison's *Beloved.*[77] Yet women moved through dangerous landscapes—Harriet Tubman led over 300 escaped slaves while other women freed themselves, especially during the Civil War. After slavery, Black women risked arrest, rape, and even lynching for resisting White-prescribed roles. Frequently, lynchings of Black men were *advertised* lengthy public affairs witnessed by Whites, including women and girls, and designed to terrify the Black community. Multiple editions of the *Green Book* (1936–1967), guided traveling Blacks to friendly motels, gas stations, and restaurants warned "Carry your Green Book with you—You may need it."[78]

Over time, landscapes change. Elite neighborhoods became islands of outdated fashion surrounded by underclass businesses, while massive urban churches became encircled by vacant lots and empty buildings. Compare a current map of the area around your museum with one from a century ago. Area maps show landscapes before development and detail changes over time. USGS maps at 1:24,000 scale provide professional-quality base maps only needing missing details. With GIS proficiency, maps reveal and share key geographic relationships and layers, bringing together watersheds, land ownership, and agricultural uses.[79] Maps can show origins and destinations, such as women traveling from Delaware farms to Philadelphia markets to sell their butter, eggs, and produce for much-needed cash to pay taxes or on trips to see their mothers.[80] Consider how much the mental map of a plantation and its surroundings differed between an enslaved woman and her slaveowner. Some landscape "defining characteristics" are obvious, others hidden. For example, "This fence was an extremely important physical and symbolic barrier that separated the private mansion yard from the very busy yards of the working plantation," with meanings of exclusion and privacy on either side.[81]

Researching Landscapes

First, determine the kind(s) of landscape(s) your museum/site has of the kinds discussed above. Using maps from your immediate museum/site area, become familiar with the topography, waterways, vegetation, and land use patterns now and historically. If available, Sanborn Fire Insurance maps give powerful insights into neighborhoods and their residents—with color-coded building construction and uses (see Chapter 5: "Visual Sources"). Cross-reference a Sanborn map with your museum's relevant manuscript census record, comparing Sanborn map neighborhood addresses with residents identified in the manuscript census by their addresses and names to "rebuild" your historic neighborhood. City directories or newer phone books provide names and addresses to cross-check data. Search particular groups associated with your area who affected your landscape. San Francisco and New York were most strongly identified with LGBTQ communities and locales with bars, baths, and parks. Northern Minnesota and Michigan Finnish communities' landscapes included special hay-drying barns and saunas (dry heat baths); elsewhere, tobacco barns stood. Road names inform research and provide "detective work" approaches to research landscapes. Street names with "ferry" or "ford" indicate former water crossings; "Glebe Road" passed a church and "Rockville Pike" was once a toll road. May Theilgaard Watts in *Reading the Landscape of America* has wonderful diagrams showing transitions from rural landscapes to urban ones.[82] An aerial view of your landscape provides information and insights unavailable elsewhere. The Farm Security Administration has 10 million images, including aerial images, available in black and white, natural colors, and infrared formats. High-quality, they include topographical landscape and cultural features. In Great Britain, aerial photographs have even located Iron Age settlements.[83] Look especially for water features, crossroads, and places where people gathered and traveled—such as rivers they traveled along—as well as places they avoided (waterfalls, rapids, or swamps). The topography around your site hints how it affected the women there (and the men too!). Tourist brochures, city guides, ships' logs, the WPA Writers Guide books, and local newspapers all help. Search out digitized photograph collections from historical societies and museums such as the Lower Eastside Tenement Museum and the New York Public Library.[84]

Restored Landscapes

Many people want to grab a shovel and start restoring their historic garden or landscape. Please don't! Use the ideas, sources, and concepts here to build your landscape file and plans. Once developed, such files as part of your Knowledge Base are useful for research, interpretation, and maintenance. Your landscape file should show changing relationships among buildings, structures, and natural features—how the landscape evolved; it should include Indigenous perspectives as appropriate. Landscapes as portions of ecosystems provide settings for all other tangible resources and provide greater insights for women's lives. At Tumacácori Mission, in a re-created garden once tended by women neophytes (converted Native Americans), 145 documented plants are raised, including peach trees, tarragon, and white sagebrush, which was used for digestive disorders, as deodorant, against Rocky Mountain Fever, and as smudge sticks in Native American ceremonies.[85] At Andrew Jackson's Hermitage in Tennessee, Rachel Jackson lovingly tended her rose garden; its design reflected her preferences and sense of beauty and provides insights into her; "I never saw anyone more enthusiastically fond of flowers than Rachel [Jackson]."[86] (See Figure 6.3—the plan for Rachel Jackson's rose garden provides insights into her life and values.) Plants growing in unexpected places often indicate earlier landscapes—a lonely rosebush marks a former garden or daffodils, a house site. Removing invasive species and restoring earlier ones requires work and patience. Some romantics cry that they want a battlefield landscape to "look just like the day of the battle."[87] Resist that notion—remind them of the horrors of wounded and dead soldiers and horses. We need to exercise caution in how "accurate" we should be, and focus on *all* the effects, which included enslaved women freed, and destroyed family farms.

Interpreting Women and Landscapes

Understanding foundational aspects of landscapes explains ways they shaped historical events and affected women's lives, provides insights into our foremothers' lives, and helps us interpret their lives with visitors. We need to interpret women as deeply involved in all these landscapes—planting corn, drying laundry, working in waterfall-powered mills, migrating northward and in every other direction, planting flowers around prairie homesteads, or raising sugar cane in Hawai'i. For example, the Lower Eastside Tenement Museum, by acquiring and preserving not only its original 97 Orchard St. but 103 Orchard St. as well, can now interpret a longer time span and include both the immediate neighborhood as well as its larger one, which included synagogues, pushcarts, shops, and ever-changing immigrant newcomers.[88] They can better interpret immigrants, immigration, and our nation's ambivalent policies and politics. The Willa Cather Foundation is restoring a 612-acre historic prairie to assist return of the native grasses, flowers, and birds that Willa Cather knew and featured in her *Song of the Meadowlark* and other books. Cather strongly identified with the prairie landscape, as she stated in her novel *My Ántonia*: "the earth was warm under me, and warm as I crumbled it through my fingers."[89] Visitors who can only imagine the ecological richness of prairies over a century ago will be able to explore them and so better understand Cather and her books.

Interpreting an *authentic* landscape will enhance your locale and provide your buildings context. Challenging, and often fascinating, reestablishing the landscape can be accomplished either physically or virtually. Landscapes with their many layers and constant changes provide many opportunities to attract visitor/community interest from gardeners, geologists, and kids who love to play in the mud—as our foremothers did. Landscapes entail a never-ending workload.

Tools for Chapter 6: Landscapes

Tool 6.1: Initial Landscape Analysis

Use your knowledge base to understand the landscape at your site/museum. Use the CESU ecosystem map and the NPS categories to determine "your" area in order to analyze it as vernacular, designed, historic, or ethnographic, as well as commercial, ranchlands, etc. Was it primarily industrial? Urban? Rural? This analysis identifies useful regional and national sources about your landscape/garden. What do you most need to know? Did major events occur here that changed your landscape—urbanization, a battle (or two), a railroad? Is your landscape famous for protests? Associated with a particular group? Collect landscape information including native, invasive, and historically available plants; methods; changes; and activities, making this organized information useful for future interpretive programs, maintenance schedules, budget development, and funding. The 1897 *Sears Catalog* lists "Choice Flower Seeds"; a superb source is Rudy J. Favretti and Joy Putnam Favretti, *Landscapes and Gardens for Historic Buildings: A Handbook for Reproducing and Creating Authentic Landscapes*.[90] Review previous research, especially archaeological and historic structure reports, and the existing landscape itself for relevant evidence. What particular factors influenced your landscape, such as availability of plant materials, contemporary styles, and preferences? Gather pertinent quotes, letters, newspaper references, photographs/drawings, garden notes, etc. Determine which females most interacted with the landscape—a wife who gardened, girls who played there, women who harvested wild berries. Understanding how women interacted with landscapes will help identify research needs and interpretive opportunities.

Tool 6.2: Establish a Landscape File and Maps

Develop landscape maps that show key features during the primary period of your museum/historic site, using evidence from the research in Tool 6.1. Key features include landforms, water features, roads and trails, structures (irrigation ditches, bridges), and buildings. Use additional transparent maps or GIS overlays to depict different time periods. Then map relevant women's movements onto the base landscape map to show patterns and raise questions to generate programs, exhibits, FAQs, and web items. For example, on the base map, locate women's daily routines and outdoor work areas such as hoeing, drying clothes, or going to school. Show routes from house to town, or factory to church to home, or house to well to chicken coop to fields. Show tangible resources or their previous locations, such as barn, shed, trellis, and fences. Assume that the landscape has changed—that many acres once surrounded farms, but only a few acres do now; or that once-flowing streams are now undergrounded; or that neighborhoods have drastically changed, making it difficult to picture historic ones.

Tool 6.3: Interpret Women's Landscapes

Develop interpretive programs that best show how women interacted with your landscapes and different ways to restore it if possible, otherwise to represent it. Programs can be as simple as growing a girl's favorite flowers, growing and processing indigo fabric dye, or cooking with seasonal herbs or chilies. Or interpretive programs can be as complex as restoring the prairie ecosystem that once surrounded your locale, as at the Willa Cather Center in Nebraska. Sharing native plants helps visitors discover the "natural supermarket" women once harvested.

Tool 6.4: Reestablish the Historic Landscape

Now, start digging!

Notes

1. Eva Mahoney, "Interview with Willa Cather," *Omaha Sunday World-Herald*, November 27, 1921; quoted in Mildred R. Bennett, *The World of Willa Cather* (Lincoln: University of Nebraska Press, 1989), 139.
2. Tara Travis, "Spider Woman's Grand Design: Making Native American Women Visible in Two Southwestern History Sites," in *Her Past Around Us: Interpreting Sites for Women's History* (Malabar: Krieger Publishing Company, 2003).
3. Willa Cather and Sharon O'Brien, *Early Novels and Stories: The Troll Garden / O Pioneers! / The Song of the Lark / My Antonia / One of Ours* (New York: Library of America, 1987).
4. Charles A. Birnbaum, "Preservation Brief 36: Protecting Cultural Landscapes: Planning, Treatment and Management of Historic Landscapes" (NPS, September 1994), https://www.nps.gov/tps/how-to-preserve/briefs/36-cultural-landscapes.htm.
5. Julie Roy Jeffrey, "There Is Some Splendid Scenery: Women's Responses to the Great Plains Landscape," *Great Plains Quarterly* 8 (1988).
6. Elizabeth Cady Stanton, *Eighty Years & More: Reminiscences, 1815–1897*, reprint 1971 (New York: Schocken Books, 1898), 293.
7. Colonial Williamsburg Foundation, Virtual Williamsburg, https://research.history.org/vw1776/3d/.
8. A national consortium of federal agencies, universities, and nonprofits. See www.cesu.org.

9. "A shabby little apartment on the bottom floor," Margaret Mitchell House, Atlanta History Center, http://www.atlantahistorycenter.com.

10. Cultural Landscape Foundation definition, tclf.org.

11. May Wynne Lamb, *Life in Alaska, The Reminiscences of a Kansas Woman, 1916–1919.* Dorothy Wynne Zimmerman, ed. (Lincoln: University of Nebraska Press, 1988).

12. Reed Engle, "Skyline Drive," NPS, Shenandoah National Park, https://www.nps.gov/shen.

13. Katherine K. Ziff, *Asylum on the Hill: History of a Healing Landscape* (Athens: Ohio University Press 2012). In 1877, they harvested 11,000 heads of cabbage, 136. See also http://ballgardens.iupui.edu/history.html.

14. Vera Norwood and Janice Monk, eds., *The Desert Is No Lady: Women Writers and Artists of the Southwest* (New Haven: Yale University Press, 1987). 2013 HALS Challenge: "Documenting the Cultural Landscapes of Women," https://www.asla.org.

15. Suzanne M. Spencer-Wood, "Gendering the Creation of Green Urban Landscapes in America at the Turn of the Century," in *Shared Spaces and Divided Places: Material Dimensions of Gender Relations and the American Historical Landscape* (Knoxville: University of Tennessee Press, 2003), 53.

16. The Cultural Landscape Foundation, "Beatrix Farrand (1872–1959)," *Pioneers* (blog), n.d., https://tclf.org/pioneer/beatrix-farrand.

17. ASLA Staff, "Vilma Pérez Blanco: A Pioneer in Puerto Rico's Landscape," ASLA Women in Landscape Architecture, December 7, 2012, https://Thefield.Asla.Org/2012/12/07/Vilma-Perez-Blanco-A-Pioneer-In-Puerto-Ricos-Landscape/Mainimages_Puntoverde.

18. See http://tclf.org/tregaron-estate-update-former-landslide-site.

19. "Beatrix Farrand Gets a Fresh Look," *"The Dirt"* ASLA, http://dirt.asla.org/2013/03/11/beatrix-farrand-gets-a-fresh-look/.

20. See http://www.annespencermuseum.com/index.php. See also https://eudorawelty.org/the-garden/.

21. See http://www.minnesotaschoolofbotanicalart.com/styled-5/index.html; see Eloise Butler, "A Collection of Garden Experiences—1916," http://friendsofthewildflowergarden.org / pages/history/ebwriting/annals_experiences1916.html.

22. See http://mountauburn.org/visit/enjoy-mount-auburn.

23. Andrew Jackson Downing, *Cottage Residences or a Series of Designs for Rural Cottages and Cottage-Villas, and Their Gardens and Grounds: Adapted to North America* (New York: Wiley & Putnam, 1842), https://archive.org/stream/cottageresidence00downrich /163/mode/2up.

24. Andrew Jackson Downing, *Cottage Residences,* Preface and 134–35.

25. *Godey's Lady's Book,* March 1852—*Plans for Flower Gardens.* More history at: http://www.accessible-archives.com/2015/04/how-to-plan-a-flower-garden-1852/#ixzz3hhKOHuDd.

26. Jill Cowley, "Place and Gender: Applying Gender Theory to the Documentation and Management of Cultural Landscapes," *CRM,* NPS, 2000.

27. Jeffery F. Burton, *Garden Management Plan: Gardens and Gardens at Manzanar* (NPS: Manzanar National Historic Site, 2015).

28. Erin Blakemore, "This Huge Women's March Drowned Out a Presidential Inauguration in 1913," January 17, 2018, https://www.history.com/news/this-huge-womens-march -drowned-out-a-presidential-inauguration-in-1913.

29. Margaret S. Creighton, *The Colors of Courage: Gettysburg's Forgotten History: Immigrants, Women, and African Americans in the Civil War's Defining Battle* (New York: Basic Books, 2005).

30. My thanks to Andy Mach, West Virginia University, for his assistance.

31. Angela Tooley, "Lucinda Hardage (1848–1940): The Last Living Link to the Battle of Kennesaw Mountain," Kennesaw Mountain National Battlefield Park, n.d.

32. Mary Ann Webster Loughborough, *My Cave Life in Vicksburg: A Woman's Account of the Siege of Vicksburg in 1863* (Bedford: Applewood Books, 1864, 2008), 98.
33. Interpretive sign, NPS, personal visit, Wilson's Creek National Battlefield, 2009.07.13.
34. Daniel Worster, *A River Running West: The Life of John Wesley Powell* (New York: Oxford University Press, 2000), 83–95.
35. Stephanie McCurry, *Confederate Reckoning: Power and Politics in the Civil War South* (Cambridge: Harvard University Press, 2010).
36. Margaret S. Creighton, *The Colors of Courage*, 2005.
37. Matilda Pierce, in Student Programming, Gettysburg NMP, *The Impact of War: The Slyder Family Farm Teachers' Guide* (Gettysburg: NPS, n.d.), 20. https://www.nps.gov/gett/learn/education/upload/Slyder_Farm_Guide.pdf.
38. Margaret Creighton, *The Colors of Courage*, 2005.
39. Margaret Creighton, *The Colors of Courage*, 2005, 154.
40. From https://www.nps.gov/wicr/learn/photosmultimedia/virtual-tour-stop-2.htm (Acc. 2016.09.10). Personal visit, 2009. Lydia Leister, http://civilwarwomenblog.com/lydia-leister-farm/; and http://dahts.tripod.com/; for HABs floorplan and elevation, domesticartshonorabletradessociety/id9.html.
41. Melissa A. Connor, "What Price Victory: Human Remains Found at Big Hole Battlefield, 1991," Report for NPS Rocky Mountain Regional Office (Lincoln: Midwest Archeological Center NPS, 1992).
42. "U.S. Military Attacks," https://www.nps.gov/biho/learn/historyculture/index.htm.
43. See Virginia Scharff and Carolyn Brucken, *Home Lands: How Women Made the West* (Los Angeles: University of California Press, 2010); L. Loendorf and L. O. Weston, "An Examination of Tipi Rings in the Bighorn Canyon-Pryor Mountain Area," *The Plains Anthropologist*, 28:146–155; "From Microcosm to Macrocosm: Advances in Tipi Ring Investigation and Interpretation," Leslie B. Davis, ed. (1983). http://www.wnpa.org/research-item/tent-circles-provide-proof-of-life-on-the-plains/; L. Loendorf and L.O. Weston, "Proof of Life: Tent Circles at Bighorn Canyon," 1983.
44. Sam W. West and Helene L. Baldwin, "The Water Supply of El Morro National Monument," Geological Survey Water Supply Paper 1766 (Washington, DC: US Geological Survey, GPO, 1965), http://pubs.usgs.gov/wsp/1766/report.pdf. Thanks to Robert Munson for his generous assistance at Cabrillo NM, April 30, 2017. See https://www.nps.gov/cabr/.
45. Oñate was first there in 1598 with 1,000 settlers; but left his inscription in 1605.
46. Barbara Pearson Yocum, "Historic Structure Report, The Stanton House," (Lowell: National Park Service Women's Rights NHP, 1998), 18–22. http://www.nps.gov/wori/learn/history-culture/upload/Stanton-House-HSR-2.pdf.
47. Travis, "Spider Woman"; Rosalyn R. LaPier, "Here's What No One Understands about the Dakota Access Pipeline Crisis: Understanding "Sacred" Sites." *Washington Post*, November 4, 2016, https://www.washingtonpost.com/posteverything/wp/2016/11/04/heres-what-no-one-understands-about-the-dakota-access-pipeline-crisis/.
48. Annette Kolodny, *The Lay of the Land: Metaphor As Experience and History in American Life and Letters* (Chapel Hill: University of North Carolina Press, 1984); Kolodny, *The Land Before Her: Fantasy and Experience of the American Frontiers, 1630–1860* (Chapel Hill: University of North Carolina Press, 2014).
49. Susan Sleeper-Smith, *Indigenous Prosperity and American Conquest: Indian Women of the Ohio River Valley, 1690–1792* (Chapel Hill: University of North Carolina Press, 2018), 61.
50. Harriet Fish Backus, *Tomboy Bride: A Woman's Personal Account of Life in Mining Camps of the West* (Portland: Westwinds Press, 1980); http://www2.ctahr.hawaii.edu/costume/quilts/brochure01.html.

51. Danielle McGuire convincingly argues for a reinterpretation of civil rights history as intimately tied to the Black community defending Black women's right to protect their bodies, especially from interracial rape, in *At the Dark End of the Street: Black Women, Rape and Resistance—A New History of the Civil Rights Movement from Rosa Parks to the Rise of Black Power* (New York: Alfred A. Knopf, 2010).

52. David M. Kennedy, "Up from Hyde Park," *New York Times*, April 19, 1992, http://www.nytimes.com/1992/04/19/books; Blanche Wiesen Cook, *Eleanor Roosevelt*, Volume One, 1884–1933 (New York: Viking Press, 1992).

53. Christina Hanhardt, "Places and Spaces of LGBTQ Collective Identity Formation," in *LGBTQ America: A Theme Study of Lesbian, Gay, Bisexual, Transgender, and Queer History* (online: National Park Service and National Park Foundation, 2016), www.nps.gov/subjects/tellingallamericanstories/lgbtqthemestudy.htm.

54. Esther Newton, *Cherry Grove, Fire Island: Sixty Years in America's First Gay and Lesbian Town*, Rev. 1993 (Chapel Hill: Duke University Press Books, 2014).

55. Stella M. Drumm, *Down the Santa Fe Trail and into Mexico: The Diary of Susan Shelby Magoffin, 1846–1847* (New Haven: Yale University Press, 1926); Kansas Historical Society, "Susan Shelby Magoffin," in *Kansapedia* (Topeka: Kansas Historical Society, May 2009), https://www.kshs.org/kansapedia/susan-shelby-magoffin/12137.

56. Harriett Bidwell Shaw, "Crossing the Plains, the Journal of Harriett Bidwell Shaw" (Kansas Memory, 1851), http://www.kansasmemory.org/item/209694/text. See Oct. 1, 1851, 7.

57. Joanne Wilke, *Eight Women, Two Model Ts, and the American West.* (Lincoln: University of Nebraska Press, 2007).

58. Virginia Scharff, "Gender and Genius: The Auto Industry and Femininity," in *The Material Culture of Gender, The Gender of Material Culture* (Winterthur: Winterthur Museum, 1997), 145. See also Heather Huyck, "Since 1918: Women in the National Park Service," *Courier*, January 1980.

59. Nell Hughes Boyle, personal communication; personal experience, 1973, Campaway, Lincoln, Nebraska.

60. Barbara Barden Margerum, *Homeless on the Range: Life on the Road in a Model T Ford during the Great Depression* (Santa Barbara: San Leandro Press, 2009), 10; Janet Robertson, *The Magnificent Mountain Women: Adventures in the Colorado Rockies* (Lincoln: University of Nebraska Press, 1990), 121–42. https://www.nps.gov/romo.

61. Teaching with Historic Places, "Adeline Hornbek and the Homestead Act: A Colorado Success Story" (NPS, n.d.), https://www.nps.gov/nr/twhp/.

62. Solomon Butcher, *The Chrisman Sisters*, 1887, Nebraska State Historical Society.

63. See Marcia Hensley, *Staking Her Claim: Women Homesteading the West* (Glendo: High Plains Press, 2008); H. Elaine Lindgren, *Land in Her Own Name: Women Homesteaders in North Dakota* (Norman: University of Oklahoma Press, 1991); Teaching with Historic Places, "Adeline Hornbek and the Homestead Act: A Colorado Success Story" (NPS, n.d.), https://www.nps.gov/nr/twhp/wwwlps/lessons/67hornbek/67hornbek.htm.

64. Barbara Howe, "Women and Architecture," in OLLI (Morgantown, 2013).

65. Charles Dawes house, kitchen window, Evanston, personal observation.

66. Atlanta History Center, "Bina Lockett," maid at Swan Mansion, personal visit, 2015.

67. Jessica Ellen Sewell, *Women and the Everyday City: Public Space in San Francisco 1890–1915* (Minneapolis: University of Minnesota Press, 2011).

68. Thanks to Beth Boland for her tour of these streets for the 1997 National Trust for Historic Preservation Conference. See Monica Domosh and Joni Seager, *Putting Women in Place: Feminist Geography Makes Sense of the World* (New York: Guilford Press, 2001).

69. Cultural geographers, Domosh and Seager, *Putting Women in Place* discussed places where women were welcome or not, and the "safety" issues involved.

70. Rosie the Riveter World War II Homefront National Historical Park, https://www.nps.gov/rori/learn/historyculture/index.htm. Special to the *New York Times*, "Industrial Deaths since Pearl Harbor 37,600, Exceeding military deaths by 7,500 Number Killed in War," *New York Times*, January 21, 1944.

71. Liza Mundy, *Code Girls: The Untold Story of the American Women Code Breakers of World War II* (New York: Hachette Books, 2017).

72. Laura Schumm, "America's Patriotic Victory Gardens," *Hungry History*, May 29, 2014, http://www.history.com/news/hungry-history/americas-patriotic-victory-gardens.

73. Stella M. Drumm, *Down the Santa Fe Trail, 1926*. Most travelers died from disease and accidents. Drumm has been criticized for her heavy editing. See Bureau of Land Management Trails websites, www.blm.gov.

74. Many women remember men's whistles and hostile calls when they walked past construction sites. California suffragists worked to make women's public presence more acceptable. See Sewell, *Women and the Everyday City*, 2011, Chapter 5, "Spaces of Suffrage."

75. Monica Domosh and Joni Seager, *Putting Women in Place*, 93. A terrific book.

76. Stephanie M. H. Camp. "The Pleasures of Resistance: Enslaved Women and Body Politics in the Plantation South, 1830–1861." *Journal of Southern History* 68, no. 3 (2002): 533–72.

77. "Margaret Garner," Ohio History Connection, n.d., http://www.ohiohistorycentral.org/w/Margaret_Garner; Toni Morrison, *Beloved: A Novel* (New York: Alfred A. Knopf, 1987).

78. Victor H. Green, *The Negro Motorist Green Book* (New York: Victor Green, 1940). See https://digitalcollections.nypl.org, and Evan Andrews, "*The Green Book*: The Black Travelers' Guide to Jim Crow America," History Channel, February 6, 2017, https://www.history.com.

79. Anne Kelly Knowles, ed., *Placing History: How Maps, Spatial Data, and GIS Are Changing Historical Scholarship* (Redlands: ESRI Press, 2008). Some land records are digitized.

80. Joan Jensen, *Loosening the Bonds: Mid-Atlantic Farm Women, 1750–1850* (New Haven: Yale University Press, 1988).

81. See http://thehermitage.com/learn/mansion-grounds/garden-grounds/landscape.

82. May Theilgaard Watts, *Reading the Landscape of America* (New York: Collier Books, 1975).

83. Christopher Taylor, *The Archaeology of Gardens*, Shire Archaeology 30 (Aylesbury, UK: Shire Archaeology, 1983). See "Aerial Archaeology Project Reveals Rich Archaeology of Norfolk" by Culture 24 Staff, *Culture 24: Art, History, Science*, Jan. 15, 2009, http://www.culture24.org.uk/history-and-heritage/archaeology.

84. See https://digitalcollections.nypl.org. and https://www.tenement.org.

85. Penny Waterstone, "Tumacácori NHP: Courtyard Garden: Plant Origins & Historical Uses" (National Park Service, 2000) in Jill Cowley, "Place and Gender: Applying Gender Theory to the Documentation and Management of Cultural Landscapes" *CRM*, no. 7 (Washington, DC: NPS, 2000).

86. Diary of Juliana Margaret Courtney Connor, September 3, 1827; University of North Carolina library, http://finding-aids.lib.unc.edu/00174. My thanks to Marsha Mullin, vice president of museum services Andrew Jackson's Hermitage; http://thehermitage.com/learn/mansion-grounds/garden-grounds/garden/.

87. Member of US House of Representatives to author, Gettysburg NMP, 1990.

88. See The Tenement Museum, www.tenement.org.

89. Mildred R. Bennett, *The World of Willa Cather* (Lincoln: University of Nebraska Press, 1989).

90. *1897 Sears Roebuck & Company Catalogue [reprint]* (New York: Skyhorse Publishing, 2007); Rudy J. Favretti and Joy Putnam Favretti, *Landscapes and Gardens for Historic Buildings A Handbook for Reproducing and Creating Authentic Landscapes*, 3rd ed. (Lanham: Rowman & Littlefield Publishers/AASLH, 2017).

7

Architecture

The Built Environment

The two doors of the Narbonne House provide poignant architectural evidence of women's lives. The front door of the steep-roofed 1675 house faces *west*, but its shed addition door that faces *north* once had stone steps leading toward Essex Street, then the main thoroughfare of Salem, Massachusetts. Nathaniel Hawthorne, who wrote *The House of Seven Gables* (1851) while working nearby, described impoverished women too old to sew or teach reduced to running "cent shops," combination drug and hardware stores. Here, in mid-nineteenth-century Salem, widowed Sarah Narbonne and her unmarried daughter Sarah ran a cent shop in their remodeled kitchen whose inside wall shows alterations.[1] Curiously, the Essex Street door was divided horizontally, barn door–style, so that its upper half could open into a sales counter while the lower half remained shut. Here, architectural evidence literally opens a door to the world of small-time female entrepreneurs selling wares from inside their homes.

Architecture encloses space and provides visual and haptic approaches for researching historical change. It serves symbolic functions as when buildings declare their purpose with their front door styles.[2] We experience spaces when we walk into a tipi, ride the eight-story *industrial* elevator at Minneapolis Mill City Museum, or bask in the opulent Main Reading Room of the Library of Congress. We sense different room heights, rough floor textures, and light levels. Worn wooden stair treads and stained wallpaper reveal tenement living, while paint layers and odd hardware reflect changing room uses. Integral to museums and historical sites, architecture is an excellent interpretive resource to make women's past lives real to present visitors. But the built environment challenges us because we learn so little about it in history classes. We don't need to know Flemish bond brick masonry or the operation of single pipe steam furnaces, but we should appreciate the shade of a dogtrot for work or recognize women's special spaces.

Buildings and structures present further challenges because most architectural history focuses on the designs of famous male architects rather than on the women who inhabited their designs. This chapter will discuss architectural basics and ways to interpret women's history using buildings and structures found in our locales, with special attention to domestic buildings.

Architecture: Buildings and Structures

Walk into a building. Usually, it can tell you about itself and the women associated with it by its entrance; its types of rooms, and their relative sizes and relationships, construction, amount of light, temperature, and relationships with the outdoors. Architectural elements such as lath and plaster walls, or an electrified gaslight chandelier, indicate their residents' financial resources and

Figure 7.1. Late-seventeenth-century Narbonne House, 71 Essex Street, Salem, Massachusetts, as documented by the Historic American Building Survey (HABS) in 1933. HABS has photographed American architecture since the 1930s and stored the high-quality images at the Library of Congress.

HISTORIC AMERICAN BUILDINGS SURVEY, CREATOR. NARBONNE HOUSE, 71 ESSEX STREET, SALEM, ESSEX COUNTY, MASSACHUSETTS. DOCUMENTATION COMPILED AFTER 1933. PDF. RETRIEVED FROM THE LIBRARY OF CONGRESS, HTTPS:// WWW.LOC.GOV/ITEM/MA0165/. ACCESSED FEBRUARY 12, 2017.

lifestyles. A cabin with all life functions consolidated into one room supported a different lifestyle than a Victorian mansion with its highly specialized rooms—pantries, billiards, and nursery—or a picture-windowed suburban tract house. Historic buildings reflect the women who lived in them through décor, wall colors, and furniture arrangements. At the Historic Ephrata Cloister in Pennsylvania, a pre-Revolutionary German community, a small, plain bedchamber with a little window, narrow wooden bench, and wall cabinet in the Saaron—the sisters' building—reveals their austere pietist theology.[3] In contrast, Emily Inman's ornate bed in the intensively decorated Swan Mansion bedroom at the Atlanta History Center epitomizes her wealth—and her long widowhood. In contrast, her housekeeper had a room upstairs with a plain metal bedstead, trunk, chair, and electric fan.[4] Revealing in a different way, California architect Julia Morgan protected the privacy of lesbian physicians Clara Williams and Elsie Mitchell when she disguised their 1915 home as a shared doctors' office.[5]

Because historic buildings exemplify *actual* lifestyles rather than *prescribed* ones, "reading" their uses and alterations increases our understanding of how women lived. Proximity of rooms and access to each other facilitated or discouraged interaction among residents; public rooms were more decorated than family ones, with more formal behavior expected. Alterations and interior arrangements often show women's actual usage rather than a building's initial construction. Exploring old houses exposes hidden realities, such as the tiny attic room where a maid slept in stifling summer heat, connecting comfort levels with class differences.

Preservationists differentiate between *buildings* that protect humans and *structures* that provide infrastructure for transportation, utilities, and storage.[6] Buildings shelter humans and animals along with their possessions and activities, while structures enable transportation, storage, communication, and manufacturing. Buildings include houses, forts, schools, bars, and offices that enclose space from hostile environments and human threats, provide comfort and status, and shape human relationships. Buildings include mansions that flaunt residents' status and churches that proclaim worshipers' theology. A Friends (Quaker) Meeting House embodied its theology of gender equality; when its center partitions were closed, the space was *evenly* divided between men and women. In contrast, Spanish mission churches in the Southwest separated the male priest at the altar from the congregation in its central nave, reflecting Roman Catholic focus on sacraments that only their priests performed. Structures include infrastructure (dams, windmills, and sewer lines) as well as transportation (roads, automobiles, boats), storage (water towers, grain elevators), and communication (telegraph lines, television cables). While underappreciated, structures powerfully changed women's lives. Plumbing, electricity, and heating, cooling and ventilation (HVAC) replaced innumerable chores of tending fireplaces, lugging clean and dirty water, and emptying chamber pots. Women's workloads were dramatically altered when infrastructures were modernized, although many women waited decades to access such "conveniences."

Figure 7.2.   Friends Meeting House, West Branch, Iowa, showing symmetry of two identical exterior doors and an interior sliding partition for women's and men's separate meetings. Quaker worship uses neither altars nor pulpits.
FRIENDS MEETINGHOUSE, HERBERT HOOVER NHS, COURTESY OF THE NATIONAL PARK SERVICE

Architecture

Good architecture matches its environment and enhances our lives. In New England, steeply pitched roofs shed snow and interior fireplaces conserved precious heat; in the South, exterior fireplaces dissipated heat, and windows sought breezes. Colonial center halls provided ventilation, workspace, and a place for their beloved dancing while barring unwelcome intruders from interior rooms. Women peeled potatoes and placed their washing machines on their porches, greeted passersby, and created female-dominated spaces away from spousal demands.[7] With crowded interior spaces, women cooked and washed laundry outdoors, as 1949 photographs from El Paso, Texas, show.[8] Author Marjorie Kinnan Rawlings's home has many features designed to cope with pre-air-conditioned Florida, including cross-ventilation and screened porches for work and sleeping, assisted by electric fans. Screens and fly covers for food show evidence of insect issues.[9]

American architecture, both formally designed and vernacular, grew from North American, European, and African roots, ranging from ancient stonewalled desert southwest homes to three-room New York tenements, where children nightly slept on beds they made by lining up kitchen chairs across from the sofa.[10] Housing ranges from providing basic protection from the elements, to demonstrating middle-class respectability and upper-class status in the late eighteenth to early twentieth centuries; or mid-nineteenth-century protection of middle-class domesticity from the industrial world; or expressing family consumerism, once known as "Keeping Up with the Joneses." Residents frequently altered building interiors substantially *after* moving in. Twentieth-century houses constructed in massive subdivisions became differentiated as their inhabitants reconfigured them in the great American home Do-It-Yourself projects by enclosing garages or adding wings. Seasonal and temporary housing included indigenous remudas (shade bowers) where Navajo women wove their famous blankets/rugs, dome-shaped Apache wickiups, and Iroquois (or Haudenosaunee) longhouses.[11] On the nineteenth-century high plains, Native American women owned and determined access to their tipi homes; they constructed their tipis by first positioning long thin logs into a circle and then placing a buffalo skin cover over them. Mobile housing, somewhat inaccurately considered less permanent, includes house trailers, which provided less expensive housing during and after the Great Depression, and camping trailers dating before then.[12] By the mid-nineteenth century, well-to-do Americans built summer housing, often called cottages in the east and cabins in the west. In the 1940s lesbians in Buffalo, New York, claimed Winters Bar as their own women-defined space.[13] Bars provided gathering places for lesbians and locations for them to join other women when the more public parks and bathhouses of gay men were unavailable to women.[14]

Architectural history focuses on architects, styles, and changing design and construction methods. It assumes ownership or at least control of buildings of all kinds. We know more about architectural design, construction, and owners than about how female occupants interacted with the buildings they occupied and the structures they used. In architectural history, women are best known as historic preservationists of Great Men's homes than as builders of any, such as Ann Pamela Cunningham, who led preservation efforts for George and Martha Washington's plantation Mount Vernon, and the Ladies' Hermitage Association, who preserved Andrew and Rachel Jackson's home. Furthermore, until the twentieth century, few women owned "real property," in contrast to personal property. Legal limitations kept most married women from owning real estate outright; single women seldom had the financial strength to do so. Obviously, millions of women lived in and used such property, but they did not own it or fully control it, brothels being an exception.[15] Historically, a husband could legally sell their jointly occupied home without her permission. A few American women owned buildings, farms, and boardinghouses, such as Revolutionary War–era widow Christiana Campbell, who advertised "genteel Accommodations, and the very best Entertainment" at her Williamsburg, Virginia, tavern, as shown in her signed receipt acknowledging that George Washington had paid his bill.[16]

Figure 7.3. "The party encamped about twenty miles from the village. The women plant the poles of their tipis firmly in the ground and cover them with buffalo skin. A fire is soon made in the centre [sic] and the corn put on to boil. Their bread is kneaded and put in the ashes to bake."
BRAUN RESEARCH LIBRARY COLLECTION, AUTRY MUSEUM OF THE AMERICAN WEST, LOS ANGELES: P10711.

Basic Architectural Considerations

Architecture encloses space and creates the built world that we inhabit, although we infrequently consider its greater effects. Buildings with nearly infinite forms, whether made from imported or local materials, may have one floor or 110 and can be rigidly symmetrical or nearly haphazard, simply shaped or complex, windowless, or nearly all glass. Some rooms declare their importance with their elegant finishes while others are deliberately stark.

More useful to interpreting women's history than often recognized, buildings can tell us much in their many purposes. Building configurations demonstrate many gender patterns, such as a canned food assembly line where a group of women seated together at a table hand-cut onions, insurance companies where women sat in many rows of desks supervised by a single man, or interior windowless desks where female employees "protected" access to higher-status males in exterior offices.[17] Buildings reveal individual women's backgrounds or aspirations, such as the *mixed* hewn logs and sawn lumber home of Navajo activist Annie Wauneka, who fought for better medical care that combined traditional Navajo and Western medicine.[18] Architectural design reflects and shapes relationships when its elements facilitate or hinder movement from one part of a building to another with stairways, elevators, or adjacent rooms. Rita, wife of artist Thomas Hart Benton, had her ironing room next to their master bedroom; his studio was in the garage.[19] She wanted close proximity for her tasks while he needed slight distance. In contrast, door locks on bathrooms and parental bedrooms have often controlled access.

Few buildings remain unchanged over time. Historic buildings have decades of accretions, such as the installation of "new" plate-glass windows so shoppers could better see goods for sale. Such changes obscure the "original fabric" of the building—"modern" linoleum floors now cover wooden ones and dropped ceilings hide earlier pressed-tin ones. Look just above the cornice level of commercial buildings to find evidence of their earlier functions. Seek all the uses that your buildings have witnessed. The 1848 women's rights convention in Seneca Falls, New York, was held in the Wesleyan Chapel, which later became an opera house, then a car dealership, and in 1961 became the Seneca Falls Laundromat—still a busy laundromat when the Women's Rights National Historical Park opened in 1981.[20] The former chapel had ten apartments rented out and businesses including a telephone company.[21]

Technological changes have been crucial in transforming the built environment. Plumbing and electricity revolutionized women's lives, providing better sanitation, lighting, heating, and cooling. Before modern sanitation provided clean water and sewage disposal, intense urban living was difficult and disease ridden; without electricity, high-rise urban life would have been impossible. Nostalgia for families gathered around a single lamp on their center table overlooks the reality that the dim and smelly lamp was the best light available. Electric lights allowed individuals to disperse to separate rooms for greater autonomy. In northern Michigan, men requested telephones for their dressmaker, nurse, and schoolteacher daughters to support women's home-based occupations.[22] Using electric lights, telephones, safe drinking water, and interstate highways required infrastructure not yet invented or generally unavailable. Expectations for housing amenities and size have changed enormously: Compare the 100 square feet that housed a middling colonial family with 325 square feet for ten people in a tenement to the upscale 5,000-square-foot homes today.

Architectural Styles, Materials, and Methods

Architectural history books focus on architects and building styles from Georgian to Federal to Queen Anne to Arts & Crafts to Art Deco and Mid-Century Modern. Understanding basic concepts, terms, and the kind(s) of architecture at your museum will enable you to read buildings and better recognize female interactions with them. Knowledge of architectural principles and vocabulary facilitates work with preservationists and work crews. Buildings require a distinct vocabulary—distinguishing joists from studs, for example—and concepts such as load limits, original fabric, bays, and as-built. A "Materials and Methods of Construction" course or textbook that provides a solid foundation for understanding both modern and historic construction will help preserve and interpret architectural resources supplemented by sources specific to the style of your buildings.[23] Key architectural concepts include the basic building unit "pen," as in a single-pen or double-pen. For example, a one-room cabin is a single-pen, a two-room house is a double-pen, and a dogtrot has a covered passageway between two pens. A "bay," a door or window opening on a façade, conveys the complexity of a building—a three-bay building usually has one door between two windows. Visual presentations of buildings, or "plans," diagram the floor space; an "elevation" or façade shows one side, and a "cross-section" is a cutaway of the inside. "Studs" are vertical building members, "joists," horizontal ones; "headers" provide needed support over doorways, and "trusses" or beams that span longer distances.[24]

Architects use many concepts and terms to discuss their craft. Anyone working at a museum or historic site will benefit from learning about your relevant architectural period. A deeper understanding of a particular architectural style greatly enhances historical understanding by knowing what was—and wasn't—possible, available, or stylish during a historical period and location. This knowledge helps with both preservation and interpretation, as it will help distinguish intervening changes that may or may not be significant. Standardized lumber sizes, as in a

"2-by-4 board" (not its actual dimensions), structural steel, high-tech glass, and plastics, as well as CAD (computer assisted drawing), make possible architectural forms once hard to imagine. Knowing the basics about relevant architecture helps you read buildings and why they were constructed as they were. The tremendous changes help us appreciate what we now have, as well as what our predecessors had, such as truly wide boards of lumber from virgin forests. Dramatic transportation and communication changes, railroads and then trucks, and airplanes created a national marketplace giving women purchasing choices and convenience. Knowing the basics helps you understand the resource and increases your credibility with maintenance workers, preservationists, and the public.

Vernacular Architecture

Architecture that professionally trained architects designed contrasts with vernacular architecture that was built with local knowledge and cultural traditions.[25] Vernacular architecture reflects different geographic regions with their distinct environmental and social patterns. Southwestern Pueblo peoples constructed their homes of pounded-earth bricks with adobe coatings, while Northeastern Haudenosee/Iroquois built longhouses of logs covered with bark sheeting. English ship-building techniques framed post-and-beam houses, as Swedish log traditions became symbolic American log cabins. The French colonial architecture of upright logs rammed into the soil still stands at the home of widow Marie Courtois Bolduc in Ste. Geneviève, Missouri.[26] Generations of Creoles built shotgun houses in Louisiana, and southern antebellum buildings reflect African traditions. Many museum buildings are vernacular, such as the 1860 Schulz farmhouse at Old World Wisconsin, with its *schwarz kuche* (black kitchen), "basically a large chimney in the center of the house," or the family home in North Carolina that African American Pauli Murray's grandfather built.[27] Vernacular architecture changed when new technology brought greater comfort, but its designs, construction, and exteriors persisted.

Women as Architects and Builders

Before architecture became a profession in the late nineteenth century, men with the necessary capital, knowledge, and connections designed and constructed major buildings. Lacking access to architectural education or apprenticeship, only a few women—often with sponsors—became professional architects. Restaurateur Fred Harvey and the Santa Fe Railroad hired Mary Jane Colter to design still-extant iconic national park buildings; newspaperman William Randolph Hearst hired Julia Morgan to design Hearst Castle in California, one of more than 700 buildings she designed, often for wealthy women and women's organizations.[28] Even today, women architects struggle for professional recognition, as one recently stated, "I Am Not the Decorator: Female Architects Speak Out."[29] A few women had major, if obscured, roles in buildings such as the Venetian-styled art museum of Isabella Stewart Gardner in Boston or the Farnsworth House in Plano, Illinois, which Dr. Edith Farnsworth had prominent architect Mies van der Rohe build for her as a retreat in 1951.[30] Gender expectations affected the complex and ambiguous relationship of Farnsworth and van der Rohe. The architecturally outstanding modernist "home" visually refutes then-prevalent norms of privacy and domesticity.[31]

Jane Addams did not *physically* build the thirteen buildings of the Hull-House settlement that once filled an entire Chicago city block, including a children's building, coffeehouse, boys' club, and others, in addition to the original 1856 mansion. With other Hull-House leaders, she oversaw the creation of a multicultural community, which provided immigrants services, and Progressives a think tank.[32] Now, only the mansion and the Arts and Crafts building remain, surrounded by

Figure 7.4.   Built for Edith Farnsworth as her private retreat, this epitome of modernist architecture designed by Ludwig Mies van der Rohe influenced the more famous Philip Johnson Glass House, while Edith's role has been obscured.

CAROL M. HIGHSMITH, PHOTOGRAPHER. FARNSWORTH HOUSE, PLANO, ILLINOIS, BETWEEN 1980 AND 2006. IMAGE RETRIEVED FROM THE LIBRARY OF CONGRESS, HTTPS://WWW.LOC.GOV/ITEM/2011631309. ACCESSED FEBRUARY 14, 2017.

the University of Illinois–Chicago Circle. Historic photographs provide crucial evidence of the massive buildings that once constituted the Hull-House operation.[33]

Close investigations of buildings *show* powerful stories. For decades, beginning in the 1860s, Hawai'ians sickened by leprosy (Hansen's disease) were exiled to isolated Kalaupapa on the island of Molokai.[34] The narrow Kalaupapa Visitors Building is divided by a high partition down its center, which allowed leprosy patients and their visitors to see but *not* touch each other—the architecture of fear. The Kalaupapa chapel floor evidences that relentless disease by three-inch-by-five-inch squares cut in its floor, allowing patients to spit out phlegm to increase their comfort and dignity. Interpretation has emphasized Father Damien, who ministered to Kalaupapa patients before dying himself from the then-fatal disease. The site should fully recognize Mother Marianne Cope and the six other Sisters of Saint Francis, originally from Syracuse, New York, who nursed patients for many decades. Now Mother Marianne's work is better recognized in a Kalaupapa National Historical Park publication, "A Place of Care: Mother Marianne Cope and the Kalaupapa Cultural Landscape," which states:

> Mother Marianne Cope advocated for a home specifically for girls and women, which opened at Kalaupapa in 1888 as the Charles R. Bishop Home for Unprotected Leper Girls and Women.

The home became an important feature of the landscape, developed as an entire complex . . . [she] saw the practical value of fruit as a food source for the home, and she understood the aesthetic value of the colorful flowers that helped cheer the spirits of the sick. In 1918, Mother Marianne passed away at Kalaupapa, leaving a landscape to tell her legacy of care.[35]

Investigating Architecture: Buildings

Using a building as a historical source for interpreting women's history focuses on how female *users* experienced it—how they shaped the building and how it shaped them. Of the many ways to analyze architecture, the elements of functionality, comfort, and access/privacy each provide different lenses to interpret women's history.

Functionality is the interplay between architecture and needs of women living or working with it. Fundamentally, architecture protects from the elements, other humans, animals, and pests, and provides adequate space for associated activities. Did the building *work* for the women with adequate space and light for their activities? Warning: Cultural values varied. What does the building's space tell us about women's *preferences* for privacy, propriety, style, circulation, cleanliness, and comfort? Did women need to accommodate themselves by moving outdoors or by rescheduling their activities? Closely related to functionality, flexibility considers how easily alterations were made when human needs changed or new technology such as electricity became available. How much have your buildings been altered? Some construction methods such as log or sod make changing room arrangements or adding plumbing/electricity difficult. Space allocation for major household activities has varied dramatically, reflecting different family compositions and household relationships. Consider how space was distributed within homes for sleep, food preparation/eating, childcare, social/family interactions, storage, quiet, reflection/prayer, reading/study, and recreation. Watch for the proportion of the space that female members had. Creativity and family support were sometimes involved. The family of prodigy-astronomer Maria Mitchell fashioned her a private study on their stairway landing while Pauli Murray's family placed her crib there.[36] Examine specialized functions such as sewing, which needed better light. Consider who was welcome in different parts of houses and under what circumstances. Most homes flow from the more public areas such as the living room to more private workspaces and personal ones. In a three-room ground-floor apartment called "the Dump," Georgia author Margaret Mitchell (1900–1949) used her front room to write and entertain, the middle room to dine, sleep, and sew at her sewing machine, and the back kitchen for her maid, Bessie Jordan, to cook.[37] Her front room was public; the middle room was shared with her husband, John Marsh, to eat and sleep; and the back kitchen was a service area, dividing "her" space from her cook's. Recognizing these spaces provides interpretive insights useful for understanding women's lives.[38]

Comfort, while not salient in the eighteenth century, now includes the control of noise, unwelcome insects and unwanted intrusions, steady temperature and humidity, the absence of mold and disgusting odors, and the presence of light, and also soft surfaces and smooth flooring. Decorating can also be embraced here with stylish textures, colors, and designs. Compare George and Martha Washington's bedroom with the reconstructed slave cabin at Mount Vernon, or a basement kitchen with a main-floor one.

Another architectural element, access/privacy, is simply the ability to exercise personal power and keep one's own actions to oneself with walls, closed doors, or signs, as in "Miss [Maria] Mitchell is Busy," which protected her from interruptions. Privacy also connotes women's ability to conceal their actions or possessions. Look for adult women who shared their bedrooms. How much privacy and/or decision-making authority did different women have in your buildings? Consider how building layouts—spaces and connections among rooms—shaped interactions among family and other household members, such as detached kitchens for enslaved workers and servants' sleeping spaces in attics or basements. Back stairways separated servants from the families who employed them. Some house plans had entrances directly into the kitchen to separate male farmworkers from private family rooms. Privacy expectations have increased; once entire families slept together, and privies had multiple seats for adults and children.[39]

Access, nearly opposite of privacy, allowed women to go where they wanted. Especially salient for women, access is both physical movement and consent. Climb a ladder into a home carved into the south-facing wall of Bandelier Canyon and duck under its low doorway into a surprisingly large circular room, where ancient soot still marks its ceiling. Imagine carrying a child up that ladder or up the dark, twisting Narbonne house stairs. Exclusion affected women's lives when they were long denied access to knowledge spaces in the home, higher education buildings, and official places. Laws and custom excluded women from jury rooms, locker rooms, pool halls, golf clubs, and saloons as "male preserves," where politically useful information was available.[40] Temperance women trespassed when they swept into saloons protesting alcohol.[41] Or a few women were allowed into architectural spaces under specific circumstances and in very small numbers, which limited the few allowed "in" as well as the majority of most women kept from decision-making locations. Women were long present in courtrooms as defendants and witnesses, but their *right* to be in jury rooms only came in 1964. In sharp contrast to today, many elite colleges and professional medical and law schools accepted women relatively recently and in extremely small percentages until the late twentieth century, such as Supreme Court Associate Justice Ruth Bader Ginsburg, who was one of nine women in her 1956 law school class of 500

Figure 7.5.   In 1920, male-only Masons expectantly waited for their dinner while the two women clearly responsible for feeding them stand almost hidden by the kitchen door in Calumet, Michigan.
COURTESY KEWEENAW NHP, THE NATIONAL PARK SERVICE.

at Harvard University.[42] In various circumstances, Japanese, Black, Irish, and Jewish women, as well as Latinas, were specifically barred from some locales. Some zoos allowed Black women only when they accompanied White children, while some churches allowed women to watch ceremonies but not fully participate.[43] Some churches prohibited women from performing their duties near the altar when menstruating.[44] In a much more gender-segregated society, women were banned as "bad luck" in mines and on ships, although female family members, such as whaling captains' wives, were allowed. Although barred from membership in men's organizations, women frequently cooked for and served dinners in their halls. Rationales for exclusion claimed that women were distracting, inferior, "unclean," or simply unwanted. Before the late 1920s, many hotels allowed women entrance only by side doors, ostensibly to protect them from unwanted male attention. That restriction clearly reinforced women's second-class status.[45]

Some women gained individual access to male domains, usually from a male family member. Decades before women could become lawyers, Judge Daniel Cady allowed his daughter Elizabeth Cady [Stanton] access to his study, where she studied his law books. In 1848, she based the "Declaration of Sentiments" on knowledge she gained there. Women were not admitted to law schools for another fifty years, and then only a very few. Enslaved young Cornelia Smith Fitzgerald was welcomed by her White grandfather into his study, where she illegally learned to read. She later raised her granddaughter, who became the distinguished lawyer-activist and first Black Episcopal woman priest Pauli Murray, an example of generational accumulation of intellectual accomplishment during American apartheid.[46]

Changing Families, Changing Domestic Spaces

Domestic spaces have continually changed uses. Early colonial parlors shifted from displaying the master bed and best possessions to become social spaces, then formal living rooms, then family rooms, while the medieval remnant "halls" became kitchens. Dining rooms—once the epitome of Victorian propriety and male prestige decorated with animal trophies—while repeatedly declared defunct, still survive for family celebrations.[47] In contrast, boardinghouses used dining rooms as their common space. Unlike earlier ones, kitchens today focus less on food preservation than food preparation and presentation. Once, family yards were small farms with barns, large gardens and even orchards. The very wealthy once had outbuildings of dairy, washhouse, and smokehouse, which were domestic work hubs. Barnyards and urban backyards had to suffice for many. Then, as plumbing came and water heaters replaced heating water on stoves, mothers no longer bathed their children in tenement sinks.[48] Cooking technology evolved from open fireplaces to stoves burning wood, then a succession of coal, gas, electricity, and microwaves that require less tending. Storage needs changed with canned, refrigerated, then frozen foods. Once, many women stored potatoes and root vegetables in cellars and dried herbs in attics, while Hispanic attics held raisins, tamale husks, and dried pears.[49]

With industrialization, the family—once an economic partnership—was transformed, as many fathers/husbands joined the wage economy and were paid for their labor while wives/mothers remained in the older exchange, "unpaid" economy. Because women have been linked so tightly to home-work and because so many museums and historic sites are historic houses, understanding how women functioned economically and socially *inside* homes is crucial. Women's roles as child-bearers, child-raisers, educators, and cultural transmitters were critical for families and the larger society to function. Visitors find intriguing the huge variety of activities women undertook in their homes. Rather than foregrounding homes as domestic spaces, we should emphasize them as women's work places—both paid and unpaid, legal and illegal—where female domestic skills generated their livelihoods and raised the next generation. For example, when Historic New England renamed and reinterpreted the "Harrison Gray Otis Mansion" to the "Otis

House," its focus enlarged from the one elite man there to include *all* the women who worked and lived there in a family home; private hospital; genteel boardinghouse; and by 1900, a lodging house that rented rooms to both sexes, with all-female staff.[50]

Even with the industrial revolution, this enormous unpaid, invisible female labor force remained as crucial as the paid labor of males, because women provided the diverse kinds of subsistence and social support men needed. Women worked hard in this domestic economy, providing goods (butter, eggs, clothing, quilts, braided straw for hats) and services (lodging, meals, tourist homes, piano lessons, refashioned clothing) on a massive scale. Wives and mothers were expected to scrimp and save and to stretch family budgets by scavenging coal, picking and selling wild berries, and haggling to purchase foodstuffs less expensively. From the genteel to the scruffy, boardinghouses were once common urban lodgings managed by women, including those from ethnic groups opposed to having women work outside their homes. To pay mortgages or simply survive economically, women ran boardinghouses that provided meals, lunch buckets, laundry, mending, and beds—while their own family members sometimes crowded into a single bedroom. A few women who managed boardinghouses made more money than their husbands.[51] President Lincoln died in the Petersen House, an upscale boardinghouse then owned by butcher William Petersen and Anna Petersen, his wife.[52] The once-elegant mansion of later-impoverished "unsinkable" Molly Brown also became a boardinghouse.[53]

By the 1920s, advertisements promoted electric appliances as "the New Servant in the House" to replace women who preferred to work in factories and retail stores.[54] During Prohibition, some women made "hooch" in their kitchens; one teenage girl delivered clean laundry and illegal booze that her widowed mother made, while another woman cooked spaghetti sauce in her basement to survive the Depression.[55] Frank Lloyd Wright claimed to design "servant-less" homes with "Usonian" simplified domestic architecture, such as the Pope-Leighey House. Sunbeam appliances, while expensive, brought efficiency and status with their Mixmaster and Coffeemaster in 1938.[56] With twentieth-century urbanization and then suburbanization, many women became primarily identified as consumers, while continuing their roles as caregivers and domestic managers. Post–World War II architects designed Cape Cod styles in suburbs such as Levittown, and compact ranch-style homes that decreased building costs and housework. Efficiency experts replaced stand-alone stoves and tables with continuous kitchen counters and electric appliances. The 1950s *Guide to Easier Living* called for informal lifestyles with only an occasional "cleaning lady."[57] Middle-class housewives found themselves isolated in the suburbs, with only the company of their children as they drove endless errands and carpools.[58] Educated women who found their assigned but constricted role deeply unsatisfying helped spawn Betty Friedan's "Problem without a Name." As they acted on their frustration, second-wave feminism blossomed.[59]

Constructing Women's Spaces, Informal and Formal

American women were deeply affected by the major historical transitions in American society in the early nineteenth century. During that era, American society shifted from a rural, agrarian-subsistence society to an urban, industrial, and commercial one, followed by a suburbanized, post-industrial one. Living in a society that often dismissed their abilities, women sometimes created and controlled their own spaces, including businesses of millinery shops and beauty parlors and organizations of college sororities and Girl Scout camps. African American women created spaces of their own in beauty parlors; because the beauticians as professionals were independent from the White world, in contrast to many Black women who were domestic workers then, they were able to organize for civil rights quite effectively—and invisibly from the White world. In African American women's beauty shops, "the ability to gather in a place of pampering and self-care led to community activism."[60]

Figure 7.6.   Domestic vernacular architecture, a home in late-nineteenth-century small-town Kansas with a nearby grain elevator, a structure that stored wheat until shipped by the adjacent railroad tracks. Filled by an immigrant family and their nine children, the front porch has since been closed in. Note the nearby grain elevator, a structure that stored wheat until shipped by train.
PHOTOGRAPH BY TONI COTTRELL, BENNINGTON, KANSAS.

Women also created crucial if ephemeral spaces with quilting bees, church women's mis-sionary projects, and Tupperware parties that combined work with socializing.[61] These gather-ings, while elusive to document, provided women with sought-after companionship, life-based insights, and alternative perspectives. Often women hosted each other in their homes. They held tea parties where activists planned the Seneca Falls convention; later, lesbians held open house parties and found friendly bars where they formed their own communities and conscious-ness.[62] Women founded female-centric institutions of public libraries, nursery schools, feminist art spaces, and later, lesbian resource centers.[63] Homes for unwed mothers—girls and women "sent away" because they were pregnant—had social stigma and imprisoning characteristics.[64] Search for locales accessible to the women/girls associated with your museum to understand how those varied places functioned in their lives. While challenging to research, such home gatherings can be an interpretive opportunity. Involve visitors to help re-create meetings where women discussed literature, educated each other, or planned activism. Many female-infused institutions opened. Women's "seminaries," colleges, sororities, normal schools for teachers, nursing schools, and woman's clubs built female-oriented spaces to provide the companionship, knowledge access, and respite men had long had in their colleges and private clubs. To open schools, settlement houses, and clubs, women had to access sufficient social and financial capital to erect buildings, both nonprofit and commercial. Consider how much access the women at your site/museum had to buildings with female-focused spaces and organizations. Lesbians met in each other's homes, in bars, and in restaurants known as welcoming. Sue Gibson, cofounder of a women-only club and restaurant in Iowa City, explained that, "Women of the present time may not understand that men had a way of taking over, of filling the spaces of classrooms, meetings, and areas of recreation with their concerns and plans and often, louder voices. Grace and Rubies [a women's-only restaurant in town in the 1970s] provided a place where women could go to share their ideas and feelings with other women and to enjoy one small space away from men."[65] Some lesbian locales that provided women respite and support lasted many years, but many did not. Sadly, as the blog lostwomynsspace notes, "Quite often, the herstorian tracking down lesbian bars finds erasure and disappearance more than neat anecdotes and personal reminiscences. And because [induced] amnesia is not uncommon in womyn's history, it is important to note and record the erasures as well."[66] Other female-oriented spaces have also disappeared.

Nineteenth-century women organized to help, even protect, younger women who moved to cities. They rented or constructed buildings. In 1860, women's organizations such as the Montana YWCA, met trains and urged traveling females to stay at the Y's newly opened boardinghouses for female students, factory workers, and teachers in order to avoid the "risks" of lodging houses.[67] The Phillis Wheatley Club in Cleveland, Chicago, and other cities provided lodging and social space for African American women. The YWCA in New York City rented rooms for both Black and White women (separately, until 1940).[68] The Philadelphia New Century Guild (1906) building served "self-supporting women" with meals, evening classes, and rooms. Hull-House in Chicago opened "Jane Clubs" for single women clerks.[69] Demonstrating the accomplishments of organized women's groups, the United Charities Building in New York City "housed some of the Progressive Era's most influential women's groups."[70] In Evanston, Illinois, the Women's Christian Temperance Union, newly triumphant with winning Prohibition against alcoholic, wayward husbands built an impressive office building. In the Midwest, ladies' restrooms provided respite for rural women during their daylong trips into town.[71] Although derided "as crazy" when they requested a $50,000 construction loan (which they successfully repaid), the Montgomery [Maryland] Farm Women's Market has sold produce and baked goods since 1932—a successful women's business.[72]

The modest house she called "Val-Kill," at the Eleanor Roosevelt National Historic Site, is one of the most famous female-oriented spaces. President Franklin Roosevelt (FDR) explained that, "My missus and some of her female friends want to build a shack on a stream in the back woods."[73] Although architect Henry Toombs formally designed it, FDR extensively marked up the architectural plans for the Dutch Colonial–style cottage. Eleanor Roosevelt used Val-Kill as a place for respite from the national spotlight and the Roosevelt mansion Springwood—and as a place where she and other politically minded women could strategize. Eleanor Roosevelt mused, "Val-Kill is where I used to find myself and grow. At Val-Kill I emerged as an individual."[74] For decades she hosted hundreds of visitors from around the nation and the world at her simple rock-and-wood house with its memorabilia, comfortable chairs, and relaxed atmosphere. Evidence of her stature (5'11") comes in her bathroom, where its mirror hangs high on the wall.

Different groups of women encountered distinct architectural forms. Religious orders lived in convents and often worked in institutional settings of hospitals or schools. Nuns designed their convent buildings following their specific order's theology, with separate wings housing sisters at each level of commitment. Before construction of their "new" 1958 convent, many School Sisters of Notre Dame professors at Mount Mary College in Milwaukee slept *in* their classrooms on foldaway beds.[75] Most dramatically, and reflecting changing attitudes toward divorce, in 1927 George Wingfield remodeled his elegant Riverside Hotel in Reno, Nevada, after successfully lobbying for a shorter, three-month divorce residency requirement to attract business.[76] Conveniently next door to the Washoe County Courthouse, unknown and famous women and men waited there. Author Clare Boothe [Luce], later editor of *Vanity Fair* and a Republican congresswoman, stayed there in 1929 to divorce her alcoholic husband.[77] Made famous by Hollywood stars, several movies featured it. More significantly, everyone in the "divorce colony," including wives of many famous men, was there to end a marriage, which affected not only personal lives but cultural attitudes toward marriage. In New York City, lesbians imprisoned in the Women's House of Detention called out to their lovers gathered on the sidewalks below; today, the Lesbian Herstory Archives fills an entire townhouse.[78]

Women Decorating Interiors

Women have had significant roles in designing, arranging, and adapting interior spaces. In 1869, sisters Catherine Beecher and Harriet Beecher Stowe authored *American Woman's Home* that proposed more efficient homes for the "ideal Christian family."[79] Together they favored dramatically changed buildings, with practical arrangements that clustered the pantry, kitchen, well, cistern, and dairy together for greater efficiency. Edith Wharton, the first woman to win a Pulitzer Prize, wrote *The House of Mirth* (1905) and *Ethan Frome* (1911) at The Mount, the 1902 house and gardens she had designed, following the principles in *The Decoration of Houses*. She coauthored this still-influential 1897 guide on good taste and Beaux-Arts design with the famous architect Odgen Codman.[80] Styles changed as generations shifted from elaborate Victorian décor to simpler designs to post–World War II "easier living" American Modern Style. Magazines such as *Better Homes & Gardens* featured the latest in decorating, while elite women hired professional decorators. At the Swan Mansion in Atlanta, "decorator" Ruby Ross Wood, owner Emily Inman, and architect Philip T. Shutze collaborated on its interiors—though Wood is credited "with many of the decorative decisions throughout the house, including paint colors, furniture placement, draperies, etc."[81] Houses reveal individual women's tastes—Mamie Eisenhower's bedroom decorated in her favorite pink, gold, and khaki colors contrasted with her husband's dark wood Eastlake bedstead and red Bokhara rug.[82]

Investigating Architecture: Structures

Structures are architectural constructions, from dams to grain elevators, which are *not* primarily intended to house humans, but which provide crucial infrastructure for utilities and transportation. Although often underappreciated, they've had major impacts on women's lives as workers, mothers, and mourners. Modern structures differentiate preindustrial worlds from ours with the architecture of power plants, complex transportation, and storage infrastructure. We typically ignore these infrastructures until essential public services of water, power, and waste removal are disrupted. Electric stoves freed women from constantly tending them, filling them with pounds of coal, and removing their ashes, while plumbing replaced filling water pitchers and emptying dirty chamber pots. Before public water and sewers, household back-yard wells and privies were often so proximate that their pollution caused fatal illnesses and childhood mortality. Rather than false romanticism, interpreters should appreciate our ongoing need for power-generating facilities, chicken-slaughtering factories, and sewage treatment plants that gradually replaced on-site work as our population grew denser. While urban White households gained modern utilities in the 1920s, and rural electrification proceeded during the Great Depression, many minorities had to wait until long after World War II. One African American girl recounted her delight in gaining running water and electric lights in her new 1955 home.[83]

Structures have greatly affected American women, who had few direct roles in construction of ports, railroads, or airports, but who gained substantial economic roles in the manufacture and consumption of goods in the ensuing economy. Traditionally, Americans have not associated open roads and cars with females.[84] One unexpected relationship between such structures and women's lives comes from Papago women in Arizona. Since the 1920s, when more adequate roads were constructed, Papago women have sold their highly artistic baskets along roadsides to eager European American tourists. These Papago women became the "most successful of all basket makers today."[85] Canals, which were major early-nineteenth-century infrastructure improvements, provided faster and less expensive transport of people, goods, news, and *ideas*. Entire families lived on canal boats, with wives doing domestic and boat-related work with children tied onto the boats to protect them from falling off. An Erie Canal spur that ran through Seneca Falls, New York, facilitated the first women's rights convention there. Bridges improved access by replacing less reliable ferries. Underappreciated in the Brooklyn Bridge construction was the indispensable role of Emily (Mrs. Washington) Roebling, who became its unofficial project manager after her engineer-husband's health failed. She mastered the complex engineering and daily inspected its construction.[86] With extensive coastlines and maritime trade, the United States once had 600 often-isolated lighthouses whose lightkeeper families lived, gardened, and kept the lights on before automation. In *Everyday Heroes: The True Story of a Lighthouse Family,* a daughter recounted how every member worked during disasters; the always-on-duty mother/wife sometimes became the official assistant lighthouse keeper.[87]

For centuries, people traveled on foot, on horse, or by watercraft. An estimated half million Americans made the six-month journey by wagon trains to California, Oregon, and Utah during the 1840s–1860s, later reduced to six days by railroad as western tourism grew. Later deluxe trains provided "maid, shower, and lounging room for ladies."[88] Changed etiquette, education, and gender role expectations accompanied these transformations. Public transportation—trolleys, railroads, and buses—were simultaneously locales of contestation. Black women were forced to ride directly behind steam engines spewing hot cinders, in foul smoking cars, or in rear bus seats. Bus seating in 1955 precipitated Rosa Parks's famous Montgomery, Alabama, bus boycott, which was woman-organized despite men serving as its public face.[89] In the 1880s, "safety bicycles" with two identically sized wheels led to a bicycle craze that loosened the design of "acceptable" women's clothing, encouraged female athleticism, and created a demand for improved roads. Automobiles provided greater freedom for commuting, work, and courting. The highly successful New Mexican extension agent Fabiola Cabeza de Baca drove thousands of miles on rural roads to teach rural women gardening techniques, poultry raising, and sewing. At the same time, she honored their traditional cultures.[90] Already bilingual in Spanish and English, she mastered Tewa to communicate with Pueblo women. Consider the kinds of public and private transportation available (or not!) to the women interpreted at your museum and how that impacted their lives. Compare their transportation access with how visitors arrive now.

Museums and historic sites must interpret these multiple revolutions, or we will miss how profoundly women's lives have changed *before* the present. Only thirty years separated the transcontinental crossing by missionaries Narcissa Whitman and Eliza Spaulding riding side-saddle on horseback to passengers riding on transcontinental trains, enabling an interpretation that recognizes the larger historical context. Automobiles allowed travelers to drive much faster over greater distances and to choose their routes. Driving cross-country—before signed paved roads, reliable cars, and gas stations—was considered an achievement for women, and many nasty jokes circulated against women drivers for decades. For families living in suburbia, automobiles became essential tools for living there, not only to get basic groceries but to ferry children to classes, sports activities, and appointments of all kinds. Mothers became family chauffeurs.

As more Americans gained leisure time to travel after World War II, gas stations, restaurants, motels, and the service industry—like the earlier Harvey Girls—often provided travel amenities at drive-in restaurants served by attractive teenage girls and motels cleaned by local staff. Private automobiles gave African Americans some freedom from Jim Crow. Yet limitations persisted. In the mid-1960s, a Black wife driving with her army husband to his next duty station in Oklahoma had to explain to their daughters why—in spite of "Vacancy" signs—they could not get a motel room and were forced to sleep in their car.[91] During World War II, women joined or replaced men as fire tower lookouts, while during the Cold War women missileers were responsible for nuclear warheads at underground nuclear launch control facilities.

Shifting our analysis from the men who predominantly designed and built structures and buildings to the women present in them gives us a quite different perspective. Careful searching of the tangible resources themselves when combined with other visual, oral, and verbal documentation can yield great insights. Spend time in these spaces and consider how the women in them experienced them; try to replace current distractions with historic ones and ask questions of the space itself. Notice how sunlight changes the rooms. If you are fortunate enough to have original flooring, study wear patterns for how the room was actually used. All these hints combine to understand women's lives.

Architectural Case Studies

These case studies provide examples of the interfaces between architectural resources and women's history interpretation. Consider how best they apply to your situation.

Case Study #1: Narbonne House: Vernacular Domestic/Commercial (See Figure 7.1)

As previously discussed, the three-centuries-old Narbonne House has a main floor with three rooms—a parlor, a bedroom, and a kitchen/cent shop—and a second-floor attic used for sleeping and storage. Many visitors picture seaports as overwhelmingly male places with ships landing and departing, but seaports such as Salem were predominantly female cities.[92] With many Salem men away at sea for months, even years, women necessarily provided community continuity and commerce. Often impoverished and lacking basic political and economic rights, women still needed to support themselves and their families.

In any building, it's crucial to trace its alterations and to question why changes were made, for whom they were made, and how they functioned. In Figure 7.1, the building itself is the best resource. Look for unusual hardware, for peculiarly shaped and sized spaces that indicate alterations, for anything that seems unusual in shape, size, symmetry, or regularity. Here, the door itself shows alterations—the enlarged opening raises questions. Consider our assumptions of women and buildings. Where were women active? How many? What did they do? What social and economic relationships did they have? Scholarship shows that women were economically much more energetic than often credited—bartering, selling, running lines of credit with merchants, paying cash, lending and borrowing at different levels of formality, and simply helping each other. Good wives brought in resources and managed them. Looking at their lives as connected both with each other and with the men in their lives shows us a more realistic history. Times when women accomplished less than usual hint at crises or competing responsibilities that required their attention. Compare a building's history with the women's life histories and their life-cycle stages as daughter, young woman, wife, mother, grandmother; weaver, entrepreneur, or dairy woman. Seek explanations for unusual patterns that may indicate natural disasters, whether storms, epidemics, or fires; or human catastrophes such as a miscarriage, poor health, broken relationships, grieving, death, "panics," or warfare. Assume that neither women's lives nor their buildings were static, and hunt for changes.

Case Study #2: Fort Snelling: Designed Military Architecture

Managed by the Minnesota Historical Society, Fort Snelling State Park, with its high stone walls and military atmosphere, does not appear an obvious women's history site. (See Figure 6.4—

Historic Fort Snelling.)[93] Historic Fort Snelling mixed military and political purposes as the young United States nation expanded westward. Located on bluffs above the Minnesota and Mississippi rivers, 500 miles upstream from St. Louis, a six-month-long winter isolated the fort and its community. Women of heterogeneous races, tribes, and backgrounds—all integral to frontier forts—lived here, worked here, traded here, and stopped here. Frontier forts' official occupants included officers' wives, children, and servants; U.S. Army laundresses; hospital matrons; teachers; and when permitted, enlisted men's spouses.[94] Each laundress had 380 square feet allocated for herself and laundry for eighteen soldiers. In contrast, Victorian mansion Maymont in Richmond, Virginia, had a separate laundry room.

Forts had nearby traders' families, Indian agents, and Native American women, such as Dakota and Ojibway women at Fort Snelling. Dakota women lived in their seasonal camps along the Mississippi River banks while fur traders' wives lived across the river. In 1835, the Indian agent and his wife, who lived near the fort, brought their slave Harriet Robinson there.[95] Years later she and her husband, Dred Scott, each sued for their freedom in St. Louis (as many other Blacks had done successfully), based on their residence at Fort Snelling in *free* Minnesota territory. But slave-owning Chief Justice Taney and the Supreme Court infamously ruled in the 1857 *Dred Scott* decision that as once-enslaved African Americans, they could neither become free nor U.S. citizens.

During our history, Americans established different kinds of forts—military, commercial, imperial, or some combination—many of which are now historic sites. Women in and near these forts lived numerous roles shaped by each fort's mission. When researching a fort, look at *everyone* who lived inside it or near it, and who visited it. Women who accompanied their husbands often had surprisingly informal roles. Civilian women sought protection in forts during warfare, travels, and personal crises; one woman during the Revolution's siege of Fort Stanwix gave birth in its bunker while under bombardment.[96] Military wives awaited their husbands' hoped-for safe return from battles. Other women stopped at forts on their travels. Susan Magoffin described Bent's Old Fort in Colorado with its multicultural population and complex politics while recuperating from her 1846 miscarriage; later, her description provided crucial evidence for its reconstruction. Magoffin joined Hispanic, Cheyenne, Arapaho, Anglo, and African American women there—women with disparate personal experiences living closely together.[97] Many forts initially traded the furs that tribal men had trapped and tribal women had tanned in exchange for European goods, especially metal objects and woven cloth. Women who traveled west overland left accounts of being assisted at Forts Laramie, Hall, and Bridger; while during the Civil War, enslaved women and men escaped to Fort Monroe, Virginia. Women lived at Fort Union in New Mexico, a fort and supply depot that proclaimed U.S. military (and governmental) power, its bugles calling the times of day. Dakota and later Apache women captured during the "Indian Wars" were imprisoned at Fort Snelling and Fort Bowie during their "pacification."

Today, Fort Snelling has very knowledgeable interpreters in several buildings, including a costumed Mrs. Abigail Snelling, wife of the commander. In their gracious quarters, a girl's doll, a woman's shawl, and a cradle mark female presence, while outside in the yard an interpreter invites visitors to wash laundry with her. Interpreters interact easily and well with visitors and portray a variety of women, although the interpretation would be strengthened by portraying Dakota women encamped by the Mississippi River. Fort Snelling interpretive programs include the stories of Harriet Robinson Scott and Dred Scott, as well as a World War I program on women's suffrage with costumed staff debating both pro and con arguments, successfully enticing public participation. Its summer day camp, "Little House in the Big Fort" with bonnet-wearing girls and straw-hatted boys, features cooking, sewing, music, stories, fishing, winter survival, and games as well as lessons in the fort's one-room schoolhouse. Multiple perspectives include American

Indian history—essential as some 1,600 Dakota, including many women and children, were imprisoned there after the 1862 Dakota uprising.

Case Study #3: West Branch School: Vernacular Educational Building

During the nineteenth century, the American educational revolution brought public elementary schools nearly nationwide, with boys and girls learning the "three Rs—reading, writing and 'rithmetic" together. West Branch, Iowa, built a one-room school that was also used for community events and worship.[98] Now restored to the 1870–1877 period, the school has student desks, as well as a stove whose original marks remain on the floor. Its eight-inch-high teacher's platform—the school's focal point with her desk, chairs, globe, bookcase, and blackboard—increased her visibility. A bell to call students, a ruler to punish them, pictures of Presidents Washington and Lincoln, and a U.S. flag all reinforced her authority, while the students' stationary desks directed their attention toward her.[99]

To encourage vivid visitor experiences, bring the schoolhouse alive. Staff your schoolhouse, share Noah Webster's *Original Blue Back Speller* and *McGuffey's Eclectic Readers*, hold spelling bees, and debate the latest "news" to interpret women's lives. Have "students" recite lessons and perform once-popular "mental arithmetic." *Be* a class rather than lecturing about one—and then discuss it. For example, the Conner Prairie schoolhouse has a "female interpreter who portrays a young unmarried woman who has just arrived in town to take over the school. She has lessons written on the board and talks about her life and role in the community."[100] Numerous teachers' memoirs describe such schools. Add recorded sounds of a crackling stove, screeching chalk, children whispering, and water dippers clanging. Consider the effects of all grades learning together in a *coeducational* setting. These centers of community life contested male-dominated saloons. Teaching elementary school expanded women's acceptable occupations. Well-known because they "boarded around" with families, teachers were respected as good catches, but they were required to quit teaching upon marriage. They helped Americans accept women in "new" roles as nurses, clerks, and secretaries. By the late nineteenth century, women sought expanded lives as some women traveled on lecture tours, drove stagecoaches, became astronomers and missionaries—and protested for women's rights.[101]

Case Study #4 St. Luke Hall: Architect-Designed Headquarters Building

Now private, the St. Luke Hall was the national headquarters of the African American beneficial organization, the Independent Order of St. Luke (IOSL) in Richmond, Virginia.[102] The 18,000-square-foot St. Luke Hall, built with three stories in 1903, was renovated in 1916 in an Italianate style with an elevator and fourth floor added, including an office suite for its renowned leader, Maggie Lena Walker.[103] Unusual for a woman, in 1925 she headed the 100,000-member organization with its insurance, a newspaper, an emporium, and a bank. The first floor had offices and manufactured ceremonial regalia; the second floor, a 500-seat auditorium; the third floor had changing rooms and meeting rooms for their rituals and the fourth floor held staff offices and Mrs. Walker's office. Members protected their bank vault and her office suite by interposing other rooms; they guarded their secret rituals by posting "Outside Sentinels."

Searches for building details provide insights in women's history. With "Love, Purity and Charity," their motto, and, unlike most such organizations, IOSL female members were equal to its male members; and with Mrs. Walker as its leader, strong "womanist" values prevailed.[104] The St. Luke Building Council held their rituals and ceremonies in five meeting rooms on its third floor, where where St. Lukes (members) were required to wear their official regalia, which were sewn and assembled by IOSL employees in the building.[105] To understand the Independent Order better, their *Ritual*, blueprints for the 1916 building renovation and expansion, and the building itself were analyzed together.[106] The blueprints clearly showed that three of the five meeting rooms could *only* be accessed through the Wardrobe Rooms. Partitions with doors created individual dressing stalls so that IOSL members could change from their work clothing into their fraternal garments. The *Ritual* emphasized the then-secret initiation rites for each of six IOSL "orders" or levels. But reading *Rituals* and seeing floorplans shows intentions, not actual behavior.

Then close inspection found two-inch cuts regularly spaced every thirty inches in the wall moldings of one of the former Wardrobe Rooms, evidence of the stalls that had been there. Elusive evidence can still be crucial. The partitions were long gone but the molding notches remained, matching the historic blueprints.[107] Carefully walking these spaces gave insights into the St. Luke's symbolic transformations from living in a predominantly White, often hostile world to being in a proud Black-determined one. Those easily-overlooked notches enhanced understanding of the power and success of this organization. Here, Black women domestic and factory workers transformed themselves in a marble-paneled setting and used complex language their employers probably never imagined. The blueprints, *Ritual*, and the building itself provided complementary clues to their spaces and community of resistance. Stop and imagine changing here

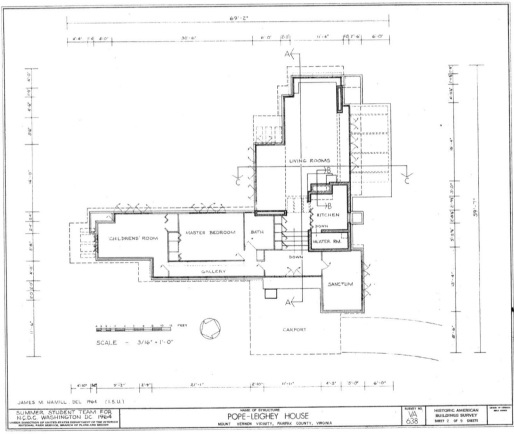

Figure 7.7.   Designed domestic architecture—the floor plan of the Pope-Leighey House, a "Usonian"-style home designed by Frank Lloyd Wright for Loren and Charlotte Pope (1940) and sold to Robert and Marjorie Leighey (1946). Note relationships between room locations and sizes.
HABS VA, 30-FALCH, 2- (SHEET 2 OF 9) - POPE-LEIGHEY HOUSE, 9000 RICHMOND HIGHWAY (MOVED FROM FALLS CHURCH, VIRGINIA), MOUNT VERNON, FAIRFAX COUNTY, VIRGINIA. LIBRARY OF CONGRESS PRINTS AND PHOTOGRAPHS DIVISION, WASHINGTON, DC, 20540 USA. HTTP://HDL.LOC.GOV/LOC.PNP/PP.PRINT.

from a workplace uniform into elegant regalia, from being addressed only by your first name, in a time that showed deliberate disrespect, to being addressed by elegant titles. Search for similar thresholds of altered treatment in the lives of the women and girls at your site. Where did they live other aspects of themselves? At church? School? At a basketball game or hairdresser?

This building provided African Americans respite and resources during American apartheid; here, Black women found jobs as clerks, stenographers, typists, secretaries, and actuaries. Consider how their pride showed in subtle ways such as the crown motif over its front canopy, the marble-walled entrance hall, and pictures of their leaders on the walls. Interpretation of this building should recognize its meaning and agency for the Black community, and Mrs. Walker's exceptional leadership as she deftly maneuvered among disparate groups in her life that exemplified intersectionality.[108]

Case Study #5: Pope-Leighey House, Designed Domestic

The 1940 Pope-Leighey House, a Frank Lloyd Wright "Usonian"-style home, presents his suburban ideal, embodying his concepts of mingling indoor and outdoor living in a compact, "open" home designed for family togetherness and informal living.[109] While much more elegant, this Usonian house shared characteristics with the less gracious and much derided Levittown homes, as both were built without basements and with simple room configurations that cut costs. The kitchens of Levittown homes were relatively roomier than those of Pope-Leighey. The latter, built for a family with two children, is the antithesis of a Victorian home; everything is wood, brick, and neutral colors except for cheerful dishes and the turquoise carpets. Entered under a carport, the house has a narrow hallway on the left with a bathroom and two small bedrooms, which Wright designed for sleeping only. To the right, a "sanctum," planned as Loren Pope's private workspace, was unavoidably used more flexibly. Four steps down, past the dining alcove and a cramped kitchen often labeled a "workroom," is the living room, with full-length windows and a bookcase wall behind Wright-designed furniture. Wright designed small closets and storage because he believed people should have few possessions; the owners later built a shed for their turkey roaster. Each wife had to accept a minimalist lifestyle in order to live here, eschewing the popular acquisitiveness, although Loren Pope later built in a dressing table and chest. The space allocation for husband and wife reflected gender expectations before second-wave feminism—Wright designed husband/father Loren Pope the private "sanctum," as a newspaper *man* needed quiet, but he built Charlotte Pope an inadequate kitchen. Interpreters passionate about Wright's architecture present this exquisitely detailed suburban home, yet they must constantly balance Wright's design with how Charlotte Pope and Marjorie Leighey *actually* lived.

These various buildings illustrate different women's lives. Such close investigations show telling elements—the doorway at Narbonne Home/Cent Shop, the notches from wooden stalls where "St. Lukes" changed from work uniforms into ritual regalia, and the nail holes delineating the schoolteacher's platform. These elements provide insights unavailable from other sources. Use their tangible reality to interpret women's experiences and perceptions.

Resources for Architectural Analysis

Search city directories and tax records to find *all* the uses of your building. In addition, look for building permits, insurance records, newspaper articles (break-ins, fires), court records, and photographs. Most of all, examine the building *very* carefully. Study what fits with its original style period—stairways, window design, size, hardware . . . any obvious changes. Look for extra stair-steps, blocked doorways, sealed windows, odd hallways, mismatched floorboards, conversions, "updates," and obsolete features. Look for new additions and doorways, mismatched tiles, and other anomalies, such as changes in floorings, wood trim, or paint color. Basements and attics often show how adjacent floors changed, with their altered framing, plumbing, and HVAC. In Anglo American common law, a widow inherited one-third of her deceased husband's estate, her "dower right" to provide for her as she was accustomed to live, with the other two-thirds of his estate protected for his children. This sometimes resulted in widows and their often-numerous children being squeezed into a few rooms of their former houses with the other rooms now rented, or even sold to other people to pay his debts.[110] Because the court sought to provide widows with spaces (domestic, social, commercial) needed for their subsistence, women frequently inherited usage rights to discontiguous rooms and spaces, including chambers, garret, cellar, garden, and "necessary." The courts frequently specified widows' right to "pass and repass" through spaces where other families now lived. Physical alterations were usually minimal because courts considered her widowhood residency temporary, ending with her remarriage or death. One can only imagine the challenges of such spatial arrangements. Look in building and written records for physical and occupancy changes after a husband died, as these provide rich interpretive possibilities infrequently interpreted, even though widowhood was common. Outside, changed stone or brick colors show additions or newer construction, as seen in the Washington Monument. Search for "stable" elements in historic paintings, drawings, and photographs, such as windows or columns in a large open room that are visible in photographs over many years. Those elements can serve as anchors for finding other changes. By understanding architectural basics and those at your museum/historic site, you have additional sources to research and interpret the lives of women present there. The National Trust for Historic Preservation's *Preservation* magazine publishes images of historic buildings, and its regional guides helpfully discuss specific architectural styles. The Vernacular Architecture Forum (VAF) and *Winterthur Portfolio* are excellent resources, as are the NPS's National Register of Historic Places (www.nps.gov/nrhp) and state historic preservation offices.

Using Architecture to Interpret Women's History

By researching and understanding women and all their impacts and motivations, a more powerful history emerges of forces that affected women living at a specific place and how the women living there affected others as well. Analysis of their social networks can untangle subtler or longer-term interactions. The Swan Mansion at the Atlanta History Center uses in-character performers not to portray the mansion's owners but to play its interior decorator, architect, and kitchen maid—each of whom plays her/his roles to interpret superbly the history of both the Inman family and the mansion. Good history requires full inclusion of everyone whose presence shaped life in these homes, but who as day employees didn't live in them. Cookbook beside her, the kitchen maid Bina Lockett explained that she lived in Summerhill, a Black neighborhood in southeast Atlanta, and commuted by streetcar.[111] To give an accurate overall portrayal and provide context, interpret other key aspects of these women's lives, families, and communities that made the Swan's high-status lifestyle possible.

Being able to read tangible resources encourages questions—and answers—to interpret women's lives. We learn through our bodily movements as well as our ears and eyes—we feel cramped building interiors and unsteady suspension bridges. These case studies can provide insights applicable to your own museum or historic site's buildings; discussing them in a group will provide additional ideas. Document your findings thoroughly—future generations will thank you. Stand in one room of "your" building and think about the women once there. What were they doing at the same time of the day/week/year? In which life stage? How did this architecture reflect and shape their lives? Make it easier or more difficult to live them? And for other women? How can buildings and structures enhance visitors' understanding of our foremothers? How can they help us understand the deeper feelings and motivations involved?

How do you interpret women's lives in your buildings and structures? Doing so literally opens up interpretive opportunities for many kinds of visitors and greatly increases our understanding of women's actual lives, just as seeing the door at the Narbonne House as a commercial location as well as a familial space does. We can find evidence all over the built environment, and link women's lives with structures we too seldom appreciate. Examine the elegance of the National Council of Negro Women, headed by the indefatigable Mary McLeod Bethune who also founded Bethune-Cookman College. The NCNW organization worked hard to increase the rights of African American women; their property reflects their confidence, propriety, and determination. Once some fluency has been mastered in architectural research, it can fascinate with its stories hidden in plain sight. The Tools below are designed to lead you through this process.

Tools for Chapter 7: Architecture

With the focal women and associated people, including men, affiliated with your museum/historic site identified, examine the building, its interior spaces, relevant structures, surroundings, and neighborhood to understand it and to interpret women's history. Together these tools provide a durable guide for interpretation, which will also assist in preservation.

Tool 7.1: Discover the Architecture of Your Building(s)

Walk around your primary building. Outside, look at its shape, construction materials, additions, and repairs to understand its history. What style was it, and what specific elements show its style? What was required for this building to function? Look at entrances and stairs and their respective locations and functions, such as the elegant front port chochère for guests and a squeezed back stairway for servants at the Maymont Mansion. Consider its location and amenities, such as a well or pumped city water. How did the amenities—or lack of them—affect the women here? Look at its neighborhood and neighbor interactions. A building that seems modest now may have once been considered ostentatious when most people lived in one- and two-room homes. How do you interpret current buildings that have replaced historic buildings, or missing buildings on empty lots?

Now, study your building room by room, beginning with its entrance and how it presented itself to the world. Look at the different rooms with their relative proportions and wall/floor conditions, the number and views from their windows; and the wall finishes and colors or designs and floor finishes. An elegant entrance that contrasted with upstairs bedrooms missing plaster on their lath walls indicated family priorities. List the primary and secondary rooms. Note the locations and sizes of rooms and the prominence of the kitchen or cooking area to identify gender assumptions in most homes or the scale of entertaining in mansion homes. What functions did each room have? How did the rooms connect (or not) with each other? What impacts did the connections have? Was there one primary room, its use depending on the time, or many rooms with specialized functions? Kitchens and bathrooms have especially had changes in technology, which affects their appliances and configurations. Bathrooms with toilets, sinks, and tubs/showers gradually and unevenly became parts of homes.[112] Before then, people washed in bedrooms with pitchers and bowls or bathed in kitchens with water heated on the fire or stove. Toilets were outdoor privies or chamber pots that needed daily emptying, an unpleasant female task. One man expressed, "It [is] very inconvenient for grown people (especially women folks) and almost impossible for small children (especially in the winter time) to use the old-fashioned toilets now in the back yard."[113] Early toilets were sometimes added to outdoor porches or basements, making access difficult.[114]

Particular rooms give insights into women's personalities and activities, the foundations for their contributions. For example, journalist Marjorie Stoneman Douglas's home was primarily her workroom; she barely used her kitchen. In contrast, Julia Child initially filmed her television show *The French Chef* in her own kitchen, now exhibited at the Smithsonian. Work room by room and consider how much each room has been altered. Take photographs and keep notes!

Next, sketch the floor plan for your building. If blueprints or floorplans are available, use copies of them. Once you have done that, imagine living there, noting the residents, visitors, and workers involved, also including men and boys. "Walk" and photograph the house, yard, and barn as well as the neighborhood to get a better sense of the lives, workloads, and skills involved. Consider cows and horses, which were often stabled in the back yard, and fuel and water procurement and disposal as well as seasonal tasks.

Map an entire if hypothetical day, including caring for a six-week-old baby and three-year-old toddler. Look around to discern how each room functioned. List the activities and chores associated with each room. What technology was available? Not available? How does this evaluation change the interpretation here? Try to "live" their lives for interpretive insights. Consider ways to include visitors and students in these explorations. A warning: I once lunged out toward an attic floor to examine it more closely, only to be sternly warned, "Stop!"—which I did. Later I learned that the "load limit" for that floor was zero. Not even squirrels should be there. Some attics, basements, and disrepaired buildings are unsafe—be careful.

Tool 7.2 Identify Women's Spaces

Now look for women's spaces. How does this building reflect the women who lived and worked in it? Men have often had dedicated spaces for writing and business, including George Washington's study and Frederick Douglass's back-yard "growlery." Few women had private spaces such as Val-Kill, built for Eleanor Roosevelt as a retreat during FDR's lifetime and a home after his death.[115] At Connemara, Carl Sandburg wrote prize-winning history in his attic study as Lillian [Steichen] Sandburg managed her prize-winning goat herd from her main floor office.[116] Frances Willard's study is impressively disheveled with scattered books and papers with a wonderful sign, "Today is My Busy Day."[117] What personal spaces were available for the women and girls you interpret?

Consider their life contexts, of social and economic prosperity or disruption, different environments, and their individual life courses; compare them with their contemporaries and with our era. Marjorie Kinnan Rawlings sat at her typewriter on a simple screened porch. If women-identified spaces remain inaccessible to visitors, as kitchens often are, their absence implicitly proclaims that women's work and lives are devalued.

By mapping out the daily activities and spaces of women in your buildings, their usage patterns will become more visible. Look for their personal spaces—kitchens, maid's rooms, service spaces, and nurseries. Look where authors lived and did their writing. The socioeconomic burdens that race and gender placed on Zora Neale Hurston show in her house, which was described as "a very modest, but substantial one story concrete-block structure with a tar and gravel roof which extends into a stoop over both the front and back door entrances . . . [with] two bedrooms, a bathroom, kitchen and front room." It's crucial to search numerous locales. For example, in the *LGBTQ Theme Study for National Historic Landmarks*, Evelyn Hooker's work and her office in the psychology department of the University of California Los Angeles is recognized for her NIH-funded research, so crucial in removing "homosexuality" from the American Psychiatric Association's *Diagnostic and Statistical Manual of Mental Disorders* in 1973.[118]

Being inclusive requires interpretation of these spaces that were foundational to the functioning of the entire building. Look at space usage. How did people share space? Find personal space? Even secret space? Who decided? How do we know? What do different architectural styles imply about gender expectations? Restricted spaces, separate entrances, and barriers enhance our understanding of formidable obstacles earlier women encountered. Compare rooms with each other. Seek the meaning of different locations. Some places hid women or things, while others became emotionally charged as women/girls experienced major life events there, whether marriage proposals or rapes.

Please map the interactions women had with people far away, whether school friends or distant family members. Draw the women's network, which might be small and close, or large and complex, extending far away, to provide context and key influences on the women living at your museum/site.

Notes

1. See Salem Maritime NHS, "The Narbonne House," *Pickled Fish and Salted Provisions* 2, no. 10 (October 2000) and "The Narbonne Family" (n.d.). Personal visit, June 2011. Thanks to Dr. Emily Murphy.
2. David Handlin, *American Architecture* (New York: Thames and Hudson, 1985); Clifton Ellis and Rebecca Ginsberg, *Cabin, Quarter, Plantation: Architecture and Landscapes of North American Slavery* (New Haven: Yale University Press, 2010); Barbara Miller Lane, ed., *Housing and Dwelling: Perspectives on Modern Domestic Architecture* (New York: Routledge, 2007); Thomas Carter and Elizabeth Collins Cromley, *Invitation to Vernacular Architecture: A Guide to the Study of Ordinary Buildings and Landscapes* (Knoxville: University of Tennessee Press, 2009); Gail Lee Dubrow and Jennifer B. Goodman, eds., *Restoring Women's History through Historic Preservation* (Baltimore: Johns Hopkins University Press, 2003); S. Allen Chambers Jr., *National Landmarks, America's Treasures: The National Park Foundation's Complete Guide to National Historic Landmarks* (New York: John Wiley & Sons, Inc., 2000); Keith Eggener, ed., *American Architectural History* (New York: Routledge, 2004).
3. Historic Ephrata Cloister. Thanks to Elizabeth Bertheaud, site manager; multiple visits.
4. Personal visit, Atlanta History Center. Emily McDougal Inman lived there for thirty-one years after her husband's death. Thanks to Michael Rose. See http://www.georgiaencyclopedia.org/file/12740.
5. Annmarie Adams, "Sex and the Single Building: The Weston Havens House, 1941–2001," *Buildings & Landscapes: Journal of the Vernacular Architecture Forum* 17, no. 1 (Spring 2010): 82–97. Meghan Drueding, "Ahead of Her Time: California Icon Julia Morgan," *Preservation*, Summer 2015, https://savingplaces.org; Nancy Loe "Julia Morgan: an Online Exhibition at Cal-Poly," http://lib.calpoly.edu.
6. The National Register of Historic Places distinguishes between buildings and structures. See https://www.nps.gov/nr/publications/bulletins/nrb15/nrb15_4.htm.
7. Sue Bridwell Beckham, "The American Front Porch: Women's Liminal Space," in *Making the American Home: Middle-Class Women & Domestic Material Culture, 1840–1940* (Bowling Green: Bowling Green State University Popular Press, 1988).
8. One photograph shows five washtubs hung from a balcony railing; in another, women stood by their tubs, 1949 El Paso. Russell Lee Photographic Collection, El Paso, Texas www.cah.utexas.edu/.
9. Marjorie Kinnan Rawlings Historic State Park, Florida, https://www.floridastateparks.org/parks-and-trails/marjorie-kinnan-rawlings-historic-state-park.
10. Personal tour of the Tenement Museum, New York, 2008.
11. The Colorado Wickiup Project. Curtis Martin, John E. Lindstrom, Holly Shelton, "The Colorado Wickiup Project Phase VII: Documentation of Selected Ephemeral Wooden Feature Sites in Rocky Mountain National Park, Colorado" (Grand Junction, Colorado, Dominquez Archaeological Research Group, 2012); Emalie Schaefer, "Apache Dwellings Version 15: American Indian Film Gallery," April 29, 2015, http://scalar.usc.edu/works/american-indian-film-archive/apache-clothing?path=apache-southwest-indians.

12. Susan Sleeper-Smith, *Indigenous Prosperity and American Conquest: Indian Women of the Ohio River Valley, 1690–1792* (Chapel Hill: University North Carolina Press, 2018) notes that Miami women also controlled their housing. Andrew Hurley, *Diners, Bowling Alleys, and Trailer Parks: Chasing the American Dream in Postwar Consumer Culture* (New York: Basic Books, 2001), 204–205.
13. Anonymous, "Winters," *Lost Womyn's Space* (blog), September 11, 2012, https://lostwomyns-space.blogspot.com/; Elizabeth Lapovsky Kennedy and Madeline D. Davis, *Boots of Leather, Slippers of Gold: The History of a Lesbian Community* (New York: Penguin Books, 1993).
14. Elizabeth Lapovsky Kennedy and Madeline D. Davis, Boots of Leather, Slippers of Gold, 1993, 382. See also Lillian Faderman, *Odd Girls and Twilight Lovers: A History of Lesbian Life in the 20th Century* (New York: Columbia University Press, 2012).
15. Catherine Holder Spude, "Engendering the Klondike Gold Rush," *CRM, Placing Women in the Past* 20, no. 3 (1997), https://www.nps.gov/CRMJournal/CRM/v20n3.pdf.
16. Julie Richter, "Christiana Campbell," *Encyclopedia Virginia* (Virginia Foundation for the Humanities, http://www.EncyclopediaVirginia.org/Campbell_Christiana_ca_1722-1792.
17. Author's observation, soup factory, Ontario, Canada, 1967; numerous online insurance and advertising office photographs show these patterns.
18. The St. Luke Building (900 St. James St.) and Maggie L. Walker NHS (110 E. Leigh St.) are in Richmond, Virginia; Carolyn J. Niethammer, *I'll Go and Do More: Annie Dodge Wauneka, Navajo Leader and Activist* (Lincoln: University of Nebraska Press, 2001).
19. Personal visit, August 2018, Thomas Hart Benton Home and Studio State Historic Site, Kansas City, Missouri.
20. Sharon Brown, "Historic Structure Report: Wesleyan Chapel, Seneca Falls, New York" (National Park Service, U.S. Department of the Interior, 1986), 6. https://archive.org/stream/historicstructur00women/historicstructur00women_djvu.txt.
21. Brown, "Historic Structure Report: Wesleyan Chapel Seneca Falls, 1986, 78, 97, 108, 111.
22. Alison K. Hoagland, *Mine Towns: Buildings for Workers in Michigan's Copper Country* (Minneapolis: University of Minnesota Press, 2010), 148.
23. Edward Allen, *Fundamentals of Building Construction: Materials and Methods*, 6th ed. (Hoboken: John Wiley & Sons, 2013).
24. Herbert Gottfried and Jan Jennings. *American Vernacular Buildings and Interiors, 1870–1960* (New York: W. W. Norton & Company, 2009). Helpful, with an excellent glossary.
25. Henry Glassie, *Vernacular Architecture* (Bloomington: Indiana University Press, 2000), 46.
26. Louis Bolduc House, St. Geneviève, Missouri. Thanks to Dr. Lesley Barker. www.frenchcoloniallife.org.
27. Excerpt from "OWW 1860s German Immigrant Farm Content Guide (v 2018.1)." Thanks to Anna Altschwager, Assistant Director, Old World Wisconsin; Pauli Murray NHL; The Pauli Murray Project, https://paulimurrayproject.org restored her family home.
28. Arnold Berke, *Mary Colter: Architect of the Southwest* (New York: Princeton Architectural Press, 2002); Meghan Drueding, "Ahead of Her Time: California Icon Julia Morgan," *Preservation Magazine*, Summer 2015, https://savingplaces.org/stories; Catherine Trujillo (curator), "Julia Morgan Papers at Cal-Poly," http://lib.calpoly.edu.
29. Robin Pogrebin, "'I Am Not the Decorator: Female Architects Speak Out,'" *New York Times*, April 12, 2016.
30. Hilliard T. Goldfarb, *The Isabella Stewart Gardner Museum: A Companion Guide and History* (New Haven: Yale University Press, 1995).
31. Alice T. Friedman, "People Who Live in Glass Houses: Edith Farnsworth, Ludwig Mies van der Rohe, and Philip Johnson" in *Women and the Making of the Modern House: A Social and Architectural History* (New Haven: Yale University Press, 2006).

32. See Jane Addams Hull-House, https://www.hullhousemuseum.org.
33. For photographs of historic Hull-House, see JAMC_0000_0134_0156, https://lib-scan. photoshelter.com/gallery-image. Date photographs by automobiles styles. Chicago History Museum "built environment" https://photostore.chicagohistory.org/cityscapes.
34. Personal visit to Kalaupapa NHP, February 2010. See www.nps.gov/kala.
35. National Park Service, "A Place of Care: Mother Marianne Cope and the Kalaupapa Cultural Landscape Kalaupapa N.H.P.," https://www.nps.gov/articles/mother_marianne_cope.htm.
36. Pauli Murray NHL, Durham, North Carolina, https://paulimurrayproject.org, visited August 2015; Maria Mitchell Association, Nantucket, www.mariamitchell.org, visited June 2008.
37. Thanks to Delana Gilmore, Margaret Mitchell House, Atlanta History Center, visited April 20, 2019.
38. Personal visit, Margaret Mitchell House, Atlanta History Center, October 2018.
39. Thanks to Patty Suttle for her insight; The Plumbing Museum, www.theplumbingmuseum.org.
40. Joan M. Jensen, *Calling This Place Home: Women on the Wisconsin Frontier: 1850–1925* (St. Paul: Minnesota Historical Society, 2006).
41. State Historical Society of Missouri, "Carrie Amelia Nation," in *Historic Missourians*, n.d., https://shsmo.org/historicmissourians/name/n/nation/#section4.
42. "Ruth Bader Ginsburg," Oyez. https://www.oyez.org/justices/ruth_bader_ginsburg.
43. Thanks to Dr. Stuart Berryhill for his account from Memphis, Tennessee, 2015.
44. Personal communication with the Rev. Dr. Jeannette Ridlon Piccard, 1976.
45. Lisa Pfueller Davidson, "'A Service Machine': Hotel Guests and the Development of an Early-Twentieth-Century Building Type," in *Building Environments*, vol. X, Perspectives in Vernacular Architecture (Knoxville: University of Tennessee Press, 2005), 113–29.
46. Pauli Murray, *Proud Shoes: The Story of an American Family* (New York: Harper & Row, 1956). Murray lived the concept of intersectionality.
47. Kenneth L. Ames *Death in the Dining Room: And Other Tales of Victorian Culture.* (Philadelphia: Temple University Press, 1992); John F. Kasson, "Rituals of Dining: Table Manners in Victorian America," in *Dining in America 1850–1900* (Amherst: University of Massachusetts, 1987).
48. Michael Olmert, *Kitchens, Smokehouses and Privies: Outbuildings and the Architecture of Daily Life in the Eighteenth-Century Mid-Atlantic* (Ithaca: Cornell University Press, 2009).
49. Holly Alonso, #28 Hacienda Peralta Food. Script, Peralta House exhibits: Friends of Peralta Hacienda Historical Park; http://www.peraltahacienda.org, Oakland, California.
50. Heather Huyck and Margaret (Peg) Strobel, eds. *Revealing Women's History: Best Practices in Interpretation at Historic Sites* (Santa Cruz: National Collaborative for Women's History Sites, 2011); www.historicnewengland.org/historic-properties/homes/otis-house.
51. Alison K. Hoagland, *Mine Towns: Buildings for Workers in Michigan's Copper Country* (Minneapolis: University of Minnesota Press, 2010).
52. "The Petersen House," Ford's Theatre NHS, www.nps.gov/foth; Molly Brown House Museum, https://mollybrown.org/.
53. Molly Brown House, 1340 Pennsylvania Avenue, in Denver's Capitol Hill neighborhood.
54. Virginia Electric Power Company bill, July 10, [1933?], Maggie Walker Collection.
55. Janet Ore, *The Seattle Bungalow: People & Houses, 1900–1940* (Seattle: University of Washington Press, 2007).
56. Olivia Mahoney, "Recipe for a Modern Kitchen," Chicago History Museum, *Exhibitions* (blog), December 18, 2018, https://www.chicagohistory.org/recipe-for-a-modern-kitchen/; the Sunbeam company made sheep-shearing and horse-trimming equipment before manufacturing early electrical household appliances, starting with irons in 1910 and mixers in 1930, https://www.sunbeam.com/history.html.
57. Mary and Russel Wright, *Guide to Easier Living*, 1950 ed. (Layton: Gibbs Smith, 2003).

58. Ruth Schwartz Cowan, *More Work for Mother: The Ironies of Household Technology from the Open Hearth to the Microwave* (New York: Basic Books, 1985). Barbara Allen, "The Ranch-Style House in America: A Cultural and Environmental Discourse," *Journal of Architectural Education* 49, no. 3 (February 1996): 156–65. Each has helpful insights; Allen blames ranch-style housing for economic and environmental ills.
59. Betty Friedan, *The Feminine Mystique* (New York: W. W. Norton & Company, 1963).
60. Tiffany M. Gill, *Beauty Shop Politics: African American Women's Activism in the Beauty Industry* (Urbana: University of Illinois Press, 2010), 108.
61. Monica Domosh and Joni Seager, *Putting Women in Place: Feminist Geography Makes Sense of the World* (New York: Guilford Press, 2001); Sarah Deutsch, *Women and the City: Gender, Space, and Power in Boston, 1870–1940* (New York: Oxford University Press, 2000).
62. Elizabeth Lapovsky Kennedy and Madeline D. Davis, *Boots of Leather, Slippers of Gold: The History of a Lesbian Community*, 1993; Lillian Faderman, *Odd Girls and Twilight Lovers: A History of Lesbian Life in the 20th Century* (New York: Columbia University Press, 2012).
63. Susan Ferentinos, *Interpreting LGBT History at Museums and Historic Sites* (Lanham: Rowman & Littlefield Publishers, Inc., 2014), 145.
64. Ann Fessler, *The Girls Who Went Away: The Hidden History of Women Who Surrendered Children for Adoption in the Decades before Roe v. Wade* (New York: Penguin Books, 2006).
65. Anonymous, "Grace and Rubies Restaurant," *Lost Womyn's Space* (blog), December 16, 2011, https://lostwomynsspace.blogspot.com/2011/12/grace-and-rubies-restaurant.html.
66. Anonymous, "Unnamed Lesbian Bar (Pittsburgh, Pennsylvania)," *Lost Womyn's Space* (blog), December 2, 2013, http://lostwomynsspace.blogspot.com/2013/.
67. Ellen Baumler, "Empowering Women: The Helena YWCA," in Martha Kohl, ed., *Beyond Schoolmarms and Madams: Montana Women's Stories* (Helena: Montana Historical Society, 2016), 70–72; "History of YWCA," YWCA, www.ywca.org.
68. Judith Weisenfeld, *African American Women and Christian Activism: New York's Black YWCA, 1905–1945* (Cambridge: Harvard University Press, 2013).
69. Page Putnam Miller, "New Century Guild National Historic Landmark Nomination," National Park Service NHL Form (Washington, DC: National Park Service, 1992). See also Page Putnam Miller, *Landmarks of American Women's History* (New York: Oxford University Press, 2003) and S. Allen Chambers Jr., *National Landmarks*, 404.
70. United Charities Building, https://www.nps.gov/nr/travel/.
71. For WCTU, see https://franceswillardhouse.org/research; and Katherine O'Bryan, "Gender, Politics, and Power: The Development of the Ladies Rest Room and Lounge in Rural America, 1900–1945" (PhD dissertation, Middle Tennessee State University, 2014).
72. Mary C. Crook, "The Montgomery Farm Women's Cooperative Market," *The Montgomery County Story*, August 1982, www.farmwomensmarket.com.
73. Franklin D. Roosevelt quote, National Park Service, "Teaching with Historic Places: First Lady of the World: Eleanor Roosevelt at Val-Kill," Eleanor Roosevelt NHS, https://www.nps.gov/nr/twhp/wwwlps/lessons/26roosevelt/26roosevelt.htm.
74. National Park Service, "Eleanor Roosevelt National Historic Site, Val-Kill Cottage, New York," *Discover Our Shared Heritage Travel Itinerary* https://www.nps.gov/nr/travel/presidents/eleanor_roosevelt_valkill.html.
75. Thanks to S. Joanne Poehlman, SSND, Mount Mary College for her assistance and insights.
76. "Riverside Hotel," Online Nevada Encyclopedia, www.onlinenevada.org.
77. https://www.nps.gov/nr/travel/nevada/riv.htm; http://renodivorcehistory.org/ library/from-eppes-hawes-to-george-bartlett/; "Clare Booth Luce: American Playwright and Statesman," in *Encyclopaedia Britannica*, https://www.britannica.com/biography/Clare-Boothe-Luce.

78. Joan Nestle, "Women's House of Detention, 1931-1974," Outhistory.org/exhibits, 2008.
79. Catherine E. Beecher and Harriet Beecher Stowe, *The American Woman's Home or, Principles of Domestic Science: Being a Guide to the Formation and Maintenance of Economical, Healthful, Beautiful, and Christian Homes* (Hartford: Stowe-Day Foundation, 1975). See www.harriet-beecherstowecenter.org/.
80. The Mount, Edith Wharton's Home, https://www.edithwharton.org/; Edith Wharton and Ogden Codman, *The Decoration of Houses* (New York, Rizzoli facsimile 2007).
81. Thanks to Jessica Rast VanLanduyt, Atlanta History Center, email, July 2016.
82. Personal visit to Eisenhower NHS, 1982. See www.nps.gov/eise. For images of American house interiors, see http://hearth.library.cornell.edu/h/hearth/index.html.
83. Personal interviews with Connie Howard, March 2013, and Debra Jones, November 11, 2016.
84. Virginia Scharff, *Twenty Thousand Roads: Women, Movement, and the West* (Berkeley: University of California Press, 2003).
85. Joan M. Jensen, *One Foot on the Rockies: Women and Creativity in the Modern American West* (Albuquerque: University of New Mexico Press, 1995), 60, 80–81.
86 Anna M. Lewis, *Women of Steel and Stone: 22 Inspirational Architects, Engineers, and Landscape Designers* (Chicago: Chicago Review Press, 2014).
87. Seamond Ponsart Roberts and Jeremy D'Entremont, *Everyday Heroes: The True Story of a Lighthouse Family* (Portsmouth: Coastlore Media, 2013); Mary Louise Clifford and J. Candace Clifford, *Women Who Kept the Lights, An Illustrated History of Female Lighthouse Keepers*, 2nd ed. (Alexandria VA: Cypress Communications, 2000).
88. Anonymous, "Lounging Room for Ladies, Louisville & Nashville Railroad," August 6, 2015.
89. Danielle L. McGuire, *At the Dark End of the Street: Black Women, Rape and Resistance—A New History of the Civil Rights Movement from Rosa Parks to the Rise of Black Power* (New York: Alfred A. Knopf, 2010).
90. Scharff, *Twenty Thousand Roads*, 2003; Michael Ann Sullivan, "Fabiola Cabeza de Baca," *New Mexico History*, http://newmexicohistory.org/people.
91. Personal interviews with Connie Howard, March 2013, and Debra Jones, November 11, 2016.
92. Elaine Forman Crane, *Ebb Tide in New England: Women, Seaports and Social Change, 1630–1800* (Boston: Northeastern University Press, 1998).
93. Thanks to Nancy Cass and Dr. Melissa McDonald of Historic Fort Snelling, Minnesota Historical Society, St. Paul, Minnesota, for all their assistance.
94. Jennifer J. Lawrence, *Soap Suds Row: The Bold Lives of Army Laundresses, 1802-1876* (Glendo: High Plains Press, 2016), 70.
95. Lea VanderVelde, *Mrs. Dred Scott: A Life on Slavery's Frontier* (New York: Oxford University Press, 2009). Superb.
96. John Luzader, Louis Torres, and Orville W. Carroll, *Fort Stanwix: History, Historic Furnishing, and Historic Structure Reports* (Washington, DC: NPS, 1976).
97. Stella M. Drumm, *Down the Santa Fe Trail and into Mexico: The Diary of Susan Shelby Magoffin, 1846-1847* (Lincoln, 1926), https://archive.org/details/downsantafetrail00mago. See Mark Lee Gardner, *Bent's Fort on the Arkansas,*" *NPS Historic Resource Study*, La Junta, Colorado, 2004. Thanks to John Carson, Bent's Old Fort NHS.
98. Heather Huyck, "Furnishing Plan for West Branch School, Herbert Hoover N.H.S." (Harpers Ferry: NPS, 1977).
99. See Andrew Gulliford, *America's Country Schools* (Washington, DC: The Preservation Press, 1984); James Johonnot, *School-Houses* (New York, 1871); J.R. Sypher, *The Art of Teaching School* (Philadelphia, 1872); and James Pyle Wickersham, *School Economy* (Philadelphia, 1864).

100. Thanks to Nathan Ryalls, professional visit, Conner Prairie, August 10–13, 2016.
101. "Stagecoach Mary" Fields drove a stagecoach in Montana, Annie Oakley joined Buffalo Bill's Wild West Show, and Maria Mitchell taught astronomy at Vassar College.
102. St. Luke Building, a designed commercial building, Richmond, Virginia. Privately owned.
103. Elsa Barkley Brown, "Womanist Consciousness: Maggie Lena Walker and the Independent Order of Saint Luke," *SIGNS: Journal of Women in Culture and Society* 14:3 (1989); Leslie Mc-Call, "The Complexity of Intersectionality," *SIGNS: Journal of Women in Culture and Society* 30: 3 (2005): 1771–1800.
104. Elsa Barkley Brown, "Womanist Consciousness."
105. See 1925 Independent Order of St. Luke, Calendar (Richmond: St. Luke Press, 1925) for photograph of regalia manufacture; W.M.T. Forrester, *Degree Ritual Independent Order of St. Luke Containing the Rules, Regulations and Ceremonies of Degrees*, revised (Washington, DC, 1894) Library of Congress.
106. Earlier blueprints were not found; the building has since been refashioned into apartments.
107. Charles Russell, "Blueprint St Luke Building Renovation 3rd floor" 1919, Library of Virginia and personal examination of St. Luke Building, February 17, 2011.
108. Not open to the public but historic photographs of the St. Luke Building can be found at www.nps.gov/mawa. Kimberlé Williams Crenshaw, "Mapping the Margins: Intersectionality, Identity Politics, and Violence against Women of Color," *Stanford Law Review* 43, no. 6 (1991): 1241–99; Jennifer Nash, "Re-Thinking Intersectionality," *Feminist Review* 89 (2008): 1–15; Lynne M. Woehrle, ed., *Intersectionality and Social Change* (Bingley: Emerald Group Publishing, 2016); Patricia Collins and Sirma Bilge, *Intersectionality* (New York: John Wiley & Sons, Inc., 2016).
109. Pope-Leighey House in Alexandria, Virginia, is a National Trust for Historic Preservation property. Steven M. Riess, *Frank Lloyd Wright's Pope-Leighey House* (Charlottesville: University of Virginia Press, 2014); Helen Duprey Bullock, *The Pope-Leighey House* (Washington, DC: National Trust for Historic Preservation, 1969).
110. Bernard L. Herman, *Town House: Architectural and Material Life in the Early American City, 1780–1830* (Chapel Hill: The University of North Carolina Press, 2005). Chapter 5, "The Widow's Dower," explains the interplay between widowhood and architecture superbly.
111. Tour, Swan Mansion, Atlanta History Center. See also Elizabeth Clark-Lewis, *Living In, Living Out: African American Domestics in Washington, D.C., 1910–1940* (Washington, DC: Smithsonian Institution Press, 1994).
112. Alison K. Hoagland, "Introducing the Bathroom: Space and Change in Working-Class Houses," *Buildings & Landscapes: Journal of the Vernacular Architecture Forum* 18, no. 2 (Fall 2011): 15–42.
113. Hicks, in Alison K. Hoagland, *Mine Towns: Buildings for Workers in Michigan's Copper Country* (Minneapolis: University of Minnesota Press, 2010), 136. These quotes come from a set of letters pleading for upgrades to copper mining company housing.
114. Some basement toilets were accessed by a trapdoor in the kitchen floor. Hoagland, *Mine Towns*, 137–41.
115. See Val-Kill, Eleanor Roosevelt NHS, www.nps.gov/elro.
116. Cultural Resource Division, Southeast Region, National Park Service, "The Swedish House: Historic Structure Report," 2005. www.nps.gov/carl.
117. See https://franceswillardhouse.org/wp-content/uploads/willard_in_office_for_opening_8nt6.jpg. Thanks to Lori Osborne.
118. Katie Batza, "LGBTQ and Health," in *LGBTQ America: A Theme Study of Lesbian, Gay, Bisexual, Transgender, and Queer History* (Washington, DC: National Park Service, 2016), https://www.nps.gov/subjects/lgbtqheritage/upload/lgbtqtheme-health.pdf.

8

Objects

Who Packed This Lunch Bucket?

"You have to read between the lines."[1]

Photographs of industrial life frequently show heavily muscled men carrying their lunch buckets into mills and mines.[2] Plain metal cylinders with two compartments and a handle, these lunch buckets sustained Michigan miners with hot black tea in the base and "pasties," meat pies of beef, potatoes, and turnips, in the upper compartment. The seldom-recognized, foundational female work that filled these ubiquitous objects shows how essential women were to industrial enterprises and how men's work affected women's lives.[3] Objects can tell us much about women and their lives and provide powerful interpretive tools. To use them interpretively, we must first understand them ourselves. Understanding objects' characteristics and their different relationships with women and men provides us a more accurate history. While many female-associated objects have been used by males as well, such as eating with knives and forks or teaching with blackboards, others were linked with specific female life stages, such as Latinas' quinceañera dresses. Sometimes objects demonstrate *female presence*: The eleventh-century Norse settlement L'Anse aux Meadows in Newfoundland has a small soapstone spindle whorl that women used for spinning then.[4] Objects hint at the range of women's experiences: a 1750 tea table at Old Salem, North Carolina; a 1930s doll; an electric refrigerator. An exhibit of purses during the twentieth century illustrates the shift from chatelaines to credit cards as well as "the changes in women's lives over time, from the necessity of carrying smelling salts to the availability of birth control pills."[5]

By definition, every museum and historic site has objects of all kinds, many female-associated. Our challenge is to understand how women created, interacted with, and were affected by objects in ways obvious and subtle. Museums and historic sites collect, research, preserve, and interpret many *millions* of primarily female-associated objects—beaded moccasins, silver tea sets, wooden mousetraps, gravestones for beloved chickens, and bridal dresses made from silk parachutes.[6] Given the millions of objects found in museums and historic sites, it's impossible to discuss them all. Instead, this chapter will focus on several different ways to research and interpret them.

The importance of objects results from many reasons. Sometimes they are rare female-associated evidence, such as the early brass thimble found at Jamestown with a girl's handwriting scrawled on a slip of paper inside it.[7] A set of objects belonging to a woman or group of women reveals their priorities and preferences in colors and designs. Some objects are valuable because they are old and unusual, such as the 1920 Edison electric hair curler; others are significant

Figure 8.1. Lunch bucket, with two compartments, commonly used by miners. Wives or "bucket girls" filled them with pasties (meat, potato, and rutabaga turnovers) or tortillas and beans, and hot tea or coffee, depending on the man's ethnicity.

PHOTOGRAPH BY NATHAN RYALLS, PRIVATE COLLECTION.

from their association with a famous woman who made or used them, such as Clara Barton's rolltop desk. Once-common objects, such as laundry agitators, wick trimmers, or carbon paper, are now rare.[8] Objects dear to earlier generations may not be valued by later ones—ornate Victorian cut-glass Castor Sets for oil and vinegar no longer decorate tables. Other objects never imagined as special are collector's items—a New York airport once exhibited a large collection of washboards.[9]

The beauty, creativity, and variety of these objects bears witness to the same characteristics in our foremothers. For example, the Museum of International Folk Art in Santa Fe houses more than 130,000 objects from more than 100 countries that show how women expressed delight through beadwork, pottery, and baskets.[10] We now know that beautiful Tiffany glass lampshades were designed by Clara Driscoll (1861–1944), head of the Women's Glass Cutting Department in the Louis C. Tiffany company.[11] Some objects have shifted gender associations, making generalizations complicated. Outfits perfect for early-twentieth-century male toddlers now appear as dresses.[12] Fashionable women now wear heels, lace, and wigs, while eighteenth-century elite men did.[13] Gender differentiation, once so emphasized, has decreased with sports-influenced clothing from the late-nineteenth-century bicycle craze to the present.

Some of the most important aspects of women's experiences are seldom found in earlier collections. Sadly, we'll never have all the tangible evidence that women once had. New England colonists had considerable appreciation for women's nursing, its cultural significance, and the associated challenges, but mothers left relatively few objects related to breast feeding in comparison to its importance, once so crucial to babies' survival.[14] Yes, there are pap boats for feeding colonial infants a bread and milk mixture, nursing bottles, and advice books on how to nurse and how to cope with nursing. Nursing a child who was sometimes given to a friend or wet nurse for medical or social reasons seldom left physical evidence.[15] If historical women at your museum nursed children—and many women did, although sometimes nursing was discouraged—it's crucial to trace their specific history as much as possible. Those of us who have not nursed our own children must seek to understand that experience from women who have, just as it's essential that those of us (female or male) who have not been pregnant or had children research and interview those who have. The insightful *Mother Is a Verb* combines historical research with one mother's specific experiences.[16]

The objects at your museum or historic site are rich research sources and interpretive tools for understanding and presenting women's lives. While curators carefully analyze the physical properties of objects, the emphasis here will be on their many other properties. This chapter first considers characteristics of objects, and then focuses on female-associated objects found in many museums and historic sites, chosen for their representation of different usages, periods, groups of women, and purposes. Visitors appreciate encountering tangible historical objects such as quilts, baskets, and lunch buckets that are simultaneously familiar and strange. Many museums sell reproductions that extend history into visitors' homes and provide income for the organization as well.

Some objects become valuable because they are old and unusual. Others become accidentally significant because they were made by or used by someone famous. Objects dear to earlier generations may not be recognized, much less valued, by later ones. As the smallest, most portable kind of tangible resources, objects were more frequently linked with women and girls than were landscapes and architecture. Colonial Anglo-American women inherited objects instead of land because they could take linens and cows with them when as brides they moved from their parental homes to their married ones. Objects included personal, household, and trade/professional tools—clothes, jewelry, pots and utensils, or butter and cheese molds used for both familial and commercial production. Jewelry and silver tea sets demonstrated wealth and status while kettles and sewing needles were utilitarian.[17] Women used locally sourced items such as wood splints to make baskets and carried other items long distances, such as immigrant women arriving at Ellis Island who brought their goose down–filled bed comforters.[18] Specific groups of people—here, deliberately defined as both vague and encompassing—used objects to proclaim their shared identity. By custom, women "owned" their personal items, although a wife could lose them to pay her husband's debts. Legally, enslaved women owned nothing, including themselves. They preferred to believe otherwise. Archaeologists have found small objects such as cowrie shells hidden in "cellars" where enslaved women lived.[19]

Analyzing Objects

Objects can be approached descriptively and analytically. Descriptive approaches study objects' physical dimensions, material, style, function, maker, and users. Curators carefully measure objects. In the case of the lunch pail, the basic description notes its physical characteristics: a 1910 twelve-inch-high and nine-inch-diameter aluminum lunch pail with two compartments, the lower one for hot tea that warmed food in the upper one, a tight-fitting lid, and a bail to carry it. For generations women made their own clothing, so by measuring a woman's dress sleeve we know her arm length. Analytical approaches, by contrast, look for deeper cultural meanings. This ubiquitous bucket documents one of the many crucial but invisible ways women provided for men in mills, canals, and factories by feeding them, washing their often-filthy clothes, and caring for them. On a daily basis, wives, boardinghouse keepers, and "bucket girls" in "commercialized domesticity" sent men off to strenuous manual labor.[20] Every day, women grew, bought, chopped, mixed, and cooked food and filled these pails. Ethnicity changed the cuisine packed in them. In northern Michigan, women filled Welsh copper miners' buckets with black tea and "pasties." A Southern Colorado Hispanic coal miner's wife, Maria de las Nieves, packed lunches for her husband, Albino Ruiz, with tortillas and beans, "maybe a bit of meat," and a sweet. She rose "before the sun to make the tortillas and tend to the beans."[21] This lunchbox has a story! Consider women's labor, sustenance, and concern packed into each one.

Characteristics of Objects

History museums and sites have *millions* of objects associated with women. Of the kinds of tangible resources, objects—with their smaller scale—are more easily exhibited and closely studied than buildings or landscapes. As less expensive and more portable than other tangible resources, objects more often belonged to women.[22]

Objects have their own life cycles of acquisition, use, and disposal, with numerous ways to acquire them. Women have gathered local reeds to make baskets, and gleaned or begged for food. Women informally borrowed objects and supplies from each other and formalized borrowing of books when they established community libraries. Other special and/or costly objects were inherited from an earlier generation, such as ceremonial baptismal gowns or handmade lace. Women "bought" objects, using barter, trade, or pawn; or with cash or scrip, employee payment that was only accepted at company stores. Many merchants gave customers credit for the butter and eggs women sold them, or until crops were harvested.[23] Tenant farmers and sharecroppers "settled up" their accounts after harvest. Since the 1920s, some department stores and oil companies gave customers charge cards. In 1950, more flexible credit cards that purchased goods and services anywhere they were accepted encouraged consumer debt. But until 1974 legislation, married women had difficulty getting credit cards without their husbands' approval. All these ways of acquiring objects show the complex economic systems in which women participated. Women also sold objects at "Mom and Pop" stores, "Cent Shops," and small to large retail; in department stores where women clerks interacted with customers on behalf of store owners;

and from mail order catalogs. The mail order catalog revolution provided women with new and impressive choices in goods at different price points and styles, and offered privacy as well. In its 1897 catalog of 708 pages, Sears, Roebuck & Co. "the Cheapest Supply House on Earth" encouraged post office or express money orders as payment and allowed postage stamps—but specifically warned customers against sending gold or silver bullion![24] Some objects were stolen—desperate women and children stole coal from train tracks and ripening fruit from fields.

Women have made and used all kinds of objects/tools such as knives, shells, hoes, and *hornos* (outdoor ovens). They have woven and sewn: Hubbell Trading Post has beautiful "Two Grey Hills" rugs woven and traded by Navajo women; the Grace Hudson Museum has elaborate baskets made by Pomo women.[25] Women have spun yarn; woven cloth; designed, cut, and stitched clothing; and mended it. Women, both colonists and indigenous, purchased cloth more frequently than our myths proclaim.[26] Susan Sleeper-Smith explains that the "fur trade" should be renamed the "cloth trade" because indigenous women traded for so much fabric.[27] Consider the range of objects in your collection and the modes of acquisition available to women there.

As tools or supplies, objects as tools were connected with specific activities—metates that ground corn or mortars and pestles that husked rice with food preparation; knitting needles and thread with needlework; pens and typewriters with clerical work. Matching cooking with cookbooks, or knives and ladles with available foods, help visitors better understand how women prepared food. Some tool assemblages reflect specific occupations, such as the enslaved women at Poplar Forest who used thimbles, needles, and pins to produce clothing for Thomas Jefferson's plantation.[28] In brothels, prostitutes left archaeological evidence of perfume bottles, fancy buttons, and bones from better cuts of meat.

Recognizing an assemblage of many objects helps identify *specific* activities and groups of people.[29] Nurses wore uniforms unique to their profession, as did nuns; female ministers, priests, and justices experimented to find robes, collars, and stoles that reflected their femininity and professions. Waitresses had uniforms that always included aprons, while a century after the first female flight attendants and park rangers undertook their duties, their uniform styles still keep fluctuating. Although limited to 2 percent of the armed forces for many years, Navy Nurse Corps and other armed forces uniforms show women's military service.[30] While objects often are tools for livelihoods, their relationship may be unexpected, requiring careful analysis. The "Root Beer Lady," Dorothy Molter, brewed and sold root beer to thirsty canoeists in the northern Minnesota Boundary Waters Canoe Area Wilderness. The Dorothy Molter Museum displays the glass bottles she repeatedly used to make and serve root beer in that remote location where using new bottles was infeasible.[31]

Objects have symbolic functions, marking women's status, their roles, and their affiliations with various religions, schools, and organizations. They provide evidence of identity, or of religious and political beliefs in myriad ways, whether a Jewish menorah or a WCTU flag. At Ephrata, an eighteenth-century German religious community, the objects in the Saaron, or Sister's Hall, cells reflect their piety. They reflect cultural differences and individual preferences. Two adjacent archaeological sites in Los Angeles—a brothel and the Chinese District—had very different *sets* of objects, with alcohol and perfume bottles in one and Chinese serving dishes in the other.[32] Objects often demonstrate cultural preferences, especially traditional designs that mothers taught their daughters. Embroidery samplers—marks of middle-class female accomplishments—had designs that varied by geography, schools, available fabrics, and eras—some with impressive individual variations. The meaning of some objects changed with new designs or materials (plastics!), or consumers wanting something different, as early Native American women bargained when they sold their furs. Objects dear to one generation were relegated to attics or became playthings. A once-treasured elegant blue silk flapper dress became a "dress-up" costume for little girls oblivious to its rebellious past. Other objects were revived by subsequent generations. With the 1876 U.S. centennial celebration, long-discarded spinning wheels became patriotic symbols.[33] Other objects marked female lineages as women willed quilts or jewelry to their daughters and female descendants.[34]

Objects such as clothing, jewelry, and home accessories reveal women's identity, beliefs, and status. The Martha's Vineyard Museum has a three-inch elegantly embroidered shoe for a Chinese woman with bound feet. Susan B. Anthony had a trademark red shawl that identified her suffragist beliefs.[35] Objects associated with twentieth-century lesbians include symbolic pink triangles and rainbow flags as well as motorcycles, leather boots, and very large earrings. The Chicago History Museum exhibit "Out in Chicago" featured the motorcycle of Debby Rios, leader of the Chicago Chapter of Dykes on Bikes.[36] Uniforms that mark wearers as members of a group affiliated with particular roles—whether WACs or Girl Scouts—signified women's or girls' status. Religious objects filled homes—Christian crosses, Russian icons, and the candlesticks Jewish women lit to welcome the Sabbath. In our more secular age, it's a challenge to recognize—and honor—how much religion deeply shaped our foremothers' lives. Omitting women's rosaries, Bibles, and prayer books disserves them and damages our understanding of their motivations and actions. At same time, cosmetics or romantic novels we hardly consider dangerous were once attacked for promoting fantasies that subversively allowed women to imagine less restrictive lives.[37]

Women employed objects as political tools to create change. American women, "prodigious consumers" of tea, "governed" their tea tables with their friends, creating private female spaces where they organized their fury at the pre-Revolution tea tax.[38] The "Daughters of Liberty" successfully boycotted imported tea. In three years, American consumption dropped 26 percent as they drank peppermint and bergamot "tea" instead.[39] Nineteenth-century American women devised and wore costumes and made signs and banners to dramatize suffrage, temperance, and other political causes. Protesters over abortion rights used objects to make tangible their positions. Opponents carrying plastic babies symbolizing fetuses were countered by proponents who carried coat hangers symbolizing women's deaths by illegal abortions.

Some objects were designed to control or punish. Many colonial chests (and subsequent reproductions) have locks on each drawer, and liquor cellarettes had locks. Rather than locking the outside perimeter as today, these locks protected objects *inside* houses from servants or slaves already inside it. Tools of slavery included whips and shackles and the dearth of objects for comfort. Jennifer Morgan in *Laboring Women: Reproduction and Gender in New World Slavery* details the complexities of African women's essential roles in American slavery.[40] Slave owners valued enslaved women for both their productivity and their reproductivity; as former slave Harriet Jacobs explained, "Slavery is terrible for men; but it is far more terrible for women."[41] Enslaved women's vulnerability to White men's sexual predation made their lives especially difficult, making historic interpretation today emotionally fraught. Formerly enslaved Lu Perkins described being for sale, standing on a wooden auction box, such as one in the Louisiana State Museum. Her horrific experience was both shared with male slaves and specific to her gender, "I 'members when they put me on the auction block. . . . They pulled my dress down over my back to my waist to show I ain't gashed and slashed up. That's to show you ain't a mean [slave]."[42]

While all objects have historic dimensions, some objects provide visceral connections to the past, such as a lock of hair from a beloved deceased relative. A small locket holds both Martha and George Washington's hair, because "hair locks served as a physical reminder of a beloved figure or family member."[43] A Hungarian refugee who kept the yellow Star of David that Nazis had forced Jews to wear explained, "I want all the children to touch it, to feel the fabric and know the real thing. . . . This little star . . . is a living memory of my family and all the others who suffered and died but [who] will not be forgotten."[44] A little girl's brown shoe was a "quietly devastating" artifact, all that remained after Anna Liebenow and 1,300 other women and children drowned in a ferry accident on the way to their Sunday school picnic in New York Harbor.[45] Embrace such objects and include them in exhibits that respect the children who once wore them.

Life Stages

Objects related to female life stages provide crucial insights, even as notions of privacy and propriety hinder our ability to locate and identify them, especially as many objects were ephemeral because they were temporary or trashed. Discussions of menarche, menstruation, birth control, pregnancy, childbirth, miscarriages, stillbirths, sterilization, menopause, abortions, and their related objects remain complicated and too-little-discussed topics for museums and historic sites. Yet they profoundly affected every woman's life and so require our attention. While many objects such as baby bottles were shared by males and females, other objects were specifically related to female biological needs and social wants. Objects symbolically marked life stages and status changes with wedding rings, caps, and new hairstyles; or the quinceañera dresses of fifteen-year-old Latinas, now women. Nuns put on their order's habit with their final vows, and nurses gained stiff white caps of authority when they graduated. From puberty until marriage, Hopi women wore their hair on the *side* of their heads "squash blossom style," but braided their hair after marriage.[46]

Infancy has its own set of objects. Cradles so emblematic of colonial babies were later replaced by cribs with their bars designed to enclose exploring babies, even as swaddling for tightly wrapped infants was exchanged for looser gowns. Cradleboards safeguarded indigenous babies on their mothers' backs for their first two years. High infant mortality rates left grieving colonial mothers who believed it was God's Will their children had died; nineteenth-century mothers blamed themselves for inadequate loving. Maternal and child death rates remained very high until the early twentieth century. Women lost pregnancies, had stillborn babies, or birthed children who lived only a few days. Babies whose mothers could not nurse them faced death. Sometimes other women nursed babies or wet nurses did so. Babies reared "by hand" with "pap boats" often died.[47]

Until the past fifty years, most Americans shared the assumption that mothers had greater responsibility for infants' care; fathers usually played minor roles for the first few years. This belief that mothers care for babies had some basis when nursing children was so crucial to babies' well-being. Seventeenth-century American women nursed for twelve to twenty-four months, while eighteenth-century women only nursed for eight to ten.[48] Most women nursed their children if they could, although upper-class nineteenth-century women used wet nurses because of fashion or their husbands' preferences.[49] Fashions affected nursing ease. Styles with low necklines made nursing more convenient than 1820s dresses with high necklines. Colonial Williamsburg has a rare dress whose "bodice front was made with a loose panel that could be unfastened at the waist and raised for nursing."[50] Nursing mothers suffered from the sheer physical strain involved, which we should interpret and appreciate in ways we seldom do.

Objects of girlhood—toys, highchairs, and clothing—illustrate their lives. Karin Calvert typifies childhood's stages as the "inchoate adult" in the seventeenth to mid-eighteenth centuries, the "natural child" until 1830, and the "innocent child" until 1900, each with its own parental expectations and associated objects.[51] These profound changes in adult expectations make matching our interpretation with particular eras important. Girls trained for their future roles as they played house with tea sets and dolls; girls' dolls have been made from rags, bisque, and plastic—a mixture of available materials and social aspirations, from baby dolls to Barbie dolls. Girls' toys often encouraged solitary indoor play in contrast to boys' outdoor games.[52] Especially physical girls were derisively labeled "tomboys."

Menarche marks sexual maturity, when girls began to menstruate and could become pregnant. We need to interpret historic girls' age of menarche because then they could bear children. The age of menarche, estimated at an average of fourteen years in medieval ages, rose with industrialization to ages fifteen to sixteen, but it has since dropped to an average of twelve to thirteen years.[53] While some cultures celebrated a girl's physical maturation into womanhood, the predominant American society has continued to shroud menstruation in shame and a sense of pollution. Women's studies professor Chris Bobel explains, "We have a very uncomfortable relationship with women's bodies, and we see menstruation as a problem that needs to be hidden or fixed."[54] Numerous medical and social theories have been advanced that have blamed menstrual and fertility problems on women's inadequacies.[55] With few clear references to women having their menstrual periods or accompanying cramps, this woman's diary entry becomes more significant: "April 19. I am flowing and have much pain all day—Regret to be so miserable for Angus' [her husband's] account."[56] Different approaches have sought to contain and conceal "menstrual products" under many euphemisms. Most women used layers of cloth (or diapers) to collect their menstruation, washing them out and reusing them; elite women had their maids do such work.[57] These napkins were truly ephemeral. A 1896 *Ladies Home Journal* advertised, "Ladies Earn Money Selling our Hygienic Comfort Belt and Supporter" with two sets of straps, one for stockings and another, a shorter higher one, "a 'double hook' fastener front and back for SPECIAL use."[58] A 1922 *Ladies Home Journal* Kotex advertisement argued, "It [Kotex] lessens the laundry problem," showing a disgruntled washerwoman who no longer had to scrub bloody stains from cloth napkins each month. Discreetly packaged disposable "sanitary napkins" eliminated that unpleasant task. Women from the 1950s through the 1970s wore garter belts to hold up stockings (replaced by pantyhose), and sanitary belts for sanitary napkins. Today, many American women use tampons. Adhesive strips attach sanitary napkins to women's underwear.

The "Museum of Menstruation" collected many such objects but closed for inadequate support and squeamishness over this basic human function. It once displayed douching powder, a 1922 "Sanitary Apron" box that advertised itself as "Indispensable for Travel, Automobiling, Athletics, Emergency Uses," indicative of changing behaviors, and a nonelastic sanitary belt marked "war duration type."[59] Women sometimes tried douches as ineffective contraception.

Products included "Vaginal Cones with Picric Acid" (an ingredient in World War I explosives), a 1928 Lysol advertisement that promised, "she stayed young within by the correct practice of feminine hygiene. . . . Buy a bottle of 'Lysol' Disinfectant at your druggist's today," and Pristeen vaginal spray deodorant, which claimed, "Unfortunately, the trickiest deodorant problem a girl has isn't under her pretty little arms."[60]

With sexual maturity, courting often followed. Since the mid-nineteenth century, mainstream American courting has had distinct chapters, from well-chaperoned young women meeting young men in parental parlors to cities allowing women more freedom with public amusements and anonymous behavior.[61] Beth Bailey argues that courting gave way to several versions of dating, from an emphasis on popularity as measured by the number of dances with members of the other sex to the ideal of "going steady" and a more commercialized approach. Young women went "steady" at earlier ages. As courting became dating, men paid directly for dates while women paid for ways to fulfill advertised impossible-to-fulfill ideals in female makeup, hair, and clothing. That change equated the value of a woman by how much a man spent on her, especially for major events such as proms, with the implicit understanding that his expenditures would translate into various degrees of her sexual availability.[62] The Great Depression then suppressed family formation; when it eased, marriage rates rose and marriage ages fell. The urgency of men leaving to fight in World War II led couples into quick marriages, which partially explains the subsequent rise in divorce rates. During World War II, men's fraternity and school class rings, engagement rings, and wedding rings given to women symbolized their relationships—and enhanced individual women's status. That approach fit with World War II advertising, which urged American women to work harder in munitions factories to bring their men safely home. Rosie the Riveter/WW II Home Front National Historical Park interprets this era with badges, tools, and even earrings made from airplane glass.[63] In addition to personal objects, dating gifts included ephemeral corsages, with orchids considered higher status than gardenias.[64] Dating patterns have repeatedly changed without any "golden age."[65]

Historically, as most women expected to marry, relevant objects provide particular insights as they demonstrate frequent changes in a social institution often assumed to be unchangeable. Different peoples had distinct expectations of marriage and women's roles in it.[66] Marriage customs followed different religions' beliefs, as seventeenth-century native peoples of New England and English colonists struggled to understand each other's marriage customs.[67] A statue of St. Anthony of Padua, patron saint for Catholic women seeking husbands, stands at Tumacácori Catholic mission in Arizona while the Russian bishop's house in Sitka, Alaska, has two wedding crowns for Russian Orthodox wedding ceremonies. Contrary to our assumption, the tradition of white wedding gowns only began with British Queen Victoria. Euro-American women had often married in their parents' parlors in their best dresses, such as the 1861 purple and white wedding dress and the 1875 blue and gray–striped one at the Autry Museum.[68] Women wore wedding rings; men less frequently. Marriage customs became more ornate in the late nineteenth century, adding floral bouquets and veils, which Jewish brides had long worn.[69] Because marriage has been considered so special, marriage-related objects including framed photographs, guest books, dried flowers, trousseau clothing, and wedding gowns have been saved and passed down from generation to generation, making them relatively common objects, especially for affluent women after the nineteenth century. Twentieth-century advertisements show household objects that women ought to acquire upon marriage, such as a "waterless cookware" sets of pans and electric coffee percolators.

Soon after marriage, pregnancy became the common state for many American women, especially for those with minimal knowledge of, or access to, birth control. As Marylynn Salmon explains, "After marriage, most seventeenth-century and eighteenth-century women spent fully twenty to twenty-five years either pregnant or nursing. . . . Their work as mothers filled their days."[70] For centuries, getting married, being pregnant, and becoming a mother were closely linked, just as caring *for* children has been tightly connected *with* women. In preparation for marriage, wealthier colonial women made or bought "suits of child-bed linen" or later a "Baby's Health Wardrobe" of clothing for their expected infants.[71] Some nineteenth- and twentieth-century women with difficult pregnancies were placed on bed rest.[72]

Linda Baumgartner at Colonial Williamsburg described women's clothing during pregnancy then:

> Many [women's] gowns fastened at the front with hidden lacings that could be let out to accommodate the new figure. If the triangular stomacher no longer fit the front of the enlarged gown, the front could be filled in with a large neck handkerchief worn much like a shawl. Petticoats usually fastened at either side with ties, and thus could continue to be worn during pregnancy by loosening the ties. Women merely tied their petticoats up over their abdomens, hiking up the hems at the front as a result. Print sources suggest that no attempt was made to adjust hemlines to make the skirts hang evenly in front.[73]

Other women who wore simpler clothing of a skirt and top made even fewer adjustments when pregnant. While the first generations of colonists had large families, by the 1780s a dramatic change occurred: The birth rate dropped and has, with some perturbations, continued to drop. Much of the American population growth has come from successive waves of immigrants, both voluntary and not. Contrary to common assumptions, before 1800, four of five women westward immigrants came from Africa, *not* Europe.[74] In the mid-nineteenth century, other northern European settlers arrived, followed by Germans fleeing political upheavals and Irish escaping the potato famine. During the late nineteenth century, millions of southern and eastern Europeans arrived. In 1890 the foreign-born population reached 15 percent, raising racist fears of "race suicide" unless northern European women had more babies. They didn't—except for the post–World War II "baby boom." Legislation severely restricted foreign immigration from 1924 until 1965, when liberalizing legislation allowed immigrants from Puerto Rico and Mexico to increase the mainland U.S. population. Such pendulum swings provide crucial contexts for women's lives, set against national and international events.[75]

Most significantly, family size for native-born Americans shrank dramatically with the "demographic transition" beginning in the 1780s—much earlier than once thought.[76] The century before, the European American population had increased at 3 percent annually, becoming *eighteen times larger*. Then the birth rate dropped dramatically in a "unique demographic evolution" not seen elsewhere.[77] Since then, the birth rate has vacillated but trended downward; immigration has brought much of the population increases. The "Mortality Revolution" began in the 1870s decreased mortality, but still left high maternal and infant death rates.[78]

Midwives assisted women giving birth, working for both mother and baby with their goal a "living mother of a living child, with a Williamsburg midwife credited with three thousand births."[79] The earlier model of a community of women and midwife helping a mother give birth at home shifted, as male obstetricians medicalized births in hospitals.

Long kept secret by male doctors, forceps were instrumental in shifting obstetrics from female midwives to male doctors.[80] First used to save maternal lives after prolonged labor had resulted in the death of their babies, forceps were later used to hasten the delivery of babies. Midwives still served minority communities until the mid-twentieth century in spite of doctors' efforts to end their practices. In *My Bag Was Always Packed: The Life and Times of a Virginia Midwife*, Claudine Curry Smith described caring for African American women and their babies. She followed official state guidance for home births, from covering beds with layers of newspapers to caring for newborn babies.

Not every woman became pregnant immediately. Historians continue to search for more evidence of how women planned and spaced their children, with nursing, which apparently suppresses ovulation, believed to be the most common approach, although coitus interruptus and abstinence, including the "rhythm method," were also used. As E. B. Connell explains:

> The transition to a more modern era in contraceptive devices was marked by the invention in 1709 of the condom, followed in the early 1800s by the contraceptive sponge and a contraceptive syringe. Although early condoms, diaphragms, cervical caps, and IUDs represented advances in terms of contraceptive efficacy, various substances inserted into the vagina were toxic and mechanical devices had the potential for both injury and discomfort.[81]

Then, in 1873, as a way to legislate morality, the Comstock Act made illegal the distribution of birth control and any advertisements or information about it. Using the U.S. mail even to send contraceptive *information* became illegal. Advertisements skirted around acknowledging contraception, as concoctions promised to cause menstrual periods; their efficacy (and safety) remains uncertain. That prohibition lasted until 1965, when the Supreme Court in *Griswold v. Connecticut* legalized it for married women and in 1972 *Baird v. Eisenstadt* for single women.[82] Obviously, availability and correct use of contraceptive methods affects their efficacy. Before *Griswold* made contraception legal in all states, older married women had to cross state lines or find a friendly school nurse to give them contraception to avoid becoming pregnant. One woman who was her family's sole support would have been fired if she became pregnant.[83] Margaret Sanger, who had opened a family planning clinic in 1916, and been arrested for it, later worked with her husband to smuggle in diaphragms with the 3-in-1 oil he imported.[84] She then worked with Katharine McCormick and Dr. Gregory Pincus to develop the first oral contraceptive, "the pill," which revolutionized women's lives with its convenience and efficacy.[85] Today, U.S. women prefer the pill, long-acting methods, and voluntary sterilization as contraceptive methods.[86] In contrast, doctors sterilized Latinas through tubal ligation, often without their permission or with coercion. In 1975, they sued to end that practice. Unfortunately, they lost.[87] The "Museum of Contraception" has over 1,100 objects and an online exhibit, "The History of Birth Control."[88] The Smithsonian National Museum of American History has another 200 objects, including an oral contraceptive dispenser. After Doris Wagner began taking oral contraceptives in 1961—"the pill"—from a bottle, its on-and-off schedule caused confusion. Her engineer husband, David Wagner, developed and patented the first dispenser.[89] During the 1930s, early pregnancy tests became available in doctors' offices, with home test kits first sold in 1978.[90]

Much of the morbid tone in Colonial and Victorian culture came from the proximity of sudden death from accidents, epidemics, and deadly childhood diseases whose names we hardly know with better sanitation practices and mass vaccinations preventing them.[91] Until the mid-twentieth century, women gave birth and faced their own deaths during and after childbirth in their homes, not hospitals. They lost their own children and were present when family members and friends died. Because death so profoundly affected many women's lives, these topics need to be thoughtfully interpreted. Deep senses of privacy make it difficult to research these life-changing events. Historian Laurel Thatcher Ulrich, in her close analysis of the *Midwife's Tale*, found a subtle reference to Martha Ballard's own daughter's death.[92] Today, while both maternal and natal death rates have substantially decreased, they remain higher for Black women. With fewer American women or their babies dying, understanding those crises depends even more on our foremothers' experiences, making such historical recapture even more important. We can barely fathom how many children families lost.

Historically, some women who were "barren" or had few children were ostracized for not fulfilling social expectations. Some women remained single all their lives by choice or because they could not find spouses; some nuns and professional women never married. Before being gay was socially acceptable, some lesbians married men or hid their partnerships to various extents. Today, with gay marriage legal and generally supported, lesbians are marrying each other and having children together. In 1900, 10 percent of women ages 45–54 were single; in 1990, 4.6 percent.[93]

For generations, some women apparently knew that ergot, pennyroyal, or savin could end pregnancies. Ladies' magazines advertised "Female medicines" that functioned as emmenagogues that induced menstruation and could cause miscarriages.[94] Under earlier U.S. law, abortions were legal until "quickening" occurred, when a woman could sense movement in her womb—before other detection methods were available.[95] Some historians claim that a silent epidemic of venereal disease rather than douching prevented pregnancies during the early twentieth century, with women unaware they were sterile from pelvic inflammatory disease.[96] Abortions were made illegal in the nineteenth century because of the danger they posed to women.[97] In the twentieth century, after abortions became illegal, some women had so-called back alley abortions, instrumental abortions often performed under unsanitary circumstances. Other women had their own doctors perform their abortions. In reaction to women dying from septic abortions, state laws began to change. After New York legalized abortion, its maternal mortality rate dropped 45 percent. In 1973, the U.S. Supreme Court made abortion legal under most circumstances under *Roe v. Wade*, which have since been restricted.[98] Objects related to these fundamentally female experiences can be found in surprising places—in advertisements for drugs to bring on menstrual periods, in medical tools such as forceps and speculums, diaphragms hidden in dresser drawers, various packages and prescriptions of contraception. Objects related to female fertility and its control need thoughtful and discreet inclusion and discussion, or misconceptions about our foremothers will persist.

Elderly women are surprisingly little studied. Some historians discuss widowhood, which was often a financial calamity, especially for women with dependent children, when women's incomes were consistently half or lower than men's. Under English common law, widows inherited one-third of their deceased husband's estates; French and Spanish women, under those legal systems of property rights, stood to inherit one half or more, legal traditions that continue in California, Louisiana, and other "common property" states. Much more research and interpretation is needed on the history of elderly women, menopause, and widowhood. Old Sturbridge Village interprets its Fenno House as home to an elderly widow and her unmarried daughter who spin, weave and house a young male boarder and rent their fields for their livelihood, illustrating a more common situation for 1830s women than we realize. In New Mexico, another living history museum, El Rancho de las Golondrinas, interprets the Abuelita's (Grandmother's) house, showing her expertise in medicinal herbs as a curandera and in homecrafts. By extending the typical lifespan interpreted, these museums help us appreciate different models of aging.[99]

Few aspects of human life have more significant impacts and have less historiography than sex! Sadly, historians often must settle for tantalizing hints rather than clear knowledge of actual earlier sexual practices and objects associated with them. Dire prescriptive warnings against sex or advertisements for all kinds of objects and substances that claim to assist or prevent pregnancy aren't evidence of actual behavior. Oral history interviewees are often reluctant to be frank, and quality historical data remains difficult to obtain. While more history of the many ways sex has been practiced is becoming more visible, the history of a fundamental human drive and activities remains inadequate.

Objects and Gender

Objects can also be analyzed by their relationships with genders. Using *binary genders* implies an either/or approach to human sexuality and related gendered behaviors. The complexity comes because different cultures define genders in diverse ways, with acceptable behavior in one cultural group rejected by another. Objects show many gendered relationships, some based on biological needs such as men's jock straps or women's breast pumps, and others culturally specific ones such as serving aprons for women or formal robes for men. Sidesaddles, hoops, and corsets have marked females as proper "ladies." Consider the variety of headgear American women have worn: caps, head wraps, mantillas, bonnets, cloches, and berets. On Sundays, women covered their hair with prayer caps, mantillas, or hats as required for worship and to show subservience. African American women traditionally wore elaborate hats, "crowns" to church, while Amish women wore white prayer caps daily and black ones on Sundays.[100] Women's hats were once so elaborately decorated with bird feathers that Harriet Hemenway and Mina Hall founded the Audubon Club in 1905 to end such massive avian killing.[101] When males and females shared clothing styles, they often wore different colors. The most formal clothing—white tie for men and long gowns for women—remains the most differentiated. Pants provide an example: In a turnabout, young boys once wore dresses, then short breeches, then pants. Women wearing bloomers were harassed. It has been illegal for anybody to wear clothing associated with the other gender. In 1851, the Chicago City Council made women wearing pants illegal—and arrested and convicted women for that outrageous behavior.[102] As recently as 1981, women were told they could not wear pants to work in a federal agency.[103] Some objects have switched gender identification—Anglo American colonial elite males wore now female-associated wigs and heels. Blue, once reserved for girls for loyalty, and pink for boys as bravery, long ago swapped meanings. Many tools were gender-specific, being closely associated with particular professions. Typewriters, while initially closely associated with men, became so affiliated with females that some women were called "typewriters." These women-associated culturally relevant objects can enrich visitor experiences by connecting historic and modern lives. In your museum's collection, which objects were once solely identified with one gender? Which ones have switched or lost their single gender identification? How do other social factors interplay with gender in these objects?

Some possessions were packed away either temporarily or permanently, until their uncertain retrieval, when women were committed to mental hospitals, sent to Japanese-American internment camps, or entered convents.[104] Other objects have been permanently lost. Some objects have been reused, such as rags once used to make paper and bottles recycled into glass. On the overland trails, people dumped beloved objects—furniture, books, and clocks that connected women with the lives they had left behind—as oxen pulling wagons flagged. Immigrants left heirlooms behind, and families lost beloved paintings when their homes burned. A dumpster near a historic site was considered too hard to climb into to gather historic records that were being thrown out . . . an egregious example of historic misbehavior. Many objects have been found in *middens* (trash piles).

Recent archaeology has worked hard to literally uncover women's lives since Janet Spector's 1993 classic *What This Awl Means: Feminist Archaeology at a Wahpeton Dakota Village* challenged others to find women everywhere in ancient middens, giving us much of what we understand about archaeology and history.[105] With careful methodology, archaeology reveals actual lives with objects left unintentionally. Many objects we know today were deliberately saved by families who bequeathed them to their descendants, often choosing the most expensive, elaborate, or personally meaningful items. These inherited objects, which often become housed in museums, have provenance, were usually well cared for, and are in reasonably good condition. They reflect not only their unusually wealthy sources, but also that they were considered special—the most special of the special—which cumulatively makes a dramatic misrepresentation of the past. For example, we see exquisite silver tea sets by Paul Revere, and reasonably but wrongly assume that many colonial women enjoyed them.

Case Study #1: Clothing Every Body

Consider all the purposes clothing played—protection from the elements (warm shawls); activities (aprons); and markers of age (girls' short dresses); status (fur muffs, long gloves); roles (American Red Cross uniforms); identity (school uniforms); special events (Christmas apron); transitions (wedding dress, widow's weeds); and ethnicity (mantillas, kimonos). Style changes give visitors insights.

Historically, women's responsibilities for clothing their families required constant work. Every "Cheyenne woman routinely carried a sewing awl . . . used daily, for sewing clothing or lodge covers, and perhaps most frequently for keeping moccasins in repair."[106] Making moccasins, the common Native American footwear, well suited to their travel was "work carried out exclusively by women."[107] Before industrialization, women sewed *all* their clothing as well as sails, sheets, tablecloths, and flags—without sewing machines, sizes, patterns, or brand names.[108] Most clothing for women and girls was custom-made until the ready-made revolution. Rather than sew new clothing, women often remade their existing ones. Working men's clothing was long commercially available for sale, and men's suits were increasingly produced assembly line fashion while most women's clothing was homemade or custom made by seamstresses or milliners until those occupations shrank dramatically around the turn of the twentieth century.[109] Dominant upper-class and middle-class Anglo-American women's fashion and silhouettes have changed every decade since the 1750s, with women adding and subtracting farthingales, petticoats, crinolines, and hoops. Frequent changes have been the only fashion constant. Enslaved women who were field hands had simple shifts and skirts of coarse cloth; other enslaved women wore somewhat better clothing.[110] At different times, fashion accentuated the bust, waist, or shoulders with styles such as huge "mutton leg sleeves" or the Sears's 1897 "Haircloth combination Hip Pad Bustle" that now seem outlandish with their exaggerated shapes of women's bodies.[111]

A major interpretive challenge is that most ordinary clothing gets worn out before being thrown out or recycled into cleaning rags. Few women wore the elegant gowns worn by some historic site interpreters or found in exhibit cases. Clothing for special events, from christening dresses to evening gowns, treasured generation by generation, can be easily found, but shifts worn as basic clothes or antique blue jeans are rare. As Mary Warner explained, the Minnesota Historical Society "collection suffered from the 'wedding dress/military uniform syndrome' that characterizes many museum clothing collections. People donate those items because they represent important events in their lives. They forget that blue jeans and t-shirts are just as important to telling their stories."[112]

During the colonial era, fabrics were expensive and limited to wool, linen, and imported silk for some, and later, cotton grown first in India or more commonly by enslaved peoples (predominantly from Africa in the Americas) under extremely harsh conditions. Transforming flax plants into linen fabric required *twenty-two* steps and many tools; wool fabric required many objects including shears and spinning wheels—and sheep. Cotton fabrics became practicable once the cotton gin could remove the seeds from the bolls; just before the American Civil War, the United States grew 75 percent of the world's cotton.[113] To meet the demand, entrepreneurs moved an estimated 1 million enslaved women and men to new cotton plantations in Arkansas, Alabama, Mississippi, and Texas. Cotton fabrics were lighter and easier to sew and clean; printed calicos became popular. During the nineteenth century, yardage *per skirt*, varying by style, ranged from three to twelve yards.[114] Synthetic fabrics that required less ironing—rayon, nylon, and polyester—only began to be manufactured during World War II.[115]

Clothing and Accessories for Life's Stages

Frequently pregnant or nursing for many years, some women wore special maternity dresses, as found at the Atlanta History Center; many women adjusted their waistlines, simply letting their skirts ride higher in front, while others wore a looser "bed gown" or "short gown."[116] A few shifts (a simple dress) still exist that women wore after giving birth and for easier nursing.[117] For generations, women wore stays and later corsets because they were "associated with feminine beauty, aristocratic display, and self-discipline, and demonstrated that a woman was not doing heavy physical work."[118] With all the layers, women could wear *thirty pounds* of clothing, useful for poorly heated rooms but clearly heavy.[119] Although corsets caused discomfort and medical concerns, they ensured erect posture, small waists, and enlarged breasts, showing desired female sexuality. Made first from reeds and "whalebone" (baleen) and later steel, stays had flexibility and strength. Whalebone corsets with incised decorations were "one of the most intimate pieces of scrimshaw a whale man could produce."[120]

The most dramatic change in women's clothing came with World War I and afterward. One dramatic illustration comes from a mother's woolen gym suit [c. 1900] and her daughter's field hockey cotton dress [1925], the one designed to conceal the female body, the latter to provide a comfortable outfit.[121] Pictures show a female silhouette more relaxed as brassieres and girdles replaced corsets. One early brassiere was simply a tie and two pieces of cloth sewn together.[122] Maidenform began manufacturing bras in the 1920s to help new, much shorter and less constructed clothing styles fit better.[123] During the Cold War, the company made the "bullet" bra as a symbol of fighting the Soviet Union.[124] One 1970s women's rights activist always wore a girdle whenever she left her house to display her cause's propriety.

Sewing Family Wardrobes

Men generally designed and patented sewing machines, "the Queen of Invention," but women *used them* constantly in another clothing revolution. As sewing machines became more common by the mid-nineteenth century, stitching speed increased dramatically. First powered by arms, then by legs pumping a treadle, and later by electricity, sewing machines were so treasured that families featured them in photographs. The time savings greatly impressed *Godey's Lady's Book*, the premier nineteenth-century women's magazine, which lauded sewing machines with comparisons of hand- and machine-made clothing, "A gentleman's shirt required one hour and sixteen minutes by machine and fourteen hours and twenty-six minutes by hand."[125] As sewing machines cost $50.00–$75.00 in the 1860s (roughly $2,000 today), *Godey's Lady's Book* recommended that families buy machines together and form clubs to share them.[126] Women lent sewing machines to those who didn't own them. Sewing machines helped expand women's wardrobes from hanging on a few pegs to cupboards to jammed master closets. Analysis of the attire worn by the early-nineteenth-century family of Sarah Snell Bryant, who lived on a Massachusetts farm, reveals her heavy workload. While each family member acquired a few new garments, she constantly mended and refashioned their existing clothing with a "relatively small number of garments made [new] in each year for each individual. Clothing kept in good repair was worn for years."[127] Some expensive nineteenth-century dresses had a modest daytime version that covered a woman's neck and arms, designed to be converted into a low-cut sleeveless evening dress.

While some men's clothes became standardized in the mid-nineteenth century, many women sewed their own clothes until the 1950s, when commercially made women's clothing became widely available.[128] Other women became professional dressmakers, forming long and intense relationships with their clients. Key to the female economy, milliners initially made and sold all kinds of female clothing and objects, but later only made intricate hats.[129] Cleaning, ironing, and mending clothing was as demanding and unceasing as the old nursery rhyme of "Wash on Monday, Iron on Tuesday," indicated, a tradition made unnecessary by electric washing machines that heated water, "agitated" the dirty clothes, then rinsed and spun them dry.

Historically, most women wore long skirts, which often became muddy or wet. Amelia Jenks Bloomer, editor of *The Lily: A Ladies Journal Devoted to Temperance and Literature*, was ridiculed when she wore loose flowing pants, covered by a short skirt with a matching jacket, soon dubbed "bloomers." Derision convinced other early feminist leaders to quit wearing the practical bloomers they preferred. Even Amelia Bloomer gave up wearing them, indicative of the resistance against women *not* wearing long skirts.[130] Much of the reaction came from men angry that this style of women's clothing was too similar in length to men's pants.[131] Anyone who has worn historic costumes knows how some can be surprisingly comfortable while others squeeze even the skinniest women. The most profound change came in the practicality of wearing and caring for clothing, a trend evident in today's knit and no-iron fabrics. Short dresses that 1920s flappers wore were actually a more dramatic change than 1960s miniskirts, as hems rose some twenty-four inches after World War I and corsets gave way to brassieres or bras. Hem styles dropped in the 1930s and rose to save fabric during World War II, before lengthening again after that war. In other words, hems rose and fell roughly decade by decade. Sleeve styles so emphasized during the nineteenth century became less enormous. Some women wore pants in private and when living on western ranches. With World War II, pants became culturally acceptable for women working as riveters and welders, because their home front efforts were recognized as crucial. Silk previously used for women's stockings was diverted for military parachutes; some women

Figure 8.2.   Sleeping bench with wooden pillow in Saaron [Sisters'] Building, Historic Ephrata Cloister. A German pietist community, Ephrata was known for its sacred music singing. Ephrata, Pennsylvania.
COURTESY EPHRATA CLOISTER, PENNSYLVANIA HISTORICAL AND MUSEUM COMMISSION.

painted "seams" on their legs as "stockings."[132] By the 1970s, some professional women risked wearing pants or pantsuits to work, although conservative resistance continued into the 1980s.

Consider what each garment shows about women's lives, when it was appropriate or not to be worn, and how most collections are skewed toward fancier clothing more frequently saved. Immaculate "museum-quality" clothing often appears pristine and "flawless," presenting an inaccurate sense of their historic condition *before* museums mended their holes, tears, and repairs. Accounts from women's travels on overland trails described dresses worn to rags. The Smithsonian's "First Ladies" exhibit inadvertently misleads us that such exquisite garments were common. Finding ordinary historical clothing—shifts, aprons, and blue jeans—remains difficult because clothes were often worn until only shreds remained. A simple calico apron worn in a Confederate hospital is rare and special.[133] The only consistency was frequent style changes.

Case Study #2: Necessities Made Art: Baskets and Quilts

Found in most cultures, baskets in their myriad shapes are simultaneously practical and artistic, made and purchased and used by women and girls—even carrying water in very tightly woven ones. Specialized baskets existed for winnowing wheat, carrying laundry, and as infant beds. Baskets used to pick berries or carry food often have residues useful for research of earlier environments or foodways. Women of all ages have used baskets, with little girls carrying personal treasures, women shopping or hawking goods, and elderly women carrying their mending. Although plastic containers have replaced many, baskets are still made in many sizes for various uses—as artwork, storage, or display. Consider the baskets at your museum/site. Were they made locally or imported? By whom and why? Handmade or manufactured? How were they used? To deliver laundry; harvest apples; collect herbs, berries, and flowers? What did they mean? What were their artistic values? So many variations for one object! This same approach can be used with other objects, always working to understand them in the context of their relationship with the women who used/owned/made them.

Some baskets demonstrated original beauty from "exacting, time-consuming work."[134] Others were quickly made. Examine objects carefully to gain a stronger understanding of women's lives. Individually made objects reflect cultural designs and available materials—grasses, feathers, wood strips—gathered from specific ecotones or by trade. Pomo women farmed in the summer and made baskets together in the winter. As sedges became rare, Pomo women substituted willow.[135] Some women made their baskets as "symbols of a living culture," with special ceremonial purposes and passed down through the generations. Pomo women were often buried with their baskets, making researching their artistry difficult.[136] To carry impressively heavy baskets, women attached tumplines or wound cloth coils on their heads.[137] Other women made baskets strictly for sale with designs modified for tourist tastes.[138] South Carolina women still sell their baskets with African-inspired designs along Route 17, "the Sweetgrass Highway."[139]

Quilts are another women-centered set of objects documenting elegance and deprivation. While mis-designated as "crafts" rather than "art," quilts, like other forms of women's creativity, *are really art*. Quilts demonstrate mastery of substance, form, design, and symbolism. Both aesthetically and technically more complex than most people realize, quilts consist of three layers, a designed top with a few to thousands of small fabric shapes precisely stitched together, a middle batting for warmth, and a bottom fabric layer. After piecing the top, the actual quilting stitches together these three layers with intricate designs. Queen-size bed quilts contain forty- to fifty-thousand small stitches, six to twelve per inch.[140] Sometimes made as objects given from one woman to another, or from one generation to another, quilts serve symbolic and practical purposes, providing comfort in nightly sleep, birth, illness, and dying, to death itself. They cover family, friends, even enemy soldiers, in the accomplished needlework of their designers and makers.[141] Their artistry comes in colors and patterns that make quilts "unnecessarily beautiful" and—more than simply bedcovers. Classic quilt patterns—"Log Cabin" and "Sunshine and Shadow"—created distinct effects with color and stitching choices. Different "schools" are easily distinguished by their designs—shapes, subject matter, colors, and fabrics. While seldom "signed," and too often anonymous, quilts are often dated by their designs and their fabrics. One woman designed and pieced a quilt top, and a "quilting bee" gathered to finish it by quilting its layers together. These community-endorsed gatherings brought women together—and created social space for them.

Pieced quilts from four different cultures show examples and raise questions for analyzing other quilts and women's lives. Four quilt styles—from Massachusetts; Hawai'i; Gee's Bend, Alabama; and Amish Pennsylvania—reflect distinct attitudes about women, their cultures, and environments. They share vibrant colors but different worlds. Massachusetts quilts have "traditional" patterns: the Double Wedding Ring and Grandmother's Garden.[142] Amish women's quilts reflect their theology with simple geometrical shapes in bold but somber colors such as Center Diamond or Stripes resembling plow furrows. Hawaiian quilts with exuberant appliquéd designs in two and three colors celebrate luxuriant native hibiscus and poinsettias. In contrast, Gee's Bend (Alabama) quilts reflect African traditions, poverty, and their isolated environment. Their quilts recycled worn-out clothes, men's jeans, and earth-tone scraps from a Sears' upholstery contract. Relatively few of these powerful Gee's Bend quilts remain, as they provided winter warmth and summer protection against mosquitos when they were burned as smudges.[143] In 1965, when Gee's Bend women rode the ferry to the county courthouse to register to vote, they were jailed instead and lost their ferry for thirty years.[144] These distinct quilt styles, which show women's responses to different life events, can be used as templates for museum and site interpretation everywhere, by connecting environments, access to resources, and cultural values with different aesthetics.

The official National Park Service definition of "Art," used as preservation policy, excludes women's baskets, quilts, and Navajo rugs from being Art as exemplars of beauty and creativity. They should be recognized as such. In her powerful *One Foot on the Rockies: Women and Creativity in the Modern American West*, Joan Jensen explores the necessary conditions for women artists to flourish.[145] Like recently "found" women landscape architects, she located many women who were once active artists but have long been forgotten. Women artists needed space, materials, emotional support, and an audience to respond and recognize them *as artists*. Finally, quilts, baskets, and other women-created art is being appreciated.

Working with Objects

Many objects that once existed no longer survive, whether destroyed by fires, floods, and theft or by simply rotting away. Objects such as thimbles, rings, and broken cups of durable metals or

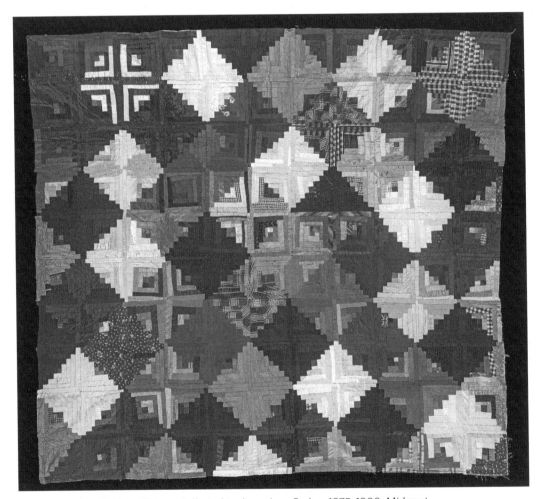

Figure 8.3.   Log Cabin quilt top, attributed to Anna Jane Parker, 1875–1900, Midwest.
COURTESY OF THE COLONIAL WILLIAMSBURG FOUNDATION. GIFT OF JEAN AND JERRY JACKSON AND BOB AND HELEN JACKSON BREWER.

ceramics survive better in archaeological excavations than organic materials of cloth and wood that disintegrate. But in the arid Southwest, objects made from organic materials, such as a yucca sandal or a turkey feather robe, survive because of their dry environment. When studying objects as evidence, consider how much environments affected their deterioration, even destruction. A display at Historic Jamestowne explains:

> Most of the objects that furnished those homes in the 17th century were made of organic materials [wood, fabrics] that generally do not survive in archaeological contexts. Metal artifacts are among the few tangible remains that show how 17th-century homes and work-places were furnished. These include iron chest locks and fittings, copper alloy curtain rings, and lead canes that held in window glass [in place].[146]

Professional museums have developed extensive protocols for handling—or more often, not handling—objects, by ensuring their careful display to minimize light fading them, protecting them from insects, securing them from theft, and rotating them to more protective storage. They routinely use complex technology to study objects to describe them, assess their condition, and determine treatments needed. Preferred treatments change but the principles of doing the least intervention necessary, documenting actions, and using reversible treatments persist. These principles help preserve objects not only in our lifetimes but for future generations as well. Professional museums use conservation departments to ensure their tangible resources are well preserved. (See Chapter 9: "Preservation.")

Women's History in Objects

Curators describe the physical characteristics of objects—their size, materials, styles, and design. They study why objects were made, how they were used, and the meanings women found in them. Colonial Williamsburg curators who reproduced a set of "Child-Bed Linen" they had assumed were baby clothes then discovered that several items were for the mother, not her baby. Such a project can involve the public in the pleasure of historical research. Atlanta History Center interpreters sew the clothing styles that they wear to show visitors the impressive amount of work and complexity involved. What did women think of these objects? How did they use them? What can they show us about women's lives? Utilitarian objects associated with women fulfill basic human needs such as food, clothing, and care for others—specifically for young, old, and sick. Women had to expend considerable effort to prepare meals—saving seeds, raising and processing plants, then storing, cooking, and serving them. Food- and cooking-associated tools reveal much about how women preserved, prepared, and served foods. A high-end 1930s kitchen with its icebox, meat grinder, and ceramic mixing bowls required different methods and culinary skills for food preparation, all requiring more effort than frozen meals popped into a microwave oven. Interpretation of such sets of food preparation needs to compare both existing period tools and the absence of modern ones. Matching cooking tools of ladles, frying pans, and mixers with historically available foods helps visitors imagine how past women cooked. Modern materials such as Tupperware plastics and Corningware ceramics provided durable materials that eased food preparation and storage.

Consider how food tools have affected women's lives and how women use them. Before the "cold chain" of refrigeration, foods were eaten in season (strawberries, watermelon) or preserved (sauerkraut). Instead of casually pulling out a bag of peas from the freezer, our foremothers had to grow, pick, and then shell them. While today we spend two minutes beating for a cake, it took them a half hour of hand-beating eggs. Diets of homemade breads, pies, and biscuits used flour from 50-pound bins rather than single canisters. In the 1880s, a Colorado high-altitude mining

Figure 8.4.   Kitchen with dual fuel stove (coal and gas) and icebox, Maggie L. Walker NHS, Richmond, Virginia.
COURTESY OF NATIONAL PARK SERVICE, MAGGIE L. WALKER NATIONAL HISTORIC SITE.

village left a rubbish pit full of hand-soldered metal condensed milk and fruit cans from foods that supplemented the flour, beans, and other staples imported there.[147] Harriet Backus, a mining engineer's young wife, detailed her struggles with cooking three meals daily at those high altitudes. One Thanksgiving, the costly turkey she had lovingly cooked had previously spoiled—its rotted meat filled their mouths.[148] Food preservation became increasingly industrialized, with crops grown in one place but processed and consumed elsewhere. Centralized hog and beef butchering and more partially prepared foods shifted the American diet, as commercial dairies replaced women's traditional small-scale butter churning and its income. National networks of finance, manufacture, transportation, and advertising contributed, as did new products—instant yeast, ready-to-eat cereals, and packaged gelatin added convenience. Consider the interaction between the lives of the women represented at your museum and the technologies available for food preservation and cooking, with the time, labor, and skill required. Technology here includes not only utilities, but also equipment to chop, mix, and stir. Food preparation offers a major opportunity to interpret women's lives—whether a frontier housewife or an urban immigrant. Toasters alone show technological advancement, from open hearths to early electric ones to high-tech toaster ovens. How can these objects help visitors understand the realities of women's historic lives? While often caring for young children, women performed these multiple tasks simultaneously, *not* one at a time. While crucial to our survival, their products were immediately consumed, not saved. When we underestimate women's workloads, we mislead visitors.

"Farmers in reality, if not in name" once applied to most American women of all backgrounds, when families and commercial economies were tightly intertwined.[149] Once, farm women drove with wagonloads of produce, fruit, baked goods, cheese, and butter (more portable, as milk spoils quickly) to town markets.[150] Objects—hoes, churns, scales, and typewriters—helped women earn their livelihoods, which included making other objects or selling them. A Salish woman with six

Figure 8.5.   Yeibachi rug, Black Mountain, Navajo Nation, Arizona, with weaver [name unknown] and purchaser Dorothy Boyle Huyck, 1963.
PHOTOGRAPH BY EARL E. HUYCK; PRIVATE COLLECTION.

children, "Oshanee . . . became an expert at Brain-tanning hides and produced soft, supple hides of superior quality, which she then made into regalia, clothing, cradle boards, and handbags decorated with beadwork." She functioned in two cultures and sold her art in several locales, "which she supplemented with seasonal income from picking apples in Washington."[151] Women used specific objects as they gave piano lessons, ran daycare facilities and IT companies, taught and tutored, wove ornate fabrics, and took catalog orders. They worked in almost every field and job while they cared for their eighty-seven-year-old mothers. Interpreting work objects—from pianos and pie pans to early mimeographs—helps visitors understand women's work and businesses. Dairying tasks alone required special pails and pans and many hours of work daily.[152] Interpreting those objects that show the complexity of dairying gives a greater sense of the demands women faced. Objects are especially crucial when women were illiterate, making our ability to read them closely essential. "We can learn about what their lives were like from artifacts. . . . Seeing these artifacts in person allows us to connect to these women in a unique way."[153] Women needed specific knowledge to accomplish those tasks, with the simplest equipment often requiring the greatest expertise. Hopi women ground corn *daily* on their stone metates using rolling pin–like manos. Hopi brides proved their worthiness for marriage by grinding and cooking corn during a four-day ordeal. Ruth Swartz Cohen in *A Social History of American Technology* lists twenty-one household skills necessary for "self-sufficiency." Work, skills, and objects match each other, allowing interpreters to use objects to reconstruct skills and demonstrate essential but often unseen work.

Carefully study existing objects (and search for missing ones) to identify activities specific to the women once present, and interpret for today's visitors. Barbells or basketballs in your collection may indicate women exercising and playing on teams, activities common during the Progressive era.[154] Some objects reflect changes in women's lives, such as "Gladys," the bicycle Miss Frances Willard of the WCTU learned to ride at age fifty-three. Willard wrote, "[B]icycling has done more to emancipate women than anything else in the world. It gives women a feeling of freedom and self-reliance. I stand and rejoice every time I see a woman ride by on a wheel . . . the

Figure 8.6. A spode soup tureen from Fort Vancouver, a frontier fort (now Washington state) with peoples from nearly all over the world, where its officers lived well.
COURTESY FORT VANCOUVER NATIONAL HISTORIC SITE, WASHINGTON, NATIONAL PARK SERVICE.

picture of free, untrammeled womanhood."[155] Objects as prosaic as lunch buckets tell us much about past women's lives—and their crucial roles that can be interpreted with the public. In their variety, objects document women's lives, show visitors their presence, and help us interpret them as well.[156] Curator Theresa Langford explains, "One of the main purposes of a museum collection is to explore histories that are not readily apparent . . . allow visitors to discover 'hidden' parts of Fort Vancouver's past through tangible objects."[157] May your objects give superb interpretive insights into women's lives. Look again at that lunch bucket and think about her work, concern, and—we hope—affection, entailed in filling it daily—and his work that it sustained.

Tools for Chapter 8: Objects

Tool 8.1: Collection Survey

Analyze the quantity and types of female-associated objects in your collection. Select ten emblematic objects, study the information you already have in your knowledge base, including their catalog records, and discuss how they can best evoke women's lives. Review their provenance, condition, rarity, cost, and any conservation needs. Consider their properties and the examples given here. Compare your collection's holdings with those objects historically present and identify objects that need to be collected, restored, etc. What is missing? Determine collection priorities by rarity, significance, and cost. Prepare a list of female-associated objects with collecting priorities.

Tool 8.2: Object Exhibition

After considering your relevant themes and stories, identify which objects can best interpret the women-associated stories of your museum/site. Connect interpretive programs and products with the key female-associated objects and either mount a new exhibit or place them in existing exhibits or rooms, such as including a shawl on a chair or a girl's toy on the floor. Plan to change the objects displayed to feature different themes—whether seasonal, life cycle, or national events. For example, the Maymont Mansion in Richmond, Virginia, powerfully used mourning objects, such as fans, cards, and mirrors draped with crepe, to interpret historic death practices.[158] An 1896 issue of *Ladies' Home Journal* provided detailed directions on mourning attire for young widows, for those who have lost their parents and distant relatives, but interestingly did not prescribe clothing for women who had lost their own children.[159] Consider using objects to interpret powerful events in past women's lives and how to exhibit them, whether joyful courting or the devastating loss of a spouse. Such changes enliven rooms and encourage return visits, but require the full use of a registration system, a key to professional management. Are some objects too fragile or controversial for display?[160]

Tool 8.3: Female-Related Objects Blog

Based on the tools above, develop a blog entry on how women and girls used and perceived these objects and how the interpretation was enhanced by greater inclusion of females. Discuss lessons learned, visitor reactions, and planned subsequent actions.

Notes

1. Bonnie Stacy, chief curator, Martha's Vineyard Museum, interview 2016.06.17, on doing women's history. Edgartown, Massachusetts.
2. Thanks to Jonathan Fairchild and Wyndeth Davis, National Park Service, Keweenaw NHP, Curto Collection, Album 12, #093 Quincy Mine, ca. 1890.
3. Margaret Byington, *Homestead: The Households of a Mill Town* (Pittsburgh: University of Pittsburgh, 1910, 1974), "I was struck by the pains taken with the mister's bucket," 64.
4. Helge and Anne Stine Ingstad, "'Discovery of the Site and Initial Excavations' of L'Anse aux Meadows, 1968–1960," Parks Canada (website), http://www.pc.gc.ca/eng/lhn-nhs/nl/meadows/natcul/decouverte_discovery.aspx.
5. Kathleen Pate, "It's What's Inside That Counts: The ESSE Purse Museum," Exhibit Review of "What's Inside: A Century of Women and Handbags, 1900–1999," ESSE Purse Museum, Little Rock, Arkansas, " https://aaslh.org/esse-purse-museum, July 12, 2019.
6. Personal visits, Martha's Vineyard Museum, June 2016, for pet chicken gravestone; Walter Magnes Teller, *Consider Poor I: The Life and Works of Nancy Luce*, reprint (Edgartown MA, 1984); and Smithsonian National Museum of American History, Washington, DC, November 2015. The Women in Military Service to America exhibit has one from 1LT Virginia Nickerson, who married Army LT Vincent DiGiacinto, https://www.womensmemorial.org/collection/detail/?s=parachutes-trousseaux.
7. Collection, Colonial National Historical Park, Jamestown, Virginia.
8. Jane C. Nylander, "Everyday Life on a Berkshire County Hill Farm: Documentation from the 1794–1835 Diary of Sarah Snell Bryant of Cummington, Massachusetts," in *The American Home* (Winterthur: Henry Francis du Pont Winterthur Museum, 1998), 103.
9. Personal observation, probably Rochester, New York, 1980s.
10. Museum of International Folk Art, Santa Fe, New Mexico, www.internationalfolkart.org.

11. Center for Women's History, "Gallery of Tiffany Lamps," New York Historical Society, https://www.nyhistory.org/womens-history/exhibitions/tiffany-gallery.

12. Karin Calvert, *Children in the House: The Material Culture of Early Childhood, 1600–1900* (Boston: Northeastern University Press, 1992), Chapter 4, "Childhood, Boyhood, and Youth."

13. The Colonial Williamsburg Foundation has excellent interactive portrayals of dressing six different groups of colonial Virginians. See "Dress the Part," https://www.history.org /History/teaching/dayInTheLife/webactivities/dress/dresspart_english/index.html.

14. Marylynn Salmon, "The Cultural Significance of Breast-Feeding and Infant Care in Early Modern England and America," in *Mothers & Motherhood: Readings in American History* (Columbus: Ohio State University Press, 1997). Hannah Rosin, "The Case Against Breast-Feeding," *The Atlantic*, April 2009, https://www.theatlantic.com/magazine/archive/2009/04/the-case-against-breast-feeding/307311/.

15. Jessica Martucci, *Back to the Breast: Natural Motherhood and Breastfeeding in America* (Chicago: University of Chicago Press, 2015).

16. Sarah Knott, *Mother Is a Verb: An Unconventional History* (Farrar, Straus and Giroux, 2019).

17. Linda Baumgarten, "Looking at Eighteenth-Century Clothing," *Colonial Williamsburg History* (blog), https://www.history.org/history/clothing/intro/clothing.cfm.

18. Thanks to Diana Pardue, Chief of Museum Services Division, Statue of Liberty National Monument and Ellis Island, National Park Service, for her assistance.

19. Patricia Samford, "Modified Cowrie Shell" (Jefferson Patterson Park & Museum, January 2008), http://www.jefpat.org/CuratorsChoiceArchive/2008CuratorsChoice/JAN 2008-ModifiedCowrieShell.html. Allison Manfra McGovern, "Rocky Point's African American Past: A Forgotten History Remembered through Historical Archaeology at the Betsey Prince Site," *Long Island History Journal* 22, no. 1 (2011).

20. Margaret Byington, *Homestead,* 1910, details women's prodigious efforts to be successful housekeepers. Mary Murphy, "The Women's Protective Union," in *Beyond Schoolmarms and Madams: Montana Women's Stories* (Helena: Montana Historical Society, 2016), 23. Thanks to Jean Ellis and Keweenaw Heritage Center, Calumet, Michigan, for their insights. Students also carried similar lunch buckets to school.

21. Thanks to Vicki Ruiz for her generous sharing. Vicki Ruiz to Heather Huyck, 2016.

22. Peoples had differing attitudes toward land ownership. Indigenous peoples who treated land as commonly held based rights on use. British common law recognized women's dower rights of one-third of marital property but otherwise practiced sole male ownership. French and Spanish colonial practices held that real property—lands and buildings—were common spousal property and gave women greater inheritance rights.

23. Minnesota Historical Society, "Harkin Store," accessed April 17, 2019, http://www.mnhs.org/harkinstore/learn.

24. *1897 Sears Roebuck & Company Catalogue* [reprint] (New York: Skyhorse Publishing, 2007).

25. Grace Hudson collected baskets and their complex histories, www.gracehudsonmuseum.org; see Birgitta Wallace, "L'Anse Aux Meadows," published 2006.11.18; http://www.thecanadianencyclopedia.ca/en/article/lanse-aux-meadows/.

26. Laurel Ulrich Thatcher, *The Age of Homespun: Objects and Stories in the Making of an American Myth* (New York: Knopf Publishing, 2001); Susan Sleeper-Smith, *Indigenous Prosperity and American Conquest: Indian Women of the Ohio River Valley, 1690–1792* (Chapel Hill: University of North Carolina Press, 2018). An indicator of the linkage between women and spinning: "spinster" originally meant one who spins. See *Oxford Living Dictionary*, n.d., https://en.oxforddictionaries.com/definition/spinster.

27. Susan Sleeper-Smith, *Indigenous Prosperity and American Conquest: Indian Women of the Ohio River Valley, 1690–1792*, 2018.

28. Barbara J. Heath, *Hidden Lives: The Archaeology of Slave Life at Thomas Jefferson's Poplar Forest* (Charlottesville: University Press of Virginia, 1999), 49.

29. Donna J. Seifert, "Mrs. Starr's Profession," in *Those of Little Note: Gender, Race, and Class in Historical Archaeology* (Tucson: University of Arizona Press, 1994), 160–65.

30. DeLois (Swoboda) Woodard Collection, Women in Military Service to America Museum, https://www.womensmemorial.org/collection/detail/?s=a-stateside-wedding.

31. Sarah Guy-Levar and Terri Schocke, *Dorothy Molter: The Root Beer Lady* (Cambridge: Adventure Publishing, Inc., 2011). See Dorothy Molter Museum, Ely, Minnesota.

32. Julia G. Costello, "'A Night with Venus, a Moon with Mercury': The Archaeology of Prostitution in Historic Los Angeles," in *Restoring Women's History through Historic Preservation* (Baltimore: Johns Hopkins University Press, 2003). ·

33. Laurel Thatcher Ulrich, *The Age of Homespun: Objects and Stories in the Making of an American Myth* (New York: Knopf Publishing, 2001).

34. Ulrich, *The Age of Homespun,* 133.

35. Lynn Sherr, *Failure Is Impossible: Susan B. Anthony in Her Own Words* (New York: Times Books, 1995), 190.

36. Jill Austin and Jennifer Brier, eds., *Out in Chicago: LGBT History at the Crossroads* (Chicago: Chicago History Museum, 2011), Chapter 1, "Exhibiting LGBT History . . ."

37. Harvey Green, *Light of the Home: An Intimate View of the Lives of Women in Victorian America* (New York: Pantheon Books, 1983), 118.

38. Mary Beth Norton, *Separated by Their Sex: Women in Public and Private in the Colonial Atlantic World* (Ithaca: Cornell University Press, 2011), 170.

39. Norton, *Separated by Their Sex,* 2011, 164–71. Laura Schenone, *A Thousand Years Over a Hot Stove: A History of American Women Told Through Food, Recipes, and Remembrances* (New York: W. W. Norton & Company, Inc., 2003), 105; thanks to Nathan Ryalls.

40. Jennifer L. Morgan, *Laboring Women: Reproduction and Gender in New World Slavery* (Philadelphia: University of Pennsylvania Press, 2004).

41. Deborah Gray White, "Female Slaves in the Plantation South," in *Before Freedom Came: African American Life in the Antebellum South* (Charlottesville: University Press of Virginia, 1991). Highly recommended.

42. Plate 12 in Edward D. C. Campbell and Kym S. Rice, eds., *Before Freedom Came,* 1991, 68.

43. "Hair as Historic Artifact," *George Washington's Mount Vernon* (blog), 2019, https://www.mountvernon.org/blog/2019/02/hair-as-historic-artifact.

44. Eva Wiegl Shankman, "In Hungary, the Holocaust's Long Reach Was Woven into a Piece of Cloth," *Washington Post Magazine,* June 9, 2016.

45. Valerie Paley, chief historian of the New York Historical Society, as quoted in Bill Schulz, "Small Relics of a Colossal Disaster," *New York Times,* June 11, 2016.

46. From http://www.everyculture.com/multi/Ha-La/Hopis.html.

47. Sarah Fox, "An Eighteenth-Century Pap Boat: Breastfeeding, Pride & Maternal Love," *Emotional Objects: Touching Emotions in History* (blog), April 4, 2014, https://emotionalobjects.wordpress.com/2014/04/04/an-eighteenth-century-pap-boat-breastfeeding-pride-maternal-love/.

48. Marylynn Salmon, "The Cultural Significance of Breast-Feeding and Infant Care," 1997, 22.

49. Marylynn Salmon, "The Cultural Significance of Breast-Feeding and Infant Care," 1997, 21.

50. Colonial Williamsburg Foundation, https://www.history.org /history/museums/clothingexhibit/ museum_explore.cfm#index=225&filter=allgenders,allclothing,alldates. Acc. Num G1990-231.

51. Karin Calvert, *Children in the House: The Material Culture of Early Childhood, 1600–1900* (Boston: Northeastern University Press, 1992). Very helpful.

52. Karin Calvert, *Children in the House,* 1992, 112.
53. Anastasios Papadimitriou, "The Evolution of the Age at Menarche from Prehistorical to Modern Times," *Journal of Pediatric Adolescent Gynecology* 29, no. 6 (2016).
54. Kvatum, "A Period Comes to an End: 100 Years of Menstruation Products," 2016.
55. Harvey Green, *Light of the Home: An Intimate View of the Lives of Women in Victorian America* (New York: Pantheon Books, 1983), Chapter 5, "Health in Body and Mind."
56. Almira MacDonald, quoted in Harvey Green, *Light of the Home,* 1983, 119.
57. Jeannette Piccard (1895–1981), explanation to author, 1973.
58. "Ladies Earn Money Selling our Hygienic Comfort Belt and Supporter," *Ladies' Home Journal,* 1896, Curtis Publishing, Philadelphia.
59. Lia Kvatum, "A Period Comes to an End: 100 Years of Menstruation Products," *Washington Post,* April 25, 2016. See also RoadsideAmerica.com, "Your Online Guide to Offbeat Tourist Attractions," "Museum of Menstruation (Closed)" n.d., https:www.roadsideamerica.com/story/2116.
60. Lia Kvatum, "A Period Comes to an End: 100 Years of Menstruation Products," 2016.
61. Kathy Peiss and Kathy Lee Peiss, *Working Women and Leisure in Turn-of-the-Century New York* (Philadelphia: Temple University Press, 2011).
62. Beth L. Bailey, *Front Porch to Back Seat: Courtship in Twentieth-Century America* (Baltimore: Johns Hopkins University Press, 1989).
63. Earring, Rosie the Riveter/WW II Homefront NHP, Object RORI 5032. The collection also includes welder's masks, goggles, and rivet guns women used.
64. Beth L. Bailey, *Front Porch to Back Seat,* 1989, Chapter 3, "The Worth of a Date."
65. Beth L. Bailey, *Front Porch to Back Seat,* 1989, 143.
66. Anne Marie Plane, *Colonial Intimacies: Indian Marriage in Early New England* (Ithaca: Cornell University Press, 2000).
67. Anne Marie Plane, *Colonial Intimacies: Indian Marriage in Early New England,* 2000.
68. Autry Museum of the American West, Dress dated 1861, Object ID98.142.2-.3; Dress dated 1875, Object ID 98.142.4; used in exhibit, "How the West Was Won," 2002. http://collections.theautry.org. Thanks to Carolyn Bruckner.
69. Bren Landon, "New DAR Museum Exhibition Showcases Vintage Wedding Dresses" (Daughters of the American Revolution Museum, April 14, 2004), https://www.dar.org/national-society/media-center/news-releases/new-dar-museum-exhibition-showcases-vintage-wedding.
70. Marylynn Salmon, "The Cultural Significance of Breast-feeding," 1997, 25.
71. Phyllis Putnam, "Child-Bed Linen," *Colonial Williamsburg* (blog), n.d.; "Baby's Health Wardrobe," *Ladies' Home Journal,* 1896, Philadelphia: Curtis Publishing.
72. Stephanie Richmond, "Clio Gets Personal, Health and Wellness: Hospital Confinement: From the 19th Century to the 21st," *Nursing Clio* (blog), April 26, 2018, https://nursingclio.org/2018/04/26/hospital-confinement-from-the-19th-century-to-the-21st/.
73. Linda Baumgarten, "Fashions of Motherhood," n.d., Colonial Williamsburg Foundation, https://www.history.org/history/clothing/women/motherhood.cfm.
74. Jennifer L. Morgan, *Laboring Women: Reproduction and Gender in New World Slavery* (Philadelphia: University of Pennsylvania Press, 2004), 199.
75. Herbert Klein, *A Population History of the United States* (New York: Cambridge University Press, 2004).
76. Susan E. Klepp, *Revolutionary Conceptions: Women, Fertility and Family Limitation in America, 1760–1820* (Chapel Hill: University of North Carolina Press, 2009). See also Herbert Klein, *A Population History,* 2004, 73.

77. Herbert Klein, *A Population History*, 2004, 72. Very useful analysis. Note that this "extraordinary growth rate" does not factor in the very high indigenous death rate.
78. Herbert Klein, *A Population History*, 2004, 112–19.
79. Laurel Ulrich Thatcher, "'The Living Mother of a Living Child': Midwifery and Mortality in Post-Revolutionary New England," *William & Mary Quarterly*, 3rd, 46 (1989).
80. Sukhera Sheikh, Inithan Ganesaratnam, and Jan Haider, "The Birth of Forceps," *Journal of the Royal Society of Medicine Short Reports*, June 5, 2013, https://www.ncbi.nlm.nih.gov/pmc/articles/PMC3704058.
81. E.B. Connell, "Contraception in the Prepill Era," PubMed, U.S. National Library of Medicine, 1999, https://www.ncbi.nlm.nih.gov/pubmed/10342089.
82. Kirsten M.J. Thompson, "A Brief History of Birth Control in the U.S.," *Our Bodies Our Selves* (blog), 2019, https://www.ourbodiesourselves.org/book-excerpts/health-article/a-brief-history-of-birth-control/.
83. Jessica Milstead and Nancy Lively, personal communication, April 2019; Used with permission. Some women became pregnant on their wedding nights (Anonymous, 2019).
84. Planned Parenthood Federation of America, Inc., "A History of Birth Control Methods" (New York: Planned Parenthood Federation of America, Inc., 2012).
85. E.B. Connell, "Contraception in the Prepill Era," 1999; Planned Parenthood Federation of America, Inc., "A History of Birth Control Methods" (New York: Planned Parenthood Federation of America, Inc., 2012.).
86. Guttmacher Institute, "Contraceptive Use in the United States," July 2018, https://www.guttmacher.org/fact-sheet/contraceptive-use-united-states.
87. Jessica Lott, "Critical Intersections: Histories of Latinos, Reproduction, and Disability," National Museum of American History, *O Say Can You See? Stories from the Museum* (blog), n.d., April 19, 2019. Sadly, they lost.
88. "Museum of Contraception," Dittrick Museum of Case Western University; https://artsci.case.edu/dittrick/collections/aritfacts/contraception-collection/.
89. Diane Wendt and Mallory Warner, "Packaging the Pill," National Museum of American History, *O Say Can You See? Stories from the Museum* (blog), June 19, 2015. Advertisement from 2000 for compact-style Ortho Personal Pak reads, "It's discreet. It's elegant. It's not what you think it is," https://americanhistory.si.edu/blog/packaging-pill. See Amanda Chau, "50th anniversary of the Pill," February 15, 2010, https://americanhistory.si.edu/blog/2010/02/50th-anniversary-of-the-pill.html.
90. National Institutes of Health, Office of History, "A Thin Blue Line: The History of the Pregnancy Test Kit," https://history.nih.gov/exhibits/thinblueline/timeline.html.
91. Michael Olmert, "This Helpless Human Tide: Bastards, Abandoned Babes, and Orphans," Colonial Williamsburg Foundation, n.d.
92. Laurel Thatcher Ulrich, *A Midwife's Tale: The Life of Martha Ballard Based on Her Diary, 1785–1812* (New York: Vintage Books, 1990).
93. Catherine A. Fitch and Steven Ruggles, "Historical Trends in Marriage Formulation, United States 1850–1990," in *Ties That Bind: Perspectives on Marriage and Cohabitation* (Hawthorne: Aldine de Gruyter, 2000).
94. Online Exhibit, "History of Birth Control," Case Western University, https://artsci.case.edu/dittrick/online-exhibits/history-of-birth-control/contraception-in-america-1800-1900/.
95. "Quickening and Fetal Development," Illinois Department of Human Resources, http://www.dhs.state.il.us/page.aspx?item=48890.
96. Allan Brandt, *No Magic Bullet: A Social History of Venereal Disease in the United States Since 1880* (New York: Oxford University Press, 1987). The Union army documented 183,000 cases of venereal disease: "The Civil War: Sex and Soldiers," Jimmy Wilkinson Meyer,

"History of Birth Control," Dittrick Medical History Center (blog), accessed April 19, 2019, https://artsci.case.edu/dittrick/online-exhibits/history-of-birth-control/.

97. Michael Olmert, "This Helpless Human Tide: Bastards, Abandoned Babes, and Orphans," Colonial Williamsburg Foundation, n.d.; Leslie J. Reagan, *When Abortion Was a Crime: Women, Medicine, and Law in the United States, 1867–1973* (Berkeley: University of California Press, 1998).

98. Leslie J. Reagan, *When Abortion Was a Crime*, 1998; Katha Pollitt, "Abortion in American History," *The Atlantic*, May 1997, https://www.theatlantic.com/magazine/archive/1997/05/abortion-in-american-history/376851.

99. See Old Sturbridge Village, https://www.osv.org/building/fenno-house/; and Traci Hodgson, "Fenno House" Chemekata Community College, 2015, http://faculty.chemeketa.edu/thodgson/262ON/unit3/OldSturbridgeVillageTour/fennohouse.html chemekata community college, 2015; Daniel Goodman and Christine Mather, *El Rancho de las Golondrinas: New Mexico's Living History Museum Guidebook* (Santa Fe: El Rancho de las Golondrinas, 2015), 29.

100. Karin Calvert, *Children in the House: The Material Culture of Early Childhood*, 1992, 43; Michael Cunningham and Craig Marberry, *Crowns: Portraits of Black Women in Church Hats* (New York: Doubleday & Company, 2000); Suzanne Fisher, "Plain Talk about the Amish: A Woman's Prayer Cap," *Amish Principles for Today's Families*, July 16, 2013, http://blogs.christianpost.com/amish-principles-for-families/plain-talk-about-the-amish-a-womans-prayer-cap-17025.

101. http://www.audubon.org/content/history-audubon-and-waterbird-conservation.

102. Jennifer Brier and Anne Parsons, "Gender Crossroads: Representations of Gender Transgressions in Chicago's Press, 1850–1920," in *Out in Chicago: LGBT History at the Crossroads* (Chicago: Chicago History Museum, 2011).

103. National Park Service, Memo to employees, 1981.

104. Darby Penney and Peter Stastny, *The Lives They Left Behind: Suitcases from a State Hospital Attic* (New York: Bellevue Literary Press, 2008); Christine Turgeon, *Art, Faith and Culture: Le Musée des Ursulines de Québec* (Québec: Monastère des Ursulines de Québec, 2004); Jeanne Wakatsuki Houston and James D. Houston, *Farewell to Manzanar* (New York: Bantam Books, 1978).

105. Janet D. Spector, *What This Awl Means: Feminist Archaeology at a Wahpeton Dakota Village* (St. Paul: Minnesota Historical Society, 1993); Donna J. Seifert, "Mrs. Starr's Profession," in *Those of Little Note: Gender, Race, and Class in Historical Archaeology* (Tucson: University of Arizona Press, 1994); Sarah Milledge Nelson, *Gender in Archaeology: Analyzing Power and Prestige* (Walnut Creek: AltaMira Press, 1997); Whitney Battle-Baptiste, "Sweepin' Spirits: Power and Transformation on the Plantation Landscape," in "Archaeology and Preservation of Gendered Landscapes," 2010, http://works.bepress.com/whitney_battle_baptiste/2/.

106. http://www.smithsonianmag.com/history/how-the-battle-of-little-bighorn-was-won-63880188/#mVsqYVhx5DDDJkXj.99, accessed November 2010.

107. Catherine Cangany, "Fashioning Moccasins: Detroit, the Manufacturing Frontier, and the Empire of Consumption, 1701–1835," *William & Mary Quarterly*, 3rd ser, 69, no. 2 (April 2012).

108. Marla Miller, *Betsy Ross and the Making of America* (New York: Henry Holt, 2010). Betsy Ross's perspective on the American Revolution. Also, Miller's *The Needle's Eye: Women and Work in the Age of Revolution* (Amherst: University of Massachusetts Press, 2006).

109. Claudia B. Kidwell and Margaret C. Christman, *Suiting Everyone: The Democratization of Clothing in America* (Washington, DC: Smithsonian Institution Press, 1974).

110. Edward D. C. Campbell and Kym S. Rice, eds., *Before Freedom Came*, 1991, 102.

111. The Fashion Institute of New York website, http://www.fitnyc.edu/museum/.
112. Mary Warner, "No Stone Left Unturned: Morrison County Photo Project Documents Uncommon Places," *Minnesota History Interpreter*, Minnesota Historical Society, March–April 2004, http://www2.mnhs.org/about/publications/interpreter/March2004.pdf.
113. "The Economics of Cotton | US History I (OS Collection)," https://courses.lumenlearning.com/suny-ushistory1os2xmaster/.../the-economics-of-cotton.
114. Jennifer Rosbrugh, "How Much Yardage Do I Need?" *19th Century Costuming for Those Who Dream of the Past* (blog), September 12, 2018, https://historicalsewing.com/.
115. Kristin Holt, "Victorian Calico Fabric–More Than Little Flowery Patterns," June 12, 2018, http://www.kristinholt.com/archives/15566.
116. Atlanta History Center, Atlanta; Linda Baumgarten, "Fashions of Motherhood," n.d., Colonial Williamsburg; https://www.history.org/history/clothing/women/motherhood.cfm.
117. Jane C. Nylander, "Everyday Life on a Berkshire County Hill Farm: Documentation from the 1794–1835 Diary of Sarah Snell Bryant of Cummington, Massachusetts," in *The American Home* (Winterthur: Henry Francis du Pont Winterthur Museum, 1998), 108.
118. Colonial Williamsburg Foundation, "Historic Threads" online exhibit. Object 99.79.3. http://www.history.org/history/museums/clothingexhibit/index.cfm. Stays as "very nearly purgatory," in Karin Calvert, *Children in the House: The Material Culture of Early Childhood*, 1992, 86. There are online classes on sewing nineteenth-century clothing, such as "Victorian Undergarments," at https://classes.historicalsewing.com/p/victorian-undergarments. HistoricalSewing.com includes a variety of fashion resources.
119. Harvey Green, *Light of the Home*, 1983, 127.
120. National Museum of American History, Exhibit "Water."
121. Laurel Thatcher Ulrich et al., *Tangible Things: Making History Through Objects* (New York: Oxford University Press, 2015), 64–70.
122. See http://museum.nps.gov/. Also see Lowell NHP, object, LOWE 12462. "A green rayon brassiere . . . trimmed with beige lace."
123. Jennifer Snyder and Mimi Minnick, "Maidenform Collection, 1922–1997, #585" (Smithsonian Archives, 1997, rev. 2005), Archives Center, National Museum of American History, http://amhistory.si.edu/archives/d7585.htm.
124. Natasha Synycia, "Domestic Containment Can't Contain this Woman: The Maidenform Woman as the American Woman." Paper delivered at Western Association of Women Historians, San Diego, April 28, 2017.
125. Harvey Green, *Light of the Home*, 1983, 82.
126. Harvey Green, *Light of the Home*, 1983, 81–83.
127. Jane C. Nylander, "Everyday Life," in *American Home*, 1998.
128. Claudia B. Kidwell and Margaret C. Christman, *Suiting Everyone: The Democratization of Clothing in America* (Washington, DC: Smithsonian Institution Press, 1974).
129. Wendy Gamber, *The Female Economy: The Millinery and Dressmaking Trades, 1860–1930.* (Champaign: University of Illinois Press, 1997).
130. Lynn Sherr, *Failure Is Impossible: Susan B. Anthony in Her Own Words* (New York: Times Books, 1995), 188–98.
131. Alia Al-Khalidi, "Emergent Technologies in Menstrual Paraphernalia in Mid-Nineteenth-Century Britain," *Journal of Design History: Technology and the Body* 14, no. 4 (2001).
132. Dorothy Boyle Huyck, personal communication, 1975.
133. Edward Campbell and Kym S. Rice, eds., *A Woman's War: Southern Women, Civil War, and the Confederate Legacy* (Charlottesville: University Press of Virginia, 1996), 125.
134. Joan M. Jensen, *One Foot on the Rockies: Women and Creativity in the Modern American West* (Albuquerque: University of New Mexico Press, 1995), 63.

135. Joan M. Jensen, *One Foot,* 1995, 62.
136. Suzanne Abel-Vidor, Dot Brovarney, and Susan Billy, *Remember Your Relations: The Elsie Allen Baskets, Family & Friends* (Berkeley: Heyday Publishing, 2005).
137. Quetzaltenango, Guatemala, July 1969, personal experience of author.
138. Joan M. Jensen, *One Foot,* 41–43
139. "Sweetgrass Baskets—South Carolina State Handicraft," *SCiway.* March 26, 2016, http://www.sciway.net/facts/sweetgrass-baskets.html.
140. See https://www.amishcountrylanes.com/.
141. "Irish Chain with Applique Quilt," in Bets Ramsey and Merikay Waldvogel, *Southern Quilts: Surviving Relics of the Civil War* (Nashville: Rutledge Hill Press, 1998).
142. Lynne Zacek Bassett, ed., *Massachusetts Quilts: Our Common Wealth* (Hanover: University Press of New England, 2009).
143. "Quilts in Amish Culture," March 23, 2016, http://worldquilts.quiltstudy.org/amishstory/historic/; Serrao Poakalani et al., *The Hawaiian Quilt: The Tradition Continues* (Honolulu: Mutual Publishing, 2007); Paul Arnett, Joanne Cubbs, and Eugene W. Metcalf Jr., *Gee's Bend: The Architecture of the Quilt* (Atlanta: Tinwood Books, 2006), 23.
144. Paul Arnett, Joanne Cubbs, and Eugene W. Metcalf Jr., *Gee's Bend,* 2006, 18.
145. Joan M. Jensen, *One Foot on the Rockies,* 1995.
146. See http://historicjamestowne.org/collections/selected-artifacts/household.
147. Harriet Fish Backus, *Tomboy Bride: A Woman's Personal Account of Life in Mining Camps of the West* (Portland: Westwinds Press, 1980); Bill Sagstetter and Beth Sagstetter, *The Mining Camps Speak: A New Way to Explore the Ghost Towns of the American West.* Denver: Benchmark Publishing of Colorado, 1998.
148. Backus, *Tomboy Bride,* 1980, 74–75. For Hawai'ian quilts, see the University of Hawai'i at Manoa, http://www2.ctahr.hawaii.edu/costume/quilts/brochure01.html.
149. Ruth Schwartz Cowan, *A Social History of American Technology* (New York: Oxford University Press, 1997), 28.
150. Pauli Murray, *Proud Shoes: The Story of an American Family* (New York: Harper & Row, 1956), 76–77.
151. Laura Ferguson, "Oshanee Cullooyah Kenmille: A Joyful Spirit," in Martha Kohl, ed., *Beyond Schoolmarms,* 2016), 116. She also taught her skills to others.
152. Cowan, *Social History,* 41 and 43. See *More Work for Mother: The Ironies of Household Technology from the Open Hearth to the Microwave* (New York: Basic Books, 1985).
153. Museum Technician Meagan Huff, Fort Vancouver NHP, 2015.
154. Rachel M. Gunter, "Her Own Hero: How Self-Defense Became Acceptable for American Women," *Nursing Clio* (blog), April 4, 2019, https://nursingclio.org/author/rachelgunter/.
155. Frances E. Willard, *How I Learned to Ride the Bicycle—Reflections of an Influential 19th Century Woman,* 1991 ed. (Sunnyvale: Fair Oaks Publishing, 1895).
156. For example, see "The Poncho Quilt—Rose Tree," which corroborates a family story by the creative but subtle repairs to their quilt. In Ramsey and Waldvogel, *Southern Quilts,* 1998.
157. Theresa Langford, curator, personal communication, Fort Vancouver NHP, 2012.
158. Maymont mansion, Richmond, Virginia, 2015.
159. Elizabeth Mallon, "Suitable Mourning Costumes," *Ladies' Home Journal,* 1896, Philadelphia: Curtis Publishing, 21.
160. Harriet Baskas, *Hidden Treasures: What Museums Can't or Won't Show You* (Guilford: GlobePequot Press, 2013).

9

Preservation

From Great-Grandmothers to Great-Granddaughters

"We've all lost a part of our heritage,"

> —A Cloutierville, Louisiana, resident mourned
> when author Kate Chopin's Creole house burned down[1]

Tangible resources connect the past with the future. Previous generations saved special places for "future generations." Now, we are those "future generations" entrusted to preserve our heritage "for future generations." Many different organizations and individuals—predominantly women—have saved historic properties. While the Mount Vernon Ladies Association is the most famous, the National Association of Colored Women preserved Frederick Douglass's home, Cedar Hill; the National Trust for Historic Preservation has been a major preservation force since 1949; and many local women's groups, as well as Latina and LGBTQ groups, have all protected our tangible past. They have identified and preserved sites and founded museums. Women's groups and family members have long played central roles in preserving historic houses, sites, and museums and continue to do so, preserving innumerable mansions, historic houses, and parks, including the Natchez Pilgrimage, the Bolduc house in St. Geneviève, and "the Alamo." Ironically, women-related resources have received little protection except as by-products of saving Great Men's domestic spaces.

Every museum collection and every historic site is rife with women-associated objects and architecture. Great Men's homes, battlefields, and collections also contain many female-associated elements. Only in the past thirty years have systematic efforts identified women's sites.[2] Such recognition has practical and aesthetic ramifications in the care given buildings and objects as well as their public recognition. For example, before Elizabeth Cady Stanton's Greek Revival house was appreciated as significant, in 1972 its owners painted it a most unhistorical *bright turquoise*. After Stanton's house became part of Women's Rights NHP, its appropriate Greek Revival white color was restored.[3] Ironically, preservation projects often appear better before preservation work is undertaken rather than during that intensive process.

Special Attraction of the Real and Challenge of the Old

Although preservation often entails saving a favorite local mansion or school, it is much more than that. Preservation entails myriad resources and actions based on interlocking principles and laws. Both "historic preservation" and "cultural resources management" (CRM) share the goals of protecting physical embodiments of the past. Here, the more inclusive term "tangible

Figure 9.1.   Pauli Murray Family Home National Historic Landmark, Durham, North
Carolina, before restoration.
PHOTOGRAPH BY BETH BOLAND.

resources" alleviates the misleading division between "natural" and "cultural" resources that so
often overlap. Preservation of tangible resources can be simply defined as extending their exis-
tence through designation, documentation, and careful physical treatments, parallel to recognizing their significance, building their knowledge base, and protecting them. Preservation helps
resources resist both natural cumulative changes as well as catastrophic destruction by flood,
fire, or disrespect.

Preservation comforts us that people have survived harder times, gives us perspective,
and shows us alternatives to embrace or avoid. We've all seen old buildings being torn down or
vacant ones falling down. Preservation battles are fiercely fought between commercial needs
and local people wanting to retain their heritage, or the "built environment" as architects call it.
Architects have long endorsed preservation of architectural treasures, as have museum curators
of objects; landscape architects increasingly recognize preservation needs. But the emphasis
on famous male architects and landscape architects and male-related objects has kept female
tangible resources from similar preservation efforts. When few *identified* resources remain from
women or other groups, visitors often conclude those groups weren't there or they accomplished
little. Reasonable as that approach might seem, it's often inaccurate. We know now that women
accomplished a great deal that has not been recognized. Much history women made had only
visible male leaders. For example, we only heard about men during the American Revolution,
before recent scholarship showed how many women accompanied the Patriot army and were
integral to its success. Now we increasingly recognize female agency from women's tangible
resources, whether Seneca orchards or the Ludlow massacre archaeological site in Colorado.[4]
We need to identify and preserve adequate evidence of women's lives and accomplishments.
We also need to reconsider the women's history present in places that focus on men—all those
battlefields that were once family farms and forts where women lived and traded. Those locations
were often connected with women who are now in the minority but once were in the majority,
such as Native American women.

Tangible resources have emotional aspects. When we walk through the home of a famous woman, knowing she climbed up the very same stairs as we are climbing, or look closely at an object of hers, we sense a frisson of curiosity, even wonder. Walking through a building that has stood for centuries, where famous and amazing people once lived, we wonder if some of their special qualities might somehow rub off on us. Or connecting with a past woman when we pick up her hairpin lost a century ago. Finding human skeletons lying just as they had been buried centuries ago is a humbling experience, seeing their teeth in excellent condition, and realizing *they were/are us but centuries ago*. That sense of connection powerfully binds us. It is curiosity, and also anticipation that we just might find something amazing, that uncovering what *seems* to be "plain dirt" could be someone's foundation, fireplace, and doorway. Glass shards may indicate a window's previous location. Discarded housewares and broken wineglasses help us piece together a lost world. A thimble, a diary, and an earring all reveal past women.

Preservationists versus Historians

Preservationists and historians have distinct approaches to the past. Preservationists *begin* with the extant tangible resources and conduct "windshield surveys," drive-by searches used to expeditiously locate buildings and structures worthy of preservation. Traditionally, historians have begun with written sources—although they increasingly use visual and oral sources—to identify people or events they deem important. These distinct approaches have ramifications for women's history, with the kinds of tangible resources that preservationists seek to preserve and the questions historians seek to research and interpret. Sometimes their approaches overlap, but other times they conflict. Preservation efforts often begin with groups and individuals passionate about protecting locally significant buildings and famous architects' designs. They approach preservation from the perspective of *what still physically remains*, especially resources deemed architecturally significant. With a tinge of nostalgia, some groups treasure a quaint train station; others focus on famous architects' works.

In contrast, historians first research a particular person or event and then seek evidence from it. Years ago, an NPS historian dismissed a National Historic Landmark designation for the home of Zora Neale Hurston, author of *Their Eyes Were Watching God*, as unimportant. He argued that its cinder blocks *lacked architectural significance* although he seemed unacquainted with this American classic novel and with African American women's history as well. The National Register nomination describes her home as "a very modest, but substantial one story concrete-block structure with a tar and gravel roof which extends into a stoop over both the front and back door entrances."[5] He rejected the insight that such common construction materials revealed much about her life situation and the forces she faced as an African American woman.[6] NPS historians questioned the designation of artist Georgia O'Keeffe's home and studio in Abiquiu, New Mexico, as a NPS unit, because they didn't believe *she* was significant(!). Unless the people charged with evaluating potential women's history–related sites know enough about women's history and are sympathetic to it, getting such sites designated and preserved can be difficult. A closely related issue is the class bias toward all things deemed elegant and the privileging of White heritage. During recent years, the NPS has worked to modify their approach to include Latinx, LGBTQ, Asian Pacific Islanders—and women. Although the National Register of Historic Places lists properties of local, regional, and *national* significance, many state historic preservation offices prefer local properties, rather than National Historic Landmarks, which require national significance.

Categories available in filling out preservation documents seldom consider the profoundly important but less visible roles women have played, recognizing public male voices over work done by women "behind the scenes." Visibility differs from effectiveness. In civil rights, for example, women of the Women's Political Council such as JoAnn Robinson, a professor at Alabama

State College, organized the 381-day Montgomery bus boycott, but Dr. Martin Luther King, pastor of Dexter Avenue Baptist Church, receives most of the credit. Mrs. Rosa Parks, a trained civil rights worker long active in the NAACP who risked her life and lost her livelihood, has often been demeaned as "being tired."[7] That double standard is a catch-22: Women did the unglamorous and tedious work of phone calling, envelope stuffing, and door knocking. Then male leaders arrived to be more visible—and the women were kept from becoming visible!

As you work on sites, watch for *gender symmetry*. Are both male- and female-related stories and objects preserved, or given equivalent titles and names? The Olympics routinely referred to "men" and "girls." Are women called "Clara" while men are called "Mr. Clark"? What spaces did each gender claim? This approach requires knowing what spaces were probably present then and how women controlled certain spaces, such as a lunchroom, or men a poolroom. History is not only flashy events; it is also long-term profound processes—as powerful as they are subtle.[8] Historians are often a solo, even lonely voice among the many professionals who manage museums and sites, requiring us to present and defend our insights.

Women-Associated Tangible Resources

Many women-associated objects were once so "common" they were frequently thrown out or have lost their provenance—who owned this wooden sock-darning egg or glass orange juice squeezer? What can a woman's house tell us about her? Tangible resources of all kinds have their own life cycles of creation, use, deterioration, and sometimes restoration—or demolition/ loss. Single-family mansions became divided into multiple units, such as the apartment Margaret Mitchell, newspaperwoman and author of *Gone with the Wind*, facetiously labeled "The Dump." The Molly Brown House was the home of Margaret Tobin Brown, famous as the "Unsinkable Molly Brown" in the *Titanic* disaster but also a strong advocate for women's causes. Her mansion became a boardinghouse but has been restored as her single-family home. Elizabeth Cady Stanton's home in Seneca Falls once was twice as large with two wings and a porch. National Park Service preservationists in the regional office blocked park efforts to rebuild those wings, which included Stanton's kitchen, arguing it was against policy and unnecessary for interpretation.[9] Rebecca Conard, in "'All Men and Women Are Created Equal': An Administrative History of Women's Rights National Historical Park," criticizes the greater weight given over preservation than interpretation, arguing that the currently much smaller Stanton House does not reflect her household philosophy, her busy life with seven children and husband, or the cultural landscape, which included a barn where her sons played billiards.[10] While some architectural styles remain stable, many people have "improved" their homes by adding rooms, enclosing porches, painting rooms the latest color, or repurposing stables into garages. Stoves replaced fireplaces; furnaces replaced stoves as each change brought increased efficiency and comfort.

The biases against preserving the whole story are subtle but real—the focus on courthouses rather than once ubiquitous boardinghouses, on restoring the parlor rather than the kitchen, on stabilizing the well-built mansion rather than crudely constructed housing for enslaved men, women, and children. In each of these cases, the gender component, whether boardinghouse keepers or enslaved field women, receives less attention than the elite or male one. A surprising number of historic sites and museums use servants' quarters and kitchens as staff offices or curatorial storage instead of restoring and interpreting those prime parts of the history. Key aspects of women's work then disappear.[11] Interpreting the whole story encourages preservation of extant tangible resources from everyone involved as much as possible.

Historic preservation has its own biases, particularly toward wealthy owners and famous architects. The oft-heard claim "they used to make things better back then" ignores the fact that poorly made objects seldom survive the tests of time, with quality ones having the greatest likelihood of survival. Just as it is much more difficult to find a pair of 1920s working blue jeans than a 1900 evening gown, an original-condition cowshed, or worker's house, is less common than a mansion. Wealth, fame, and architectural distinction often reinforce each other. On most sites, some buildings and structures no longer exist, having rotted, collapsed, or been torn down. Some preservationists ferociously oppose building any "new" construction, such as infilling any dependencies or other smaller buildings that shape a farmstead. These secondary buildings were especially at risk of neglect and demolition due to their size, their original construction, and their significance—or lack of it. Having the mansion/farmhouse on land without all the smaller structures that once supported it misrepresents the past landscape when the woodshed, barn, slave housing, or country store are gone. Having some buildings present but others missing distorts the visual landscape. It's problematic to know what one has lost if one never knew it was once there! The often-glib response that interpretation can replace missing tangible resources for visitors is wishful thinking. Yes, iPads and websites can successfully help visitors understand the Lincoln Cottage in Washington, D.C. As will be discussed in the next chapter, however, interpretation cannot substitute for inadequate tangible resources and claim to be "place-based interpretation."

Preservation requires 1) identifying and preserving tangible resources associated with women's lives; and 2) caring for what has been saved—protecting *both* the Civil War cavalry sword and the homespun dress. Museums have many thousands of women-related objects that need recognition and care. Putting images of women-associated objects online, in exhibits, programs, and other media, shows their heritage to more people, increasing support for those museums and telling a more truthful history. It entails identifying objects people have stashed away or nearly thrown out, convincing owners of their value and encouraging their protection. Preservation also requires protecting the knowledge base associated with a landscape, building, or object. In addition to knowing the provenance (its ownership genealogy), it's crucial to have information about its creation, use, damage, and past treatments.

Museums and historic sites require preservation expertise and activities because their purpose would disappear without their tangible resources. People are fascinated to get close to a "real" historic dress or imagine being at sea when they step belowdecks inside a historic ship. Preservation requires knowledge about a resource, knowing how to care for it, being able to afford to do so, and, finally, doing it correctly. Preservation principles have been developed from various disasters. A classic mistake has been repointing (replacing) the mortar in old brick walls with Portland cement. The much harder cement causes softer historic bricks to spall, or pop out, leaving defaced and damaged buildings. Through such painful lessons, preservationists and cultural resource managers have developed the principles of using the gentlest repair methods possible and respecting original designs, methods, and materials.

Preservationists can sound fussy, insisting that every object and every treatment be documented, that repairs be reversible, and that extreme care be taken in handling everything such as "Never pick up baskets by their handles," or not allow any ink or liquids near historic papers. But preservationists know that these cultural resources are irreplaceable. Unlike plants and animals, buildings and objects cannot grow back (not all living creatures can survive either). If a priceless work of art gets broken, it can be restored but never returned to its original condition. Buildings, structures, and landscapes, exposed to weather, further lose their original materials when repaired. Although we imagine that well-preserved tangible resources are the exact same materials that our predecessors knew and used, that is seldom the case. Good preservation practice *repairs* damaged resources, such as using epoxy on wood rather than *replacing* it, and it emphasizes replacing "in-kind" using the same materials if possible. Sometimes original materials, such as chestnut wood from forests killed by the 1930s blight, are no longer available. In other instances, the original but now severely damaged tangible resources have elements that contained irreproducible information, such as the notes the Chinese cook wrote on the walls of a Montana ranch cookhouse or the markings from clothes hangers Alice Paul left on her mantelpiece, evidence of her decision not to spend time hanging up clothing.[12] Preserved architecture is as close to the original version as possible.

Ironically, we often only see objects in their discarded versions rather than in their new or still-being-used ones. Many historic objects show considerable amounts of wear or outright damage; it's hard to imagine that the rusty "sad" clothes iron or a cracked bowl was ever usable. Sometimes damages occurred since clothing was worn, such as a now-moth-eaten dress. When objects cannot function as originally intended or a shopping mall has replaced the cornfields of a historic farmstead, confusion easily follows. That makes interpretation more difficult because these distractions need explanations before interpretation can focus on the story itself. When missing parts have been replaced—the often-photographed canopy at the entrance to the Great Hall at Ellis Island—people looking at the object or building should be able to see its repaired or replaced parts but not be distracted by them. Preservation and CRM work to protect tangible resources from deterioration. When a building has not been maintained with paint, gutters, and an intact envelope (walls, windows, and roof), weather and humans damage it surprisingly quickly. Much preservation work is routine maintenance, creating optimal environmental conditions for object storage and protection from theft or other human damage. Obviously preserving a cultural landscape requires somewhat different tools and techniques than preserving a shed, butter churn, or shawl, but the principles are similar.

We want tangible resources to be as original as possible because they can contain information that we cannot yet unlock and answer questions we will someday want to ask. Objects preserved from particularly awful and difficult aspects of our history, such as slave shackles, bring reality to us. Without such tangible evidence of slavery, racist myths of gracious living easily persist. We see the elaborately carved *punkah*, a huge wooden paddle over a dining room table that fanned its diners before electricity.[13] That seems gracious only if we ignore the enslaved child pulling its rope and see the preserved accoutrements that bound her life.

Much of preservation is "simply" taking good *care* of tangible resources to ensure that treasured parts of our heritage survive. It's a multidisciplinary effort with archaeologists, curators, architects, maintenance crews, conservators, and historians working together. Historians of women must hone our arguments as to *why* tangible resources of women's history matter and need preservation. Accuracy, fairness, research, and calm authority best counter touchy opponents. Techniques vary by the specific resource. Tangible resources related to women's history have especially suffered from inadequate respect and inadequate knowledge. Fewer people have cared. Museums have often given women and girls' tangible resources less attention.

Damage, Restoration, Maintenance

Preservation includes all the actions taken to protect landscapes, buildings, and objects from ignorance, theft, bulldozers, or rot. Not everything can be saved forever because wood rots and paper disintegrates. Preservation practices range from local recognition of favorite buildings to highly technical analyses of historic resources. Techniques include everything from "sistering" joists together when original ones have weakened, removing hazardous materials, filling out and removing hazardous materials, to applying for tax credits. Actions range from the dramatic relocation of the Cape Hatteras lighthouse to prevent it from toppling into the Atlantic Ocean to dusting lampshades with soft brushes. Preservation does not ensure a building no longer leans or is now "pretty"—showing original materials and wear marks has priority. Construction that once used wood and stone, then iron and steel, now includes materials such as plastics not found in nature, complicating preservation challenges. Preservation helps counter the many ways tangible resources are lost to us and future generations. Tangible resources related to women's history have faced—and continue to face—several threats that need to be countered if our whole story is to be told. They are:

- *Damage by inadequate respect.* Destruction by neglect occurs when resources or the women who created them are deemed unimportant and get inadequate attention. Some objects precious to our foremothers simply aren't as valuable to us. Photographs of dead children and jewelry made from human hair may seem disgusting until we appreciate that these objects were often the *only* physical connections left to grieving families. Fortunately, museum policies have protected such objects. Burning women's letters, misusing inherited treasures, or allowing a dog to chew a handwoven Navajo rug all disrespect the women who made and used them.
- *Damage by inadequate knowledge.* Cleaning objects incorrectly often damages them—dishwashers pit sterling silver items and acidic cleaners turn marble surfaces grainy. In West Texas, candelillas plants were gathered, and then processed at local factories into wax as key ingredients of gum and cosmetics. Archaeologist Curs Tunnell, who documented the camps, concluded that no women worked in them *because he didn't see any women* there. Twenty years later, in the 1990s historian JoAnn Pospisil found daughters, wives, and other female *candelillerias* gathering the plants and processing their wax and a 1917 photograph of a candelillerias camp that showed a woman working away. Their ephemeral camps of simple thatched shelters used for gathering the candelillas had not left clear archaeological evidence, while brick foundations remained from the metal-roofed wax-processing factories. Consider that without the gathering camps, the factories lacked candelillera wax to process.[14]
- *Damage by inadequate care.* After Rachel Jackson and Andrew Jackson died, her beloved garden declined. The Ladies' Hermitage Association initially found its "beds were weedy, fences broken and shrubs and trees were dead or dying."[15] Many historic buildings deteriorate before their rescue—or are permanently lost. Before its restoration, the second floor of the Main Hall on Ellis Island had holes three feet across. Poor protection can damage tangible resources. A woman who mailed a black-on-black earthenware plate made by the famous potter Maria Martinez inadequately wrapped it. Consequently, the San Ildefonso Pueblo plate arrived broken into thirteen pieces. Unbroken, it would fetch thousands of dollars; now its value remains in its exquisite beauty and linkage to an amazing artist.

Preservation Issues: Additions, Subtractions, Modification

Ironically, poverty sometimes "preserves" buildings, as when owners of antebellum Natchez, Mississippi, mansions could not afford to update them after the Civil War. Charlestown, South Carolina, "was saved by a combination of calamity and tradition," as Stewart Brand explains in *How Buildings Learn: What Happens after They're Built.* Most buildings are modified over the years as uses, styles, and occupant needs change, making the key preservation concept "period of significance" sometimes difficult to determine. That concept focuses and limits which physical elements are preserved, restored, or removed in the preservation of a specific building. Brand shows how difficult maintaining buildings in their "original" states is, even as he praises time-kindly buildings as both flexible and sustainable, characteristics many historic buildings have.[16] Brand demonstrates how changing lifestyles affect buildings, such as modern pueblo dwellers, who moved the entrances to their homes from ladders going down into them to doors on their sides. He also discusses preservation "sins" such as "slipcovering" buildings with metal grilles that hide historic fabric.[17] Museum and historic site staff often feel ambivalent in appreciating old buildings while struggling with their realities. When many middle-class Americans migrated from urban to suburban living, they increased preservation challenges when they abandoned an enormous but deteriorating urban infrastructure of once-magnificent buildings.

Preservation Law: Identification, Research, Designation, Treatments, and Maintenance

Preservation handles real property within a formal framework of laws, processes, and regulations derived from the National Historic Preservation Act of 1966 (NHPA) and sister laws. These laws extend from local to all federal entities and set out different historic preservation responsibilities. Federal, state, local, tribal, and especially private partners identify, document, and preserve cultural resources, all playing crucial roles. Preservation efforts are strengthened when local governments, state historic preservation offices, and/or the National Trust for Historic Preservation, along with the National Park Service as "Keeper" of the National Register of Historic Places, are involved, as they can provide technical expertise, official recognition, and sometimes funding. While dated, the National Trust's *A Layperson's Guide to Historic Preservation Law: A Survey of Federal, State, and Local Laws Governing Historic Resource Protection* provides an excellent summary in a thoughtful framework.[18]

The famous Section 106 of the NHPA establishes a *process* for determining whether a proposed federal action will damage a historic resource either already on, or eligible for listing on, the National Register of Historic Places. Because federal "undertakings" include an immense variety of actions, including funding, permits, and loans, a great many projects require NHPA compliance, including highway and housing construction. Resources *eligible for* the National Register are also protected. Because protection is process-based, not absolute, only court decisions and local ordinances are legally binding. Properties can be razed even if the preservationists have done everything required. Public opinion, the strongest protection, requires activated and organized public opposition.

Preservation Identification

Traditionally, preservationists drove areas looking for potentially interesting architecture in "windshield surveys." Identifying women's history–related resources has been somewhat more complicated. Twenty years ago, with Congressional direction and funding, Dr. Page Miller added twenty-three female-focused National Historic Landmarks. Secretary of the Interior Kenneth Salazar called for a workshop, which was then held at Sewall-Belmont House, now, Belmont Paul Women's Equality NM, in December 2012 with the National Collaborative for Women's History Sites. That workshop eventually resulted in the National Historic Landmark designation of the Pauli Murray Family home, Marjorie Stoneman Douglas home, and nomination of the Annie Wauneka Navajo Tribal Council House. Recent NHL designations include the homes of Frances Perkins and Mary Baker Eddy.

Existing resources to identify more tangible resources in women's history include state historic preservation offices, organized women's groups, academia, local heritage groups such as state women's halls of fame, and focused organizations for sports, fashion, education, and religion interested in preserving tangible resources related to their fields. For example, quilt museums preserve and interpret women's needle arts in Paducah, San Jose, Lincoln, Golden, and LaGrange.[19] Matching important women and organizations with state and local tangible resources can help identify more sites. The National Trust has sought to identify additional "National Treasures" for preservation and support, and the Smithsonian is undertaking analysis of its massive holdings. Many more museums and historic sites are strengthening the tangible resources in their collections. But recently the president of a local historical society explained that she wanted to include women's history but had *no idea* how to begin or if she could even find any women's history. Many museums and historic sites large and small still remain sadly lacking in women's history.

Many more sites should be designated, especially the home of Estelle Griswold, next to the former Planned Parenthood office in New Haven that precipitated *Griswold v. Connecticut*, the 1965 Supreme Court case that legalized contraceptive information for married women. Many other locations related to computer pioneer Admiral Grace Hopper; Jeannette Piccard, who piloted a balloon into the stratosphere in 1934; Phyllis Schlafly, activist who masterminded opposition to the Equal Rights Amendment; Betita Martinez, Latina organizer; Gerda Lerner, founding mother of women's history; Pearl Hart, lesbian attorney and activist; Anita Bryant, singer and anti-gay activist; and Cherokee leader Wilma Mankiller. All their related properties lack a key step to their preservation. Fast-food restaurants that simplified feeding families and shopping malls that made consuming a leisure activity and have so changed women's lives need preservation too.[20] Additional sites of women's education and economic roles need identification and preservation.

Many more women properly deserve such recognition—dancers, boardinghouse keepers, swimmers, scientists, academics, and activists of all kinds. Museums and sites must preserve the stories, objects, and places of those who opposed women's and human rights to document the difficulties women faced in obtaining greater rights, as well as recognizing more women than those who were involved in rights struggles. The organizations that opposed women's rights, the individuals against lesbian rights, and the institutions that embodied patriarchal values need preservation too. More research, preservation, and interpretation are needed for properties associated with all underrecognized women. Rather than the usual architecture/art history stylistic approach, preservation needs to emphasize vernacular architecture, suburban locations where so many mid-twentieth-century Americans lived, and women of all kinds and beliefs to ensure that the whole story be told.

Preservation Research

Earlier chapters have covered research using the Sanborn maps and many written and oral sources. Because preservation so often deals with real estate, land records, deeds, city directories, and tax records are helpful. Photographs and archaeology are especially useful because they can "see" what other sources cannot. Photographs show building elements not described elsewhere. Years ago, working in Iowa with Henry Wagner, a terrific historic architect, to restore the one-room schoolhouse at Herbert Hoover NHS, I said I was quite certain the schoolhouse door was originally in its gable end. When the restoration began, the door was on the long side. Had the door been moved when the schoolhouse was converted into a house? When Wagner asked me why I thought the schoolhouse door was in the gable end, I admitted I didn't know. To humor me, he gently swung his hammer at the gable end and found the header where the doorway had been. (A header runs across two vertical studs to carry the load across an opening.) He restored the door to its original position. Later, I realized that in my research on one-room schools, I'd studied many photographs that *always* showed the teacher standing proudly with her students in front of her school—with the door in the gable end.

Photographs can also provide preservation information in unexpected ways. A recent preservation project used a historic photograph that showed the original façade of the building being restored reflected in a glass window *across the street*. Measurements taken from photographs can be used to calculate missing building elements. Aerial photographs show patterns of human activity invisible from the ground, helping archaeologists determine where to excavate (or not). When working with historic buildings, finding photographs of similar buildings helps greatly. Good preservation practice demands documenting preservation processes, showing original damaged resources with all recent accretions removed and the preservation techniques used to care for them. Blueprints provide baselines when they illustrate how buildings were to be constructed, with as-built drawings and photographs of later alterations invaluable for preservation work.

Archaeologists make particular contributions to preservation, especially when undertaking "salvage archaeology," which is undertaken in preparation for construction of roads and subdivisions that disturb underground resources. Such before-the-bulldozer work is often required by the National Historic Preservation Act. Because this work is driven by location, not research goals, it seldom focuses on preserving women's history. Unless archaeologists find burials, where bones clearly differentiate males from females, it can be difficult to identify women's lives because so few objects are definitely female-specific and so much female activity left little tangible evidence. Clearly female-associated sites such as the Betsy Prince site where an African American widow lived for twenty years are rare. Here, Section 106 of the National Historic Preservation Act, which requires surveys for potentially significant historic resources for every highway project that involves federal permits or funding, resulted in a significant archaeological discovery. In New York, Route 25A highway widening uncovered Prince's 11-by-13-foot home. Prince, listed as a free Black woman on the 1820 U.S. census, lived in a free Black community, where she was integral to that rural economy. The 8,000 artifacts recovered "represents a rare assemblage of material culture from [her] free African American household." [21] In another example, the Connecticut Department of Transportation, which oversaw the excavation of four sites to understand eighteenth-century "middling class" life ways, found milk pans, extensive foodways remnants, and even lice combs. [22]

Preservation Designation

Having properties "listed" on the National Register of Historic Places gives them the preservation equivalent of a Good Housekeeping Seal of Approval. Being listed attests that the tangible resource is significant at a local/regional or national level, is (usually) at least fifty years old, and has enough "original fabric" to have physical integrity. Official recognition requires documentation of a resource's importance. Such actions require strong community support, research, and quantities of documentation. Preparing a nomination for a city, a state, the National Register, or designation as a National Historic Landmark simply takes a lot of work. Nobody wants to designate the "wrong" place—which has happened. Local Historic District Commissions (HDC) and Historic Property Commissions (HPC) also exist as entities of local governments that enforce preservation regulations. [23]

For a site to become a National Historic Landmark requires national significance and considerable public support. There are 94,000 properties listed (as of 2019) in the National Register, representing 1.8 million contributing resources—buildings, sites, districts, structures, and objects. Properties are assessed on having historic *significance* ("the importance of a property to the history, architecture, archeology, engineering, or culture of a community, state, or the nation as achieved in association with events, activities, or patterns; association with important persons; distinctive physical characteristics of design, construction, or form; or potential to yield important information"); *integrity* (location, design, setting, materials, workmanship, feeling, and association); and *context* (theme, place, and time that "link historic properties to important historic trends"). [24] Properties become eligible for tax credits as well as some federal grants. There are 2,600 properties designated as National Historic Landmarks that require "a high degree of integrity" and *national* significance. [25] An NPS website showcases already-identified sites, "Telling All Americans' Stories: Introduction to Women's History," at https://www.nps.gov/articles/taas-womenshistory-intro.htm.

Preservation Treatments

Most preservationists recognize different approaches to tangible resources, which involve increasing degrees of intervention: stabilization, restoration, preservation, and reconstruction. The appropriate treatment depends on whether the tangible resource is designed, vernacular, historic, or ethnographic; the level of significance and documentation; the needs; and the technical and financial resources available. Some preservationists joke that physical preservation needs depend on how carefully resources are examined.

Stabilization entails minimal action, as it seeks to halt further deterioration of the physical components of the site as feasible. It does not restore architecture to an earlier period. Stabilization slows but does not repair any damage so that, for example, the Kennecott mine, mill, and village will continue to deteriorate from Alaskan winters but more slowly than without any intervention.

Restoration returns a building (or structure) back to a defined "period of significance" and limits the elements treated. The defined "period of significance" specifies when a building or structure was considered most important, a process that often has omitted women. A Great Man's home is defined as "significant" only while he lived there, not for the years when others lived there. One redefinition of significance changed a house restoration from focused on one

Table 9.1.   Historic Preservation Treatments.

Activity	Elements	Results	Comments
Stabilize Vacant commercial building	Original materials but little public access Commercial needs dictate history saved.	Least action-involved— close building envelope to slow deterioration; protect from vandalism.	May be ugly but "real." Often lose key elements— copper pipes stolen . . . water damage . . .
Rehabilitate/ Adaptive Reuse Church now a library	Original materials but new uses. Exterior same except stained glass windows removed. Interior altered.	Non historic use—a church now a library or a warehouse, condos but building saved and active.	Good choice when traditional use is now impracticable. How many vacant churches or schools can be preserved?
Restore Clara Barton home/Red Cross Headquarters	Original materials; repair/replace damaged and missing elements; new materials removed.	Similar to original historic period. Modern utilities and structural members hidden	Best for historic interpretation; Historic fabric often discovered during process of restoration.
Reconstruct Bents Old Fort	New materials, old uses, lacks information from the original fort. Expensive and some conjecture required.	Appears original but lacks original materials; often smaller scale. Can help visitors envision historic place but can also confuse.	Pretty but not "real." May help interpretation when it restores landscape's missing elements—housing for enslaved people or utility buildings; original scale often changed.

Figure 9.2. Adaptive reuse, a church becoming a library, shows historic preservation policies at work.
PHOTOGRAPH BY TONI L. COTTRELL, PERSONAL COLLECTION.

prominent man to cover its entire history, which included it becoming a women-run private hospital. Restorations may replace a few missing elements—such as a stair spindle or may ensure buildings meet code requirements, with changes as discreet as possible.[26] (See Figure 9.2.) "When modern wallpaper was removed in July 2013, the original location of the door opening to [Emily] Dickinson's room was revealed. . . . The original doorway had been sealed over with new plaster, and its outline stood out clearly from the yellow painted plaster."[27] Restoration returned the room to the configuration she knew.

Preservation practices have evolved far from the simple approaches used early on, to more sophisticated ones, including a range of materials and methods. Nondestructive technology can locate sites and elements and can analyze their components. Because old materials are often recycled into new construction or abandoned nearby, missing elements are frequently found in attics, basements, or adjacent buildings. During restoration, the Clara Barton house's bright cranberry-colored stained-glass Red Cross doors, once discarded in her Glen Echo basement, were re-placed on her office doors to proclaim her headquarters again.

Reconstruction starts from the beginning and builds what was once there and is no longer, using the best documentation possible. Reconstruction is generally the least-preferred, although sometimes the appropriate approach, such as adding back small buildings in the landscapes that are profoundly misleading without them. Kitchen, slave houses, laundry, dairy, dovecote—all these service functions are often ignored. Missing such female work buildings from landscapes results in "magic" landscapes. This preservation bias has particular impact on preserving women's workplaces because so much of their work occurred in the chicken coop, dairy house, buttery, and especially the yard, as seasons permitted.

Adaptive reuse recycles buildings, keeping some original elements but gaining new uses. Office buildings and warehouses often become condos. Recently, Kansas town activists, for example, saved a vacant 1911 church by reopening it as a much-needed community library. Such adaptive reuses preserve exteriors while altering their interiors. The exterior of the appropriately named Church of the Transfiguration remains, with library shelves and community activities inside.[28]

Preservation Maintenance

To remain "on the Register," property owners—whether private, state, local, or national—must then follow professional preservation practices. These practices strive to maintain as much of the past's physical evidence as possible to protect it for the future. While preservation focuses on human made resources, tangible resources include natural ones also crucial to our history. Various plants and animals and insects, once integral to prairie ecology, are now "missing" from such landscapes—bison, wolves, bees, and snakes—with some species unlikely to return. True preservation would restore those elements but is highly unlikely; exhibits and films can help interpret how those elements interacted with women's lives, whether harvesting wild bee honeycombs or playing haunting howls of coyotes once heard often. When historic buildings are in "good condition," defined as "only" needing routine and cyclic maintenance, they still need ongoing maintenance, even as care for their different elements sometimes conflict. For buildings, routine maintenance of cleaning gutters and replacing roofs remain; for commemorative works such as statues, cleaning and waxing is still necessary. Spiderwebs must be cleaned off the Lincoln Memorial to prevent greater preservation problems from birds and their droppings. A sign reads "Maintenance Is Preservation" to remind visitors of the near-constant cleaning, clearing, and repointing of masonry required. A few years ago, a contractor brought a proprietary product for cleaning marble statues in Washington, D.C. The salesman whose company applied for the job claimed it was *so safe* one could put one's bare hands in it. To demonstrate their "perfectly safe" solution, the owner poured it into his palm. But the cultural resource manager noticed that he then kept rubbing his hands in discomfort—and she did not acquire their product.

Occasionally, major work is required, such as the multimillion-dollar Statue of Liberty restoration. The preservation team researched, cleaned, and restored the statue before its 1986 centennial. Galvanic action (disparate metals touching) between the iron skeleton and the copper skin had corroded "her" skin and her iconic arm was in danger of falling off. Historic housekeeping, an art in itself, is an important form of preservation. Historic housekeeping manuals reinforce the *relentless care* required in simply dusting shelves without breaking unusual tchotchkes. The Minnesota Historical Society has published a useful and friendly *Historic Housekeeping Handbook*.[29] The NPS Technical Briefs and Training Modules provide guidance to avoid serious mistakes and argue that specialists can best solve uncertainties. Caution preserves the irreplaceable. Many preservation techniques are quite technical, using advanced chemistry to determine the best methods of diagnosis and treatment. Find curators and conservators who know what can safely be handled and what could cause irreparable harm. Ironically, it's often safer to handle an eighteenth-century letter than one from 1928 because the older paper was less acidic or prone to "inherent vice." The Association for Preservation Technology International not only has excellent preservation guidance but also provides access to numerous historic catalogs and trade publications, which include period stoves, furniture, decorating, kitchen designs, etc., all useful for analyzing women's homes and lives, in its Building Technology Heritage Library.[30] Warning! It's a fascinating time sink.

Tradeoffs are plentiful in preservation treatments, such as the ivy covering a building that appears quaint but simultaneously damages its mortar and bricks. HVAC maintains an even temperature and humidity inside but changes the historic relationship between a building's envelope and its environment. Not electrifying a building seems more historic but decreases environmental and security controls, risking its museum collection. Light that helps visitors see objects better can damage those objects—and is not historically authentic. Balancing these different risks

Figure 9.3.   Pauli Murray Family Home National Historic Landmark, during restoration.
COURTESY OF THE PAULI MURRAY CENTER FOR HISTORY AND SOCIAL JUSTICE.

requires constant work, especially as megastorms and human misbehavior threaten tangible resources. Preservation includes managing the hydrology of a swamp so that its basket-making reeds survive or countering the effects of sea level rise as much as possible to protect near-shore historic properties. Other preservation work involves mitigating environmental risks such as keeping curatorial objects and paper under strict temperature, humidity, air quality, and security controls that slow their deterioration. Historic preservation commissions must cope with inappropriate "infill," jarring architecture adjacent to historic buildings, owners who cannot maintain their properties resulting in "demolition through neglect," and development pressures. These issues affect women's sites when historic scenes helpful in understanding a locale are damaged or buildings associated with women's history are lost. There are some major tradeoffs, best negotiated with curators and object conservators. Watching *This Old House* shows isn't enough to master the technical issues involved.

Legal Framework

In addition to the cornerstone National Historic Preservation Act of 1966 discussed above, several other key laws guide U.S. preservation as well as some court cases. The National Environmental Policy Act, which mandates Environmental Impact Statements, applies to historic tangible resources as well as to living creatures, and the Department of Transportation Act of 1966 includes its Section 4(f) for compliance. While not specific to historic preservation, these major laws often play substantial roles in protecting tangible resources from all kinds of threats, as long as there is a federal connection through permits, funding, and the like (which can often be found). A working knowledge of these laws helps protect our history.

The Historic Sites Act of 1935 established National Historic Landmarks; made education a responsibility of the NPS; and authorized cooperative agreements between NPS, academics, and nonprofit organizations so that partners can undertake projects with the NPS using federal dollars. Other key legislation includes the 1979 Archeological Resources Protection Act (ARPA) to protect underground resources from damage, looting, and trafficking. Grave robbers have stolen unique objects and destroyed archaeological sites to sell ancient pottery, baskets, and jewelry found in them. The Abandoned Shipwreck Act protects maritime and underwater resources from treasure hunters who indiscriminately dig up tangible resources in ways that destroy their associated knowledge base. The Native American Graves Protection and Repatriation Act (NAGPRA) ensures that sacred objects and human remains of Native Americans and Native Hawai'ians are treated respectfully and returned to their originating tribes. The first federal preservation law, the Antiquities Act of 1906, empowers the president to protect natural and cultural resources by declaring them National Monuments (NMs) *if* the property is already federally owned. To the fury of Congress, presidents of both parties have repeatedly invoked the Antiquities Act to protect tangible resources by designating them national monuments. Court cases also play a crucial role in preservation. The landmark 1978 case *Penn Central Transportation Co. v. City of New York* recognized the validity of historic preservation statues and protected New York City's Grand Central Station from demolition. The National Trust monitors such cases as part of its professional services. The Trust published Julia H. Miller's very helpful *A Layperson's Guide to Historic Preservation Law: A Survey of Federal, State, and Local Laws Governing Historic Resource Protection*, which discusses court cases as well as key concepts and terms useful to understand this particular legal ecosystem.[31] In addition to federal and state laws and local ordinances, tax credits have leveraged $96.87 billion preservation dollars and easements have preserved many buildings by ensuring that their exteriors and landscapes are protected even as interior modifications are allowed.[32]

Hard Lessons Distilled

Historic preservationists have learned much about what to do—and what *not* to do. Decades of hard-won experience, disappointments, and occasional triumphs have been distilled into "The Secretary of the Interior's Standards for the Treatment of Historic Properties," known as "the Secretary's Standards," listed as seemingly pithy principles. These basic principles test the appropriateness of proposed actions without giving detailed specifics that would probably not fit in many situations given this country's diversity of landscapes, structures, and buildings. The emphasis here is on the tangible resources, not on the history they reflect or the publics who comprise their audiences. This results in more consideration of physical needs of tangible resources—think earthquake proofing—rather than their knowledge base needs.

Behind those standards are many technical requirements that often require specialists' involvement. But as the NPS says, "The Standards are to be applied to specific rehabilitation projects in a reasonable manner, taking into consideration economic and technical feasibility."[33] Buildings must comply with modern codes, the Americans With Disabilities Act of 1990, and seismic requirements. Lead paint and asbestos in floors, exterior walls, etc. must be removed extremely carefully, but they seldom reach the crisis level so often portrayed on home improvement television. These requirements—codes are condensed learning—often differ from historic methods and materials, but they can usually be met with some creativity. For example, proper insulation now involves more than Clara Barton tacking old envelopes inside her walls to decrease air flow. Generally, buildings are not to be moved, although occasionally they need to be. Alexander and Eliza Hamilton's "Grange," originally chosen for its countryside setting, was relocated after New York City had surrounded it.[34]

Key Organizations

The National Park Service (NPS) has major responsibilities for historic preservation, by "keeping" the National Register of Historic Places, by working for the secretary of the interior to nominate National Historic Landmarks, and by managing over 400 national park units, the NPS's best-known responsibility. *Every* park unit has women's history.[35] Unfortunately, the NPS preservation approach greatly needs revision so that women's lives and accomplishments are fully recognized and preserved. The NPS provides excellent online training on its website, www.cr.nps.gov; makes grants from the Historic Preservation Fund; and has oversight of the State Historic Preservation Programs. The Advisory Council on Historic Preservation and federal preservation officers work together with state historic preservation officers, tribal preservation officers, and certified local governments to identify, nominate, and treat their cultural resources. The NPS argues that historic preservation is sustainability in that "Historic preservation has proven economic, environmental, and social benefits. Studies show that historic districts maintain higher property values, less population decline, more walkability, and greater sense of community."[36] Reflecting our federal system, states and localities have their own preservation offices with parallel but not identical approaches as with states having their own laws. For example, some states specifically protect cemeteries. The National Conference of State Historic Preservation Officers coordinates among the states and provides advocacy, training, and tools. Other relevant organizations are listed in the Appendix.

Since being chartered in 1949, the National Trust for Historic Preservation, with 800,000 members, has worked to preserve special American places, through education, funding, and advocacy.[37] It also owns twenty-seven sites, a wide range of houses from ordinary to extraordinary, including the Pope-Leighey house, which Marjorie Leighey donated to the National Trust when the I-66 highway was being built across her land (see Figure 7.7). Designed by Frank Lloyd Wright with his usual elegance, the 1,200-square-foot house is a template for post–World War II suburban housing with its low-slung horizontal shape, separate living and bedroom wings, dining "area" (no dining room), carport, and indoor-outdoor permeability. Charlotte Pope "wrangled" with Wright over the rug color, which, unusually, he agreed to change; she also added a fire screen to protect her children. Montpelier, the mansion of James and Dolly Madison, and the Cooper-Molero Adobe are National Trust properties. The Trust also owns the architecturally outstanding (Edith) Farnsworth House in Plano, Illinois, built in 1951, which Dr. Edith Farnsworth had famous architect Mies van der Rohe build as her retreat. Sadly, her roles as client and financier are obscured by calling it the Farnsworth House.[38]

Available Training

These recommended organizations have expertise for training in preservation and treatments:
- American Association for State and Local History (AASLH) provides technical leaflets, webinars, and training courses.
- Association for Preservation Technology International offers its *Bulletin*, its online Building Technology Heritage Library, conferences, etc.
- Colonial Williamsburg provides guidance online for object conservation of paper, fabric, musical instruments, and mechanical arts, as well as preventive preservation following the adage "an ounce of preservation is worth a pound of cure." See Colonial Williamsburg's quilt preservation, that classic women's art form including an exquisite Log Cabin quilt by African American Anna Jane Parker, on the cover of this book.[39]
- National Center for Preservation Technology and Training has over 600 online entries, such as removing mold from paper, iron conservation, preservation of timber structures, and 3-D

Figure 9.4.   Pauli Murray Family Home National Historic Landmark, after restoration.
PHOTOGRAPH BY MEL GODWIN, COURTESY OF THE PAULI MURRAY CENTER FOR HISTORY AND SOCIAL JUSTICE.

documentation. It hosts numerous training courses and conferences. It emphasizes architectural preservation, but it works with many different preservation issues.

- The National Park Service provides technical guidance, including fifty *Preservation Briefs*, https://www.nps.gov/tps/how-to-preserve/briefs.htm.
- The National Trust for Historic Preservation has *Preservation*, annual meetings; its *Preservation Forum* is specifically for preservation professionals.

Practicalities to consider: Keep reading women's history and other fields—fascinating research continues to be published, and many older works are intriguing. We all have busy lives, but we still need to keep reading the wondrous outpouring in women's history literature. Twenty minutes every night over a lifetime helps (advice I have followed since the seventh grade). Go regularly to professional conferences if you possibly can. Share rooms, drink cheap coffee, and eat PB&J sandwiches, but go and be energized. Build your network by joining organizations such as the National Trust for Historic Preservation, American Association for State and Local History, National Council for Public History, National Collaborative for Women's History Sites, Vernacular Architecture Forum, Organization of American Historians, and their regional affiliates. Go to the Berkshire Conference on the History of Women and Gender held every three years; it combines rigorous scholarship with a memorable summer camp atmosphere. Build your networks and communities. Master the legal and preservation technicalities. Some can be learned by careful online study or at conferences. For in-depth understanding, take public history courses, maximize on-the-job-training, and seek wide experience. Visit every museum and historic site you can—it's your Life List. Going as a visitor can give key insights.

Preservation applies to more than buildings and landscapes, although most preservation laws focus on those resources and reflect the priorities of architects and archaeologists rather than historians and curators. Traditionally, but fortunately changing, architects, curators, and archaeologists preserved *tangible resources* while historians and archivists preserved the *knowledge base*. Both are needed. Full understanding of the past melds tangible resources with knowledge base. Genuine comprehension requires understanding how the landscape shaped fighting on a battlefield or how women experienced wearing corsets. Corsets were often made from whale baleen, the same keratin protein as our fingernails which is strong but much more flexible than "whalebones."[40] Preservation extends both the tangible aspects of our history and our knowledge base. Tangible resources themselves testify to the past as well as helping us remember it, although the resources need their historic context, so crucial for meaning. By sharing our stories, we preserve them and ourselves—anyone who lacks "their" history through blind adoption or enslavement suffers from this profound loss. We can all be enriched.

Tools: Practicing Good Preservation

Preservation requires a mind-set of protecting "forever"—many generations from now. Implementing these tools take commitment, time, and money. The extent and timing of implementation depend on available resources, but developing the attitude of stewardship by everyone and simply getting started are crucial. Sharing preservation principles and practices with visitors and involving everyone in the work necessary to preserve our tangible resources increases appreciation for and support of our history. Many people are intrigued by being close to original tangible resources—involve them.

Tool 9.1 Significance: Support and Strengthen

Continue to argue for, and support, the importance of fully including the presence and actions of women and girls in our history, needed to garner financial and political resources. Seek tie-ins with contemporary events, news, and popular culture. Keep reaching out to "new" audiences and market to them. Sustain relationships; as the Girl Scouts used to say, "Make new friends but keep the old." Seek ways to connect your history and tangible resources in new ways and with new groups; in other words, find new opportunities to share women's history.

Tool 9.2 Knowledge Base: Identify and Document

1. Develop a strong knowledge base—use general women's history books, articles, and memoirs relevant to your time and place. Also research technical and online sources and develop site-specific research projects such as "Nineteenth-Century Quaker Theology in West Branch, Iowa," that documented female ministers at Herbert Hoover NHS Partner with local colleges and universities to prepare such research.
2. List all eligible buildings and structures on the National Register of Historic Places, fully including women's history aspects in them. Revise old nominations as necessary.
3. Collect or create historic architectural drawings and photographs that show the baseline conditions for landscapes, buildings, structures, and objects. Keep a set of architectural drawings *somewhere else* in case your storage facility is destroyed (fires happen).
4. Prepare Historic Structure Reports for buildings and structures that evaluate their history, and recommend future treatments. Especially document spaces that women and girls used, whether a garden plot or sewing spot by a window. Research and document the landscape/buildings/objects/site, by walking it carefully and studying your collection thoroughly, photographing it, and using current technology to research hidden elements nondestructively.
5. Have a basic understanding how historic preservation works, if your site/museum is private, local, or state owned and managed or how cultural resource management, its twin sister, works if a federal property.

Tool 9.3 Tangible Resources: Restore and Maintain

1. The most serious threat is not taking seriously female-related resources. Inadequate public recognition and appreciation results in irreplaceable important resources being trashed. Many people don't know how important women's actions were. Involving everyone in your larger community *from the beginning* helps. Treat female-associated rooms the same as others. If the parlor is restored, then restore the kitchen, maid's room, and other female-associated spaces.
2. Consult specialists on major repairs and follow preservation tenets from professional sources. Avoid damaging irreplaceable resources. Remediate common risks of lead, asbestos, and mold. Update all electrical systems—no more knob and tube wiring!
3. Practice good housekeeping and integrated pest management. Document all preservation actions thoroughly so future stewards will know what you did.
4. Identify major local threats, whether earthquakes or floods, and mitigate risks as possible. Have disaster plans in place *before* emergencies strike. Partner with local emergency responders to ensure they understand your resources and want to protect them.
5. Objects get stolen or structures vandalized. Protect your tangible resources—think like a thief or vandal and harden them accordingly.

Tool 9.4 Interpret Preservation

1. Work with women's history experts to ensure proper preservation of female associated resources. Develop support for your museum/site to fully include women's history in its context. Include males associated with your museum/site.
2. Provide *ongoing* interpretive and preservation training in women's history for all staff and interested people.
3. Educate visitors and stakeholders about the purpose and need for preservation work, important because so much preservation work is invisible but expensive.
4. Interpret preservation work for visitors. Most preservation techniques and practices relate to specific kinds of tangible resources. Include female-related preservation issues such as bird feathers on turn-of-the-twentieth-century women's hats that pose preservation problems.

Women's Historic Preservation Agenda

1. Identify key women, movements, and concepts crucial in women's history that need recognition, including both obvious women and "hidden figures": scientists, artists, religious figures, and women active in all kinds of family enterprises. Be truly inclusive! Include women and girls in site interpretation as intrinsic parts of every museum and site. Monitor interpretation at sites—especially state and federal ones we pay for. Identify key women's organizations/schools, sororities, clubs, teams with significant girls'/women's activity, women's markets, clinics, etc. Ensure full demographic diversity. Recognize and include the multiple facets of women's lives. Consider which women affected the museum/site, then research them, their histories, and tangible resources. Work across disciplines with archaeologists, architects, tribal members, curators, etc.
2. Identify, preserve, and make accessible additional women's history sites. This includes women's history at places named for women and at places *not* named for them—battlefields, forts, villages, farms, etc. Recognize women's presence at every site. Rename and enlarge the interpretation of sites named for families—more accurate—at least, "John Walker and Family" or "Otis Family." Always include females—and not only in stereotyped ways. Do not

obscure females under "his family." Identify female-related tangible resources everywhere. Include gender and intersectionality in basic management categories. Interpreting women must not be optional for managers or individual interpreters. Avoid losing tangible resources (buildings, collections, documents). Marjorie Merriweather Post's female-designed Mar-a-Lago in Florida and Georgia O'Keeffe's home and studio in New Mexico were *temporarily* NPS units. It's crucial to identify potential sites/collections and to have site/museum management involved with potential donors in ongoing, *appreciative* ways.

3. Work with partners such as the National Trust to designate and preserve National Treasures, with NPS/SHPOs/owners on National Register and NHL properties, and other preservation organizations. Treat partners as coworkers, not as subordinates or "just volunteers." If you see a dumpster being filled with history, determine what's being thrown out. Encourage people to recognize, save, and donate important tangible resources. Integrate historic properties and tangible resources into classes on American history and other disciplines; work with academics to identify additional potential tangible resources and to keep your interpretation current. Share "best practices" with each other—NCWHS can help here—www.ncwhs.org. Work with travel organizations, chambers of commerce, and state welcome centers—it's surprising how few even think of women's history, except as suffrage, which is important but there's so much more! Establish *permanent connections among* museums, sites, relevant organizations, and academia, and encourage personal connections among them. Sites/museums have significance, tangible resources, knowledge bases, and visitors, while academics create different knowledge bases and have students; nonprofit organizations often support museums and sites nationwide. All are needed, with their stronger integration better women's history.

Notes

1. Doris Roge, http://voicesofthepast.org/2008/10/01/kate-chopin-house-burns.
2. Marion Tinling, *Women Remembered: A Guide to Landmarks of Women's History in the United States* (Westport: Greenwood, 1986); Lynn Sherr, *Susan B. Anthony Slept Here: A Guide to American Women's Landmarks* (New York: Three Rivers Press, 1994); U.S. Congress report language; see Page Putnam Miller, "Women's History Landmark Project: Policy and Research," *The Public Historian*, 15, no. 4 (Autumn 1993) resulted in twenty-three more National Historic Landmarks; Secretary of the Interior Kenneth Salazar called for a workshop that was held in December 2012 with NCWHS. It resulted in NHL nominations for homes of Pauli Murray, Marjorie Stoneman Douglas, and Annie Wauneka. See also NPS website, "Telling All Americans' Stories: Introduction to Women's History," https://www.nps.gov/articles/taas-womenshistory-intro.htm, 2019.
3. Barbara Pearson Yocum, *The Stanton House: Historic Structure Report Women's Rights National Historical Park* (Lowell: National Park Service, 1989).
4. National Park Service, "Secretary's Standards for Rehabilitation," https://www.nps.gov/tps/standards/rehabilitation/rehab/stand.htm.2. See Susan Sleeper-Smith, *Indigenous Prosperity and American Conquest: Indian Women of the Ohio River Valley, 1690-1792* (Chapel Hill: The University of North Carolina Press, 2018), 63; Joan R. Gundersen, *To Be Useful to the World: Women in Revolutionary America, 1740-1790* (Chapel Hill: The University of North Carolina Press, 2006), especially Chapter 9, "Daughters of Liberty"; "Working American: The Human Experience of the Colorado Coalfield Strike of 1913-1914," *Teach Ludlow*, 2004, http://www.teachludlowco.com/dotnetnuke/Exhibit/womenandchildren.aspx..
5. Page Putnam Miller, "National Historic Landmark Nomination Form, Zora Neale Hurston House" (Washington, DC: National Park Service, June 19, 1991).

6. Personal conversations with National Park Service personnel, Washington Office, 1981–1983.
7. J. Todd Moye, "Discovering What Is Already There," in *Mississippi Women: Their Histories, Their Lives* (Athens: The University of Georgia Press, 2010). See Danielle L. McGuire, *At the Dark End of the Street: Black Women, Rape and Resistance—A New History of the Civil Rights Movement from Rosa Parks to the Rise of Black Power* (New York: Alfred A. Knopf, 2010); Lynne Olson, *Freedom's Daughters: The Unsung Heroines of the Civil Rights Movement, 1830–1970* (New York: Touchstone Books, 2001); Keisha N. Blain "This unheralded woman actually organized the Montgomery bus boycott: Jo Ann Robinson is unfortunately overlooked by history," *Timeline*, January 19, 2017, https://timeline.com/this-unheralded-woman-actually-organized-the-montgomery-bus-boycott-db57a7aa50db.
8. See Margot Lee Shetterly, *Hidden Figures: The American Dream and the Untold Story of the Black Women Mathematicians Who Helped Win the Space Race* (New York: William Morrow and Company, 2016). Shetterly has many examples.
9. Barbara Pearson Yocum, "The Stanton House: Historic Structure Report Women's Rights NHP," 1989. The actor Alan Alda donated the key $10,000 to purchase the Stanton House and attended the park's dedication. Personal knowledge.
10. Rebecca Conard, "'All Men and Women Are Created Equal': An Administrative History of Women's Rights National Historical Park" (National Park Service and Organization of American Historians, April 2012).
11. See Marsh-Billings-Rockefeller NHP and Clara Barton NHS; Jennifer Pustz, *Voices from the Back Stairs: Interpreting Servants' Lives at Historic House Museums* (DeKalb: Northern Illinois University Press, 2010) agrees. I have long complained about the non-restoration of women's spaces.
12. Personal visit. Grant-Kohrs NHS, Deer Lodge, Montana, 1999.
13. Eve Kahn, "How Ceiling Fans Allowed Slaves to Eavesdrop on Plantation Owners," *Atlas Obscura* (blog), May 14, 2018, https://www.atlasobscura.com/articles/punkah-project-fans-antebellum-south.
14. See http://www.texasbeyondhistory.net/waxcamps/today.html.
15. The Andrew Jackson Hermitage, http://thehermitage.com/learn/mansion-grounds/garden-grounds/garden/ in 1889.
16. *How Buildings Learn: What Happens After They're Built* (New York: Penguin Viking, 1994), 76–77.
17. Brand, How Buildings Learn, 144–45.
18. Julia H. Miller, *A Layperson's Guide to Historic Preservation Law: A Survey of Federal, State, and Local Laws Governing Historic Resource Protection*, 2008 ed. (Washington, DC: National Trust for Historic Preservation, 2008). https://forum.savingplaces.org/glossary.
19. These quilt museums, among many, have distinctive approaches and collections, some focused on historic quilts and others on current controversies in quilts. See National Quilt Museum, www.quiltmuseum.org, Paducah, Kentucky; San Jose Museum of Quilts & Textiles, www.sjquiltmuseum.org, San Jose, California; The International Quilt Study Center & Museum, www.quiltstudy.org, Lincoln, Nebraska; The Rocky Mountain Quilt Museum, www.rmqm.org, Golden, Colorado; and the Texas Quilt Museum, www.Texasquiltmuseum.org, LaGrange, Texas.
20. Lizabeth Cohen, *A Consumers' Republic: The Politics of Mass Consumption in Postwar America* (New York: Vintage Books, 2003).
21. See http://www.nysm.nysed.gov/research-collections/archaeology/historical-archaeology/collections/betsey-prince-site.
22. Ross K. Harper, Mary G. Harper, and Bruce Clouette, *Highways to History: The Archaeology of Connecticut's 18th-Century Lifeways* (The Connecticut Department of Transportation and The Federal Highway Administration, 2013).

23. Connecticut Trust for Historic Preservation, *Handbook for Historic District Commissions and Historic Property Commissions in Connecticut*, 2010, http://lhdct.org/documents/Handbook%20for%20Historic%20District%20Commissions%20in%20CT.pdf; See also James K. Reap and Melvin B. Hill, "Law and the Historic Preservation Commission: What Every Member Needs to Know," National Park Service (Washington, DC: 2007).

24. See https://www.nps.gov/subjects/nationalregister/what-is-the-national-register.htm and https://www.nps.gov/nr/publications/bulletins/nrb16a/nrb16a_II.htm#gathering.

25. See https://www.nps.gov/subjects/nationalhistoriclandmarks/nr-and-nhl.htm.

26. The James J. Otis house interpretation shifted to the Otis House and included later women.

27. Bedroom Restoration, Emily Dickinson Museum, http://www.emily dickinsonmuseum.org / Emily%20Dickinson%20bedroom%20restoration.

28. Interview with Vanessa Everhart, Bennington Community Library, Bennington, Kansas, February 2, 2018. Judy Swagerty helped her establish the library.

29. Minnesota Historical Society, *Historic Housekeeping Handbook* (St. Paul: Minnesota Historical Society, 2000).

30. See https://archive.org/details/buildingtechnologyheritagelibrary?&sort=-downloads&page=3.

31. Julia H. Miller, *A Layperson's Guide to Historic Preservation Law: A Survey of Federal, State, and Local Laws Governing Historic Resource Protection*, 2008 ed. (Washington, DC: National Trust for Historic Preservation, 2008), https://forum.savingplaces.org.

32. See "Tax Incentives for Preserving Historic Properties," Technical Preservation Services, National Park Service (Washington, DC: 2019); https://www.nps.gov/tps/tax-incentives.htm.

33. NPS, Introduction, "The Secretary of the Interior's Standards for Rehabilitation," https://www.nps.gov/tps/standards/rehabilitation/rehab/stand.htm.

34. Lighthouses are frequently moved as banks erode. Hamilton Grange NHS in New York City was moved to give it a more suitable environment; the Hull-House was rotated as part of the University of Illinois–Chicago Circle construction.

35. In 1978, 55 million acres of Alaskan parks were declared national monuments, which 1980 legislation separated into different parks, wildlife refuges, etc. See G. Frank Williss, "'Do Things Right the First Time': Administrative History of the National Park Service and the Alaska National Interest Lands Conservation Act of 1980" (Denver: National Park Service, 1985). Recent National Monuments include Sewall-Paul Women's Equality NM, Harriet Tubman NM, and Pullman NM.

36. National Park Service, "Certified Local Government Program & Local Preservation Tools," *Certified Local Government Program*, n.d., https://www.nps.gov/clg/index.html.

37. Thanks to Priya Chhaya, National Trust for Historic Preservation, February 2017.

38. Alice T. Friedman, "'People Who Live in Glass Houses: Edith Farnsworth, Ludwig Mies van der Rohe, and Philip Johnson,'" in *Women and the Making of the Modern House: A Social and Architectural History* (New Haven: Yale University Press, 2006).

39. See Anna Jane Parker, *Quilt Top Log Cabin Quilt*, 1875–1900, Colonial Williamsburg Foundation, donated by Jean and Jerry Jackson and Bob and Helen Jackson Brewer; emuseum.history.org; https://www.history.org/history/museums/conservation/index.cfm; Quilt Index, University of Nebraska-Lincoln, Program of Textiles, Merchandising and Fashion Design, www.quiltindex.org/about.php; see International Quilt Study Center & Museum, University of Nebraska-Lincoln, "Beyond the Myths," World Quilts: The American Story, worldquilts.quiltstudy.org/americanstory/quiltsare/beyondthemyths; and Rocky Mountain Quilt Museum Golden, www.rmqm.org.

40. https://us.whales.org/whales-dolphins/what-is-baleen/. Accessed January 11, 2020.

Part IV

Interpretation

10

Interpretation

Sharing Women's History *with* Visitors

"Welcome, please come in—we're so glad you're here."

Interpretation as Hospitality

An attitude of hospitality assures visitors that we want to share something special with them. Visitors as our lifeblood enjoy discovery just as we do. We want them to be fascinated with our foremothers and to become engaged in our museum community. We hope they will leave excited at encountering women's history everywhere and to appreciate the centrality of women in American history. Given cultural biases against women and girls—much of it not conscious—this is no small project.[1]

Previous chapters discussed emotional, intellectual, and physical aspects of women's history. This chapter focuses on the best methods for interpretation of women's history with the public by sharing historical meanings and current relevance that connects them with the peoples, places, and resources of the past. We can do this by strengthening interpretation at existing locales, by nominating more women-associated National Historic Landmarks and National Register of Historic Places properties, and by recognizing women's ephemeral spaces, whether on riverbanks or in private lesbian clubs.

Interpretation has several meanings—to translate between languages, to analyze and explain research, and to present tangible resources to the public. The first is used cross-culturally, the second academically, and the third by historic sites, museums, and parks. Here, interpretation uses all meanings. The academic usage applies to the knowledge base and recognizes that interpretations of existing data change as does locating new data, which requires us to keep current as academic interpretations change. Consider the dramatic reinterpretation of Sally Hemings and her relationship with Thomas Jefferson—long denied, then dismissed, but now acknowledged for their long and significant relationship. Hemings's room at Monticello, obscured as a bathroom, again has physical connections to Jefferson's rooms.[2] We do not need to participate in every academic argument, but we need to know changes that profoundly affect our interpretation. Having solid partnerships with academics who research women's history and being active members in organizations that "do" women's history makes the difference. (See Appendix.) Go to major and regional conferences to network and learn current scholarship and techniques. Read key journals/magazines and go to JSTOR for relevant articles and research published by state and local historical societies. Fear not footnotes! Watch for major books that reinterpret long-held ideas about women such as Laurel Thatcher Ulrich's book *The Age of Homespun: Objects and Stories in the Making of an American Myth* and Susan Sleeper Smith's book, *Indigenous Prosperity and American Conquest: Indian Women of the Ohio River Valley, 1690–1792*.[3] Their lives and the ecology of the Ohio River Valley were destroyed by Revolutionary War veterans claiming their promised lands. Because academic interpretations build on each other and sometimes refute each other, it's important to stay aware of new scholarship and changing perspectives.

The third kind of interpretation, long practiced by the National Interpretive Association, the National Park Service, and similar organizations, defines it as a "mission-based communication process that forges emotional and intellectual connections between the interests of the audience and meanings inherent in the resource."[4] That recognizes emotional connections (significance), intellectual connections (knowledge base), and resources (tangible resources) but includes mission-based directions and audience interests. Doing good women's history interpretation builds on natural and cultural tangible resources with diverse audiences through excellent programs, projects, and products and assists public audiences in making intellectual and emotional connections. Long-term preservation requires that people care about resources with their visits, votes, and financial/time resources. The interpretation of women and girls as central to American history strengthens our stewardship. As the National Parks Conservation Association says, "Your Parks, Your Turn." That's true for all our historic museums and places and a special challenge when so many other activities compete for attention. We're the stewards of these special places that belong to us; it's our responsibility to pass them on by telling the *whole story.*

The shift from hosting tourists to discovering past women's lives *together* involves understanding that visitors cocreate interpretation. History *already* belongs to visitors at places where we as stewards preserve, research, and share. We don't relinquish our hard-won expertise to emphasize visitors' interests; we respond to our visitors' needs and their cultural moment with ongoing relationships, not one-night stands. Traditionally, interpreters led visitors on tours between barricades designed to protect both collections and visitors. On a recent historic house tour, the interpreter announced that the young girl following us was to "make sure none of you touch anything." Her condescending attitude interfered with my appreciation for the fascinating woman who had once lived there. Expecting visitors to stand still and be silent while we talk at them risks transforming pleasurable visitor discoveries into tedious chores. Visitors on vacation are often expected to be solemn in once-noisy places. Yet families and groups enjoy talking among themselves, which often enhances interpretation, rather than interrupting it.

We need to change our asymmetrical relationship from experts to visitors to a mutual relationship. The interpretation guru Freeman Tilden preached that interpretation should "provoke" visitors, an inherently hierarchical relationship.[5] Instead we need to provide the historic context and then intentionally work *with* visitors to assemble their chosen experience. This approach recognizes their impressive range of historical understanding, interests, and styles. Some visitors just want to read labels, while some come primed with questions but many don't know what to ask. Others bring peculiar preconceptions and even hostility to learning about women. We need to welcome and work with all. Watch body language—smiles erupt when friendly participation is invited rather than didactic passivity expected. We must respond simultaneously to visitors' needs and interests while providing core content and safety messages, which is why surveys such as AASLH's "Visitors Count" are so important.[6] We must discern preferences and capacities—it's not fun to be embarrassed as a visitor! Rather than canned talks, conversations built with each group engage visitors while increasing our connections.

Our hospitality is grounded in skillful research and planning, ongoing preservation, and solid interpretive principles. We do not want to overwhelm visitors with the complexities of metal conservation technology nor debates over intersectionality or heteronormality, even as we preserve metals and incorporate those important concepts.[7] Hospitality precludes pretension. Consequently, we distill scholarship to connect with the many different publics and the women's history in our museums and historic sites. We need to see visitor experiences from their perspective, not ours, and encourage their connections with historic women. As public historians, we share these tangible resources, encouraging visitors to share their insights while making our expertise accessible. Thoughtful and authoritative—*not* authoritarian—we facilitate robust yet civil conversations so that visitors feel welcome to participate. A dialogue approach works well when the audience has sufficient knowledge to be comfortable, but participation can be complicated because many visitors learned little women's history in school. Ask visitors to find meaningful or interesting tangible resources and share their insights.

Knowing women today differs from knowing women's history. Similarly, interpreting a woman's biography differs from presenting women's history, a risk that biographical sites particularly have when an individual woman's background and accomplishments are featured at museums and sites named for individual women, whether Marjorie Kinnan Rawlings or Clara Barton. Include her friends, relatives, and foes, and discuss the events and milieu she experienced to ensure visitors understand her context. Such context helps us to avoid underestimating the forces arrayed against the changes women sought. At a time when a high percentage of medical and law students are female, the plea for women's professional education in the 1848 "Declaration of Sentiments" sounds quaint rather than the radical statement it actually was.[8]

More Women's History Resources for Us All

In the past decade, many historic sites and museums have enhanced their interpretation of women's history, by adding programs, integrating women into some exhibits, and hosting special events. These improvements reflect absorption of the scholarly outpouring and greater presence of knowledgeable staff who support women's history. The Smithsonian joined this effort with its "American Women's History Initiative," with interpretive programs at its many museums, including the Library of Congress has the public making suffrage centennial buttons like the now-memorabilia ones "Votes for Women," transcribing women's papers, hearing gallery talks, and "meeting" actors portraying famous historical women, including Mary Church Terrell and Susan B. Anthony. The NPS has developed "Telling All Americans' Stories: Introduction to Women's History," which showcases National Historic Sites, National Historic Landmarks, and National Register properties.[9] Its website lists thirteen parks as women's history ones rather than recognizing women's history being ubiquitous—in every park.[10] AASLH has a Women's History Affinity Committee, is working with the Organization of American Historians to do joint webinars on women's history topics, and has "Historic House Call," a webinar on women's history for historic house museum staff. The National Trust is incorporating the "breadth of women's experiences," including a track entirely on women's history at its PastForward conference with sessions that include storytelling, interpretation, and discussion about the national discourse around ratification of the Nineteenth Amendment as well as interesting "Women's Heritage Stories." The National Collaborative for Women's History Sites has long documented and interpreted places of women's history.[11]

Despite such efforts, general knowledge and full integration of women's history still remains inadequate. We cannot assume that arriving visitors have any particular interest or knowledge in women's past, given our cultural fascination with shiny new things and our stereotypes about women. Our hospitality decreases the uncertainty some visitors feel toward women's history. We need to emphasize that historic women's lives and experiences are part of the core story that makes our places so important. Conscious hospitality helps avoid making visitors feel defensive about past mistreatment of women; it's important to separate historic attitudes and structural patriarchy from our lives. Specific visitors cannot and should not be held responsible from other people's past actions. We can't be responsible for history before our lifetimes but we must strive to understand what happened then—and to accept responsibility for our actions during our lives, which we can affect.[12] Further, as Susan Ferentinos thoughtfully explains, while current scholarship recognizes that gender roles are socially constructed, the general public (and some staff) with much less exposure to this key concept may "find it a challenging notion" and so react.[13] Our efforts to interpret LGBTQ history may also elicit rejoinders—another advantage of an accessible knowledge base. Some locales need reexamination of sexual relationships as obvious as two women sharing their bedroom. Tangible resources, and a strong knowledge base, help visitors encounter our "messy," often complex past. History that omits or distorts women's past is fiction instead.

Strong interpretation helps museums and historic sites present rich and varied stories that integrate women's history through exhibits, programs, sale items, and tours. Encountering historic women strengthens us with their courage and challenges us by their accomplishments. The Dorothy Molter Museum interprets a fiercely independent woman who lived year-round in the northern Minnesota *wilderness* fifteen miles of lakes and trails from the nearest road. She modeled resilience and generosity, living off the grid with below-zero winter temperatures.[14] Sharing her struggles and humor introduces visitors to women guide stars. When people proclaim that today is "worse" than any other, we reference *their* lives in times of epidemics, wars, and atrocities and draw on their emotional strength. Programs that implicitly compare our foremothers' lives with our own helps us appreciate our fortune—although we mourn losses of whippoorwill cries.

Interpreting Women on Their Own Terms

As historic interpreters, we first need to understand women *on their terms*, not ours. It's surprisingly difficult to shed our own skins but crucial, because we tell *their* stories when they cannot. How? First, by respecting the sheer varieties of women's experiences and accomplishments: women and girls from many different groups and situations, by applying concepts of intersec-

Figure 10.1.   Upstairs bedroom in eighteenth-century Brush Everard House, interpreted for daughters with girls' objects—an effective way to indicate female presence.
COURTESY OF THE COLONIAL WILLIAMSBURG FOUNDATION, WILLIAMSBURG, VIRGINIA.

tionality, and by showing genuine comprehension of our sources. Second, by understanding that "proper" roles for women have been much more flexible and varied than recognized. Gender roles, as social constructions, change as influenced by their societies. Major changes have altered our lives, not uniformly but profoundly. While agrarian societies needed muscle, postindustrial ones require intellectual acuity. Now, with generally effective birth control, women can determine the timing, number, and spacing of children, dramatically affecting our lives. Third, we need to recognize deep commonalities women share historically—life cycles, as daughters and in other relationships (as stepmothers), potential motherhood, social and legal disempowerment, and a range of sexual orientations.

When we recognize that women and girls were historically present and active, stories emerge. For example, while a man legally owned a colonial tavern, his wife managed it with him; her work needs to be interpreted alongside his. Weaving, dairying, even brewing beer have been fervently assigned to one gender and then to the other. In Scandinavia, men handled dairying; here, American women milked some surprisingly large herds. We must be cautious in assuming that activities were exclusive to either gender, lest we inadvertently reinforce inaccurate stereotypes. We need to interpret women at *every* site and museum. Developing better interpretation of women's history entails alternating between large social patterns and specific locale-related details. Changing a site name to recognize everyone there immediately signals the significance of more than one man. For example, the James Otis House became the Otis Family House accompanied by major interpretive and exhibit alterations. Museums/sites have many opportunities to invigorate their interpretation of women's history, by asking different questions and applying other knowledge. For example, the Betsy Ross house and workshop bases their interpretation on the scholarship of Marla Miller in *Betsy Ross and the Making of America* to emphasize Elizabeth Claypool Ross's trade and revolutionary life, a shift from hagiography to thoughtful women's history. "We depend on that book" a staff member explained.[15] Historic schoolhouses should expand interpretation of single women teachers' lives to include their community roles, boarding with students' families and that teachers, while considered especially eligible, were fired upon marriage. Museums should reference women who worked behind the scenes on assembly lines and as clerks, secretaries, miners, and telegraph operators. Interpretation should include how women needed cash or credit, which illustrates the possibilities and constraints of their lives. Recognize women as financially responsible for their family members, a reality contrary to the myth of male providers. Milliner-editor-suffragist Abigail Scott Duniway had a disabled husband; biologist-editor-author Rachel Carson supported her elderly mother and adopted son.[16] Include women's neighborhoods where they shopped, worshiped, rallied, and traveled—few women spent all their time in their homes. We need to interpret their larger worlds.

Scholarship has identified much the greater impacts "minority" women had on our history, which requires changed interpretation at museums and historic sites. Indigenous women had central roles and impacts within their societies—and were crucial Native American intermediaries with early European-American men. Black women were integral to the American Civil War—now recognized as our greatest slave uprising—when they fled on perilous journeys or sabotaged slave-supported plantations. Interpretation of Navajo women requires revising older scholarship, working closely with these women, and honoring their culture.[17] Newer scholarship reveals that Navajo women weavers received pittances for their internationally recognized artistry. Share with visitors the lesbian-occupied spaces in existing sites, such as Willa Cather's childhood home and Jane Addams Hull-House, where a visitor survey encouraged greater recognition of Addams's partner, Mary Rozet Smith.[18] Interpret places of all kinds, including softball fields and safe spots that were "ephemeral—a favorite stoop on which transgender women would hang out."[19] In addition to the historical context, provide the geographic context—the post office, church, or hair salon that particular groups of women frequented. The Kennecott Copper Mine site in Alaska only permitted company employees (nurses and teachers) and managers' wives and daughters to live there. Now Wrangell-St. Elias National Park needs to interpret the miners' families, boardinghouse keepers, and sex workers (then called "prostitutes") who lived five miles away in the village of McCarthy, as well as miners who sent remittances to their faraway families. Map the local geography using tax records or Sanborn maps to virtually reconstruct surrounding buildings or landscapes so that interpretation of historic house denizens includes the myriad interactions women had with other people and institutions. Immediate surroundings have often drastically changed, with spacious landscapes now subdivisions or previously mixed commercial and residential neighborhoods replaced by sleek high-rises. Massive change makes envisioning the historic scene difficult for visitors, making such mapping needed. Otherwise a woman's life becomes reduced to her house only, inadvertently squeezing her life in ways inaccurate and inappropriate. Consider also all the places she traveled during her/their lifetime to give greater context. Include the geographies of people who were major influences on her life, such as a woman whose then very pregnant grandmother had pulled a handcart 1,400 miles from Illinois to Utah in a Mormon brigade.[20] This approach offers additional connections with visitors.

Interpretation should connect visitors with historic women in ways that excite and educate. In recent years, visitor preferences have shifted *interpretation* from lecture-style presentations to active visitor participation.[21] Visitors who grew up playing interactive computer games and project-based learning find lectures boring. They want to discover for themselves, even as such programming actually requires considerable background preparation by interpreters. It's challenging to compress quantities of research into powerful presentations that intrigue. Such distillations simultaneously require intellectual rigor and effective communication to diverse audiences. With the self-empowerment of the internet, many visitors want more personal engagement. Our role shifts from lecturers to discovery facilitators as we discuss women's objects, rooms, and places with each group. This requires that we quickly evaluate visitor groups to match our best approach. The hospitality model works best when everyone feels comfortable and participates (but no one dominates). Understanding different visitor groups and assisting their shift from being observers to participants increases public support and organizational viability. Some visitors can only come once, others return repeatedly, while neighbors seek history and/or community. Seeing everyone as a potential partner, as the Hacienda Peralta Historic Site and Harriet Beecher Stowe Center do, enriches everyone and fulfills our civic duty as entities that benefit from public support.

Hospitality invites visitors to become our partners. For example, at the Harriet Beecher Stowe Center, visitors are invited to take an "interactive" tour at a "non-traditional" site.[22] In a combination immersive and guided tour, visitors first encounter their interpreter and each other while sitting by an exhibit showing Stowe's *Uncle Tom's Cabin* among other generative books on a wall labeled "Words That Changed the World," providing literary and historical context. They walk into the former pantry of the Beecher Stowe House to read and discuss quotes about *Uncle Tom's Cabin*, critical and complimentary, stenciled on bright red walls. In the dining room and back parlor, visitors hear how family history led to her famous novel as they hand around, decipher, and discuss facsimiles of a Beecher family circular letter. Later, visitors in the front parlor read copies of "Slave Sales and Runaway" advertisements, which brings the realization that the 1850 Fugitive Slave Act forced northerners to enforce the slave system. Upstairs, her bedroom mantlepiece holds copies of her less-famous books while interpreters explain her literary life at her desk there. The adjoining room wallpapered with scenes from the book startles with museum cases exhibiting *Uncle Tom's Cabin*–related objects. Going downstairs, visitors are invited to sit again, at "her" kitchen table covered with brown paper, given colored pencils, and encouraged to respond with personal commitments to Beecher Stowe's vision and activism.

Two fundamental approaches exist to center women at museums and historic sites: The first strategy is invigorating existing locales; the second strategy is identifying and developing new ones. We need to mine our existing museums and historic sites for fresh insights and pro-gramming to *fully* interpret historic women and girls. With fresh analysis, identify significant female-associated landscapes, buildings, and artifacts, including "missing" ones to interpret women's lives at your locale. Purists hate "reconstructions," but portrayals of honest landscapes need some long-disappeared female-associated workplaces: root cellars, housing, outhouses, and sheds. The Atlanta History Center has reconstructed a multi-seat outhouse, evidence of his-toric privacy practices.[23] Invigoration reinterprets existing collections (including archaeological ones) to identify needed acquisitions and exhibits, and examines whether its tangible resources accurately reflect the materiality of past women's lives—and how they can best interpret wom-en's history. For example, the Louisa May Alcott House interprets the archway between the parlor and dining room where the Alcott sisters staged her plays to show Alcott's creativity.[24] Use "un-expected" tangible resources. For example, the Martha's Vineyard Museum exhibits its maritime heritage with "try pots" that rendered whale blubber into whale oil. Why? To show that brighter oil-lit antebellum lamps fueled an outburst of women-oriented publications. Recent exhibits have included an alcohol-making still juxtaposed by a temperance water-drinking set, while Maymont Mansion in Richmond interpreted Victorian mourning practices and Valentine's Day decorations. Sites and museums have so many *domestic* objects, we need to remember the many *other* things women did—as insurance clerks, postmistresses, and "human computers."[25]

In addition to the research discussed in this book to find and integrate women's history, the search for miscataloged, undiscovered, or "lost" collections and other tangible resources enhances the history being portrayed. As vice president Anne Digan-Lanning at Deerfield Village stated about a painting, "Sometimes when an object enters the collection you just know that it has the potential to tell a fascinating story."[26] Identifying "missing" objects—i.e., physical evidence once present that may have been lost, stolen, or miscataloged—entails knowing primary sources and carefully working through scenarios of women's and girls' common and unusual events. In each room, develop a chart of women's daily activities in different life stages or seasons to iden-tify their probable material possessions, whether a nursing bra or a Jewish menorah. (One site misidentified a gynecological speculum as a Civil War surgeon's instrument.)[27] Because many women and girls were illiterate, objects must substitute for letters or accounts. Fortunately, "We can learn about what their lives were like from artifacts. Seeing these artifacts in person allows us to connect with these women in a unique way."[28] As well as the objects themselves, interpre-tation needs to include the *processes* of production and consumption of goods, their makers and *users.* Cobblers made shoe soles in their shops; women then attached shoe uppers in their homes. When only men's trades of smithy or cobbler are interpreted while women's work is invisible, women's lives are misrepresented. Look for *gender symmetry* to identify women's hidden roles—if male doctors, female midwives. Fur trappers get much attention with minimal interpretation of tribal women who performed the nasty labor that transformed animal carcasses into pelts.

Engaging Your Audience: Planning Visitor Experiences

As public historians in museums and historic sites, we connect tangible resources and our knowl-edge of the past with present visitors. As professionals, we respect women both past and present, and locate ourselves firmly between past and future. We are here now but were not there then. We cannot take credit for past women's accomplishments simply because we weren't *there*. Nei-ther can we be blamed for past occurrences—we could not have changed them even as we may deplore them now. While we can deplore our ancestors' actions, we need not feel guilty. Instead we must claim and act upon our own accountability. By taking responsibility for the present and for our depictions of the past, we can help facilitate difficult but crucial conversations and actions. We recognize that gender, class, sexual orientation, ethnicity, and race—along with many other factors—intersect and intermix in infinite variety because every woman and girl is simultaneously part of multiple groups. We must interpret how their lives overlapped and diverged, in ways obvious and subtle.

An inclusive planning process builds on significance. The discipline of *design thinking* works well; it focuses on identifying solutions to construct exemplary visitor experiences with *all* key parties involved in the planning process.[29] Good planning includes the "usual suspects" of museum curators, historians, interpreters, exhibit designers, educators, and supportive academic partners but must include key stakeholders and the "general public," in person or online. This approach may seem contentious, even risky, but good facilitation results in quality plans. Women's history must be integral to *all* planning—it's not frosting. Every program needs to consciously integrate women's history. When interpreting specific cultural groups, planning *must* immediately include credible representatives of the heritage being interpreted. Cultural groups (here, females) tire of explaining themselves to others, but it's integral to the planning process. Invite women and men with a range of attitudes toward women's rights, of different generations and backgrounds. Avoid embittered or angry people. Good facilitation and refreshments help overcome discomfort when participants encounter profound differences.

Knowing your significance, knowledge base, and tangible resources, as well as institutional capacity, provides the basis for your mission (WHY) and long-term goals. This should be followed by defining your "success" (WHAT). *Only* then should you focus on implementation of your plan (HOW). Many groups begin with "how" to achieve goals without really articulating them—and then argue incessantly! Planning must consider the environment, such as respecting neighbors' concerns and differentiating among audiences. To encourage men to better appreciate women's lives and accomplishments, develop programs that specifically welcome them, such as father-daughter programs. To build cross-racial bridges, sponsor shared projects with clear tasks and strong interpretive products. Although sometimes fraught, this builds relationships, and when done well, everyone gains.[30] Building relationships of sufficient trust that stories and subtleties are shared and incorporated into interpretive products requires time, careful listening, genuine humility, generosity, and forgiveness. As people share deeper insights, they can awaken their own pain, which needs to be treated kindly. A common project provides focus to work together; women from different backgrounds find their relationships strengthened. Examine your prejudices. Having believed I was relatively free from deep prejudices, I was appalled when working as part of a multiracial group to discern my inappropriate attitudes and privilege that I then consciously confronted and changed. As a White woman, I found this a sometimes painful but amazing process. Public planning processes provide forums to identify themes that will resonate with intended target audiences. As planners love to assert, planning is an iterative process with cycles of increased understanding punctuated by "BFOs," or "Blinding Flashes of the Obvious," insights that envision the best connections between audiences and resources. Lesley Barker encourages us to look obliquely at inter-gender encounters for often-missed insights.[31] Watch for relationships of power and dependency between genders, as well as affection such as fathers who gave their daughters custom-made armoires and fiancés who made ornate bride boxes. Much is missed if not perceptively reexamined.

Focusing on the entire visitor encounter with the women at your museum/site helps ensure success. We know how much visitors vary with their different needs and wants. Some come great distances for once-in-a-lifetime destination visits, others are regional seasonal visitors, while others are locals stopping for afterwork drinks-and-history programs. Museum and site managers should tailor programming to meet diverse visitor interests, whether games, book readings, or rug hooking. Destination visitors want "it all" in their single visit; regional visitors generally prefer special programs; and locals seek a community gathering place as much as a historic experience. Some visitors search for your museum while others are driving by or find it on the history app

Clio.[32] Visitors' needs affect museum experiences whenever they are hungry, have difficulty standing or climbing stairs, carrying squirming children, or struggling to understand. Smart museums schedule programming during lunch hour or right after work for younger audiences, and during daylight for older ones uncomfortable with night driving. Responding to visitors' needs encourages them to stay, enjoy, and return.

There are many approaches to interpretation that respect historic women and link us to them. Instead of flooding visitors with mini-lectures of catalog-style object descriptions, encourage them to join in discovery that engages both children and adults. Examine photographs that show intensively gardened back yards behind every house. Discuss relevant medical crises and long-term effects of injuries or illnesses, and how women's deaths affected their families. Share the multigenerational impacts from unequal gender access to educational opportunities, memberships, medical care, and workspaces. Study period newspapers for ways in which popular culture debated women's roles in movies, radio shows, music, and plays. Anti-suffrage cartoons still resonate. Study "insignificant" objects—girls' hairpins—for insights. Look beyond the obvious to subtle forces that link historic women with us. People are fascinated with "behind the scenes" tours or when they can peer at (but not touch) objects unseen in centuries or read letters never intended to be shared. Archaeologists have long involved the public in their excavations, garnering additional labor and crucial community support with professionals supervising trained volunteers. Historic sites can likewise shift visitor experiences from passive viewing to active participation using activities and sensory stimuli. Visitors can be invited to decide where to reposition a video microscope to examine historic needlework or hand-sew twenty-two stitches to the inch to appreciate women's workloads. People enjoy the challenge of deciphering 1930s handwriting. Because handling rare and fragile original objects risks damaging them, enlist and train volunteers, student workers, and civic groups to share our resource stewardship. Difficulty of preserving resources decreases when people understand the risks of inept document handling or the constraints of historic buildings with low load limits. Visitors who want more participation can join projects to transcribe digitized historic documents or deeply analyze and contextualize objects. Include your partners in preparing the Tools in this book. With encouragement, the sense of discovery gives participants strong senses of accomplishment and empathy with historic women.

When visitors then find treasured historical mythology has been challenged become upset, deep learning, accessible knowledge bases, and FAQs provide thoughtful responses. (Few visitors suspect the meticulous work that precedes professional interpretation.) Include the public and visitors as we research. Research guided by experts in women's history, interspersed with questions that arise from objects such as an icebox, can enthrall people. This approach slows research but builds public interest enhanced by visitor insights and recollections. Invite scholars, members of local communities, and descendants of women whose history is being interpreted. Involve people with deep cultural knowledge of women being interpreted—do *not* wait until you open an exhibit about Latinas to involve MALCS (*Mujeres Activas en Letras y Cambio Social*) and similar groups as well as local Latinx Studies departments. Invite the public to monthly brown bags with public and academic historians to share women's history and build your community. Have staff choose core readings, share collections and programs, and hold ongoing educational sessions.

Most of all, visitors are our essential partners who expect greater activity and involvement—to "feel" rooms and objects and have "special" treatment. Unfortunately, irreplaceable historic objects cannot be handled much before they deteriorate; landscapes, too, are fragile. Some sites allow visitors to sit on reproductions or handle "period pieces." Visitors become engaged when staff "argue" in dramatic skits, such as girls having to quit school at age fourteen to care for sick relatives. Debates for and against women's suffrage, temperance, child labor, and immigration "reform" work well. Develop interpretive activities that recognize women's lives, accomplishments, and artistic creativity to entice public involvement. The Emily Dickinson Museum invites visitors to write poetry in her bedroom (for a fee); the Dorothy Molter Museum sells her root beer; and the Atlanta History Center has weekend performances, including Rosalyn Walton, one of the Atlanta Nine, accompanying their city-focused exhibit, *Gatheround*.[33] Museums and historic sites have been creative in their activities but need to avoid well-intentioned activities that inadvertently belittle or misrepresent our foremothers. Gathering Easter eggs when anachronistic is inappropriate. Tea parties should not be the *only* female-related occasion, because interpreting women solely with a tea party belittles their lives. Ask, "Would our foremothers really have done this?"

Historic sites/museums need to attract many visitors and members; don't ignore *any* major segment of your potential audience/market. Building audience is a long-term effort, based on enticing programs that make a museum a gathering place, usually with a mix of informal activities (fun, food and drink, games, and mysteries) and serious presentations. President Lincoln's Cottage in Washington, D.C., where he drafted the Emancipation Proclamation, held in-depth workshops entitled "Students Opposing Slavery" on slavery, historical and modern. After the 2016 election, its local community spontaneously gathered there as a safe, nonpartisan place to process conflicted reactions. Director of Programming Callie Hawkins states, "[We] need to make museums a gathering place, essential to people's lives."[34] The Harriet Beecher Stowe Center challenges visitors to "Be Inspired by the Woman whose words changed the world."[35] It seeks to "inspire commitment to *social justice and positive change*." Stowe Center's "Salons 101" teaches "skills to facilitate effective group discussions, bringing critical thinking and dialogue to your organization."[36]

Interpretive Approaches

Nearly ubiquitous, tours of museums and historic sites provide live interpretation that allows visitors to ask questions, make comments, and get immediate responses. Tours ensure visitors don't jump on beds (unless allowed) or damage exhibits or themselves. Tours "meet" different groups wherever they are; tour introductions should whet visitor curiosity and provide interpreters an assessment of each group's interests and knowledge of women's history. Asking where people come from opens a nonthreatening dialogue. Singling anyone out for their ignorance shames them and mars their experience.

Visitors' experiences are enhanced when they encounter unfamiliar objects and ask questions that interpreters link to the historical context. Practicing hospitality entails dropping our "teacher's voice"; our expertise becomes obvious as tours proceed. Good interpreters include everyone and reinforce each visitor's contributions to the group conversation. What appears relaxed is actually more demanding work than canned speeches because interpreters must actively respond to every group participant and share basic information about the key women within their larger historical context. Tours can be structured to include key points in ways that engage visitor activities, such as having them analyze written documents, seek girl-related objects on "treasure hunts," or explore how rooms were originally used. This approach requires that museums use their planning process to develop the crucial takeaways for visitors.

Museums and historic sites vary in their interpretive approaches. At Andrew Jackson's Hermitage, a Black woman reenacting enslaved Hannah Jackson greets visitors at the front door, implicitly inviting a discussion of slavery. Being in costume enhances her impression. Historically, family and high-status visitors entered by the ceremonial front door; everyone else was relegated to the back door. Costumed interpreters can help visitors understand social expectations by how women dressed; costumes vary from excruciatingly accurate clothing to highly romanticized frilly dresses to slapdash polyester ones never worn historically. Total accuracy, while actually impossible, would require many female interpreters to wear boned corsets, garments few women want. But we can—and should—wear historic fabrics and styles and avoid distracting inappropriate sunglasses, hairstyles, tattoos, and jewelry. Fort Snelling, a Minnesota Historical Society site, practices stationary interpretation with well-costumed interpreters in the commander's home and open-hearth kitchen, sutler's store, and barracks, each presenting short introductions and answering questions as visitors wander inside the fort. Stationary interpreters frequently shift roles and locations, especially useful during busy times. These "third person" interpreters do not portray specific women, which allows female employees to interpret in all locations without inviting consternation of women interpreting "male" spaces. At the Atlanta History Center, the Smith Family Farm promises, "No boring tours, no hands-off antiques—the farm and its artifacts are touchable history."[37] Visitors are invited to wander through the Smith Family Farm house with an open house format featuring costumed interpreters who initiate conversations that enliven our historic places. Smith Family Farm visitors encounter characters portraying family members, their neighbors, and enslaved workers who provide insights into the challenges of daily life on a rural Georgia farm during the Civil War.[38] Rather than the older approach, where visitors watched costumed women spin thread, here visitors are encouraged to ask questions and be responsible for their visit's success. Interpreters focus on their interpretation itself rather than on spinning or cooking. And because visitors ask questions based on what they *already* know—which seldom includes women's history—interpreters must weave women's history into their conversations.

Living history, long practiced at Plimoth Plantation, is first-person interpretation on a grand scale, in farmhouses, courtrooms, villages, and battlefields. Interpreters (and reenactors) have striven for historic accuracy and honesty in period in clothes, demeanor, and language. At Plimoth Plantation, interpreters mix performing activities with depicting a specific woman. There are several challenges. While Plimoth's seemingly unkempt gardens and dirt floors enhance their authentic living history portrayal, it still remains distant from historic reality, when pregnant colonial women toiled *and* cared for infants. With immersive living history, it's difficult to convey historical *processes.* At the Swan Mansion in the Atlanta History Center, interpreters use first-person interpretation, speaking to visitors as if they were in the past. Portraying a specific woman requires the whole shebang, as is well done at the Swan Mansion at the Atlanta History Center, which uses character actors coached in historic posture, diction, and overall verisimilitude. There, a character actor superbly portrayed famed 1930s (White) interior designer Ruby Ross (Pope) (Goodnow) Wood in full 1930s hairstyle and period makeup that enhanced her realism.[39] In the kitchen, the interpreter who plays African American Bina Lockett, the cook's assistant, explained her work for the Inman family, her streetcar commute, and her home life in the Black community, providing poignant context. Her clothing, *lack* of makeup, and historic hairstyle contributed greatly to her effectiveness. Some women are more actors than classic interpreters, while others present well-rehearsed presentations describing their lives, often countering our expectations.

At the Sutter Fort State Historic Park in Sacramento, California, a costumed woman roasted four chickens over a campfire, producing hunger-inducing smells as costumed elementary school students enthusiastically made wooden stools, baked bread, and washed laundry. They participated in activities that the historic women being interpreted did. Specific skills of beading and embroidery fascinate some visitors. Consider how long different tasks take, how sensual they are, and how visitors can safely participate in them. Long-favored cooking demonstrations need to discuss that stirring the pot was a minor step in making stew. Demonstrations can be as simple (packing a valise for a suffrage lecture tour) or complex (reenacting a major protest) as resources allow. They engage visitors with their movement, whether stitching clothing or typing on a manual typewriter, a demonstration more interesting than older generations imagine.

Figure 10.2.   Interpreter Anita Badertscher portrays Sra. María Rita Duran, a once-ignored Alta Pimera woman, who with many other women and girls lived, worked, and worshiped at Tumacácori mission.
COURTESY TUMACÁCORI NATIONAL HISTORICAL PARK, ARIZONA, NATIONAL PARK SERVICE.

Greater Reality with Sensory Experiences

Sensory experiences provide another enlivening opportunity as an entire field of historic study is investigating our changing sensory experiences, especially sounds, tastes, and smells. Introducing life-size cutouts (or shadows) of historic women facing visitors helps us "see" them, as Monticello recently did for Sally Hemings. Smells, both pleasant and disgusting, are crucial to avoid inaccurate romanticism; some scents are now commercially available. "Deerfield changed seasonally as its population of cattle waxed and waned. It also smelled and looked a great deal different than it does now, with piles of manure."[42] Reproductions or sacrificial not-museum-quality period objects allow visitors to touch objects—handling solid "sad" irons effectively conveys the weight of women's work. Low light levels reflect dimmer lantern power. Cooking smells add greatly to realism. Although fire prevention laws and food safety regulations prohibit serving visitors directly from open fireplaces, museum restaurants can feed them. Mount Vernon even supplies home-distilled whiskey. A Plimoth Plantation fundraiser has served drinks from eight distilleries, a brewery, and a meadery, reflecting the historically heavy alcohol consumption there although drunkenness was discouraged.[43] Its restaurant has Pilgrim and Wampanoag–themed food of venison stew and corn bread; Colonial Williamsburg restaurants feed visitors Brunswick stew and sweet potato muffins.[44] Visitors viscerally connect when they touch reproduction fabrics, including coarse "Negro Cloth."[45] Greater realism with dirty aprons and patched clothing shows women as people rather than mannequins. Women did not wash their hair daily; images show women with their hair "up" or covered with caps.[46]

More history museums should adopt the very effective prerecorded audio programs that many art museums use to enhance visitor experiences. At Andrew [and Rachel] Jackson's Hermitage, a curator narrates an audio program about its grounds complete with birdcalls. Sounds of women's life-cycle events add powerful realism, with birth groans, moans, death rattles, or simply sighs. To restore historic soundscapes, kitchens can add audible water pouring, food frying, a baby fussing, and a woman humming period songs. Different spaces and events (hiding in the basement during battles as many women did) had specific accompanying sounds. Adding these sensory elements enhances our understanding of the past. Which sounds would be most evocative? Add radiators hissing, violins playing, wolf howls, or coal scuttles being cleaned, and most of all, women's voices. Identify appropriate activities and sounds in interpretive spaces and restore the historic soundscape. Repopulate it with women and girls replicating historic accents, vocabulary, and speech patterns. Sounds from specific events enhance realism—a 1920s telephone ring; *The Women's Forum Hour*, a radio show for farm wives; a 1940s radio FDR *Fireside Chat*; even the Beatles on the 1964 *Ed Sullivan Show*. Outside Chicago, the industrial housing remains at Pullman NM, but the factories where people worked are gone, resulting in a visually and sonically distorted landscape. Restoring that industrial soundscape would help visitors contextualize this once-busy space.[47]

Visitor Activities

Special events lure people to visit historic places they have driven past for years. Demonstrating considerable creativity, Women's Rights NHP held a temperance event that combined a barge trip on the local canal with staff "arguing" for and against alcohol. Visitors heard reason and passion on both sides. During a "Night at the Museum," Girl Scouts completed several projects for their "Girl Scout NPS" badge, including drafting new sections of the 1848 "Declaration of Sentiments" while the Girl Scouts and their leaders were "locked in" for a sleepover. Historic Fort Snelling hosted suffrage debates as staff deliberately riled up the crowd while they presented arguments for and against women voting. These programs match relevant stories and audiences with activities that draw visitors to "Live History." Many programs are social justice/conscience–themed and some are just fun—try drinking on a barge while arguing temperance! Alexander Ramsey House events include a "Victorian Séance" and "From Ladies Musicale to the 130-year-old Shubert Club," which performed music. Their "History Happy Hour" series includes two drinks, a presentation, and "time to mingle in the mansion"—history combined with social gatherings. These programs encourage visitors to consider different aspects of women's lives. At Colonial Williamsburg, four Black women interpreters performed the evocative "A Gathering of Hair," which featured a group of African American women, both enslaved and free, preparing for their friends' wedding while discussing their lives and still-present racial issues. "Out of the Fiery Furnace" portrayed women's lives at Revolutionary-era Hopewell Furnace NHS.[48] Other museums and sites have harvest festivals, birthday celebrations, concerts, and readings that interpret and enliven women's history.

Another approach, object-oriented programs, link experts with the public. As archaeologists have long done, historians, curators, and archivists should include the public in processing museum or site collections. With careful project selection, training, and supervision, involving strongly interested members of the public to join in, developing metadata or working with collections benefits everyone. Visitors delight in going "beyond the ropes" to get close to and even touch the "real stuff." That works if done carefully but damages tangible resources if overdone. People are especially tempted to touch objects that someone famous once had—as if magic will rub off! One class at a famous museum allowed students to move fragile historic teacups around on a heavily padded table to examine them closely, which minimized risk of damage. People love tours of curatorial storage of objects not on display. Anyone researching women's history should request an in-depth collection tour to identify female-associated objects.

Several historic sites and museums are enlarging their missions with educational programs especially designed to develop girls' leadership. The Jane Addams Hull-House, whose mission melds "research, education, and social engagement," holds a "Feminism Is for Everybody!" program for Girl Scouts in grades 6–8 so girls can "learn about the radical history of women who dared to fight for racial, gender, immigration, and labor justice." After touring the house, the girls could "create your own 'zine to celebrate powerful women in your life, imagine the world you would like to create, and earn your Book Artist Badge."[49] Some historic sites expand their history mission with social action. The Alice Paul Institute offers "History Detectives" and "Meeting Alice." Its Girls Leadership Council programs "members leave meetings better equipped to engage in meaningful conversation on different topics including human rights, gender stereotypes, and intersectionality."[50] With lifelong learning, we can present women's history short courses to interpret more of our foremothers' lives, motivations, and sentiments. In their off season, museums and sites can offer Sierra Club–style work trips that bring together skilled volunteers to undertake needed projects and enjoy intensive visits.

Museum and historic site shops sell products that extend visits and encourage return ones. These include handbooks about the museum, books about specific exhibits or individuals, and children's books; "Votes for Women" mugs and T-shirts; period reproductions of high-end furniture and furnishings, Jamestown glass, courting candlesticks, earthenware bowls, soaps, and wooden boxes; children's toys and games; and "kits" from easy to excruciating for making doll-sized quilts and covered wagons. How visibly are women's history products displayed? At Colonial Williamsburg, a girl's "pocket" to carry her small necessities provides insights while an eighteenth-century milking stool, probably used by women and girls, has been renamed a

Figure 10.3.   Visitors in Stowe kitchen responding to their tour of Harriet [and Calvin] Beecher Stowe house, Hartford, Connecticut, 2018.
PHOTOGRAPH BY JOHN GROO. COURTESY HARRIET BEECHER STOWE CENTER, HARTFORD, CONNECTICUT.

"Randolph [Tavern] Kitchen Stool."[51] Is there a range from scholarly to children's books, current events to fun? At Civil War museums, is path-breaking scholarship sold or "Lost Cause" books? Some apologist books have been reprinted with fresh covers. Are reproductions accurate and appropriate? How well do these products reflect historic women's lives?

Historic sites and museums are great places to meet our foremothers. They are primary locations where the public accesses professional history to appreciate who we are as a nation and where we've come from. Preserving and interpreting women's history at our museums and historic sites is especially crucial for visitors whose classroom education included little women's history. Four decades, and many thousands of books, dissertations, and research projects, have together built a stronger American history where it's clear that women have continually played key if less-visible roles. This historical understanding *fits* more closely with what actually happened; now we need to recognize our paradigm shift and fully incorporate it into our interpretation. When we seek more women's tangible history at existing museums and historic sites, we'll find more than expected. We need to search scholarship to identify key locations of historical women, movements, and events worthy of designation and preservation. Every interpretive program, tour, and exhibit needs to recognize women's history. Recognition of the significance of women should permeate the atmosphere rather than be left to individual interests or whims. By defining visitation broadly, developing specific programs for various visitors, and enlivening their experiences, museums have amazing opportunities to recognize and share how essential women and girls have been to creating us as Americans in our full diversity. For example, the Marian Anderson Historical Residence and Museum in Philadelphia, located in her former home, sponsors the National Marian Anderson Historical Society Artist Scholars who perform diverse music to spread "her music and humanitarianism internationally."[52] Historic sites and museums preserve and research women-associated tangible resources and build their knowledge base, which reinforces public interpretation.

Identify and Preserve Additional Historic Sites, Monuments, and Parks

Other approaches are also needed. In Salem, Massachusetts, a low granite stone square marks where the accused witches were hanged in 1692. This poignant memorial witnesses a significant but nondescript space where women died. We need to identify, research, restore, and interpret many such places, happy and awful, that witness women's experiences. To inscribe women's history upon our national landscape so that preserved properties match American history, more research, identification, and marking of women's sites and special places is needed, as well as preservation of existing but not yet designated sites. Streets could be named for historic women as well as for men!

The U.S. preservation system, a bricks-and-mortar approach, needs private, state, and federal entities to recognize and preserve many more women's history locations. (See Chapter 9.) All of its categories need many more properties on the National Register, as National Historic Landmarks, or as state or federal parks/historic sites. Every Famous Man Mansion needs recognition as a women's workplace.

Another approach is to create museums that focus on specific aspects of women and their lives, such as quilt museums, the Women in Military Service to America Memorial, or the "Women at Work" museum, focused on women scientists and engineers.[53] Assembled collections of washboards, dolls, and even nutmeg graters provide insights unavailable elsewhere—how these objects were made, functioned, used, and their meaning for the women who used them. Displayed together, samplers unmistakably demonstrate different girl's subjects, skills, and designs, harder to discern in historic sites when surrounded by many other objects. Our national collection includes the National Women's Hall of Fame, ten state Women's Halls of Fame, and specialized museums such as the Cowgirls National Hall of Fame and Museum in

Texas, and the Women's Basketball Hall of Fame in Tennessee. Establishing new museums, large and small, involves complex and challenging legal, financial, and social elements. Credibility and political support require that objects be collected and curated, research conducted, and numerous logistical and fund-raising hurdles surmounted. Two promising women's museums closed in 2002 and 2011.[54] The African American History and Culture Museum in Washington, D.C., that succeeded after decades of hard work had the advantage of a politically active well-defined racial group. They are not necessarily a model for the best women's history because they perpetuate gender segregation and the narrative that male and female lives are separate when they are profoundly intertwined (no matter what an individuals' sexual orientation or a groups' ideology may be). Integrating women's history fully into all museums and historic sites recognizes that such separation is fictious while separation encourages men and boys to skip over the historical experiences and accomplishments of women and girls. The separatist approach ironically perpetuates the mostly-male version of our past, a version that has been disassembled article by article, book by book, archaeological dig by archaeological dig documenting that women and girls were integral to almost every human community. It hinders the full restructuring of American history that recognizes the indispensability of everyone in forming our past. Decades of scholarship have shown that genuine inclusion of women and girls lives and accomplishments rewrites our past so that historic events and their present interpretation fit much more closely. As half or more of humanity, human females are not a minority group, as eminent historian Gerda Lerner explained years ago in *The Majority Finds Its Past: Placing Women in History*, nor one that can be genuinely segregated.[55] Separate, "all women" museums perpetuate the false equivalence of *all* female humanity with *any* single racial/ethnic group. Instead of segregating the history of women, *every* museum should fully interpret women in American history. Another approach to recognizing women on the larger landscape is to create routes, trails, and networks that highlight locations of women's historical events such as "First Woman Who . . ." or of women-focused communities, such as private recreational camps. This approach identifies and marks places and sometimes preserves and interprets them as well. Generally, "trails" connote historic routes, but there is enthusiasm for developing new ones that mark suffrage related sites for the 2020 suffrage centennial, such as the "National Votes for Women Trail."[56] Men had to vote affirmatively for women to gain their suffrage.

Historically, women met together in many places that varied in duration and visibility, with many transitory and some now unknowable. A photograph shows smiling Victorian women enjoying their back-yard tea party in a "room" of blankets hung on clotheslines and rugs on the ground. Their outdoor celebration lasted only a few hours but was long savored. On riverbanks, women washed clothes together; in rivers, their baptisms marked life passages with religious rituals. In remote areas of plantations, enslaved women furtively worshiped together in the "invisible church." Some women's events left few marks on the public landscape even as it shaped those events, such as the infamous 1913 suffragists' march in Washington or contralto Marian Anderson's 1939 concert at the Lincoln Memorial. Lesbians frequented particular bars, clubs, parks, and protest sites to build and maintain their community.[57] Feminists gathered in bookstores, coffee shops, and rape and pregnancy crisis centers. Semi-public spaces, such as church basements and beauty shops, as well as private homes, provided places for women to gather, support each other, and organize. Some significant locales remain difficult to research and preserve, but their significance *demands* that we recognize them.

Opportunities and Challenges

Sometimes additional knowledge and intervening generations are necessary before women are properly interpreted. In transformational interpretation, the Monticello Foundation took twenty-five years to reinterpret Sally Hemings's life and her six children by Thomas Jefferson. Scholarship on slavery, the Hemings family, and site-specific research (archaeological, oral history through the Hemings family, and DNA tests) reinforced each other. Analysis revealed that Hemings's windowless room connected to her children and to Jefferson.[58] At Little Bighorn Battlefield, National Park Service interpretation, long focused on George Armstrong Custer, now features Native American men, but still slights Northern Cheyenne women. Archaeology and Northern Cheyenne oral history revealed that Cheyenne women camping beside the nearby Big Horn River first raised the alarm over to the U.S. Army's presence.[59] Buffalo Calf Woman who fought in the battle, and the U.S. Army wives who futilely awaited their husbands' return, need interpretation. This example illustrates the pernicious risk we all face: that "we don't know what we don't know." Sometimes the research has been done but not adequately interpreted to the public. Women who were Mexican American cannery workers and Japanese American wholesale florists have been researched but need more interpretation at museums and as context for historic sites. Too often when such women are not interpreted as they ought to be, the public assumes they never existed! The public relies on those of us who present past women to the present generations to reflect that past well. We need to counter such erroneous assumptions by preserving, researching, and interpreting telling the stories of all women.

Much about past women's lives remains barely known. Many women—barely literate, economically marginal, or physically impaired—have little presence in museums and sites. There are many other omissions. We know that historically women became addicted to alcohol and morphine in their patent medicines, or died in childbirth, or had their health permanently damaged from unsafe abortions. Multigenerational and sibling patterns of women need much more research and presentation. Since colonization, women have experienced profound social changes of decline of religiosity, access to contraception (which altered the experience of sex itself), and the industrial-scientific-technological-digital revolutions. Our collective knowledge base in women's history must continue to grow and be interpreted with the public.

Today, museums and historic sites have myriad ways to interpret tangible resources, the virtual and the physical. Traditionally, visitors arrived, parked, used the restrooms, watched a film, saw the museum, and encountered interpreters as they wandered around. Visitors now make decisions and acquire quantities of information online (excellent and squirrelly), which makes an electronic presence crucial to encourage in-person visitors. Special events and other activities that can *only* be enjoyed on-site, such as live performances of women's music and sensory museum experiences, become more crucial. People mistakenly think that seeing an image online is the same as seeing it in a museum, but the online revolution forces us to differentiate "real" exhibits. The opportunities are delicious, but the demands, especially on smaller organizations, are daunting. Now visitors use different media—iPhones, podcasts, and webinars. Partnerships with other museums and sites becomes even more necessary, as well as with schools, organizations, and commercial ventures. Websites and smartphones now share women's history in ways once unimaginable. Interpreters at President Lincoln's Cottage use iPads loaded with documents and images that enhance visitors' tours in a minimally furnished house that focuses on concepts because furnishings can support or distract from interpretive tours. With iPads, visitors can "see" empty rooms refurnished and "hear" historic women speak. The actual rooms where the Lincoln family summered, combined with technology, foster high-quality interpretation. At Ulysses S. Grant NHS, a "Magic Mirror" hung above the front room fireplace is actually a video screen. Visitors see Grant arguing about slavery with his father-in-law, intently watched by his wife, Julia Dent Grant, and their enslaved cook, Harriet Robinson giving visitors a powerful vignette. Museums and historic sites are adapting even newer technologies, including augmented reality ("AR"). At Highland, James Monroe's Virginia home, AR can "re-place" historic women and men. Augmented reality allows visitors to envision sites' historical appearances without interrupting

Ulyss, have you heard from your sister yet about her visit?

Figure 10.4. The "Magic Mirror" at U.S. [and Julia Dent] Grant home turns on a video showing U.S. Grant arguing about slavery with his father-in-law, "Col." Frederick Dent, while wife, Julia Dent Grant, and enslaved cook, Mary Robinson, listen. An effective interpretive tool.
COURTESY ULYSSES S. GRANT NATIONAL HISTORIC SITE, ST. LOUIS, MISSOURI.

archaeological excavations: "You can see buildings or look closely at foundation stones while still protecting them."[60] At Ulysses S. Grant NHS, a "Magic Mirror" hung above the front room fireplace is actually a video screen. Visitors see Grant arguing about slavery with his father-in-law, watched intently by his wife, Julia Dent Grant, and their enslaved cook, Harriet Robinson. With iPads, visitors can "see" empty rooms refurnished and "hear" historic women speak. The actual rooms where the Lincoln family summered, combined with technology, fosters high-quality interpretation.

We can use technology to help women speak for themselves, show their lives, and increase our understanding. For example, DNA tests identified a woman-smoked pipe stem in the African American Boston Saloon in Virginia City, a caution against assuming that artifacts belonged to men.[61] Someday, DNA may provide new insights by identifying specific villages where Africans originated before enslavement. As the technology develops, we'll be able to immerse visitors into past scenarios with impressive power and realism. We can now electronically project images onto original landscapes to "see" historic women, and "hear" their original languages and soundscapes. We can make historical women seem more three-dimensional. Finally, historical organizations can now access visitors' comments, surveys, and tweets and respond accordingly.

Partners improve results and support the never-ending need for resources. Partnerships require intense investments—constant effort, thoughtful learning, and a willingness to support partners' needs that otherwise would be unimportant. Their continuing challenge is well worth it. Support sometimes comes from unexpected sources—women with unsuspected talents and connections, or "outsiders" who nudge us out of ruts and potholes. Focusing together on meaningful common work strengthens relationships and creates lively communities of people involved in our museum/site's mission. Partner with local scholars and researchers of similar historical periods; descendants of the women being interpreted bring insights and credibility.

Some museums and historic sites partner with educational institutions to provide students real-world work—and to gain personnel. Hull-House works closely with the University of Illinois at Chicago, whose campus surrounds it. For years, public and academic women historians held monthly brown bag lunches at the Smithsonian in Washington, D.C., to share their projects and research, encourage each other, and build community—a basic but effective model. Today, digital technology, conference calls, blogs, and webinars support similar presentations and virtual meetings that build community. The American Association for State and Local History routinely uses these techniques, complemented by annual meetings, as do the National Council on Public History (NCPH) and the National Collaborative for Women's History Sites (NCWHS). They span distance and provide real-time support that strengthens women's history interpretation.

Many museums and sites consciously link current issues with their larger communities. The Harriet Beecher Stowe Center holds many events discussing current topics with those she grappled with, such as slavery, eviction, and other "contemporary social justice issues." A Pauli Murray NHL event constructed a labyrinth from old shoes in honor of her 1954 *Proud Shoes*, as well as exhibits at local galleries, plays, and religious events as living memorials to her activism. The Pauli Murray Project states, "We believe that broad-based, guided history-telling . . . is a step toward reconciliation and racial healing. We will begin by collecting and soliciting stories and asking questions through community dialogues, oral history research, panel discussions and reading circles."[62] At Hull-House, Jennifer Scott presented "Activating Marginalized Histories: Museums as Catalysts for Social Change," which continues its original vision that links research, education, and social engagement.[63] In California, Hacienda Peralta organizes many cross-cultural programs joining together Hmong, Hispanics, Cambodians, and other groups intensively sharing dissimilar cultures. A Colonial Williamsburg program with Black and White interpreters playing historic roles in "Journey to Redemption" concludes with a discussion of interpreters' feelings about playing such racially charged roles. Historic sites/museums link current issues with past ones to explore how previous generations responded—or didn't—to their overriding issues. We are challenged to connect with our foremothers to build better lives.

Women's history can also be approached by focusing on programs with specifically male appeal. From childhood, girls and boys encounter different toys, games, and rules, and historically, received different educations. Their individual differences are often shaped by the social expectations and opportunities they encounter. Research shows that male and female characteristics overlap a great deal with significant diversity within each gender. In 1906, Maggie Walker gave a speech, "Benaiah's Valour, an Address for Men Only," when she spoke frankly to her audience and told them to support Black women as their sisters, mothers, and daughters.[64] Such a male-only approach to women's history may work, especially if presented as "Everything You Wanted to Know about Women's History but Knew Better Than to Ask." To build the support necessary to preserve and interpret women's history, we *must* share it with men, emphasizing that "their" history is tightly intertwined with women's, and that real American history requires everyone. Men such as Frederick Douglass and Jimmy Carter are heroes to women, as well as many not-famous men. A male barbershop quartet and free ice cream (outside only!) brought crowds to Clara Barton NHS, while another site lured male visitors by featuring an antique Pierce Arrow car. Sadly, some men find women's history baffling and declare it extraneous, or they are openly hostile. One high-ranking manager completely dismissed women's history as neither interesting nor significant. Others denigrate women's history and resist calls for inclusivity, calling a massacred woman "Granny." Disrespect must be challenged. Legislation establishing one park service site directed that the wife "shall" be interpreted as well as her husband, appropriate because the property had been *her* family's farm. Instead, interpretation of her life has vacillated with managers' preferences. People are especially shockingly oblivious of women of color. Staff at one historic site distracted their problematic board with the excitement of archaeological excavations while they researched slave housing. Obviously, the more allies, the better—politicians, historians, and board members. As professionals, we must resist diminishing or "silencing" women's history, which damages all of us, our museums, and our historic sites. Exclusion of anyone distorts our understanding of who we are and where we have come from.

Interpretive Principles

History both consoles and challenges us. Interpreting women's history must be:

- *Authentic*: The tangible resources and accompanying interpretation must be as faithful to the original as possible, following historic women's lives and countering bogus and harmful versions: "The Autry Museum of the West has worked hard to show First American Women as core to its history, implicitly honoring historic facts rather than Hollywood myths."[65] Such authenticity is grounded in our knowledge bases. Don't confuse history with myths.
- *Inclusive*: Port Chicago NM in California is best known for its horrific World War II naval magazine explosion, which killed 320 Black (male) sailors. But its interpretation needs to include the NAACP women who supported those sailors subjected to local White hostility, as well as the sailors' grieving families and impacts on their lives. *Every* historic community member, female and male, those both directly and indirectly involved, need to be interpreted. One approach is conceptualizing a series of concentric circles, with those directly impacted (the African American sailors), and indirectly impacted (the NAACP women and the sailors' families), as well as the larger war effort. Telling the whole story interprets colonial (male) Spanish missionaries *and* the thousands of indigenous Christianized women who lived at the missions, farmed their fields and orchards, and re-plastered their adobe walls. When tangible resources no longer exist, interpretation using maps, models, and digital reconstructions makes visible communities of women and men, as Tumacácori National Historical Park does.
- *Nuanced*: Different experiences of each generation shape its distinct perspective. We ask, "How *could* they have done that? Thought that? Treated others that way?" To respect historical women, we must attempt to perceive the world *as they did* and to articulate their perceptions. Otherwise we may appear to believe we are "better" than they were. This stance is not about "letting people off" for beliefs we find disturbing. We need to be thoughtful with the names, words, gestures, and anecdotes we choose. We must also honor profound cultural differences. For example, Navajo women valued the *process* of weaving more than their *products* of treasured blankets and rugs. As part of their spirituality, weaving has secrets never to be shared with outsiders; respect for Navajo women requires that we accept incomplete knowledge.

  Interpreting women (and men) whose work made our lives possible places a moral demand on us. For all our very real issues, American women have options few could have imagined two centuries ago, in more gender-equalitarian attitudes and access to education, occupations, and health care. Without understanding those changes, we distort the context of women's lives. A century ago, when industrial accidents killed or disabled men, widows who were suddenly solely responsible for feeding their families had little public support and few employment choices. The integral roles women had and prices they paid during our wars need full interpretation, including women who died from Civil War munitions explosions or World War II shipyard pneumonia.[66] Interpreters frequently distill history; sometimes we need to *complicate* our accounts to more accurately convey women's past realities.
- *Intimate*: Without care, interpreting the most personal aspects of female lives can seem intrusive, even salacious. Historic women experienced menstruation, pregnancy, miscarriages, childbirth, and nursing, commonalities we share. Few historical accounts of pregnancy and

delivery (or sex) were written by women. Researching linguistic history helps, including slang. For menstruation, the derisive phrase "on the rag" ("sanitary napkins") hints that monthly cloths were used, then washed, a practice elderly woman confirm. Such intimate aspects need more inclusion, as do beauty products—makeup, hair products, and even cancer-causing radium paste that some early-twentieth-century women disastrously used to remove their unwanted facial hair.[67]

Few museums or sites interpret life-changing experiences of sexual molestation and abuse, incest, rape, and the lasting sorrow from children stillborn or lost to disease; or impacts from domestic violence, sexual discrimination, or harassment. Diaries and letters rarely mention them, making our knowledge incomplete. Darlene Clark Hine in "Some Preliminary Thoughts on Rape, the Threat of Rape and the Culture of Dissemblance," gave her forthright analysis and called for "an array of analytic frameworks."[68] Two excellent

Figure 10.5. Narbonne House kitchen/Cent shop interior showing door to Essex St., Salem.
PHOTOGRAPH BY EMILY MURPHY, SALEM MARITIME NHS, COURTESY OF THE NATIONAL PARK SERVICE.

books that discuss many details in women's lives are *Keeping House: Women's Lives in Western Pennsylvania, 1790–1850* and *Calling This Place Home: Women on the Wisconsin Frontier, 1850–1925*.[69] With only scraps of historical information about sexual behavior (and misbehavior), we need much more research. Changing experiences of and attitudes toward sex, sexuality, and sexual orientation pose additional opportunities and challenges. How best to recognize women who had richly rewarding nonsexual female relationships in a gender-segregated society or to present sexual orientations well? Historian Susan Ferentinos explains, "Different historical time periods understood sexual identity and expression differently."[70] It's important to recognize lesbians and their life experiences even as we respect women who clearly would not want to be "outed."

- *Worldly*: Interpretation that focuses only on the woman-in-the-house misleads—few women lived strictly in their kitchen and bedroom! Trace the organizations to which women belonged, from informal knitting circles and prayer groups to well-organized American Red Cross volunteer groups, clubs, missionary groups, or political parties. Women-focused organizations provided infrastructures for women to know each other and work together. A broader focus offers insights and interpretive programming possibilities.

Doing Women's History in Public

Fully including women's history in our museums and historic sites accomplishes more accurate history and appropriately respects the women who built America—including our friends, mothers, sisters, wives, and great-great-grandmothers. Remember the lunch buckets, the poll tax receipts, the rugged landscapes—and the women who lived them. Our fundamental challenge is integrating women's history everywhere, making full interpretation of women's history "natural," ending distortions from misinformation or omission. While the temptation exists to claim that some women's history is too faded to research, preserve, or interpret, past successes should encourage us—few people imagined how much has already been found. As Elizabeth Cady Stanton told us, "Failure is impossible." By appreciating the significance, identifying the knowledge base, and preserving the tangible resources, a different perspective on American women emerges with greater opportunities to interpret their centrality. Genuine American history requires full interpretation of the history of all American women.

Tools for Chapter 10

These tools can be implemented in different stages. If you have been implementing the tools throughout this book, you have already begun. Review what you have done and add as appropriate. You're making a real difference for all of us. Thank you.

Tool 10.1: Basic

- Know the historical women at your museum/site and their significance. Understand where she/they relate to their historical context through women's history scholarship. Avoid the embarrassment of overblown claims. Identify women historically present at your site, their significance, the knowledge base about them and their era, and all the relevant tangible resources. (See Chapters 1 and 2.) Emphasize that women and girls were *not* a minority, with half of all "minorities" women and girls. Women and girls are central to our history. Recognize and interpret the substantial, essential, but often invisible work that women did. Candle dipping was a minor activity! Think of all the work it took to keep a farm and household functioning or to support the public presentation of key men by performing household, agricultural, organizing and professional tasks from selling goods to emptying chamber pots, checking mining reports to making paper flowers hour after hour.

- Ensure support from senior management. If they are not supportive, find champions to work with them. Establish a Women's History Team (with women and men of different backgrounds, perspectives, and ages). Identify people most able to effect needed changes. Avoid naysayers. Especially involve fathers of daughters. Task the team to review museum programs, products, and publications (paper and electronic) to assess how text and images depict women. *Count* how many women and girls are portrayed—you may be surprised.
- Build support for practicing visitor hospitality—and grow your market share and diversity. Entice men and boys to increase their interest in more women's history. Develop women's history programs for men, emphasizing their interests and connections with female relatives.
- Identify local and national partners and work with them. Review other locales' interpretation of women's history. Engage local classes to do relevant women's history projects. Network!

Tool 10.2: Intermediate

- Analyze, then reduce, barriers that hamper fully incorporating women's history. Build community knowledge about historical women. Invite women's history experts to speak and inspire your locale to think about *all* the women at your site. Consider how doing more women's history will enhance your site's ability to interpret the past it portrays and reach more people. Identify historic women associated with your powerful stories and tangible resources that ought to be interpreted, for example, consider women's workspaces, such as the desk where Laura Ingalls Wilder wrote the famous *Little House* books. Find parallels between women's historic experiences and current ones.
- Build a strong argument for more women's history. *Imagine* spending a leisurely meal with several historical women from your museum/site and current stakeholders, listen to their thoughts and reactions, and together write up insights from your "conversation." Recognize women from many different groups. There are many *different* Spanish-speaking/identified women, just as there are many different Asians and European women, who identified with their specific villages, not with entire continents ("I'm from Donegal"). Have your Women's History Team for consistency develop projects of varied sizes that build community and bring people together. Conference calls work well for people who *already* know each other. Celebrate successes. Generally, younger generations support women's history more than older ones. Sadly, anyone can be miseducated by media misportrayals (no bras were burnt!). Having people from several generations and backgrounds encourages different viewpoints; frequent informal social events build your community and reward volunteers. When facing difficult discussions, prepare for them, choose the best times/locations, and provide chocolate.
- Establish an ongoing analysis of the condition of your knowledge base and associated tangible resources. Evaluate *all* existing exhibits, publications, websites, and programs to improve and update women's history. Like the quiet phase in capital campaigns, this is foundational for subsequent actions. Integrate intersectionality of gender and race, a complex and crucial concept, into interpretation. For example, consider the horrors that resulted from the attitude, as articulated by Thomas Jefferson, "I consider a woman who brings a child every two years as more profitable than the best man of the farm. What she produces is an addition to the capital."[71] Women were shaped by their backgrounds, experiences, and events. While most such significant characteristics are obvious, others are subtle, if still important. Pho-

tographer Dorothea Lange felt "different" because of her polio-induced limp, a disability that needs more interpretation.

- Seek some women's history-specific donations to show visible outside support. Identify new people interested in becoming involved and recognize them publicly.
- Provide key staff time and support. Encourage attendance and participation at regional and national meetings and introduce newcomers extensively. Experiment how best to incorporate women's history specific to your situation—and then *just do it*.

Tool 10.3: Advanced

- With your Women's History Team and champions, set up specific tasks for different people, mixing groups up. A facilitator can help identify the best mix of people, give authority to the project, and take on some of its challenges. Use an outside facilitator to identify opportunities and barriers. Work to assuage recalcitrant people (who may be female) who fear change. You may need to work around people who resist change. Don't give up on them, but don't let them impede progress.
- Hold women's history programs to build public interest, not only in March but all year long. Women should be part of all heritage history months, such as Asian American in October. Identify and sell women's history merchandise, both museum-specific and generic.
- Celebrate success when local historical women are recognized by the community and new programs and exhibits are on display. The historic house is now the Ryan Family House, or the Kara and Colin Ryan House, no longer just *his* house, and all programs routinely include speakers who focus on women's history; all speakers incorporate women into their historical presentations. Visitation is up, and you're just beginning . . .

Author's Note

This chapter benefited especially from interviews with the following colleagues: Kimberley Szewczyk (Women's Rights NHP); Lucy Beard (Alice Paul Institute); Callie Hawkins and Erin Mast Carlson (President Lincoln's Cottage); Nancy Cass and Dr. Missy McDonald (Fort Snelling); Jean Federico; Michael Rose, Kelly Whitfield Bradley, and Jessica Rast VanLanduyt (Atlanta History Center); Marsha Mullin (Andrew Jackson's The Hermitage); Dr. Barbara Lau (Pauli Murray NHL); Elizabeth Burgess and other Harriet Beecher Stowe Center staff; Sarah Guy-Levar (Dorothy Molter Museum); Tracy Fortman and Meagan Huff (Fort Vancouver NHP); Phil Wallis, Bonnie Stacy, Ann DuCharme, and Linsey Lee (Martha's Vineyard Museum); Dr. Emily Murphy (Salem Maritime NHS); Ajena Rogers, Dr. Andrea DeKoter, Dr. Benjamin Anderson, and Ethan Bullard (Maggie L. Walker NHS); the Maggie Walker Community; Doris Crump Rainey, Jean Ellis (Keweenaw Heritage Center); Susan Barron and Dan Schwartz (Pope-Leighey House); and Dr. Lesley Barker (Bolduc House).

Notes

1. Allan G. Johnson, *The Gender Knot: Unraveling our Patriarchal Legacy*, 3rd ed. (Philadelphia: Temple University Press, 2013). Iris Bohnet, *What Works: Gender Equality by Design* (Cambridge: Belknap Press of Harvard, 2016).
2. Philip Kennicott, "Jefferson's Monticello Finally Gives Sally Hemings Her Place in Presidential History," *Washington Post*, June 13, 2018; Annette Gordon-Reed, *The Hemingses of Monticello: An American Family* (New York: W. W. Norton & Company, 2008).

3. Laurel Ulrich Thatcher, *The Age of Homespun: Objects and Stories in the Making of an American Myth* (New York: Knopf Publishing, 2001) and Susan Sleeper-Smith, *Indigenous Prosperity and American Conquest: Indian Women of the Ohio River Valley, 1690–1792* (Chapel Hill: The University of North Carolina Press, 2018).

4. National Association for Interpretation, "Interpretation," 2007, http://www.definitionsproject.com/definitions/def_full_term.cfm.

5. Freeman Tilden, *Interpreting Our Heritage*, 4th ed. Revised and enlarged (The University of North Carolina Press, 2008).

6. "Visitors Count!" AASLH survey program, see https://aaslh.org/programs/visitorscount.

7. *LGBTQ America: A Theme Study of Lesbian, Gay, Bisexual, Transgender and Queer History* (Washington, DC: NPS, 2016), Chapter 14, 10.

8. See "Declaration of Sentiments," https://www.nps.gov/wori/learn/historyculture/declaration-of-sentiments.htm.

9. See https://womenshistory.si.edu/; https://www.nps.gov/articles/taas-womenshistory-intro.htm; https://www.nps.gov/museum; "Telling Stories with Objects" includes Maggie Walker, Clara Barton, and Eleanor Roosevelt. The site emphasizes the history of suffrage and the 19th amendment.

10. Belmont-Paul Women's Equality NM; Clara Barton NHS; Eleanor Roosevelt NHS; Ellis Island, part of Statue of Liberty NM; First Ladies NHS; Harriet Tubman NHP; Harriet Tubman Underground Railroad NHP; Lowell NHP; Maggie L. Walker NHS; Mary McLeod Bethune Council House NHS; Rosie the Riveter WWII Home Front NHP; and Women's Rights NHP. See https://www.nps.gov/experiencemore/related-content.htm?subjectID=64E34781-0066-46A9-9304-738A 91A3DD50#park.

11. AASLH Affinity Group, Women's History, https://aaslh.org/resources/affinity-communities/womens-history/ and blog, https://aaslh.org/category/womens-history/; Library of Congress, https://www.loc.gov/collections/?fa=subject:women%27s+history, and https://www.loc.gov/free-to-use/womens-history-month; NPS, https://www.nps.gov/subjects/tellingallamericansstories/womenshistory.htm; and *CRM*: "Placing Women in the Past" (1997); http://npshistory.com/newsletters/crm/crm-v20n3.pdf; The National Trust for Historic Preservation, https://savingplaces.org/story-categories/womens-heritage-stories#.XTXxDuhKjD4; Smithsonian Institution, American Women's History Initiative, https://womenshistory.si.edu/.

12. Allan G. Johnson, *The Gender Knot*, 2016.

13. Susan Ferentinos, "Interpreting LGBTQ Historic Sites," *LGBTQ America*, 2016. See also Ferentinos, *Interpreting LGBT History at Museums and Historic Sites* (Lanham: Rowman & Littlefield Publishers, Inc., 2014), and Paula Martinac, *The Queerest Places: A Guide to Gay and Lesbian Historic Sites* (New York: Henry Holt and Company, 1997).

14. Sarah Guy-Levar and Terri Schocke, *Dorothy Molter: The Root Beer Lady* (Cambridge: Adventure Publishing, Inc., 2011). Personal visit, June 2013.

15. Personal visit, October 2019. See Marla Miller, *Betsy Ross and the Making of America* (New York: Henry Holt, 2010). Her recent book, *Entangled Lives: Labor, Livelihood, and Landscapes of Change in Rural Massachusetts* (Baltimore: Johns Hopkins University Press, 2019) provides more insights into different women's economic and social lives applicable to many sites and museums.

16. See Scott Duniway in entry on Abigail Scott Duniway, https://oregonhistoryproject.org/articles/biographies/abigail-scott-duniway-biography/#.XSK7O-hKjD4. Rachel Carson owned a midcentury modern ranch home in Silver Spring Maryland, outside of Washington, DC, where she lived with her mother Maria McLean Carson and her adopted son Roger, and used

her yard as a laboratory. Owned by Rachel Carson Landmark Alliance; http://rachelcarson-landmarkalliance.org/about-the-landmark. Personal tour, April 2019.

17. Kathy M'Closkey, *Swept Under the Rug: A Hidden History of Navajo Weaving* (Albuquerque: University of New Mexico Press, 2002). She researched Hubbell Trading Post financial records and conducted oral history interviews with Navajo women.

18. Gail Lee Dubrow, "The Preservation of LGBTQ Heritage," *LGBTQ America*, 2016. See other excellent essays in Megan Springate, ed., *LGBTQ America: A Theme Study of Lesbian, Gay, Bisexual, Transgender, and Queer History* (online) (Washington, DC: National Park Service and National Park Foundation, 2016), www.nps.gov.

19. Christina Hanhardt, "Places and Spaces of LGBTQ Collective Identity Formation," *LGBTQ America* (National Park Service and National Park Foundation, 2016).

20. My thanks to Margaret Bagley for this example.

21. Franklin D. Vagnone and Deborah E. Ryan, *Anarchist's Guide to Historic House Museums* (Walnut Creek: Left Coast Press, Inc., 2016).

22. Personal visit, June 2, 2018, and later communications with Harriet Beecher Stowe Center staff; see www.harrietbeecherstowecenter.org.

23. Atlanta History Center; Linda Veiking, Plumbing Museum, Watertown, Massachusetts.

24. "Louisa May Alcott" (C-SPAN, 2017.06.19), https://www.c-span.org/video/?430723-1/orchard-house-louisa-may-alcott.

25. Margot Lee Shetterly, *Hidden Figures: The American Dream and the Untold Story of the Black Women Mathematicians Who Helped Win the Space Race* (New York: William Morrow, 2016).

26. Anne Digan Lanning, "Sally Rogers: The Celebrated Paintress," *Historic Deerfield Magazine*, Summer 2012.

27. Clara Barton NHS, 1979. Personal experience.

28. Meagan Huff, Fort Vancouver NHP concerning Hudson's Bay Company women.

29. Design thinking stresses results and customer satisfaction; see https://www.ideou.com.

30. Expertise gained from years in NPS strategic planning and the Maggie Walker Community.

31. Lesley Aileen Pendleton Barker, "Repurposing Museum Interpretation in American Historic House Museums" (PhD, University of Leicester School of Museum Studies, 2017).

32. Eliza Newland and Caroline B. Watts, "Sharing History with a Smartphone App 'CLIO,'" *AASLH* (blog), March 12, 2018, http://blogs.aaslh.org.

33. See https://www.emilydickinsonmuseum.org; Dorothy Molter Museum, https://www.root-beerlady.com/; personal visit, June 2013; https://www.atlantahistorycenter.com. Multiple personal visits.

34. Callie Hawkins, "The Discourse We All Need So Seriously: An Evening of Reflection at the Lincoln Cottage," *The Public Historian* 40, no. 1 (February 2018).

35. Thanks to Elizabeth Burgess, Harriet Beecher Stowe Center.

36. Harriet Beecher Stowe Center, www.harrietbeecherstowecenter.org; personal visit, June 2017.

37. Smith Family Farm, Atlanta History Center, Smith Family Farm, http://www.atlantahistory-center.com. Personal visit, October 2015.

38. Smith Family Farm, Atlanta History Center, Smith Family Farm, http://www.atlantahistory-center.com. Personal visit, October 2015.

39. Personal visit to Swan Mansion, Atlanta History Center October 2012. Thanks to Jessica Rast VanLanduyt, Vice President for Guest Experiences, Atlanta History Center. Email from Jessica Vanlanduyt, 2016.07.17.

40. Smith Family Farm, Atlanta History Center, Smith Family Farm, http://www.atlantahistory-center.com. Personal visit, October 2015.

41. Personal tour, January 2019, with American Historical Association.

42. J. Ritchie Garrison, "Listening to the Past in an American Landscape," *Historic Deerfield Magazine*, Autumn (2011). Melanie A. Kiechle and Paul S. Sutter, *Smell Detectives: An Olfactory History of Nineteenth-Century Urban America* (Seattle: University of Washington Press, 2017).

43. http://www.mayflowerfaces.com/mayflower-faces-blog-last-update-11220/archives /04-2017.

44. "Join us for Living Proof: Celebrating the Makers, Plimoth Plantation's Spring Fundraiser," Plimoth Plantation, March 2017. "Eat Like a Pilgrim," "Two Cultures," and "Wampanoag Feast," Plimoth Plantation special meals, http://www.plimoth.org. Personal visit, June 2015.

45. Eulanda A. Sanders, "The Politics of Textiles Used in African American Slave Clothing," *Textile Society of America Symposium Proceedings*, September 2012, Lincoln.

46. The *New York Times* in 1908 recommended that hair be washed "as often as every two weeks" using castile or tar soap shavings.

47. Christine Emmert, author, "From Out of the Fiery Furnace," "portrays runaway slaves, 'fallen women,' indentured servants, orphaned children . . ." Hopewell Furnace NHS, https://www.nps.gov/hofu/learn/historyculture/play.htm.

48. Girl Scout Program Overview, https://www.hullhousemuseum.org.

49. See http://www.harrietbeecherstowecenter.org; Girls' Leadership Council, http://www.alice-paul.org/programs/glc/.

50. See Colonial Williamsburg Foundation, http://shop.colonialwilliamsburg.com/Randolph -Kitchen-Stool; and http://shop.colonialwilliamsburg.com/Cascading-Floral-Blossoms -Girls-Pocket.

51. The Marian Anderson Museum and Historical Society preserves the house she purchased at 762 S. Martin St., Philadelphia. See http://mariananandersonhistoricalsociety.weebly.com/.

52. Women at Work Museum, Attleboro, focuses on women's achievements and expertise in math, science, engineering, and technology, http://www.womenatworkmuseum.org/about. html.

53. The Women of the West Museum (1991–2002, merged into the Autry Museum of the American West); the Women's Museum: An Institute for the Future (2000–2011).

54. Gerda Lerner, *The Majority Finds Its Past: Placing Women in History*, 2005 ed. (Chapel Hill: The University of North Carolina Press, 1979).

55. See National Collaborative for Women's History Sites, www.ncwhs.org.

56. Megan Springate, ed., *LGBTQ America*, NPS, 2016.

57. Philip Kennicott, "Jefferson's Monticello Finally Gives Sally Hemings Her Place in Presidential History," *Washington Post*, June 13, 2018. See www.monticello.org; Annette Gordon-Reed, *The Hemingses of Monticello: An American Family* (New York: W. W. Norton & Company, 2008); Fraser Neiman, Leslie McFaden, and Derek Wheeler, "Archaeological Investigation of the Elizabeth Hemings Site (44AB438)," Technical Report, Series Number 2 (Charlottesville: Monticello Foundation, 2000).

58. Jerome Greene, "Little Bighorn Battlefield: Closing the Circle on Indian Testimony" (Friends of Little Bighorn, Crow Agency, June 27, 2008).

59. Rediscovering James Monroe's Home, https://culturallandscapes.arch.virginia.edu, accessed February 8, 2018.

60. Kelly J. Dixon, *Boomtown Saloons: Archaeology and History in Virginia City* (Reno: University of Nevada Press, 2005).

61. See https://paulimurrayproject.org; house address is 609 Carroll Street, Durham, North Carolina.

62. At Jane Addams Hull-House, Jennifer Scott presented "Activating Marginalized Histories: Museums as Catalysts for Social Change," http://hullhouse.uic.edu/hull/rec/audio.html.

63. Maggie L. Walker, "Benaiah's Valour: An Address for Men Only," Richmond, Virginia, March 1, 1906; Maggie L. Walker NHS.

64. Carolyn Brucken, PhD, curator of Western Women's History, Autry Museum of the American West, interview January 1, 2017.

65. Morris F Collen, M.D., Bryan Culp, and Tom Debley, "Rosie the Riveter's Wartime Medical Records," *Permanente Journal* 12, no. 3 (Summer 2008), www.ncbi.nlm.nih.gov.

66. A'Lelia Bundle, *On Her Own Ground: The Life and Times of Madam C.J. Walker* (New York: Scribners, 2002); Deborah Blum, *The Poisoner's Handbook: Murder and the Birth of Forensic Medicine in Jazz Age New York* (New York: Penguin Press, 2010).

67. Darlene Clark Hine, "Some Preliminary Thoughts on Rape, the Threat of Rape and the Culture of Dissemblance," *SIGNS: Journal of Women in Culture and Society* 14, no. 4 (Summer 1989): 912–20.

68. Virginia K. Bartlett, *Keeping House: Women's Lives in Western Pennsylvania, 1790–1850* (Pittsburgh: University of Pittsburgh Press, 1994), and Joan M. Jensen, *Calling This Place Home: Women on the Wisconsin Frontier, 1850–1925* (Minneapolis: University of Minnesota Press, 2006); Mary Ann Irwin and James F. Brooks, eds., *Women and Gender in the American West* (Albuquerque: University of New Mexico Press, 2004).

69. Susan Ferentinos, "Entering the Mainstream: Interpreting GLBT History" (Nashville: *AASLH History News*, Autumn 2012).

70. Thomas Jefferson to John Wayles Eppes, June 30, 1820, quote from Monticello Foundation, www.monticello.org.

Appendix

List of Organizations, Websites, and Journals

American Alliance of Museums (AAM), www.aam-us.org

American Association for State and Local History (AASLH), https://aaslh.org; History News and other publications

American Historical Association (AHA), https://www.historians.org

American Institute of Architects (AIA), www.aia.org

American Society Landscape Architects (ASLA), https://www.asla.org

Association of Black Women Historians, truth.abwh.org

Association for Living History, Farm and Agricultural Museums (ALHFAM), https://www.alhfam.org

Association for Preservation Technology International (APTI), http://www.apti.org

Association for Study of African American Life and History, https://asalh.org; *The Journal of African American History*

Berkshire Conference on the History of Women and Gender, https://berksconference.org

Committee on Lesbian, Gay, Bisexual, and Transgender History, www.clgbthistory.org

Daughters of the American Revolution (DAR), www.dar.org

Ephemera Society of America, www.ephemerasociety.org

H-Net, http://www.h-net.org

US International Council on Monuments and Sites (ICOMOS), www.usicomos.org

Lesbian Herstory Archives, https://www.lesbianherstoryarchives.org/digital.html

Library of Congress, https://www.loc.gov

Mujeres Activas en Letras y Cambio Social Chicana/Latina Studies, MALCS http://malcs.org

National Archives and Records Administration (NARA), https://www.archives.gov

National Association for Interpretation (NAI), http://www.interpnet.com

National Collaborative for Women's History Sites (NCWHS), www.ncwhs.org

National Conference of State Historic Preservation (NCSHPO), www.ncshpo.org

National Park Service (NPS), https://www.nps.gov/index.htm; https://www.nps.gov/parkhistory/online_books

National Register of Historic Places (NR), https://www.nps.gov/nr

National Register of Historic Places Travel Itineraries, https://www.nps.gov/subjects/heritagetravel/discover-our-shared-heritage.htm; Teaching with Historic Places Lesson Plans, https://www.nps.gov/subjects/teachingwithhistoricplaces/index.htm

National Historic Landmarks (NHL), https://www.nps.gov/nhl

National Trust for Historic Preservation (the Trust), https://savingplaces.org; *Preservation and Preservation Forum*

National Council on Public History, https://ncph.org, *The Public Historian*

National Parks Conservation Association, https://www.npca.org

Organization of American Historians, https://www.oah.org; *Journal of American History*
Preservation Action, www.preservationaction.org
Smithsonian Institution, https://www.si.edu; *Smithsonian*
Society for American Archaeology, www.saa.org
Society for Historical Archaeology, https://sha.org
Society for Industrial Archaeology, http://www.sia-web.org
Society for the Study of Gloria Anzaldua (SSGA), http://www.gloriaanzaldua.com
Southern Association of Women Historians, thesawh.org
Vernacular Architecture Forum (VAF), vernaculararchitectureforum.org; *Buildings & Landscapes*
Western Association of Women Historians, https://wawh.org

Relevant Journals

Ethnohistory (indigenous), https://www.dukeupress.edu/ethnohistory
Family Tree Magazine, familytreemagazine.com
Frontiers: A Journal of Women's Studies (western and multicultural), https://frontiers.utah.edu
Gender and History, https://onlinelibrary.wiley.com/loi/14680424
Internet Genealogy, https://internet-genealogy.com
Journal of the Gilded and Progressive Era, *Journal of Southern History* (American South): https://thesha.org/jsh
Journal of Women's History, https://www.press.jhu.edu/journals/journal-womens-history
National Genealogical Society Quarterly, https://www.ngsgenealogy.org
SIGNS: Journal of Women in Culture and Society, www.signsjournal.org
The *Western Historical Quarterly* (American West), https://academic.oup.com/whq
William & Mary Quarterly (colonial), https://oieahc.wm.edu/publications/wmq
The *Winterthur Portfolio: A Journal of American Material Culture*, https://www.winterthur.org/education/academic-programs/winterthur-portfolio

Bibliography

This is divided into several sections and includes books most relevant to researching, preserving, and interpreting women's history at museums and historic sites. Provides key works only.

Women's History General

Brown, Leslie, Jacqueline Castledine, and Anne Valk, eds. *U.S. Women's History Untangling the Threads of Sisterhood.* New Brunswick: Rutgers University Press, 2017.

Evans, Sara. *Born for Liberty.* New York: Touchstone Books, 1994.

Kerber, Linda et al. *Women's America: Refocusing the Past*, 8th ed. New York: Oxford University Press, 2016.

Kleinberg, S. Jay, Vicki Ruiz, and Eileen Boris, eds. *The Practice of U.S. Women's History Narratives, Intersections, and Dialogues.* New Brunswick: Rutgers University Press, 2007.

Lerner, Gerda. *The Majority Finds Its Past: Placing Women in History*, 2005 ed. Chapel Hill: University North Carolina Press, 1979.

Miller, Marla. *Betsy Ross and the Making of America.* New York: Henry Holt, 2010.

———. *Entangled Lives: Labor, Livelihood, and Landscapes of Change in Rural Massachusetts.* Baltimore: Johns Hopkins University Press, 2019.

Ruiz, Vicki and Ellen Carol DuBois, eds. *Unequal Sisters: A Multicultural Reader in U.S. Women's History*, 4th ed. New York: Routledge, 2007.

Ware, Susan. *American Women's History: A Very Short Introduction.* London: Oxford University Press, 2015.

Reference

Hewitt, Nancy and Anne Valk. *A Companion to American Women's History.* Malden: Wiley-Blackwell, 2020.

Hinding, Andrea and Ames Sheldon Bower, eds. *Women's History Sources.* New York: A. A. Bowker, 1979.

James, Edward T., Janet Wilson James, and Paul. S. Boyer, eds. *Notable American Women: A Biographical Dictionary*, 1607–1950. 3 vols. Cambridge: The Belknap Press of the Harvard University Press, 1971.

Sherr, Lynn. *Susan B. Anthony Slept Here: A Guide to American Women's Landmarks.* New York: Three Rivers Press, 1994.

Sicherman, Barbara et al., eds., *Notable American Women: The Modern Period.* Cambridge: The Belknap Press of the Harvard University Press, 1980.

Tinling, Marion. *Women Remembered: A Guide to Landmarks of Women's History in the United States.* Westport: Greenwood, 1986.

Ware, Susan and Stacy Braukman, eds., *Notable American Women: A Biographical Dictionary, Completing the Twentieth Century.* Cambridge: The Belknap Press of the Harvard University Press, 2004.

Women's Many Varieties: A Sampling

Austin, Jill and Jennifer Brier, eds. *Out in Chicago: LGBT History at the Crossroads.* Chicago: Chicago History Museum, 2011.

Castañeda, Antonia. "Engendering the History of Alta California, 1769–1848," *California History,* vol. 76, no. 2/3 (1997).

Chan-Malik, Sylvia. *Being Muslim: A Cultural History of Women of Color in American Islam.* New York: NYU Press, 2018.

Clark-Lewis, Elizabeth. *Living In, Living Out: African American Domestics in Washington, D.C., 1910–1940.* Washington, DC: Smithsonian Institution Press, 1994.

Collins, Patricia and Sirma Bilge. *Intersectionality.* New York: John Wiley & Sons, Inc., 2016.

Deutsch, Sarah. *No Separate Refuge: Culture, Class, and Gender on an Anglo-Hispanic Frontier in the American Southwest, 1880–1940.* New York: Oxford University Press, 1987.

Faderman, Lillian. *Odd Girls and Twilight Lovers: A History of Lesbian Life in the 20th Century.* New York: Columbia University Press, 2012.

Ferentinos, Susan. *Interpreting LGBT History at Museums and Historic Sites.* Lanham: Rowman & Littlefield Publishers, Inc., 2014.

Heidenrich, Linda, ed. *Three Decades of Engendering History: Selected Works of Antonia Castañeda.* Denton: University of North Texas Press, 2014.

Hine, Darlene Clark. *Hine Sight: Black Women and the Re-Construction of American History.* Indianapolis: University of Indiana, 1997.

Hine, Darlene Clark and Kathleen Thompson. *A Shining Thread of Hope: The History of Black Women in America.* New York: Broadway Books, 1998.

Hune, Shirley and Gail M. Nomura, eds. *Asian/Pacific Islander American Women: A Historical Anthology*. New York: New York University, 2003.

Johnson, Allan G. *The Gender Knot: Unraveling our Patriarchal Legacy*, 3rd ed. Philadelphia: Temple University Press, 2013.

Klein, Laura F. and Lillian A. Ackerman, eds. *Women and Power in Native North America*. Norman: University of Oklahoma Press, 1995.

Martinac, Paula. *The Queerest Places: A Guide to Gay and Lesbian Historic Sites*. New York: Henry Holt and Company, 1997.

Morgan, Jennifer L. *Laboring Women: Reproduction and Gender in New World Slavery*. Philadelphia: University of Pennsylvania Press, 2004.

Murray, Pauli. *Proud Shoes: The Story of an American Family*. Boston: Beacon Press, 1999.

Newton, Esther. *Cherry Grove, Fire Island: Sixty Years in America's First Gay and Lesbian Town*, Rev. 1993. Chapel Hill: Duke University Press Books, 2014.

Nomura, Gail M. "Filipina American Journal Writing: Recovering Women's History," in *Asian/Pacific Islander American Women: A Historical Anthology*. New York: New York University, 2003.

Odo, Franklin, ed. *Finding a Path Forward, Asian American and Pacific Islander National Historic Landmarks Theme Study*. Washington, DC: National Historic Landmarks Program, National Park Service, 2017.

Ruiz, Vicki L. and Virginia Sanchez Korrol, eds. *Latinas in the United States: A Historical Encyclopedia*. Indianapolis: Indiana University Press, 2006.

Samanta, Suchitra. "Making Visible Asians and Asian Americans in Introductory Women's Studies Courses: The Personal Voice in Pedagogy, Making Feminist Connections across Diversity." *Feminist Teacher*, vol. 25, no. 2–3 (2015): 94–110.

Slater, Elinor and Robert Slater. *Great Jewish Women*. Middle Village: Jonathan David Publishers, 2015.

Sleeper-Smith, Susan. *Indigenous Prosperity and American Conquest: Indian Women of the Ohio River Valley, 1690–1792*. Chapel Hill: University North Carolina Press, 2018.

Smith, Jessie Carney, ed. *Notable Black American Women*: Books I–III. Gale Publishing, 1991.

Springate, Megan, ed. *LGBTQ America: A Theme Study of Lesbian, Gay, Bisexual, Transgender, and Queer History* online: National Park Service and National Park Foundation, 2016, www.nps.gov/subjects/tellingallamericansstories/lgbtqthemestudy.htmwww.nps.gov/subjects/tellingallamericansstories/lgbtqthemestudy.htm.

Vo, Linda Trinh, Marian Sciachitano, Susan Armitage, Patricia Hart, and Karen Weathermon, eds. *Asian American Women: The Frontiers Reader*. Lincoln: University of Nebraska Press, 2004.

Regional and Era-Specific but Excellent and Applicable Elsewhere!

Bartlett, Virginia K. *Keeping House: Women's Lives in Western Pennsylvania, 1790–1850*. Pittsburgh: University of Pittsburgh Press, 1994.

Blair, Karen J. *Women in Pacific Northwest History*. Revised. Seattle: University of Washington Press, 1988.

Creighton, Margaret S. *The Colors of Courage: Gettysburg's Forgotten History: Immigrants, Women, and African Americans in the Civil War's Defining Battle*. New York: Basic Books, 2005.

Hoagland, Alison K. *Mine Towns: Buildings for Workers in Michigan's Copper Country*. Minneapolis: University of Minnesota Press, 2010.

Holt, Marilyn Irvin. *Linoleum, Better Babies & The Modern Farm Woman, 1890–1930*. Lincoln: University of Nebraska Press, 1995.

Irwin, Mary Ann and James F. Brooks, eds. *Women and Gender in the American West*. Albuquerque: University of New Mexico Press, 2004.

Jensen, Joan M. *Calling This Place Home: Women on the Wisconsin Frontier, 1850–1925*. Minneapolis: University of Minnesota Press, 2006.

———. *Loosening the Bonds: Mid-Atlantic Farm Women, 1750–1850*. New Haven: Yale University Press, 1988.

———. *One Foot on the Rockies: Women and Creativity in the Modern American West*. Albuquerque: University of New Mexico Press, 1995.

Kohl, Martha, ed. *Beyond Schoolmarms and Madams: Montana Women's Stories*. Helena: Montana Historical Society, 2016.

McCurry, Stephanie. *Women's War: Fighting and Surviving the American Civil War*. Cambridge: Belknap/Harvard, 2019.

Miller, Marla R. *Betsy Ross and the Making of America*. New York: Henry Holt, 2010.

———. *Entangled Lives: Labor, Livelihood, and Landscapes of Change in Rural Massachusetts*. Baltimore: Johns Hopkins University Press, 2019.

———. *The Needle's Eye: Women and Work in the Age of Revolution*. Amherst: University of Massachusetts Press, 2006.

Murphy, Lucy Eldersveld. "Her Own Boss: Businesswomen and Separate Spheres in the Midwest, 1850–1880," *Illinois Historical Journal*, vol. 80, no. 3 (Autumn 1987): 155–76.

Norton, Mary Beth. *Liberty's Daughters: The Revolutionary Experience of American Women, 1750–1800.* Ithaca: Cornell University Press, 1980.

Romney, Susanah Shaw. *New Netherland Connections: Intimate Networks and Atlantic Ties in Seventeenth-Century America.* Chapel Hill: University North Carolina Press, 2014.

Scharff, Virginia. *Twenty Thousand Roads: Women, Movement, and the West.* Berkeley: University of California Press, 2003.

Scharff, Virginia and Carolyn Brucken. *Home Lands: How Women Made the West.* Los Angeles: University of California Press, 2010.

Simmons, Marc. *Kit Carson & His Three Wives: A Family History.* Albuquerque: University of New Mexico Press, 2003.

Turino, Kenneth C. and Max A. Van Balgooy, eds., *Reimagining Historic House Museums: New Approaches and Proven Solutions.* Lanham: Rowman & Littlefield Publishers / AASLH, 2019.

VanderVelde, Lea. *Mrs. Dred Scott: A Life on Slavery's Frontier.* New York: Oxford University Press, 2009.

Sexuality/Female Life Cycle

Apple, Rima and Janet Golden, eds. *Mothers & Motherhood: Readings in American History.* Columbus: Ohio State University Press, 1997.

Beales Jr., Ross W. "Nursing and Weaning in an Eighteenth-Century New England Household," in *Families and Children.* Boston: Boston University, 1987.

Benson, Susan Porter. *Household Accounts: Working-Class Families Economies in the Interwar United States.* Ithaca: Cornell University Press, 2007.

Brown, Victoria Bissell. "Queer or Not: What Jane Addams Teaches Us About Not Knowing," in *Out in Chicago: LGBT History at the Crossroads.* Chicago: Chicago History Museum, 2011.

Calvert, Karin. *Children in the House: The Material Culture of Early Childhood, 1600–1900.* Boston: Northeastern University Press, 1992.

Costello, Julia G. "'A Night with Venus, a Moon with Mercury': The Archaeology of Prostitution in Historic Los Angeles," in *Restoring Women's History Through Historic Preservation.* Baltimore: Johns Hopkins University Press, 2003.

D' Emilio, John and Estelle B. Freedman. *Intimate Matters: A History of Sexuality in America*, 3rd ed. Chicago: University of Chicago Press, 2012.

Gordon, Linda. *Woman's Body, Woman's Right: A Social History of Birth Control in America.* Urbana: University of Illinois Press, 2002.

Haines, Michael R. and Richard H. Steckel, eds. *A Population History of North America*. Cambridge: Cambridge University Press, 2000.

Knott, Sarah. *Mother Is a Verb: An Unconventional History*. New York: Farrar, Straus and Giroux, 2019.

Leavitt, Judith Walzer. *Brought to Bed: Childbirth in America, 1750–1950*. New York: Oxford University Press, 1988.

Martucci, Jessica. *Back to the Breast: Natural Motherhood and Breastfeeding in America*. Chicago: University of Chicago Press, 2015.

Montague Benes, Jane eds. *Families and Children, The Dublin Seminar for New England Folklife Annual Proceedings, 1985*. Boston: Boston University, 1987.

Murray, John E. "Poor Mother, Stepmothers and Foster Mothers in Early Republic and Antebellum Charleston," *Journal of the Early Republic*, vol. 32, no. 3 (Fall 2012).

National Park Service, "Eleanor Roosevelt National Historic Site, Val-Kill Cottage, New York," *Discover Our Shared Heritage Travel Itinerary*, "American Presidents," https://www.nps.gov/nr/travel/presidents/eleanor_roosevelt_valkill.html.

Newton, Esther. *Cherry Grove, Fire Island: Sixty Years in America's First Gay and Lesbian Town*. Rev. Chapel Hill: Duke University Press Books, 2014.

Olmert, Michael. "This Helpless Human Tide Bastards, Abandoned Babes, and Orphans." *CW* [Colonial Williamsburg] *Journal* (Autumn 2014), https://www.history.org/Foundation/journal/Autumn14/orphans.cfm.

Pillow, W.S. "Sex and Race in the Corps Expedition," in *Connexions: Histories of Race and Sex in North America*. Urbana: University of Illinois Press, 2016.

Ulrich, Laurel Thatcher. *A Midwife's Tale: The Life of Martha Ballard Based on Her Diary, 1785–1812*. New York: Vintage Books, 1990.

Genealogy

Carmack, Sharon DeBartolo. *Organizing Your Family History Search: Efficient and Effective Ways to Better and Protect Your Genealogical Research*. Cincinnati: Betterway Books, 1999.

Helm, Matthew L. and April Leigh Helm. *Genealogy Online for Dummies*. 6th ed. Hoboken: Wiley Publishing, 2011.

Hendrickson, Nancy. *Unofficial Guide to Ancestry.Com: How to Find Your Family History on the #1 Genealogy Website*. Cincinnati: Family Tree Books, 2014.

McCullough, Dana. *Unofficial Guide to FamilySearch.Org: How to Find Your Family History on the Largest Free Genealogy Website*. Cincinnati: Family Tree Books, 2015.

National Archives and Records Administration. *Guide to Genealogical Research in the National Archives*. Washington, DC: National Archives Trust Fund Board, US General Services Administration, 1982.

Powell, Kimberly. *The Everything Guide to Online Genealogy: Use the Web to Trace Your Roots, Share Your History, and Create a Family Tree*. 3rd ed. New York: Everything, 2014.

Rose, Christine. *Courthouse Research for Family Historians: Your Guide to Genealogical Treasures*. San Jose: CR Publications, 2004.

Written Sources

1897 Sears Roebuck & Company Catalogue [reprint] New York: Skyhorse Publishing, 2007.

McDaid, Jennifer Davis. "Using Women's History Sources in the Archives at the Library of Virginia" *Research Notes* Number 10.

Nylander, Jane C. "Everyday Life on a Berkshire County Hill Farm: Documentation from the 1794–1835 Diary of Sarah Snell Bryant of Cummington, Massachusetts," in *The American Home*. Winterthur: Henry Francis du Pont Winterthur Museum, 1998.

Schlereth, Thomas J. "'Mail Order Catalogs as Resources in Material Culture Studies,'" in *Artifacts and the American Past*. Nashville: American Association for State and Local History, 1980.

Schmidt, Laura. "Using Archives: A Guide to Effective Research," Society of American Archivists. www2.archivists.org/usingarchiveswww2.archivists.org/usingarchives.

Sharpless, Rebecca. "'Cookbooks as Resources for Rural ResearchCookbooks as Resources for Rural Research,'" *Agricultural History*, vol. 90, no. 2 (Spring 2016): 195–208.

Van Eck, Dale. "Probate Inventories: Voices from the Past," Colonial Williamsburg Foundation, https://www.history.org/history/teaching/enewsletter/volume2/april04/primsource.cfm.

Young, Sandra Florand and Margaret (Peg) Strobel. *Don't Throw It Away! Documenting and Preserving Organizational History*. Chicago: Special Collections Department, The University Library, University of Illinois at Chicago and Jane Addams Hull-House Museum, 2006, http://www.uic.edu/depts/lib/specialcoll/pdf/DTIA.pdf.

Oral Sources

Barnickel, Linda. *Oral History for the Family Historian: A Basic Guide*. Carlisle: Oral History Association, 2006.

Baylor Institute for Oral History. *Introduction to Oral History*. Waco: Baylor University, 2016.

Kennedy, Elizabeth Lapovsky and Madeline D. Davis. *Boots of Leather, Slippers of Gold: The History of a Lesbian Community*. New York: Penguin Books, 1993.

Library of Congress. "American Women: Music Division," https://memory.loc.gov/ammem/awh-html/awmusic8/index.html.

Martin, Patricia Preciado. *Songs My Mother Sang to Me: An Oral History of Mexican American Women*. Tucson: University of Arizona, 2016.

Oral History Association. "Principles and Best Practices," 2009, http://www.oralhistory.org/about/principles-and-practices-revised-2009/.

Ritchie, Donald A. *Doing Oral History: A Practical Guide: Using Interviews to Uncover the Past and Preserve It for the Future*. New York: Oxford University Press, 2003.

Visual Sources

Library of Congress. "Women's History Resources in the Library of Congress Prints and Photographs Division," March 2011, https://www.loc.gov/rr/print/coll/237_path.html.

Middle Tennessee State University. "Discovering American Women's History Online," http://digital.mtsu.edu/cdm/landingpage/collection/women.

National Archives and Records Administration. "Teaching with Documents: Documents and Photographs Related to Japanese Relocation During World War II," www.archives.gov.

National Park Service. "Photographic Images- Learning Historical Research," http://www.nps.gov/hafo/upload/Historic-Resource-Study-MIIN-A-L-Meger.pdf.

Newhall, Beaumont. *The History of Photography from 1839 to the Present*. New York: The Museum of Modern Art, 1982.

Opdycke, Sandra. *The Routledge Historical Atlas of Women in America*. New York: Routledge, 2000.

Spirn, Anne Whiston. *Daring to Look: Dorothea Lange's Photography & Reports from the Field*. Chicago: University of Chicago, 2008.

Landscapes

Adams, Denise Wiles and Laura L.S. Burchfield. *American Home Landscapes: A Design Guide to Creating Period Garden Styles*. Portland: Timberland Press, 2013.

Archer, John, Paul J.P. Sandul, and Katherine Solomonson, eds. *Making Suburbia: New Histories of Everyday Life*. Minneapolis: University of Minnesota Press, 2015.

Birnbaum, Charles. "Protecting Cultural Landscapes: Planning, Treatment and Management of Historic Landscapes." Washington, DC: National Park Service, 1994.

Conzen, Michael P., ed. *The Making of the American Landscape.* Boston: Unwin Hyman, 1990.

Cronon, William. "Sources: How to Read a Landscape," *Learning Historical Research*, 2009, http://www.williamcronon.net/researching/landscapes.htm.

Crowley, Jill. "Place and Gender: Applying Gender Theory to the Documentation and Management of Cultural Landscapes," *CRM.* Washington, DC: National Park Service, 2000.

Deutsch, Sarah. *Women and the City: Gender, Space, and Power in Boston, 1870–1940.* New York: Oxford University Press, 2000.

Domosh, Monica and Joni Seager. *Putting Women in Place: Feminist Geography Makes Sense of the World.* New York: Guilford Press, 2001.

Favretti, Rudy J. and Joy Putnam Favretti. *Landscapes and Gardens for Historic Buildings A Handbook for Reproducing and Creating Authentic Landscapes.* 3rd ed. Lanham: Rowman & Littlefield Publishers, 2017.

Groth, Paul and Todd W. Bressi, eds. *Understanding Ordinary Landscapes.* New Haven: Yale University Press, 1997.

Gundaker, Grey. "Tradition and Innovation in African-American Yards," *African Arts*, vol. 26, no. 2 (April 1993): 58–71.

McDowell, Linda. *Gender, Identity & Place: Understanding Feminist Geographies.* Minneapolis: University of Minnesota Press, 1999.

McMurry, Sally. "Women in the Vernacular Landscape," *Material Culture*, vol. 20, no. 1 (1989): 33–49.

Sewell, Jessica Ellen. *Women and the Everyday City: Public Space in San Francisco 1890–1915.* Minneapolis: University of Minnesota Press, 2011.

Spain, Daphne. *Gendered Spaces.* Chapel Hill: The University of North Carolina Press, 1992.

———. *How Women Saved the City.* Minneapolis: University of Minnesota Press, 2001.

Stilgoe, John R. *Common Landscape of America, 1580 to 1845.* New Haven: Yale University Press, 1982.

Valentine, Gill. *From Nowhere to Everywhere: Lesbian Geographies.* Binghamton: Harrington Park Press, 2000.

Watts, May Theilgaard. *Reading the Landscape of America.* Rochester: Nature Study Guild Publishers, 1999. Classic sketches.

Westmacott, Richard. *African-American Gardens and Yards in the Rural South.* Knoxville: University of Tennessee Press, 1992.

Workers of the Writers Program of the Work Projects Administration in the State of Wyoming. *Wyoming: A Guide to its History, Highways, and People, American Guide Series.* New York: Oxford University Press, 1941. Dated, but like all of the WPA guides, very useful.

Architecture

Allen, Edward. *Fundamentals of Building Construction: Materials and Methods.* 6th ed. Hoboken: John Wiley & Sons, 2013.

Beckham, Sue Bridwell. "The American Front Porch: Women's Liminal Space," in *Making the American Home: Middle-Class Women & Domestic Material Culture, 1840-1940.* Bowling Green: Bowling Green State University Popular Press, 1988.

Borrman, Kristina. "One Standardized House for All: America's Little House," *Buildings & Landscapes: Journal of the Vernacular Architecture Forum,* vol. 24, no. 2 (Fall 2017): 37-57.

Breisch, Kenneth A. and Alison K. Hoaglund, eds. *Building Environments.* Vol. X. Knoxville: University of Tennessee Press, 2005.

Carter, Thomas and Elizabeth Collins Cromley. *Invitation to Vernacular Architecture: A Guide to the Study of Ordinary Buildings and Landscapes.* Knoxville: University of Tennessee Press, 2009.

Clark, Clifford. *The American Family Home, 1800-1960.* Chapel Hill: The University North Carolina Press, 1986.

Cromley, Elizabeth Collins. *Gender, Class and Shelter: Perspectives in Vernacular Architecture V.* Knoxville: University of Tennessee Press, 1995.

Dolkart, Andrew S. *Biography of a Tenement House in New York City: An Architectural History of 97 Orchard Street.* Santa Fe: The Center for American Places, Inc., 2002.

Ellis, Clifton and Rebecca Ginsberg. *Cabin, Quarter, Plantation: Architecture and Landscapes of North American Slavery.* New Haven: Yale University Press, 2010.

Elwood, Sarah A. "Lesbian Living Spaces: Multiple Meanings of Home," *Journal of Lesbian Studies,* vol. 4, no. 1 (2000): 11-27.

Foy, Jessica H. and Thomas J. Schlereth. *American Home Life, 1880-1930: A Social History of Spaces and Services.* Knoxville: University of Tennessee Press, 1992.

Friedman, Alice T. "Shifting the Paradigm: Houses Built for Women," in *Design and Feminism: Re-Visioning Spaces, Places, and Everyday Things,* 85-97. Joan Rothschild, ed. New Brunswick: Rutgers University Press, 1999.

——. *Women and the Making of the Modern House: A Social and Architectural History.* New Haven: Yale University Press, 2006.

Gottfried, Herbert and Jan Jennings. *American Vernacular Buildings and Interiors, 1870-1960.* New York: W. W. Norton & Company, 2009. Wonderful!

Harris, Dianne. *Little White Houses: How the Postwar Home Constructed Race in America*. Minneapolis: University of Minnesota Press, 2013.

Herman, Bernard L. *Town House: Architectural and Material Life in the Early American City, 1780–1830*. Chapel Hill: The University of North Carolina Press, 2005.

Hoagland, Alison K. "Introducing the Bathroom: Space and Change in Working-Class Houses," *Buildings & Landscapes: Journal of the Vernacular Architecture Forum*, vol. 18, no. 2 (Fall 2011): 15–42. See also *The Bathroom: A Social History of Cleanliness and the Body*. Santa Barbara: ABC-Clio, 2018. Part of a series on Human Spaces, including the kitchen, tavern, factory, and schoolroom.

Hunter, Christine. *Ranches, Rowhouses and Railroad Flats: American Homes: How They Shape Our Landscapes and Neighborhoods*. New York: W. W. Norton & Company, Inc., 1999.

Hurley, Andrew. *Diners, Bowling Alleys, and Trailer Parks: Chasing the American Dream in Postwar Consumer Culture*. New York: Basic Books, 2001.

Jennings, Jan and Herbert Gottfried. *American Vernacular Interior Architecture, 1870–1940*. New York: Van Nostrand Reinhold, 1988.

Kwolek-Folland, Angel. "Gender as a Category of Analysis in Vernacular Architecture Studies," in *Gender, Class, and Shelter: Perspectives in Vernacular Architecture*, 3–25. V.E. Cromley and C. Hudgins, eds. Knoxville: University of Tennessee Press, 1995.

——. "The Gendered Environment of the Corporate Workplace, 1880–1930," in *The Material Culture of Gender, The Gender of Material Culture*. Winterthur: Winterthur Museum, 1997.

Maloney, Robin. "The Narbonne House," *Pickled Fish and Salted Provisions Pickled Fish and Salted Provisions*. Salem Maritime National Historic Site, vol. 2, no. 10 (2000).

McAlester, Virginia and Lee McAlester. *Field Guide to American Houses*. New York: Knopf, 1984.

McMurry, Sally. *Families and Farmhouses in Nineteenth-Century America: Vernacular Design and Social Change*. Knoxville: University of Tennessee Press, 1997.

National Park Service. Technical Preservation Services, "Preservation Brief 17: Architectural Character." Washington, DC: National Park Service, September 1988.

O'Bryan, Katherine. "Gender, Politics, and Power: The Development of the Ladies Rest Room and Lounge in Rural America, 1900–1945." PhD dissertation, 2014.

Olmert, Michael. *Kitchens, Smokehouses and Privies: Outbuildings and the Architecture of Daily Life in the Eighteenth-Century Mid-Atlantic*. Ithaca: Cornell University Press, 2009.

Ore, Janet. *The Seattle Bungalow: People & Houses, 1900–1940*. Seattle: University of Washington Press, 2007.

Rothschild, Joan. *Design and Feminism: Re-visioning Spaces, Places, and Everyday Things.* New Brunswick: Rutgers University Press, 1999.

Sanfilippo, Pam. "'Sunlight and Shadow: Free Space/Slave Space at White Haven,'" in *Her Past Around Us: Interpreting Sites for Women's History.* New York: Krieger Pub Company, 2003.

Strasser, Susan. *Never Done: A History of American Housework.* New York: Pantheon, 1982.

Thompson, Eleanor McD. ed. *The American Home: Material Culture, Domestic Space, and Family Life.* Winterthur: Henry Francis du Pont Winterthur Museum, 1998.

Upton, Dell, and John Michael Vlach, eds. *Common Places: Readings in American Vernacular Architecture.* Athens: University of Georgia Press, 1986.

Wells, Camille. "The Planter's Prospect: Houses, Outbuildings, and Rural Landscapes in Eighteenth-Century Virginia," *Winterthur Portfolio*, vol. 28, no. 1 (1993): 1–31.

Yocum, Barbara Pearson. "The Stanton House: Historic Structure Report, Women's Rights National Historical Park." National Park Service, U.S. Department of the Interior, 1989.

Objects/Curation (Museums) and Artifacts (Archaeology)

American Association for State and Local History. "Online Course AASLH Collections Management March 21–May 6 [2016]" AASLH, 2015, http://resource.aaslh.org/view/online-course-collections-management.

Campbell, Edward and Kym S. Rice, eds. *A Woman's War: Southern Women, Civil War, and the Confederate Legacy.* Charlottesville: The University Press of Virginia, 1996.

——, eds. *Before Freedom Came: African-American Life in the Antebellum South.* Charlottesville: The University Press of Virginia, 1991. Material culture of slavery. Pathbreaking publication for temporary exhibit.

Clark, Bonnie J. *On the Edge of Purgatory: An Archaeology of Place in Hispanic Colorado.* Lincoln: University of Nebraska Press, 2011.

Cooper, Grace Rogers. "The Sewing Machine: Its Invention and Development." Online Exhibition," NMAH Smithsonian, http://www.sil.si.edu/DigitalCollections/HST/Cooper/CF/view.cfm.

Cowan, Ruth Schwartz. *A Social History of American Technology.* New York: Oxford University Press, 1997.

Deetz, James. *In Small Things Forgotten: The Archeology of Early American Life.* Garden City: Anchor Books, reprint 1996.

Gamber, Wendy. *The Female Economy: The Millinery and Dressmaking Trades, 1860–1930.* Champaign: University of Illinois Press, 1997.

Green, Harvey. *Light of the Home: An Intimate View of the Lives of Women in Victorian America.* New York: Pantheon Books, 1983. Discusses many objects.

Harvey, Karen. *History and Material Culture.* Routledge Guides to Using Historical Sources. 2nd ed., New York: Routledge, 2017.

James, Ronald M. *Virginia City: Secrets of a Western Past.* Lincoln: Bison Books, 2012. See Chapter 6: "Women on the Mining Frontier."

Little, Barbara J. *Historical Archaeology: Why the Past Matters.* Walnut Creek: Left Coast Press, Inc., 2007.

Martinez, Katharine and Kenneth L. Ames, eds. *The Material Culture of Gender, The Gender of Material Culture.* Winterthur: Henry Francis du Pont Winterthur Museum, 1997.

McDonald, Travis. "Rat Housing in Middle Virginia," in *Building Environments, Vol. X, Perspectives in Vernacular Architecture.* Knoxville: University of Tennessee Press, 2005.

Miller, Leslie Shannon. "The Many Figures of Eve: Styles of Womanhood Embodied in a Late-Nineteenth-Century Corset," in *American Artifacts: Essays in Material Culture.* East Lansing: Michigan State University, 2000.

National Park Service. *National Park Service Museum Handbook—Complete Version, Three Parts with Quick Reference—[Museum]Collections, Records, Use, Preservation, Conservation, Emergency Plans, Handling, Pest Management, Storage.* Washington, DC: U.S. Government, 2015. [Three parts: Museum Collections, Museum Records, and Museum Collections Use.], https://www.nps.gov/museum/publications/handbook.html.

Penney, Darby and Peter Stastny. *The Lives They Left Behind: Suitcases from a State Hospital Attic.* New York: Bellevue Literary Press, 2008.

Pierce, Geo. N. & Co. *Illustrated Catalogue of Refrigerators and Ice Chests.* Buffalo: Baker, Jones & Co., Printers, 1893, http://pds.lib.harvard.edu/pds/view/2845018?n=4&printThumbnails=no.

Rosbrugh, Jennifer. "Dispelling the Myth of the Itsy Bitsy Teeny Weeny Waist, 19th Century Costuming for Those Who Dream of the Past." Blog. June 11, 2017, historicalsewing.com/historicalsewing.com/.

Rose, Vivien and Ann Derousie. "History You Can Touch: Teaching Women's History Through Three Dimensional Objects," in *Clio in the Classroom: A Guide for Teaching US Women's History.* New York: Oxford University Press, 2009.

Sagstetter, Bill and Beth Sagstetter. *The Mining Camps Speak: A New Way to Explore the Ghost Towns of the American West.* Denver: Benchmark Publishing of Colorado, 1998.

Scott, Elizabeth M. *Those of Little Note: Gender, Race, and Class in Historical Archaeology.* Tucson: University of Arizona Press, 1994.

Sheumaker, Helen, and Shirley Teresa Wajda, eds. *Material Culture in America: Understanding Everyday Life*. Santa Barbara: ABC-Clio, 2008. Reference work.

Spector, Janet D. *What This Awl Means: Feminist Archaeology at a Wahpeton Dakota Village*. St. Paul: Minnesota Historical Society, 1993.

Spude, Catherine Holder, Robin O. Mills, Karl Gurke, and Roderick Sprague, eds. *Eldorado! The Archaeology of Gold Mining in the Far North*. Lincoln: University of Nebraska Press, 2011.

St. George, Robert Blair, ed. *Material Life in America, 1600–1860*. Boston: Northeastern University Press, 1988.

Ulrich, Laurel Thatcher. *The Age of Homespun: Objects and Stories in the Making of an American Myth*. New York: Knopf Publishing, 2001. Excellent case studies.

Ulrich, Laurel Thatcher et al. *Tangible Things: Making History Through Objects*. New York: Oxford University Press, 2015.

Warner, Mark and Margaret Purser, eds. *Historical Archaeology Through a Western Lens*. Lincoln: University of Nebraska Press, 2017.

Preservation

Dubrow, Gail Lee. "The Preservation of LGBTQ Heritage," in *LGBTQ America: A Theme Study of Lesbian, Gay, Bisexual, Transgender and Queer History*. Washington, DC: National Park Service, 2006.

Dubrow, Gail Lee and Jennifer B. Goodman, eds. *Restoring Women's History through Historic Preservation*. Baltimore: Johns Hopkins University Press, 2003.

Miller, Julia H. *A Layperson's Guide to Historic Preservatio Law: A Survey of Federal, State, and Local Laws Governing Historic Resource Protection*. Washington, DC: National Trust for Historic Preservation, 2008, https://forum.savingplaces.org/glossary.

Miller, Page Putnam, ed. *Reclaiming the Past: Landmarks of Women's History*. Bloomington: University of Indiana Press, 1992.

Minnesota Historical Society. *Historic Housekeeping Handbook*. St. Paul: Minnesota Historical Society, 2000.

National Park Service, National Register of Historic Places Bulletins—available for free download at www.nps.gov/history/nr/publications.

Interpretation

Bohnet, Iris. *What Works: Gender Equality by Design*. Cambridge: Belknap Press of Harvard, 2016.

Donnelly, Jessica Foy, ed. *Interpreting Historic House Museums.* Walnut Creek: AltaMira Press, 2002.

Ekirch, A. Roger. *At Day's Close: Night in Times Past.* New York: W. W. Norton & Company, Inc, 2005. Fascinating, different perspective.

Ham, Sam H. *Interpretation: Making a Difference on Purpose.* Golden: Fulcrum Publishing, 2013. Leader in interpretation.

Huyck, Heather and Margaret (Peg) Strobel, eds. *Revealing Women's History: Best Practices in Interpretation at Historic Sites.* Santa Cruz: National Collaborative for Women's History Sites, 2011.

Huyck, Heather. "Beyond John Wayne: Using Historic Sites to Interpret Western Women's History," in *Western Women: Their Land, Their Lives.* Albuquerque: University of New Mexico Press, 1988.

———. *Women's History: Sites and Resources.* 2nd ed. Santa Cruz: National Collaborative for Women's History Sites, 2009.

Kaufman, Polly Welts and Katharine T. Corbett. *Her Past Around Us: Interpreting Sites for Women's History.* Malabar: Krieger Pub Co., 2003.

Levy, Barbara Abramoff, Sandra Mackenzie Lloyd, and Susan Porter Schreiber. *Great Tours! Thematic Tours and Guide Training for Historic Sites.* Walnut Creek: Rowman & Littlefield Publishers, Inc., 2002.

Niven, Penelope and Cornelia Wright. *Old Salem: The Official Guidebook.* Winston-Salem: Old Salem Museums & Gardens, 2011.

O'Leary, Elizabeth L. *From Morning to Night: Domestic Service at Maymont and the Gilded-Age South.* Charlottesville: University of Virginia Press, 2003.

Pustz, Jennifer. *Voices from the Back Stairs: Interpreting Servants' Lives at Historic House Museums.* DeKalb: Northern Illinois University Press, 2010.

Reid, Deborah. "Making Gender Matter: Reinterpreting Male and Female Roles in Historic House Museums," in *Interpreting Historic House Museums.* Walnut Creek: AltaMira Press, 2002.

Reinarz, Jonathan. *Past Scents: Historical Perspectives on Smell.* Urbana: University of Illinois Press, 2014.

Smith, Mark M. *Sensing the Past: Seeing, Hearing, Smelling Tasting and Touching in History.* Berkeley: University of California Press, 2007.

Vagnone, Franklin D. and Deborah E. Ryan. *Anarchist's Guide to Historic House Museums.* Walnut Creek: Left Coast Press, Inc., 2016. Current thinking.

Index

References to figures are italicized.

About the Author

Heather A. Huyck is a public historian long fascinated by past women and dedicated to "tell the whole story" and interpret quality women's history. She has participated in the emergence of women's history as a vibrant field working to bridge academic and public history. During her career, she has worked with all kinds of interpretive sources, programming, and products, and visited and worked in museums and historic sites throughout the United States and Canada. As a public historian, she has researched and interpreted myriad parts of American History—one-room schools, bear-proof pigpens, and Italian American immigration. An activist-scholar as well as a park ranger, manager, and organizer, she has a PhD in American history and a MA in cultural anthropology from the University of Minnesota, where she worked on the foundational Women's History Sources Survey, which identified women's written sources when many people assumed they didn't exist, and documented social change using oral history.

Later as the site manager at the Clara Barton National Historic Site, she designed interpretive programs and worried about a 10,000-square-foot historic building, shoveling snow off its high roof, waxing its hallway floor, and presenting public programs while appreciating how tangible resources shape and are shaped by the people who live with them. As a professional staff member who worked on eighty-one enacted laws in the U.S. House of Representatives, she worked on historic preservation policy, the Abandoned Shipwreck Act that protected maritime cultural resources, and to establish more parks in African American and women's history, from Natchez National Historical Park, Women's Rights, and revision of the NPS "thematic framework." She has formally taught women's history to the National Park Service and the College of William & Mary and has made numerous professional conference presentations. Heather Huyck has organized several women's history groups and served as president of the National Collaborative for Women's History Sites, where she worked on the designation of the (Rev. Dr.) Pauli Murray family home as a National Historic Landmark as well as developing and presenting women's history conferences and webinars.

She is an Organization of American Historians Distinguished Lecturer, American Historical Association (AHA) Congressional Fellow, and AHA Feis Public History Award recipient. She worked as part of the Maggie Walker Community to preserve Maggie Walker documents and serves on the Mary McLeod Bethune Federal Commission. She loves to wake up in her tent, listen to owls, and paddle her canoe. When not discovering more history, she now lives in Maryland with her landscape-architect husband.